fedora

10

Linux

Desktop

To my nephew,
Justin

Fedora 10 Linux Desktop

Richard Petersen

Surfing Turtle Press

Alameda, CA

www.surfingturtlepress.com

Please send inquires to: editor@surfingturtlepress.com

ISBN   0-9820998-2-7

ISBN-13   978-0-9820998-2-7

Library of Congress Control Number   2008911540

Copyright Richard Petersen, 2008

All rights reserved

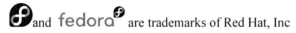

Preface

This book examines Fedora for the user. Though administrative tools are covered, the emphasis is on what a user would need to know to perform tasks. The emphasis here is on what users face when using Fedora, covering topics like installation, applications, software management, the GNOME and KDE desktops, shell commands, and both the Fedora administration and network tools. Desktops are examined in detail, including configuration options. Applications are reviewed. This book is designed for the Fedora 10 desktop, with all the latest features of interest to users.

Part 1 focuses on getting started, covering Fedora information and resources, Fedora Live CD/DVDs, Live USBs, installing and setting up Fedora, and basic use of the desktop as well as device access. Recovery with FirstAidKit is also reviewed.

Part 2 keys in on applications and software management. Repositories and their use are covered in detail, including the new PackageKit interface. Covered in detail is the RPM Fusion repository, which integrates and replaces the third party repositories Livna, Freshrpms, and Dribble. These older repositories are now empty, with one exception. Then office, multimedia, mail, and Web applications are examined. It includes coverage of the PulseAudio sound interface and a review of the Java OpenJDK and Omega multimedia spin.

Part 3 covers the two major desktops, GNOME and KDE4, discussing features like panels, applets, and file manager views. Desktop effects (compositing window managers) for both GNOME and KDE are covered. Unique KDE4 features like the dashboard and the Zoom User Interface are also explored. In addition, the shell interface is also explored, including features like history, file name completion, directory and file operations, among others.

Part 4 deals with administration topics, first discussing system tools like the GNOME system monitor, the Disk Usage Analyzer, temperature monitors, and SELinux configuration tool. Then a detailed chapter on Fedora system administration tools for managing users, the date and time, is presented, along with service management and file system access. The network administration chapter covers a variety of network tasks, including configuration of network connections, Wireless connections, 3G wireless, Firewalls, and Samba Windows access. The Printing chapter examines the new system-config-printer interface with personal printers and online drivers.

Appendix B reviews new additional desktop, including XFCE, LXDE, Sugar (OLPC), and Openbox.

Overview

Contents

Part 1

Getting Started

Part 2

Applications

Part 3

Interfaces

Part 4

Administration

Part 1: Getting Started

Introduction

Installation

Usage Basics

1. Fedora 10 Introduction

Linux Overview

Fedora Linux

Fedora Documentation

Fedora 10 changes

Standard Fedora features

Fedora Live DVD/CD

Fedora 10 Desktop Look and Feel:

Open Source Software

Operating Systems and Linux

A Short History of Linux and Unix

Red Hat Enterprise Linux

Linux is an fast, stable, and open source operating system for PC computers and workstations that features professional-level Internet services, extensive development tools, fully functional graphical user interfaces (GUIs), and a massive number of applications ranging from office suites to multimedia applications. Linux was developed in the early 1990s by Linus Torvalds, along with other programmers around the world. As an operating system, Linux performs many of the same functions as UNIX, Macintosh, Windows, and Windows NT. However, Linux is distinguished by its power and flexibility, along with being freely available.

Technically, Linux consists of the operating system program, referred to as the kernel, which is the part originally developed by Linus Torvalds. But it has always been distributed with a massive number of software applications, ranging from network servers and security programs to office applications and development tools. Linux has evolved as part of the open source software movement, in which independent programmers joined together to provide free quality software to any user. Linux has become the premier platform for open source software, much of it developed by the Free Software Foundation's GNU project. Many of these applications are bundled as part of standard Linux distributions. Currently, thousands of open source applications are available for Linux from sites the Fedora software repository, its integrated third party Fedora repositories supported by **http://rpmfusion.org**, along with independent repositories like KDE's **www.kde-apps.org**, and GNOME's **www.gnome.org**. Most of the GNOME and KDE applications are incorporated into the Fedora repository, using software packages that are Fedora compliant. You should always check the Fedora repository (System | Administration | Add/Remove Software) first for the software you want.

Linux does all this at the right price. Linux is free, including the network servers and GUI desktops. Unlike the official UNIX operating system, Linux is distributed freely under a GNU General Public License as specified by the Free Software Foundation, making it available to anyone who wants to use it. GNU (the acronym stands for "GNU's Not Unix") is a project initiated and managed by the Free Software Foundation to provide free software to users, programmers, and developers. Linux is copyrighted, not public domain. However, a GNU public license has much the same effect as the software's being in the public domain. The GNU general public license is designed to ensure Linux remains free and, at the same time, standardized. Linux is technically the operating system kernel—the core operations—and only one official Linux kernel exists.

Like UNIX, Linux can be generally divided into three major components: the kernel, the environment, and the file structure. The *kernel* is the core program that runs programs and manages hardware devices, such as disks and printers. The *environment* provides an interface for the user. It receives commands from the user and sends those commands to the kernel for execution. The *file structure* organizes the way files are stored on a storage device, such as a disk. Files are organized into directories. Each directory may contain any number of subdirectories, each holding files. Together, the kernel, the environment, and the file structure form the basic operating system structure. With these three, you can run programs, manage files, and interact with the system.

With the K Desktop Environment (KDE) and the GNU Network Object Mode l Environment (GNOME), Linux now has a completely integrated GUI interface. You can perform all your Linux operations entirely from either interface. KDE and GNOME are fully operational desktops supporting drag-and-drop operations, enabling you to drag icons to your desktop and to set up your own menus on an Applications panel. Both rely on an underlying X Window System, which means as long as they are both installed on your system, applications from one can run on the other desktop. The GNOME and KDE sites are particularly helpful for documentation, news, and software you can download for those desktops. Check their Web sites at **www.gnome.org** and **www.kde.org** for latest developments. As new versions are released, they include new software.

Fedora Linux

The Fedora release is maintained and developed by an Open Source project called the Fedora Project. The release consists entirely of open source software. Development is carried out using contributions from Linux developers, allowing them free rein to promote enhancements and new features. The project is designed to work much like other open source projects, with releases keeping pace with the course of rapid online development. The Fedora project features detailed documentation of certain topics like Installation and desktop user guides at **http://doc.fedoraproject.org** (see Table 1-1).

The Fedora versions of Linux are entirely free. You can download the most current version, including betas, from **http://fedoraproject.org** or **http://download.fedoraproject.org**. The **http://download.fedoraproject.org** address will link to the best available mirror for you. You can update Fedora using the Update System (PackageKit) to access the Fedora repository. Access is automatically configured during installation.

Fedora Documentation

Documentation for Fedora can be found at **http:/docs.fedoraproject.org**, with specialize topics provided at fedoraproject.org/wiki/Docs (see Table 1-1). The Fedora installation guide provides a detailed description of all your install procedures. The Fedora desktop users guide covers basic desktop operations like logging in, using office applications, and accessing the Web. Several dedicated Fedora support sites are available that provide helpful information, including fedoraforums.org, **www.fedoraproject.org**, and **www.fedoranews.org**.

The **www.fedoraforums.org** site is a Fedora Project–sponsored forum for end-user support. Here you can post questions and check responses for common problems. One of the more useful sites is the unofficial Fedora FAQ at www.fedorafaq.org. Here you will find solutions to the more common problems like graphic card issues and enabling MP3 support.

Your Firefox Browser will already be configured with panels for accessing popular documentation and support sites. These include the Fedora Project home page, the Fedora Weekly News, community support from Fedora forums as well as communication page, and the Red Hat Magazine.

Fedora maintains detailed specialized documentation, like information on understanding how udev in implemented or how SELinux is configured. For much of the documentation you will have to rely on installed documentation in **/usr/share/doc** or the Man and info pages, as well as the context help button for different applications running on your desktop. Web sites for software like those for GNOME, KDE, and OpenOffice.org will provide extensive applicable documentation. For installation, you can use the Fedora Installation Guide at **http://docs.fedoraproject.org/install-guide**.

Red Hat also maintains an extensive library of documentation for Red Hat Enterprise Linux, much of which is applicable to Fedora. From the Red Hat home page, you can click to its support page, and then on its Documentation page. The documentation page provides a pop-up menu from which to select products. Documentation covers topics like virtualization, the Global

File System (GFS), Logical Volume Management (LVM), and the Installation Guide. Tip, HOW-TO, and FAQ documents are also provided. All the Red Hat documentation is freely available under the GNU General Public License. Before installing Red Hat Enterprise Linux on your system, you may want to check the online Installation guide. The Red Hat Magazine provides information on the latest features.

Web Site	Name
www.fedoraproject.org	Fedora Resources
http://download.fedoraproject.org	Fedora repository, mirror link
http://mirrors.fedoraproject.org	Fedora mirrors list
http://download.fedora.redhat.com	Fedora repository site (CD)
www.fedoraproject.org/wiki/Tours/Fedora10	Fedora 10 tour, with images and videos
www.fedoraproject.org/wiki/Tools/yum	YUM tools
http://docs.fedoraproject.org/install-guide/f9/en_US/	Fedora Installation guide
www.fedoraproject.org/wiki/CommunityWebsites	Fedora Community Web sites
www.fedoraproject.org/wiki/Overview	Fedora Project Overview
www.fedoraproject.org/wiki/FAQ	Fedora FAQ
http://docs.fedoraproject.org	Documentation and support tutorials for Fedora releases.
www.fedoraforum.org	End-user discussion support forum, endorsed by the Fedora Project. Includes FAQs and news links.
www.fedorafaq.org	Unofficial FAQ with quick help topics such as enabling MP3 and 3-D graphic card support.
www.fedoranews.org	Collects the latest news and developments on Fedora.
www.linux-foundation.org	The Linux Foundation, Official Linux development.
www.kernel.org	Latest Linux kernels.
www.redhat.com	The Red Hat Web site
www.redhat.com/magazine	Red Hat Magazine with specialized articles on latest developments.
www.centos.org	Community Enterprise Operating System, CENTOS (Red Hat based)

Table 1-1: Fedora sites

Fedora 10

The new release of Fedora features key updates to critical applications as well as new tools replacing former ones. There is a new configuration tool for managing firewall, system-config-firewall. The default sound interface is now PulseAudio, though ALSA still provides sound drivers. A demo of the GNOME Online Desktop provides easy access to online services like mail, Google docs, and flickr.

Installing Fedora continues to be simplified. You can install from a standard DVD or from Live CD/DVDs. A core set of applications are installed, and you add to them as you wish. Following installation, added software is taken either from the disk or from online repositories, depending on which is more up to date. You will find that the software on your disk becomes quickly obsolete. Most software will be retrieved from the online Fedora repository. Install screens have been reduced to just a few screens, moving quickly through default partitioning, network detection, and time settings, to the package selection. Firewall and SELinux configuration are part of the post-install configuration procedure.

The Fedora distribution of Linux is available online at numerous FTP sites. Fedora maintains its own FTP site at **http://download.fedora.redhat.com** along with a mirrors listing at **http://mirrors.fedoraproject.org**, where you can download the entire current release of Fedora Linux, as well as updates and additional software. The Web page **http://download.fedoraproject.org** links to an available mirror for you. Install DVDs can be downloaded from mirrors. The following information is derived for the official Fedora 10 Release notes. Consult these notes for detailed information about all new changes. The Fedora release notes are located on the all the Fedora spins as an HTML file on the top directory. You can also fine the release notes at:

```
http://docs.fedoraproject.org/release-notes/f10/
```

For a tour of Fedora 10 with images and video, check the following site.

```
www.fedoraproject.org/wiki/Tours/Fedora10
```

Desktop Changes

- The major third party Fedora compliant repositories have been integrated into one repository, RPM Fusion (**http://rpmfusion.org**). The repositories integrated include Livna (**http://rpm.livna.org**) Freshrpms (**www.freshrpms.net**), and Dribble (**http://dribble.org.uk**). Software packages are no longer available on these sites (Freshrpms still provides older packages). RPM Fusion provides both free and non-free collections. Simply download and install the RPM Fusion YUM configuration package from the RPM Fusion Web site, to automatically configure YUM and PackageKit to access all the third party repository software. There are separate configuration packages for free and non-free collections.

- With the NetworkManager, you can automatically select wireless connections. NetworkManager now supports mobile broadband 3G connections. NetworkManager can also configure IP, PPP, and DSL connections.

- Fedora 10 supports wireless connection sharing, allowing other systems to use a Fedora wireless system as a wireless network node, setting up an ad hoc local wireless network.

`http://fedoraproject.org/wiki/Features/ConnectionSharing`

> ➢ Improved interface for the printing tool, system-config-printer. New job queue and printer configuration window, as well as support for both personal and system defaults.

`http://fedoraproject.org/wiki/Features/BetterPrinting`

> ➢ New theme and background called Solar.

> ➢ PulseAudio sound server has now uses timer-based audio scheduling instead of the interrupt-driven methods. Provides cleaner audio with power savings. The Pulse Audio server applet provides direct access to all Pulse Audio applications.

`http://fedoraproject.org/wiki/Features/GlitchFreeAudio`

> ➢ Gstreamer codec packages can be made Gstreamer detectable. When a new codec is required, its package can be installed directly by PackageKit (YUM), if available. Codeina has been replaced by this PackageKit support.

> ➢ Totem supports backends, no longer requiring recompilation to support additional playback capability. In particular the Totem Xine backend provides Xine support on Totem (**totem-xine** package). Use the **totem-backend** command to change backends.

> ➢ Updated version of bluetooth.

> ➢ Empathy instant messenger (GNOME 2.24) with telepathy plugin framework.

> ➢ GNOME Display Manager (GDM) is updated with PolicyKit control. Still no configuration support (manual editing of **/etc/gdm/custom.conf**).

`http://live.gnome.org/GDM/2.22/Configuration`

> ➢ Codeina codec installation helper has been replaced by direct PackageKit support for Gstreamer codec detection and installation.

> ➢ For KDE, users can use KPackageKit, the KDE version of PackageKit, to manage software.

> ➢ Fedora also supports numerous games.

`http://fedoraproject.org/wiki/Games`

> ➢ KDE 4.1 desktop with file manager (dolphin), theme (oxygen), and desktop/panel (Plasma), with hardware integration (Solid) and multimedia support (Phonon).

> ➢ To better allow access by users to system level applications, /sbin and /usr/sbin have now been added to all user PATHs, allow direct use of configuration features for applications like Network Manager by users.

> ➢ The LXDE desktop (Lightweight X11 Desktop Environment) is available for smaller systems like netbooks, OLPC, embedded systems, and older computers.

> ➢ Sugar desktop for OLPC computers can now be used on Fedora installs.

> ➢ Automatic detection of InfraRed remote control devices (LIRC), now supported directly by an LIRC daemon. Configuration supported by lirc, lirc-remotes, and gnome-lirc-properties (System | Preferences | Hardware | Infrared Remote Control). Plugins provided for Totem, Rythmbox, and XMMS. Also PulseAudio support.

`http://fedoraproject.org/wiki/Features/BetterLIRCSupport`

  ➢ Additional WebCAM drivers.

`http://fedoraproject.org/wiki/Features/BetterWebcamSupport`

Administration and System Changes

  ➢ The Red Hat Graphical Boot (RHGB) has been replaced by Plymouth, a much more streamlined, efficient, and faster graphical boot that does not require X server support. It relies on the kernel's Kernel Modesettings (KMS) feature that provides direct support for basic graphics. With the Direct Rendering Manager drivers Plymouth can make use of various graphical plugins. KMS support is currently provided for ATI graphics cards with Intel in development. Nvidia does not support KMS.

`http://fedoraproject.org/wiki/Features/BetterStartup`

  ➢ Input devices (mice and keyboards) are now managed as hotplugged devices by HAL. HAL provides support directly to the Xorg **evdev** driver. Input devices are no longer configured in **/etc/X11/xorg.conf**. All references to input devices are removed from this file. Input devices are now configured by HAL **.fdi** files (**10-x11-input.fdi**). If you are using a customized **xorg.conf** file, be sure to edit it to remove the input device entries.

  ➢ Firstaidkit automated recover tool provides recovering operations for common problems. The tool uses pluggable components so that new recovery operations can be added easily. FirstAidKit is meant to work in Rescue mode from a Rescue CD/DVD disc or Live CD/DVD, first diagnosing the problem and then suggesting a plugin to run to fix it. The user can then choose to run the plugin, fixing the problem.

`http://fedoraproject.org/wiki/Features/FirstAidKit`

  ➢ Kernel Modesettings (KMS) provides faster boot, fast user switching, and seamless X server switching (available for ATI graphics cards).

  ➢ Virtualization now supports storage access outside of the Virtual disks. Virtual systems can now mount and access partitions, LVM volumes, and iSCSI storage.

  ➢ The sectool SELinux utility performs security audits on your system for intrusion detection, **sectool** and **sectool-gui** packages.

  ➢ RPM 4.6 is a major rewrite of the Red Hat Package Manager (RPM). Commands and interface remain the same. RPM 4.6 also supports a new compression method, LZMA (Lempel-Ziv-Markov chain-Algorithm), for faster download and space savings. Better lower level integration with YUM.

`http://rpm.org/wiki/Releases/4.6.0`

  ➢ Support for managing online account information and access. Online account information like that for Google can now be stored by GConf with GNOME Keyring, and on the online account service provided by **online.gnome.org**. Currently only the Online Desktop is supported (for Google and Twitter), but other applications may soon be supported.

  ➢ MySQL has been upgraded to version 5.0 with numerous changes.

`http://dev.mysql.com/doc/refman/5.0/en/releasenotes-cs-5-0-67.html`

> ➤ OpenJDK 6, open source JAVA, is now installed for the JAVA Runtime Environment service. The java-gcj-compat collection is still available and provides Java runtime environment compatibility.

Installation Issues

> ➤ Install from a Live image running in RAM or on a USB drive

> ➤ For IDE drives, the device name hd has been deprecated, and is replaced by sd (except for PPC Fedora versions). IDE drives are no longer referred to as /dev/hd*x*, but as /dev/sd*x*.

> ➤ Most motherboard RAID controllers are supported by Fedora using the **dmraid** module. If your motherboard RAID is not supported, you can use Linux software RAID.

> ➤ If you computer has multiple network interfaces (NIC or PXE), it may not assign eth0 to the first network interface (see release notes).

> ➤ All hard disks, including SATA and IDE, are limited to 15 partitions per disk (SCSI device specifications), instead of 63 (IDE device specifications). If your hard disk has more than 15 partitions, you should migrate them to an LVM volume.

> ➤ During installation, NTFS support is implemented with **ntfs-3g**. NTFS partitions on your system will automatically be detected and mounted for you at subdirectories in the **/media** directory. The subdirectory names will use the partition labels or the name **disk**.

Upgrade Issues

> ➤ Device labeling is required for upgrading systems using direct hard disk partitions, instead of LVM devices. The kernel now handles device names hd*x* and sd*x* differently from previous releases. The install process sidesteps this confusion by identifying drives by their labels instead of their device names. This means that all drives now have to be labeled before installations. If upgrading from a previous version of Fedora, be sure your hard drive partitions are all labeled. If not, then label them before upgrading. Upgrading cannot proceed unless all disks are labeled.

> ➤ If you are using LVM partitions (the default for previous Fedora installations), your devices are already labeled.

> ➤ Use the following block ID command to check if your devices are already labeled. Each device should have a LABEL field.

```
/sbin/blkid
```

> ➤ If you add a label, be sure to also add the same label in the devices corresponding entry in the **/etc/fstab** file.

> ➤ Should you have to add a root device label, be sure to add the label entry in the kernel line of the **/etc/boot/grub.conf** file. Usually your root device will likely be already labeled. By default, previous installations will assign a / label to the root device.

> ➤ Be sure to test your changes by rebooting and making sure everything mounts and starts up correctly.

> ➢ When upgrading be sure to backup your **/home** and **/etc** directories (also **/opt** and **/usr/local** for any customized packages).

Fedora ISO images

Fedora disks are released as a set of spins that collect software for different purposes. Currently there are five spins available: The standard DVD image for desktops, workstations, and servers, the Live CD/DVD (GNOME Desktop), Fedora KDE Live CD, Fedora Developer Live CD, and Fedora Electronic Lab (FEL) Live CD. The regular Fedora DVD spin includes a collection of workstation and server software, but not the entire collection. Spins are created with Pungi, which you can use to develop your own customized spins. You can find out more information about spins at: **https://fedoraproject.org/wiki/SIGs/Spins/10/**, which also describes Custom Spins.

Fedora Live CD: The Fedroa GNOME desktop live CD, available in i386 and x86_64 versions.

Fedora live DVD: The Fedroa install live DVD with more complete selection of software, available in i386 and x86_64 versions.

Fedora KDE live CD: The Fedroa KDE desktop live CD, available in i386 and x86_64 versions..

Fedora Custom Spins

Custom spins are also available and can be located at the Fedora Projects Spins Tracker. Torrents for these can be These can be downloaded from **http://spins.fedoraproject.org**,

Fedora Developer Spin: i686 only. Includes GNOME desktop with development applications like Eclipse IDE, along with debugging and profiling tools, as well as documentation.

Fedora FEL Spin: Fedora Electronics Lab spin.

Fedora Edu/Math Spin: Fedora Educatonal and Math spcin.

Fedora BrOffice: Brazillian-Protugese spin with OpenOffice.org.

Fedora AOS Spin: JeOS spin for building system images for virtual appliances.

Fedora XFCE Desktop Spin: Features the light-weight XFCE desktop instead of GNOME or KDE.

Fedora specialized spins

In addition there are several specialized spins, still under development, with version currently avaialbe. They have their own locations. These include the Omega and Sugar Fedora spins.

Omega: Fedora Multimedia spin with complete set of multimedia codecs from both RPM Fusion and Livna. Currently at:

```
ftp://ftp.infradead.org/pub/spins/
```

Sugar Spin: OLPC desktop, Currently at:

http://alt.fedoraproject.org/pub/alt/olpc/0.82/

Linux Kernel

Three kernel builds are available. One is the Native version used on most systems, one is a specialized kernel for PAE (32 bit over 4 GIGs of memory), and the other is a debugging kernel used in development. For each of these kernels there may be 32bit, 64bit, and ppc versions. Both the Native and PAE versions include support for Kdump, SMP (Hyper-threading), and Xen Para-virtualizations (separate kernels for these features are no longer required).

The kernel spec file is named just **kernel.spec** instead of including the kernel version.

Multimedia

Though licensed multimedia formats like MP3 and DVD are still excluded. Open Source formats are all included, such as Vorbis, Ogg, Theora, Speex, and FLAC. Multimedia codecs with licensing issues can be directly downloaded with Packagekit, once you have configured YUM to use the RPM Fusion repository on your system (just install the **http://rpmfusion.org** configuration package for Fedora 10 which is available from that site). The RPM Fusion repository is not configured by default.

You can obtain full licensed codecs free or cheaply for GStreamer applications from Fluendo (**www.fluendo.com**).

X Window System

The X server sever is designed to automatically detect and configure your graphics hardware, significantly reducing the entries in the **/etc/X11/xorg.conf** file. Only the graphics driver information is placed in the **xorg.conf** file. Other devices including the monitor, keyboard, and mouse are configured automatically by HAL. The monitor is queried for correct resolution and frequency. You can change the resolution with the System | Preferences | Hardware | Screen Resolution tool. If your monitor or graphics card is incorrectly detected, you can use System | Administration | Display to choose the correct monitor or graphics card. Backup the **/etc/X11/xorg.conf** file first.

Standard Fedora features

Listed here are some of the features that are now standard for Fedora.

➢ A free and open source Flash player, **swfdec**, is now included with Fedora.

➢ Consolidated dictionary support for applications like Thunderbird, Firefox, GNOME, and OpenOffice.org.

➢ The Thunderbird mail client is included in this release.

➢ FreeIPA integrates auditing, identity, and policy management using a Web page interface. You can easily configure NTP, Kerberos, and DNS. Combines the Fedora directory server and Free RADIUS.

➢ Development support for the **ext4** file system, which is more scalable with better performance. Useful for large files.

➢ Service management is now handled by the Upstart init daemon, replacing the older System V init daemon. Upstart is event driven, and is much more flexible in handling services. Originally developed for Ubuntu, it is now standard for Fedora. System V Init structure is still emulated by Upstart which most services still use.

➢ Browsing Windows shares and remote printers with Samba is enabled from Gnome, through the Gnome virtual file manger. You can use system-config-firewall to enable Samba Windows browsing.

➢ Localized Common User Directories (xdg-user-dirs) automatically sets up Documents, Video, and Music directories in user home directories.

➢ A demo version of the GNOME Online Desktop provides a panel and links to online resources like Google mail and flickr (online-desktop).

➢ Removable devices like USB printers, digital cameras, and card readers are automatically detected. CD/DVD discs are treated as removable devices, automatically displayed and accessed when inserted. Input devices are now treated as removable devices.

➢ The IDE hard disk drivers are now supported by the Serial ATA drivers. All IDE devices are named with an **sd** prefix, not the **hd** prefix.

➢ A wide range of multimedia applications are included, such as a video player and a TV viewer, along with compatible support from various multimedia applications and libraries available from **http://rpmfusion.org**, such as DVD and DivX support.

➢ Information about hot plugged devices is provided to applications with the Hardware Abstraction Layer (HAL) from freedesktop.org. This allows applications like GNOME to easily display and manage removable devices.

➢ To better manage SELinux configurations, you can use setroubleshoot, which will notify you of any problems.

➢ PackageKit is used to automatically update your Fedora system and all its installed applications, from the YUM Fedora online repositories.

➢ With the alternative compiz window manager, desktop AIGLX effects can be enabled. From the Administration | Preferences | Look And Feel | Desktop Effect entry, choose Enable Effects. You will see wobbling windows when moved, and rotating workspaces with the workspace switcher.

Fedora Live DVD/CD

With the Fedora Live DVD/CD you can run Fedora from any DVD/CD-ROM drive. Some images use CDs and others use DVDs. In effect, you can carry your operating system with you on just a DVD/CD-ROM. New users could also use the Live-DVD/CD to check out Fedora to see if they like it. Files and data can be written to removable devices like USB drives, but the OS configuration cannot be changed. You could also mount partitions from hard drives on the system you are running the Live DVD/CD on. You can find out more about the Fedora Live DVD/CD at **www.fedoraproject.org/wiki/FedoraLiveCD**.

The Live DVD/CD provided by Fedora includes a very limited set of software packages. OpenOffice applications are not provided, just Abiword for word processing and Gnumeric for spread sheets. Servers are not included. For desktop support you use GNOME. Other than these limitations, you have a fully operational Fedora desktop. You have the full set of administrative tools, with which you can add users and change configuration settings while the Live DVD/CD is running. When you shut down, the configuration information is lost.

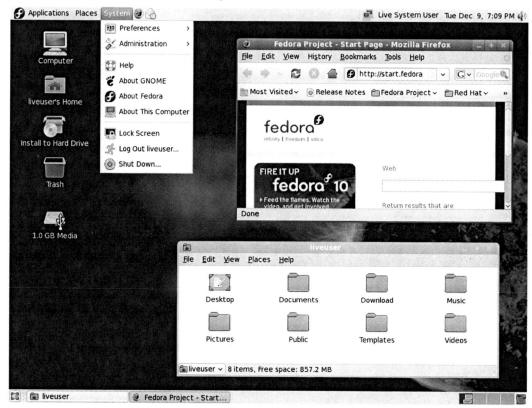

Figure 1-1: Fedora Live CD

You can logout, but this will display a login screen with a simple login button and a language menu. You can use the language menu to change your language. But you cannot shut down or restart from the login menu. You can only do that from the desktop.

The Live DVD/CD enables NetworkManager by default, automatically detecting and configuring your network connection. The Live DVD/CDs have a default username that has no password.

Fedora provides both official and custom spins. The Live CD images are available from **http://fedoraproject.org/get-fedora** page, on the LiveCD segment. Fedora provides a GNOME and KDE desktop official Live CD spins.

Fedora Live: Available for i868, x86_64, and ppc. Includes Gnome desktop and productivity applications. 686 is a Live CD, x86_64 and ppc are DVDs.

Fedora KDE Live: Available for i686 and x86_64. Includes KDE desktop. 686 version is a CD, x86_64 is a DVD.

Starting the Live DVD/CD

When you first boot, you can press the spacebar to display the boot options. These include: booting up the Live DVD/CD directly (default), verifying the disk media first, performing a memory test, or to boot another OS already on your hard disk. If you press nothing, then the Live DVD/CD starts up automatically. After your system starts up, you will be presented with the standard Login screen (the KDE disk will boot directly to the desktop). You will be automatically logged in. The GNOME (see Figure 1-1) or KDE (see Figure 1-2) desktop will then start up.

An easy way to save data from a Live session is to use a USB drive. On GNOME, the USB drive will appear as an icon on the desktop. Double click on it to open a file manager window for the USB drive. You can then copy files generated during the session to the USB drive. Remember to eject the drive before removing (right-click on icon and select Eject).

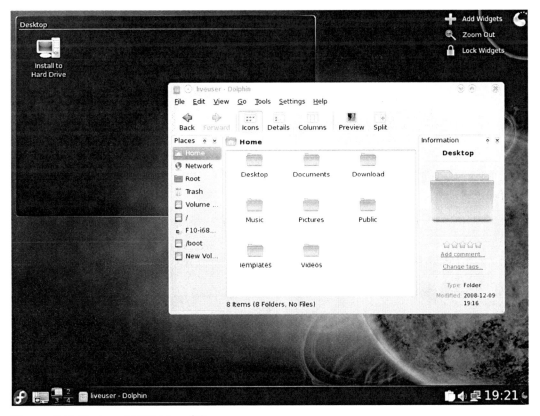

Figure 1-2: Fedora KDE Live CD

Using USB drives on KDE

The KDE Live CD uses the new Plasma desktop and panel. USB drives are no longer displayed as icons on the desktop. An icon for the USB drive will appear on the Kickoff Computer menu, in the file manager sidebar, and the New Device Notifier applet (computer screen image next to Fedora menu image on the left side of the panel). To mount the drive, just click its entry in any of these locations, usually the New Device Notifier. A mount emblem will appear on the drive (see Figure 1-3). On the file manager window, click the USB drive entry in the sidebar to open the USB drive file listing. You can then save files to the drive.

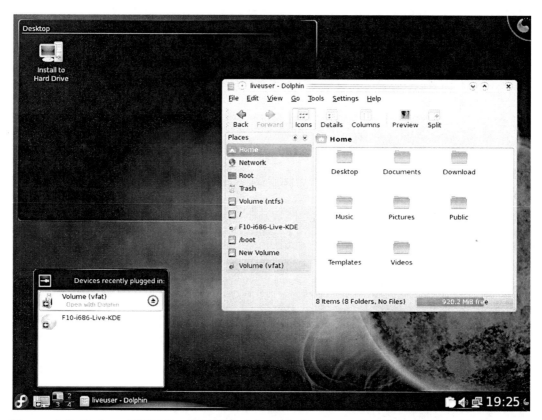

Figure 1-3: Fedora KDE Live CD USB drive as shown on the New Device Notifier (lower left) and the file manager sidebar (last entry).

To remove a USB drive using either the Kickoff menu or the New Device Notifier, pass your mouse over the USB entry in either. An Eject button will appear. Click on that button to unmount the USB drive. You can then remove it. On the file manager sidebar entry, right-click on the USB entry. This opens a menu with an option to "Safely remove Volume". Select this option to finish writing any data to the drive. The mount emblem will disappear from the USB icon and you can then safely remove the USB drive.

Installing Fedora from a Live CD

The Live CD can also be used as an installation disk, providing its limited collection of software on a system, but installing a full fledged Fedora operating system that can be expanded and updated from Fedora online repositories (see Chapter 4). In this case you would not have to download a complete set of Fedora installation disks, just the Live CD, and add packages later from repositories. Double-click on the "Install to Hard Drive" icon on the desktop to start the installation (see Chapter 2, Figure 2-1). Installs from a Live disk will enable NetworkManager by default and disable the SSH daemon (sshd).

Create your own Live CD

You can also create your own Live CD which you can have include your favorite software. From an installed Fedora system, you can use the **livecd-creator** to create your own Live CD (**livecd-tools** package). Install the **livecd-tools** package, if not already installed. The **livecd-creator** tool uses a configuration file set up in kickstart syntax to create a Live CD ISO image. Live CD kickstart configuration files for a minimal, desktop (GNOME), and KDE package selection is located at **/usr/share/livecdtools**.

The livecd-creator help option provides a complete listing of options with examples, **--help**. You use the **--config** option to specify a kickstart configuration file, the **--label** option to name your disk, and the **--repo** option to specify any special repositories. Check the README file in /usr/shard/doc/livecd-tools version for detailed information. The livecd-creator tool will first create a disk image, then download specified packages and install them on the image, install the boot loader, and then create the ISO image. The image and packages are held in the /var/tmp directory. The following creates a simple GNOME desktop Live CD (entered as one line).

```
livecd-creator --config=/usr/share/livecd-tools/livecd-fedora-desktop.ks --fslabel=MyFedora-Live
```

In the configuration file you set start up options like language, firewall, xconfig for graphical start up, and specific services like NetworkManager and DHCP for network connections. The repositories used are specified in the **repo** entries. You can use the desktop, minimal, and KDE configuration files as a base to work from. Packages are listed after the **%packages** entry. For individual packages you simply specify the package's unique name. Kickstart syntax for groups of packages conforms to the same categories and subheadings use in Add/Remove Software category sidebar panel (PackageKit). These are useful when you have to select an extensive set packages like those used for the GNOME or KDE desktops. Be sure to prefix a group name with the @ symbol, like **@Base** for the base packages. .

USB Live Disk

You can also install Fedora Live images to a USB disk. The procedure is not destructive. Your original data on the USB disk is preserved. To create a Live USB drive, you can either use the liveusb-creator application (**liveusb-creator** package), or the livecd-iso-to-disk command (**livecd-tools** package).

liveusb-creator

The liveusb-creator application is a GNOME application with an easy to use interface for creating a Live USB image from a Live CD iso image file. Once installed you can start liveusb-creator from Applications | System Tools | liveusb-creator. This opens the Fedora LiveUSB Creator window as shown in Figure 1-4. Use the Browse button to locate the USB image or download one using the Download Fedora pop-up menu. The selected image will appear in the pane below. Use the Target Device pop-up menu to select the USB drive to use, if more than one. The Persistent Storage slider allows you to create an overlay memory segment on which changes and added data can be saved. When you are ready, just click the Create Live USB button on the bottom of the window.

Figure 1-4: Fedora LiveUSB Creator

livecd-iso-to-disk

You can also install Fedora Live images to a USB disk using the **livecd-iso-to-disk** command to install the image (part of the **livecd-tools** package). This is a command line tool that you enter in a Terminal window. Use the Live image and the device name the USB disk as your arguments.

```
/usr/bin/livecd-iso-to-disk    F10-i686-Live.iso    /dev/sdb1
```

Each Live CD also provides a **livecd-iso-to-disk** script in its LiveOS directory.

Live USB Persistence Storage

If you want to be able to make changes to the Fedora OS on the USB Live version, you set up an overlay memory segment on the USB drive. To do this, use the **--overlay-size-mb** option with the size of the overlay in megabytes. Be sure your USB drive is large enough to accommodate both the overlay memory and the CD image. The following allows for 512 MB of persistent data that will be encrypted.

```
livecd-iso-to-disk --overlay-size-mb 512   F10-i686-Live.iso  /dev/sbd1
```

Persistent Home Directory

If you want to be able to save data to a **/home** directory on the USB Live version, you set up a home directory memory segment. To do this, use the **--home-size-mb** option with the size of the home directory segment in megabytes. Be sure your USB drive is large enough to accommodate the home memory and the CD image, as well as a memory overly if you also want to enable changes to the operating system. Your **/home** directory memory segment will be encrypted by default to protect your data in case it is lost or stolen. Upon creating your overlay, you will be prompted for a passphrase. Whenever to boot up your USB system, you will be prompted for the passphrase. The following allows for 1024MB **/home** directory that will be encrypted.

```
livecd-iso-to-disk --home-size-mb 1024   F10-i686-Live.iso  /dev/sbd1
```

If you do not want the data encrypted, add the **--unencrypted-home** option when creating the disk.

Combining both the overlay and the /home memory would use a command like the following. In all about 3 GB of disk space would be required.

livecd-iso-to-disk --overlay-size-mb 512 --home-size-mb 1024 Fedora-10-Live-i686.iso /dev/sbd

Fedora 10 Desktop Look and Feel:

Fedora 10 features a desktop look and feel with a Fedora logo, as well as the new default Fedora solar screen background. The logo depicts an F encased in a blue circle. On the main panel you will now see the blue Fedora logo as the icon for the Applications menu. The default background is the Fedora blue F logo encased in a bubble and surrounded by other rising bubbles. The logo even has its own package, fedora-logos.

The logo is designed to represent three features of the Linux community and development: freedom, communication, and infinite possibilities - the **f** for freedom, which melds into the Infinity symbol, both encased in a speech bubble evoking communication (voice). Free and open software with infinite possibilities developed through global communication. The idea is to evoke the spirit and purpose of Linux development as one of infinite freedom given a voice. The logo incorporates the four basic ideals of Fedora: open, free, innovative, and forward looking (see Figure 1-5). See **http://fedoraproject.org/wiki/Logo** for more details. A description of the logo as shown on the site is shown here.

infinity   freedom   voice

Figure 1-5: Fedora Logo

The default theme is Nodoka, a GNOME theme designed for Fedora. Buttons and windows are easier to use, and appear more pleasing to the eye. Of course numerous other themes are available from the Gnome theme manager (see Figure 1-6).

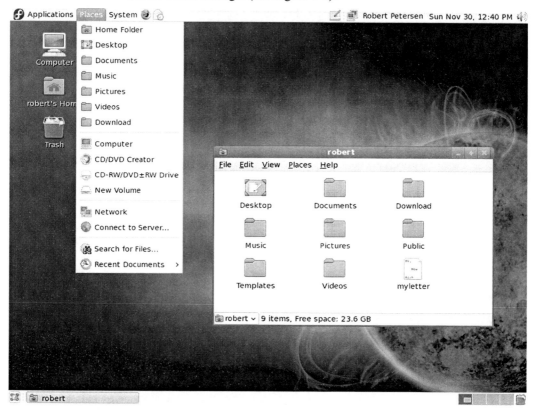

Figure 1-6: Fedora 10 desktop with Fedora logos

Open Source Software

Linux was developed as a cooperative Open Source effort over the Internet, so no company or institution controls Linux. Software developed for Linux reflects this background. Development often takes place when Linux users decide to work on a project together. The software is posted at an Internet site, and any Linux user can then access the site and download the software. Linux software development has always operated in an Internet environment and is global in scope, enlisting programmers from around the world. The only thing you need to start a Linux-based software project is a Web site.

Most Linux software is developed as Open Source software. This means that the source code for an application is freely distributed along with the application. Programmers over the Internet can make their own contributions to a software package's development, modifying and correcting the source code. Linux is an open source operating system. Its source code is included in all its distributions and is freely available on the Internet. Many major software development efforts are also open source projects, as are the KDE and GNOME desktops along with most of their applications. The Netscape Communicator Web browser package has also become open source, with its source code freely available. The OpenOffice office suite supported by Sun is an open source project based on the Star Office office suite (StarOffice is essentially Sun's commercial version of OpenOffice). Many of the open source applications that run on Linux have located their Web sites at SourceForge (**www.sourceforge.net**), which is a hosting site designed specifically to support open source projects. You can find more information about the Open Source movement at **www.opensource.org**.

Open source software is protected by public licenses. These prevent commercial companies from taking control of open source software by adding a few modifications of their own, copyrighting those changes, and selling the software as their own product. The most popular public license is the GNU General Public License provided by the Free Software Foundation. This is the license that Linux is distributed under. The GNU General Public License retains the copyright, freely licensing the software with the requirement that the software and any modifications made to it always be freely available. Other public licenses have also been created to support the demands of different kinds of open source projects. The GNU Lesser General Public License (LGPL) lets commercial applications use GNU licensed software libraries. The Qt Public License (QPL) lets open source developers use the Qt libraries essential to the KDE desktop. You can find a complete listing at **www.opensource.org**.

Linux is currently copyrighted under a GNU public license provided by the Free Software Foundation, and it is often referred to as GNU software (see **www.gnu.org**). GNU software is distributed free, provided it is freely distributed to others. GNU software has proved both reliable and effective. Many of the popular Linux utilities, such as C compilers, shells, and editors, are GNU software applications. Installed with your Linux distribution are the GNU C++ and Lisp compilers, Vi and Emacs editors, BASH and TCSH shells, as well as TeX and Ghostscript document formatters. In addition, there are many open source software projects that are licensed under the GNU General Public License (GPL). Many of these software applications are available at different Internet sites, and these are listed in Table 1-2. Chapter 4 describes in detail the process of downloading software applications from Internet sites and installing them on your system.

Under the terms of the GNU General Public License, the original author retains the copyright, although anyone can modify the software and redistribute it, provided the source code is included, made public, and provided free. Also, no restriction exists on selling the software or giving it away free. One distributor could charge for the software, while another one could provide it free of charge. Major software companies are also providing Linux versions of their most popular applications. Oracle provides a Linux version of its Oracle database. (At present, no plans seem in the works for Microsoft applications.)

Fedora Software Repositories

For Fedora, you can update to the latest software from the Fedora YUM repository using Update System (see Chapter 4). Your Update System tool is already configured to access the Fedora repositories.

The Fedora distribution provides a comprehensive selection of software ranging from office and multimedia applications to Internet servers and administration services (see Table 1-2). Many popular applications are not included, though Fedora-compliant versions are provided on associated software sites. During installation, YUM is configured to access Fedora repositories.

URL	Internet Site
`http://fedoraproject.org/get-fedora`	Download page for the latest Fedora releases, includes direct, jigdo, and bittorrent downloads.
`http://mirrors.fedoraproject.org`	Page listing Fedora mirrors
`http://download.fedoraproject.com`	Link to best available mirror
`http://download1.rpmfusion.org` `http://rpmfusion.org`	Fedora applications not included with the distribution due to licensing and other restrictions. RPM Fusion is an official extension of the Fedora Project, integrating Livna, Freshrpms, and Dribble.
`http://download.fedora.redhat.com`	Fedora repository, primary site
`http://sources.redhat.com`	Open source software hosted by Red Hat
`http://torrent.fedoraproject.org`	Fedora BitTorrent site for BitTorrent downloads of Fedora distribution ISO images

Table 1-2: Fedora Software Repositories and download sites

Due to licensing restrictions, multimedia support for popular operations like MP3, DVD, and DivX is not included with Fedora distributions. You can download free licensed MP3 GStreamer plug-in from **www.fluendo.com**. A Fedora Project–associated site, RPM Fusion, **http://rpmfusion.org**, does provided support for these functions. Here you can download support for MP3, DVD, and DivX software. Fedora does not provide support for the official Nvidia or ATI vendor released Linux graphics drivers. This site integrates support previously provided by Livna, Freshrpms, and Dribble (see Chapter 4). Fedora does include the generic X.org Nvidia and ATI drivers, which will provide all the capabilities most people need. You do not have to use the Nvidia or ATI vendor drivers.

The associated Fedora repositories, like RPM Fusion, will have Fedora-compliant YUM configuration files that you can download and install as an RPM package. You can then use the software manager or the yum command to select, download, and install software from the associated repository directly.

Third-Party Linux Software Archives

Though almost all application should be included in the Fedora software repository or its associated repositories like **http://rpmfusion.org**, you could download and install software from third-party software archives. Always check first to see if the software you want is already in the Fedora or Fedora associated repositories. If it is not available, then you would download from a third-party online site.

Several third-party repositories make it easy to locate an application and find information about it. Of particular note are **www.sourceforge.net**, **www.gnu.org**, **www.rpmfind.net**, **www.gnomefilefs.org**, and **www.kde-apps.org**. Sites for Linux software are listed in Table 1-3, along with several specialized sites, such as those for commercial and game software. When downloading software packages, always check to see if the versions are packaged for your particular distribution. For example, **www.rpmfind.net**, **www.freshmeat.net**, and **www.sourceforge.net** are also good places for locating RPM packages.

URL	Internet Site
`www.sourceforge.net`	SourceForge, open source software development site for Linux applications
`www.gnomefiles.org`	GNOME applications
`www.kde-apps.org`	KDE software repository
`www.freshmeat.net`	New Linux software
`www.rpmfind.net`	RPM package repository
`www.gnu.org`	GNU archive
`www.happypenguin.org`	Linux Game Tome
`www.linuxgames.com`	Linux games
`www.fluendo.com`	Licensed multimedia codecs for Linux, including free MP3 code.

Table 1-3: Third-Party Linux Software Archives

Linux Documentation

Linux documentation has also been developed over the Internet. Much of the documentation currently available for Linux can be downloaded from Internet FTP sites. A special Linux project called the Linux Documentation Project (LDP), headed by Matt Welsh, has developed a complete set of Linux manuals. The documentation is available at the LDP home site at **www.tldp.org**. The documentation includes a user's guide, an introduction, and administrative guides. These are available in text, PostScript, or Web page format. You can also find briefer explanations, in what are referred to as HOW-TO documents. The Linux documentation for your installed software will be available at your **/usr/share/doc** directory. As previously noted, some Fedora-specific documentation is available at **http://doc.fedoraproject.org**. The **www.gnome.org** site holds documentation for the GNOME desktop, while **www.kde.org** holds documentation for the KDE desktop.

Operating Systems and Linux

An *operating system* is a program that manages computer hardware and software for the user. Operating systems were originally designed to perform repetitive hardware tasks, which centered on managing files, running programs, and receiving commands from the user. You interact with an operating system through a *user interface,* which allows the operating system to receive and interpret instructions sent by the user. You only need to send an instruction to the operating system to perform a task, such as reading a file or printing a document. An operating system's user interface can be as simple as entering commands on a line or as complex as selecting menus and icons on a desktop.

An operating system also manages software applications. To perform different tasks, such as editing documents or performing calculations, you need specific software applications. An *editor* is an example of a software application that enables you to edit a document, making changes and adding new text. The editor itself is a program consisting of instructions to be executed by the computer. For the program to be used, it must first be loaded into computer memory, and then its instructions are executed. The operating system controls the loading and execution of all programs, including any software applications. When you want to use an editor, simply instruct the operating system to load the editor application and execute it.

File management, program management, and user interaction are traditional features common to all operating systems. Linux, like all versions of Unix, adds two more features. Linux is a multi-user and multitasking system. As it is a *multitasking* system, you can ask the system to perform several tasks at the same time. While one task is being done, you can work on another. For example, you can edit a file while another file is being printed. You do not have to wait for the other file to finish printing before you edit. As it is a *multi-user* system, several users can log in to the system at the same time, each interacting with the system through a terminal.

As a version of UNIX, Linux shares that system's flexibility, a flexibility stemming from UNIX's research origins. Developed by Ken Thompson at AT&T Bell Laboratories in the late 1960s and early 1970s, the UNIX system incorporated many new developments in operating system design. Originally, UNIX was designed as an operating system for researchers. One major goal was to create a system that could support the researchers' changing demands. To do this, Thompson had to design a system that could deal with many different kinds of tasks. Flexibility became more important than hardware efficiency. Like UNIX, Linux has the advantage of being able to deal with the variety of tasks any user may face. The user is not confined to limited and rigid interactions with the operating system. Instead, the operating system is thought of as making a set of highly effective tools available to the user. This user-oriented philosophy means you can configure and program the system to meet your specific needs. With Linux, the operating system becomes an operating environment.

A Short History of Linux and UNIX

As a version of UNIX, the history of Linux naturally begins with UNIX. The story begins in the late 1960s, when a concerted effort to develop new operating system techniques occurred. In 1968, a consortium of researchers from General Electric, AT&T Bell Laboratories, and the Massachusetts Institute of Technology carried out a special operating system research project called MULTICS (the Multiplexed Information and Computing Service). MULTICS incorporated many new concepts in multitasking, file management, and user interaction.

UNIX

In 1969, Ken Thompson, Dennis Ritchie, and the researchers at AT&T Bell Laboratories developed the UNIX operating system, incorporating many of the features of the MULTICS research project. They tailored the system for the needs of a research environment, designing it to run on minicomputers. From its inception, UNIX was an affordable and efficient multi-user and multitasking operating system.

The UNIX system became popular at Bell Labs as more and more researchers started using the system. In 1973, Dennis Ritchie collaborated with Ken Thompson to rewrite the programming code for the UNIX system in the C programming language. UNIX gradually grew from one person's tailored design to a standard software product distributed by many different vendors, such as Novell and IBM. Initially, UNIX was treated as a research product. The first versions of UNIX were distributed free to the computer science departments of many noted universities. Throughout the 1970s, Bell Labs began issuing official versions of UNIX and licensing the systems to different users. One of these users was the Computer Science department of the University of California, Berkeley. Berkeley added many new features to the system that later became standard. In 1975, Berkeley released its own version of UNIX, known by its distribution arm, Berkeley Software Distribution (BSD). This BSD version of UNIX became a major contender to the AT&T Bell Labs version. AT&T developed several research versions of UNIX, and in 1983, it released the first commercial version, called System 3. This was later followed by System V, which became a supported commercial software product.

At the same time, the BSD version of UNIX was developing through several releases. In the late 1970s, BSD Unix became the basis of a research project by the Department of Defense's Advanced Research Projects Agency (DARPA). As a result, in 1983, Berkeley released a powerful version of UNIX called BSD release 4.2. This release included sophisticated file management as well as networking features based on Internet network protocols—the same protocols now used for the Internet. BSD release 4.2 was widely distributed and adopted by many vendors, such as Sun Microsystems.

In the mid-1980s, two competing standards emerged, one based on the AT&T version of UNIX and the other based on the BSD version. AT&T's Unix System Laboratories developed System V release 4. Several other companies, such as IBM and Hewlett-Packard, established the Open Software Foundation (OSF) to create their own standard version of UNIX. Two commercial standard versions of UNIX existed then—the OSF version and System V release 4.

Linux

Originally designed specifically for Intel-based personal computers, Linux started out as a personal project of a computer science student named Linus Torvalds at the University of Helsinki. At that time, students were making use of a program called *Minix,* which highlighted different UNIX features. Minix was created by Professor Andrew Tanenbaum and widely distributed over the Internet to students around the world. Linus' intention was to create an effective PC version of UNIX for Minix users. It was named Linux, and in 1991, Linus released version 0.11. Linux was widely distributed over the Internet, and in the following years, other programmers refined and added to it, incorporating most of the applications and features now found in standard UNIX systems. All the major window managers have been ported to Linux. Linux has all the networking tools, such as FTP file transfer support, Web browsers, and the whole range of network services such as e-mail, the domain name service, and dynamic host configuration, along with FTP, Web, and print servers. It also has a full set of program development utilities, such as C++ compilers and debuggers. Given all its features, the Linux operating system remains small, stable, and fast. In its simplest format, Linux can run effectively on only 2MB of memory.

Although Linux has developed in the free and open environment of the Internet, it adheres to official UNIX standards. Because of the proliferation of UNIX versions in the previous decades, the Institute of Electrical and Electronics Engineers (IEEE) developed an independent UNIX standard for the American National Standards Institute (ANSI). This new ANSI-standard UNIX is called the Portable Operating System Interface for Computer Environments (POSIX). The standard defines how a Unix-like system needs to operate, specifying details such as system calls and interfaces. POSIX defines a universal standard to which all UNIX versions must adhere. Most popular versions of UNIX are now POSIX-compliant. Linux was developed from the beginning according to the POSIX standard. Linux also adheres to the Linux file system hierarchy standard

(FHS), which specifies the location of files and directories in the Linux file structure. See **www.pathname.com/fhs** for more details.

Linux development is now overseen by The Linux Foundation (**www.linux-foundation.org**), which is a merger of The Free Standards Group and Open Source Development Labs (OSDL). This is the group that Linux Torvalds works with to develop new Linux versions. Actual Linux kernels are released at **www.kernel.org**.

Red Hat Enterprise Linux

As a company, Red Hat provides software and services to implement and support professional and commercial Linux systems. Red Hat has split its Linux development into two lines, Red Hat Enterprise Linux and the Fedora Project. Red Hat Enterprise Linux features commercial enterprise products for servers and workstations, with controlled releases issued every two years or so. The Fedora Project is an Open Source initiative whose Fedora release will be issued every six months on average, incorporating the most recent development in Linux operating system features as well as supported applications. Red Hat freely distributes its Fedora version of Linux under the GNU General Public License; the company generates income by providing professional-level support, consulting services, and training services. The Red Hat Certified Engineers (RHCE) training and certification program is designed to provide reliable and highly capable administrators and developers to maintain and customize professional-level Red Hat systems. Red Hat has forged software alliances with major companies like Oracle, IBM, Dell, and Sun.

Red Hat also maintains a strong commitment to open source Linux applications. Red Hat originated the RPM package system used on several distributions, which automatically installs and removes software packages. Red Hat is also providing much of the software development for the GNOME desktop, and it is a strong supporter of KDE.

Red Hat provides an extensive set of configuration tools designed to manage tasks such as adding users, starting servers, accessing remote directories, and configuring devices such as your monitor or printer. These tools are accessible on the System | Administration menu, as well as by their names, all beginning with the term "system-config" (see Chapters 13 and 14).

The Red Hat Enterprise line of products is designed for corporate, research, and business applications (www.redhat.com). These products focus on reliability and stability. They are released on a much more controlled schedule than the Fedora Project versions. What was once the low-cost consumer version of Red Hat Linux has been replaced by a scaled-down commercial desktop version for consumers and small business.

Red Hat provides both desktop and server versions of Red Hat Enterprise Linux. The desktop versions are offered as a simple desktop, a full workstation, or either a simple desktop or workstation with virtualization support (multi-OS). Keep in mind that the lowest level product, the simple desktop, does not include certain networking features like Samba and NFS servers, limiting the ability to share data. The workstation desktop versions have no system memory limit, provide software development support, and include Samba and NFS servers. The workstation virtualization version features unlimited guest OS support,

Red Hat Enterprise Linux is valued for its stability, often providing more stable implementations than Fedora. It is licensed as an open source GPL product, so is technically available to anyone. The versions that Red Hat sells include commercial products and support that are not open source. Red Hat does, however, freely provide its open source enterprise versions for download from its FTP site, **ftp.redhat.com/pub/redhat/linux/enterprise**. Earlier Enterprise versions are available in binary and ISO formats, though without any commercial features. The current Enterprise version is available as source files only.

CENTOS: Community Enterprise Operating System

Should you want to take advantage of the stability and reliability of Red Hat Enterprise Linux and not purchase the product, you can, instead, use CENTOS, the Community Enterprise Operating System (www.centos.org). CENTOS make no claim to have any official association with Red Hat. Instead, under the GPL license and Red Hat's open source distribution policies; it makes use of Red Hat Enterprise Linux source files to provide its own Linux distribution. In effect, with CENTOS, you can enjoy the stability, reliability, and enterprise capability of Red Hat Enterprise Linux, without the commercial support. Keep in mind that CENTOS is an independent operation that builds its own distribution. It has none of the support or guarantees that Red Hat provides for its products. (2)Red Hat and Fedora Documentation

2. Installing Fedora 10

Install Strategies

Minimal Install with Fedora Live

Install CD and DVDs

Upgrading Fedora

Installing Fedora

Custom partitioning

Additional Software Repositories

GRUB

Setup

Login and Logout

Rescue

Re-Installing the Boot Loader

This chapter describes the installation procedure for Fedora 10 Linux. Red Hat Enterprise Linux and Fedora use the same Anaconda installation program; it is designed to be easy to use and helpful, while at the same time efficient and brief, installing as many services and applications as possible. Detailed help panels explain each procedure, every step of the way. A Fedora 10 Installation Guide is also available online. First check the new Fedora Installation guide at:

```
http://docs.fedoraproject.org/install-guide/f10/
```

Note: With Fedora 10, IDE hard drives are no longer referenced with the hd prefix. Instead the sd prefix is used, the same as for Serial ATA (SATA) disk drives. This change requires that all hard drives be labeled before installation. Labels are now used to identify hard drives, instead of their device name.

Install Strategies: Making Use of Repositories

With Fedora 10, for installation you can use either the Fedora Install DVD or one of two Live CD/DVDs, Live desktop with GNOME or Live KDE with KDE. The Fedora Install DVD allows you to download from specified repositories during installation as well as select the packages you want installed. It also includes a more extensive set of packages on disc than the Live CD/DVDs.

A simple and effective install strategy is to install a minimal desktop, using just a Fedora Live DVD/CD (Gnome or KDE). You would only need to download the Fedora Live DVD/CD, use it to install, and then rely on the Fedora repository to update and install any other software. The reasoning behind this approach takes into consideration the dramatic impact of software repositories used for Fedora software installations, along with the very painless and simple process for automatically updating software. Keep in mind that software is continually being updated. This includes all software applications, including office, Internet, and graphics applications. Software is, in a sense, dynamic and fluid, in a state of constant change; on Fedora with its YUM enabled repositories, updates are performed for you automatically. This means that much of the software on the Install DVD becomes obsolete rapidly.

This noted, one major advantage of the Install DVD, is its flexibility in the selection of software packages during installation. The Live CD/DVDs install only a predetermined small set of packages. The Fedora Install DVD allows you to select the packages you want to install, offering a much larger selection to choose from. The Fedora Install DVD is an extensive collection of the more popular applications (servers, development, and desktop).

The Fedora Install DVD also allows you to install packages from the Fedora repository as well as from any associated repository you may choose, like **http://rpmfusion.org**. With the Fedora Install DVD, you can choose to download additional packages from the Fedora repository which are not included on the Fedora DVD. During installation you can elect to install packages from the Fedora repository, downloading them directly as part of the install process.

This can be helpful if you want to install packages for proprietary drivers like the Nvidia or ATI graphics drivers or certain multimedia applications not included on the Fedora repository (both available from **http://rpmfusion.org**).

With the Fedora Install DVD, you also have the option, in effect, to install everything, including those software packages from the repository. Once you have set up access to the Fedora repository, you could simply select all the packages. Depending on your Internet connection speed, this could take some time.

If you have no high-speed network connection to support extensive downloads and you want a more extensive collection of software than in available on the Live CD/DVDs, you would need to use the Fedora Install DVD. .

Also, when installing new software, you can choose to first check the Install DVD for current versions, and install from the DVD instead of having to perform a download. Much of the software is infrequently updated.

Live CD/DVD advantages

➢ Quick download of small install disk (about 800 MB)

➢ Can check out the desktop operations on a Live CD interface

➢ Install basic desktop quickly (cannot select packages)

➢ After the install, add current packages from online repositories as needed

Fedora Install DVD advantages

➢ Larger collection of initial software packages: servers, administration, multimedia, office. (much larger initial download of Fedora DVD image, 3 GB).

➢ Can install more packages without having a high-speed connection for downloading from repositories

➢ Can specify what packages to install

➢ Can download from the Fedora repository during installation.

➢ Can select a specific Fedora compliant repository for installing packages during installation, like **http://rpmfusion.org** for vendor graphics drivers from Nvidia or ATI (this action can always be performed after the installation).

➢ You will always have a more extensive set of install packages on hand for other installs.

Minimal Install Strategy with Fedora Live: First Time Installs

If you are installing Fedora for the first time, and want to download the software quickly, you can just install from Fedora Live. Fedora Live also allows you to first see what Fedora is like, without having to install it. Should you then want to install Fedora on your system, you can do so using just the Fedora Live CD or Install DVD. You would not have to separately download an installation disk like the Fedora Install DVD. You can then later download and install software you want from the Fedora repository.

Fedora Live includes the Gnome desktop. If you want to use the KDE desktop, you can use the Fedora Live KDE. The Fedora Live and Fedora Live KDE have i686 (32 bit x86 systems), x86_64 (64 bit systems), and ppc (Mac G4 systems) versions. The i686 versions are CDs, whereas all the others are DVDs, though still only about 800 MB.

Once you download and burn the Fedora Live-CD, boot your system from it. The system will start up automatically. Pressing the space bar will display a start up menu with four options:

Boot

Verify and Boot

Memory Test

Boot from local drive

The first option is the default. The second will first test if your CD/DVD media is OK. The third performs a hardware memory test. The last will boot a local OS on a connected hard drive, if there is one.

Once you boot up Fedora, the login screen is displayed. The login user name will be Automatic Login. Press Enter (no password will be required) to start up Fedora from the CD (see Chapter 1). The KDE Live disk will start up directly to a KDE desktop.

You can now use your desktop. Some applications will already be installed. You an install other packages, but they last only for the duration of the current session. You will have full network access. You can write to your Fedora directory, but the files only last for the session. Removable media that you insert, such as USB drives, you can write to, allowing you to save any data.

Figure 2-1: Fedora Install window on Fedora Live Desktop

On the screen there will be an icon of the Fedora F symbol with the label "Install to Hard Drive". If you want to install Fedora directly on your system, click this button. Clicking this button will start the standard install procedure (anaconda) as described in this chapter. You will be installing Fedora just as you would from the standard Fedora install DVD. The only difference is that only the small subset of applications already on the Fedora Live-CD will be installation. You will not have the option to choose applications during the install process.

When you start the Install to Hard Drive process, a window will open, showing the initial install screen, letting you choose to install Fedora (see Figure 2-1).

The install process show fewer screens than the standard process, but performs all necessary tasks. The screens shown are as follows.

Keyboard: Here you select your keyboard language and layout

Hostname: Here you enter the host name for your computer, your computer name. The default is **localhost.localdomain**.

Time Zone: Select your city from the map or the pop-up menu.

Password: Enter a password for the root user. This is your administrative password.

Partitions: Here you set up your partitions. You have the option to use a default set up, or mange your own. See the section on Partition, Raid, and Logical volumes for more information

Bootloader: Here you set up your bootloader, selecting any other operating systems to boot.

Format and software install: Your partitions are formatted and all the software from Fedora Live is installed.

When you reboot, you will start up the Fedora installation on your hard disk. Initially you will only have the same software available as was on the Fedora Live CD/DVD, but you can use Applications | Add/Remove Software to install other applications, like OpenOffice. You may also have to update many of the applications installed from Fedora Live. Click the update notification icon on the top panel, which will automatically appear, to start the update process. Applications and updates will be downloaded from the Fedora repository and automatically installed.

Obtaining the CDs and DVDs

To obtain Fedora 10, just go to the Fedora Project Web site and click on the Get Fedora link. Here you will see links for the jigdo, bittorrent, and direct downloads for the different Fedora Install DVD and Fedora Live versions.

Jigdo

The preferred method for download is Jigdo. Jigdo combines the best of both direct downloads and Bittorrent, while maximizing use of the download data for constructing various spins. In effect, Jigdo sets up a bittorrent download operation using just the Fedora mirror sites (no uploading). Using the Fedora Project Mirror Manager infrastructure, Jigdo automatically detects the mirror sites that currently provide the fastest download speeds and downloads your spin from them. Mirror sites accessed are switched as download speeds change. If you previously downloaded directly from mirrors, with Jigdo you no longer have to go searching for a fast download mirror site. Jigdo finds them for you.

Jigdo organizes the Fedora download into central repository that can be combined into different spins. If you download the Fedora DVD, and then later a CD, the data already downloaded for the DVD can be used to build the CD, reducing the actual downloaded data by as much as 95 percent. Most of the CD data is already in the downloaded DVD.

Direct Download

The Direct downloads link to a currently available mirror site.

```
http://www.fedoraproject.org/get-fedora
```

You could also directly access a Fedora mirror site by entering the following URL. You would then need to navigate through the releases and 8 directories to find the Fedora and Live directories where the Fedora Install and Live iso images are kept.

```
http://download.fedoraproject.org
```

You can also access a specific mirror at the following URL. Here will be listed the current Fedora mirror and their addresses.

```
http://mirrors.fedoraproject.org
```

A detailed description for all the Fedora download options, including all the ISO discs you will need and links to mirror sites is available at the following URL. Check this site for the latest download procedures.

http://www.fedoraproject.org/wiki/Distribution/Download

Alternatively, you can also still download directly from the Fedora site using the following link at **http://download.fedoraproject.org**. This site does not have the DVD, only the CDs and package files.

```
http://download.fedora.redhat.com/pub/fedora/linux/releases/
```

The direct downloads can be very fast with broadband DSL or cable, using an FTP client like **gFTP** (Applications | Internet menu). Web-client download with browsers like Firefox tend to be slower.

To download Fedora 10 for installation from a DVD/CD-ROM drive, you download either the Fedora Install DVD image or a Fedora Live image. The Fedora Install and Live images are large files that have the extension .iso. The Fedora Install DVD resides within the Fedora subdirectory, under the respective version (i386, x86_64, or ppc), in an iso directory (Fedora/i386/iso). The Live images reside in the Live subdirectory, under the respective versions (i686, x86_64, and ppc). Once they are downloaded, you burn them to a disc using your CD or DVD writer and burner software, like the Nautilus file browser or K3b on Fedora.

There are ISO images for 64-bit system support and for the standard x86 (32-bit) support. Download the appropriate one. You cannot run a 64-bit version on an x86 (32-bit) system.

You do not have to download the images to a Linux system. You can just as easily download them on a Windows system and use Windows CD/DVD burner software to make the discs.

Bittorrent

You can use any FTP or Web client, such as gFTP or Firefox, to download the CD image files. The DVD image, though, is a very large file that can take a long time to download, especially if the FTP site is very busy or if your have a slow Internet connection. An alternative for such very large files is to use BitTorrent. BitTorrent is a safe distributed download operation that is ideal for large files, letting many participants download and upload the same file, building a torrent that can run very fast for all participants. The Fedora 10 BitTorrent files are located both at **http://fedoraproject.org** and at

```
http://torrent.fedoraproject.org/
```

You will first need to install the BitTorrent client. For Fedora, there are several BitTorrent clients available, including **azureus**, **transmission**, **ktorrent**, and the original **bittorrent**. A search on "bittorrent" in Add/Remove Software will display them (notice that bittorrent has two 't's and two 'r's in its spelling). Just install the ones you want.

Installation Overview

Installing Linux involves several steps. First, you need to determine whether your computer meets the basic hardware requirements. These days, most Intel-based PC computers do. The Fedora 10 Installation Guide is now available at `http://docs.fedoraproject.org/install-guide/f8/en_US/`. Check this guide before installing Fedora 10. It provides detailed screen examples.

Install Sources

Fedora supports several methods for installing Linux. You can install from a local source such as a CD/DVD-ROM or a hard disk, or from a network or Internet source. For a network or Internet source, Fedora supports NFS, FTP, and HTTP installations. With FTP, you can install from an FTP site. With HTTP, you can install from a Web site. NFS enables you to install over a local network. For a local source, you can install from a CD-ROM or a hard disk. You can start the installation process by booting from your DVD-ROM, or from boot disks that can then use the DVD-ROM or hard disk repository. Fedora documentation covers each of these methods in detail.

To select an install source, you will need to first boot the install kernel, either from a Fedora 10 CD or DVD disc, or from a Fedora CD boot image (you can also use USB disks and PXE servers). At the boot prompt you enter the option **linux askmethod**, as shown here:

```
boot: linux askmethod
```

Install Configurations

The Fedora Install DVD currently supports three pre-selection install configurations: Office and Productivity, Software development, and Web server. They differ in the partition they will set up by default and the group of packages they will install. Office and Productivity are selected by default. If you know what packages you want, you can select the Customize Now option. This will invoke the Pirut Package Manager to let you choose the packages by group or individually that you want on your system.

In addition to the Fedora DVD packages, you can also choose to download packages from the online Fedora repository as well as the latest updated versions of already selected packages.

These will be listed as Installation repo, Fedora 10, and Fedora 10 Updates. Fedora 10 and Fedora 10 Updates will be further qualified by the architecture you are installing, i386 or x86_64.

Office and Productivity	Office, mail, and Web applications
Software Development.	Includes software development
Web Server	Includes the Apache Web server
Customize Now	Select from all software packages
Installation repo	Select additional packages from Fedora install source
Fedora 10	Select additional packages from Fedora repository
Fedora 10 Updates	Download updated packages from Fedora repository

Install Procedures

Once the installation program begins, you simply follow the instructions, screen by screen. Most of the time, you only need to make simple selections or provide yes and no answers. The installation program progresses through several phases. First, you create Linux partitions on your hard drive, configure your network connection, and then install the software packages.

Once your system is installed, you are ready to start it and log in. Normally, you will log in using a graphical login, selecting the desktop you want and entering your username and password. Alternatively, you can log in to a simple command line interface. From the command line, you can then invoke a desktop such as GNOME or KDE that provides you with a full graphical user interface.

Installing Dual-Boot Systems

If you have another operating system already installed on the same computer as your Linux system, your system will be automatically configured by GRUB, the bootloader, for dual booting. Should you have both Linux and Windows systems installed on your hard disks; GRUB will let you choose to boot either the Linux system or a Windows system. Manually configuring dual boots can be complicated. If you want a Windows system on your computer, you should install it first if it is not already installed. Windows would overwrite the boot loader that a previous Linux system installed, cutting off access to the Linux system. You would then have to use the rescue option on the boot disk to access your Linux system and then reinstall the Grub boot loader. Check the link for **"Configuring a Dual-Boot system"** on

http://fedoraproject.org/wiki/Distribution/Download/

Simple Graphical Install with DVD/CD-ROMs

If you are installing from DVD/CD-ROMs, installation is a straightforward process. A graphical installation is very easy to use, providing full mouse support and explaining each step with detailed instructions on a help pane.

Most systems today already meet hardware requirements and have automatic connections to the Internet (DHCP).

They also support booting a DVD-ROM or CD-ROM disc, though this support may have to be explicitly configured in the system BIOS.

Also, if you know how you want Linux installed on your hard disk partitions, or if you are performing a simple update that uses the same partitions, installing Fedora 10 is a fairly simple process. Fedora 10 features an automatic partitioning function that will perform the partitioning for you.

If you choose package collections from the three preconfigured packaging installations, you will not even have to select packages.

For a quick installation you can simply start up the installation process, placing your DVD or CD disc in your optical drive and starting up your system. Graphical installation is a simple matter of following the instructions in each window as you progress. Many of them are self-explanatory (for LCD displays you may have to use the **nofb** option at the boot prompt). The steps involved are as follows:

Boot Menu or Prompt At the initial menu select Install or Upgrade and press ENTER. For text installs, press ENTER at the boot prompt.

Media Check DVDs and CDs are often burned discs from downloaded ISO images. The media check can make sure your DVD/CD-ROMs is being read correctly.

Language Selection A default is chosen for you, like English, so you can usually just press Next.

Keyboard Configuration A default is chosen for you; you can usually press Next.

Hostname Enter the host name for your system, your computer name.

Time Zone Use the map to choose your time zone.

Root Password Select a password to use for the root users. This enables administrative access. Be sure to remember the password.

Disk Partitions For automatic partitioning you have the option of replacing any partitions already present: either all partitions or just Linux partitions (preserving any Windows partitions). You can also choose no partitions and use available free space. This is used to either preserve your old partitions or for new drives. Check the Review option to have the partitioning tool show your partitioning selections and let you make changes.

Upgrade/Install Option Choose whether to install or upgrade. If you already have a Fedora system installed, Upgrade will already be chosen.

Network Configuration Most ISPs and routers now use DHCP, and this will be selected for you by default. Just press Next. You do have the option of entering in your own network information, including IP addresses and DNS servers.

Boot Loader You can then configure your boot loader (GRUB). Primarily this is used to choose a different operating system such as Windows to boot by default; otherwise, you can accept the current configuration and press Next.

Install Software Here you choose one or more of the following: Office and Productivity, Software Development, and Web Server. You can also choose to Customize now, letting you select particular packages. You can also choose to install additional packages directly from the Fedora repository. A working Internet connection is required.

About to Install At this point nothing has been done to your system. You can opt out of the installation at this point. If you click Next, then the install process will take place, making actual changes. The system will first be formatted, then packages installed, with installation progress shown, and then a post-install will perform default configurations for your packages.

After the install, you will be asked to remove your DVD/CD-ROM and click the Reboot button. This will reboot your system (do not reboot yourself).

On reboot, you will enter a Fedora Setup Agent procedure where you will be able to set the date and time, check your sound card, and create a standard user, which you can use to log in for normal use (not as root). More users can be created later. Here you select the level of support you want for SELinux. Enforcing is selected by default, but it is recommended that you change this to the Permissive level until you can configure SELinux yourself. For the firewall, you can check services to allow through. Trusted interfaces allow any host connected to that interface to access all services provided by your system. They are usually used if your system operates as a server for your local network. You may want to select samba to allow Samba browsing from your desktop.

After Setup, your login screen will display and installation will be complete.

Hardware, Software, and Information Requirements

Before installing Linux, you must ensure that your computer meets certain minimum hardware requirements. You also need to have certain specific information ready concerning your monitor, video card, mouse, and CD-ROM drive. All the requirements are presented in detail in the following sections. Be sure to read them carefully before you begin installation. During the installation program, you need to provide responses that reflect the configuration of your computer.

Hardware Requirements

Listed here are the minimum hardware requirements for installing a standard installation of the Linux system on an Intel-based PC:

A 32-bit or 64-bit Intel- or AMD-based personal computer. At least an Intel or compatible (AMD) Pentium-class microprocessor is required. A 400 MHz Pentium II or more is recommended for a graphical interface and 200 MHz for text. Fedora 10 is currently optimized for a Pentium 4.

For 64-bit systems, be sure to use the 64-bit version of Fedora 10, which includes a supporting kernel.

A CD-ROM or DVD-ROM drive. Should you need to create a bootable CD-ROM, you will need a CD-RW drive.

Memory requirements: Normally at least 128MB RAM for text, and 192 MB for a graphical interface,
with 256 MB recommended. For 64-bit systems, you will need 128 MB for text and 384 MB for graphical, with 512 MB recommended. (Linux can run on as little as 12MB RAM.)

Hard disk requirements: 3GB or more is recommended for desktop installation and 700MB for a command line interface–only installation. The full set of packages, including all those on the Fedora repository, requires about 9 GB. You will also need 64MB to 2GB for swap space, depending on the amount of RAM memory you have. You will also need availability for at least two primary partitions on your hard disk, one for the kernel (boot), and the other for the main system. Partitions on IDE hard drives are limited to four primary partitions.

Hard disk requirements depend on the kind of installation you want. The three choices, Office and Productivity, Software Development, and Web Server each add a basic configuration package for those tasks. You can then add many more as you wish in different categories. Fedora now uses a new software manager to install software. The software manager is able to download packages from Fedora repositories during installation, which will provide you with a massive selection of software to choose from during installation. You can also use the software manager after installation to install packages from any Fedora – supported repository. This kind of capability means that install sizes for different systems can vary greatly, depending on each system's particular needs. Approximate standard install sizes for command line and desktop systems are shown here:

> Command line (minimum): 700MB

> Desktop: 3GB

Keep in mind that the disk space requirements represent the amount of space used after installation. The install process will also require an additional amount of space for the install image (**/Fedora/base/stage2.img**) and selected RPM packages. Figure on 100MB for a minimum install and 200MB for a full installation.

Hard Drive Configuration

These days, Linux is usually run on its own hard drive, though it can also be run on a hard drive that contains a separate partition for a different operating system such as Windows or OS-X.

If you want to install Linux and Windows on the same hard drive, you can use a partition management software package, such as fdisk, fips, Parted, or PartitionMagic, to set up your Windows and Linux partitions. If you have already installed Windows on your hard drive and configured it to take up the entire hard drive, you would resize its partition to free up unused space. The freed space could then be used for a Linux partition. See the Fedora Installation Guide for more details.

Information Requirements

Part of adapting a powerful operating system like Linux to the PC entails making the most efficient use of the computer hardware at hand. In almost all configurations, your Linux installation process will automatically detect and configure your hardware components. Sometimes, however, particularly with older or very recent hardware, your installer may not be able to correctly identify a component. If you have such components, such as a new model monitor or video card, you should first check their manuals and take note of certain configuration settings.

Note: Network connections are now automatically configured by Network Manager during installation.

If you are sharing with Windows, decide how much of the hard disk space you want for Windows and how much for Linux.

Decide how much space you want for your swap partition. This is selected automatically for you if you use default partition configurations. Your swap partition should be about the same size as your RAM memory, but it can work with as little as 64MB. For systems with smaller RAM configurations, the swap disk should be twice the size of the RAM. Your swap partition is used by Linux as an extension of your computer's RAM.

Know what time zone you are in and to what time zone your hardware clock is set. This can be Greenwich Mean Time (GMT), also called Universal Coordinated Time (UCT), or your local time zone.

Network connections are now automatically detected and configured by Network Manager. You do not have to enter network information at the time of installation. If you need to, after installation you use Network Manager to configure your connection manual.

Mice are now automatically detected. Fedora no longer supports serial mice. The system-config-mouse utility has been dropped. If you should need to later configure your mouse, you can use the GNOME mouse configuration tool (System | Preferences | Hardware | Mouse).

Note: Monitors and video cards are automatically configured during installation. If you have problems, you will have to configure your system after installation using tools like system-config-display (see Chapter 13). You may need to provide the manufacturer's model, in case the detection is wrong. Find out the manufacturer for your monitor and its model, such as Dell 2405. You can find a complete list of supported cards at **www.x.org**. For older CRT monitors, the vertical and horizontal refresh rates are particularly important.

Boot Source Options

Normally you would boot from a DVD-ROM. Most systems currently support booting from a DVD-ROM drive. If you are installing from the Fedora 10 DVD-ROM, you will need a DVD-ROM drive on your computer to read the DVD-ROM disc. If your system supports bootable CD-ROMs, then it will boot from this DVD-ROM, letting you install your Fedora 10 system from the DVD-ROM directly.

Fedora 10 also supports several booting options should you not wish to use a DVD/CD disc. Take note that floppy disk boots are no longer supported. The 2.6 kernel is too large to fit on a floppy.

If you have an older system or DVD-ROM that will not support booting, and you can boot from a CD-ROM disc, you can create a CD-ROM boot disc, using **images/boot.iso** to burn the disc. Alternatively, you could use a USB drive or PXE network boot if these are supported for your system. Once installation begins, your DVD-ROM will be used to continue installation.

If you are installing with CD-ROMs, most systems and CD-ROM drives are now bootable. You can use the CDs directly. If your system for some reason does not support bootable CD-ROMs, you will have to set up an alternative boot method such as a USB disk with **diskboot.img** or a PXE server.

You can create a bootable CD-ROM disc with which to start the installation. The CD-ROM boot disc image is located in the **images** directory and is called **boot.iso**. You can also use this disc to install from alternate sources such as a hard drive or a network location such as an NFS, FTP, or Web site.

With the **diskboot.img** file (also in the **images** directory) you can boot from small USB drives or any bootable device large enough to hold the 2.6 kernel (the size of the **diskboot.img** file, about 6MB). This is a VFAT file system. Check first if your system can boot from the USB drive.

You can also boot from the PXE (Pre-Execution Environment) server using the **initrd.img** file in the **images/pxeboot** directory. A PXE server operates through DHCP and tftp servers off a Linux system. Check the PXE documentation file, **pxelinux.doc**, in the **/usr/share/syslinux-3.61** directory (install **syslinux** package).

Upgrading Fedora Linux

Be sure to first backup your system, including the home, etc, and boot directories.

Your keyboard and language are first selected. You are then given the option to either Upgrade an older installed version or Install an entirely new system. For upgrading, the root partition of the installed system will be shown on a pop-up menu.

"Install Fedora"

"Upgrade an existing system"

If you choose Upgrade, a boot loader configuration screen presents you with three loader options:

➢ Update boot loader configuration

➢ skip boot loader updating

➢ create a new boot loader configuration

Several steps are then automatically performed.

➢ Check for installed packages, updating with new corresponding versions

➢ Check dependencies

➢ Start install process

➢ Prepare install transactions

➢ Packages are then installed, as they are during a standard installation

Your installation will complete, and, if all goes well, you system should restart normally, using Fedora 10 but with your original configuration.

Installing Fedora Linux

Installing Linux involves several processes, beginning with creating Linux partitions, and then loading the Linux software, configuring your network connection, installing the Linux boot loader (GRUB) that will boot your system, and creating new user accounts. The installation program used on Fedora is a screen-based program that takes you through all these processes, step-by-step, as one continuous procedure. You can use either your mouse or the keyboard to make selections. When you finish with a screen, click the Next button at the bottom to move to the next screen. If you need to move back to the previous screen, click Back. You can also use TAB, the arrow keys, SPACEBAR, and ENTER to make selections. The installation screens will display a help panel explaining each step in detail. You have little to do other than make selections and choose options. Some screens provide a list of options from which you make a selection. In a few cases, you are asked for information you should already have if you followed the steps earlier in this chapter. Hardware components will be automatically detected and displayed as you progress. During installation, you will be able to perform administrative tasks such as configuring your network connections, creating users, and setting the time. Keep in mind that such administrative tasks can also be performed after installation. You are now ready to begin installation. The steps for each part of the procedure are delineated in the following sections. This should not take more than an hour.

The installation process will first install Linux, including all selected packages, on your system. It will then reboot and start a Setup process to let you fine-tune certain settings, including your display settings, sound check, and time and date.

Starting the Installation Program

If your computer can boot from the DVD/CD-ROM, you can start the installation directly from the Live DVD/CD-ROMs or the Install DVD-ROM. Just place the disc in the DVD/CD-ROM drive before you start your computer. After you turn on your computer, the installation program will start up.

The installation program on the DVD install disc or first CD install disc will start, presenting you with a menu listing the following options:

Install or Upgrade an existing system

Rescue installed system

Boot from local drive

Memory test

Use the arrow keys to move from one menu entry to the next, and then press ENTER to select the entry (see Figure 2-2). Should you need to add options, say to the Install or Upgrade entry, press the TAB key. A command line is displayed where you can enter the options. Current options will already be listed. The options will be different for each entry, for example, the Rescue entry will display a **rescue** option on its command line. Use the backspace key to delete and arrow keys to move through the line. Press the ESC key to return to the menu.

TIP: To boot from a CD/DVD-ROM, you may first have to change the boot sequence setting in your computer's BIOS so that the computer will try to boot first from the DVD/CD-ROM. This requires some technical ability and knowledge of how to set your motherboard's BIOS configuration.

Your system then detects your hardware, providing any configuration specifications that may be needed. For example, if you have an IDE CD-RW or DVD-RW drive, it will be configured automatically. If for some reason it cannot do so, your system will ask you to select your DVD/CD-

ROM from a list. If you still have difficulty, you may have to specify the DVD/CD-ROM at the boot prompt or in the option command line (**sd** prefix replaces the **hd** prefix used in previous releases).

```
sdx=cdrom
```

Replace the *x* with one of the following letters, depending on the interface the unit is connected to, and whether it is configured as master or a slave: a (first IDE controller master), b (first IDE controller slave), c (second IDE controller master), d (second IDE controller slave).

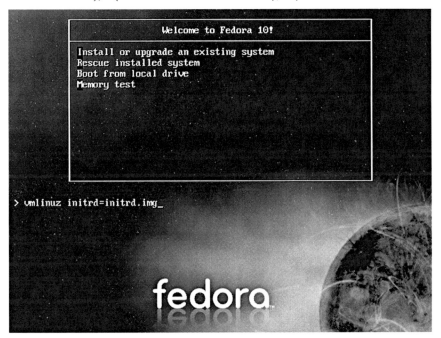

Figure 2-2: Install Menu with rescue and boot options

If you cannot start the install process and you are using an LCD display, you should press TAB on the Install entry and enter **nofb** (no frame buffer) in the options command line.

```
nofb
```

As each screen appears in the installation, default entries will be already selected, usually by the auto-probing capability of the installation program. Selected entries will appear highlighted. If these entries are correct, you can simply click Next to accept them and go on to the next screen.

Check disk media

You are then asked to check the DVD/CD disc for errors (see Figure 2-3). This check can take several minutes. You can skip the procedure by pressing the TAB or arrow keys to move to the Skip button, and then press ENTER.

Your graphical install screens will then start up.

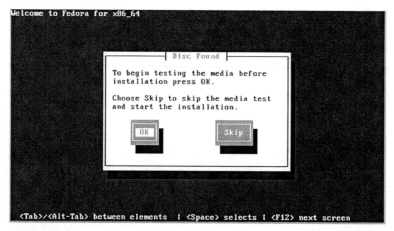

Figure 2-3: Disc check

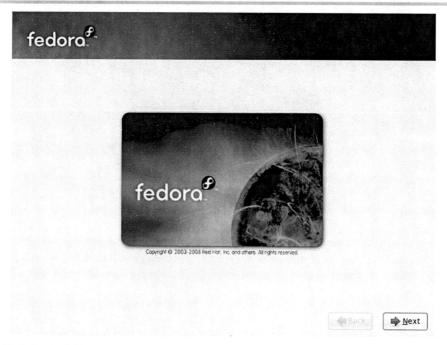

Figure 2-4: Install Screen

Initial Setup

If your basic device and hardware configuration was appropriately detected, a Welcome screen will be displayed, with a Next button on the lower-right corner. Once finished with a step, you click Next to move on. In some cases you will be able to click a Back button to return to a previous step. On most screens, button the lower left will display the release notes

The first screen will show the Fedora install image (see Figure 2-4). Press Next to start the install process.

Tip: Your mouse will be automatically detected. If you have a USB mouse that is not being detected, try reinserting the USB connector for mouse one or two times. It should be detected then.

You will then be asked to select your language, and then a keyboard configuration. A default language will already be selected, usually English (see Figure 2-5).

"What language would you like to use during the installation process"

You will then be asked to select a keyboard—the default is already selected, such as U.S. English (see Figure 2-6).

"Select the appropriate keyboard for the system"

You are then given the option to either Upgrade an older installed version or Install an entirely new system (see Figure 2-7). For an Upgrade, a drop-down menu will list partitions with installed Fedora systems. If there should be more than one on your system, they will be listed. It is possible that some systems may have several versions of Fedora installed, each on its own partition.

"Install Fedora"

"Upgrade an existing system"

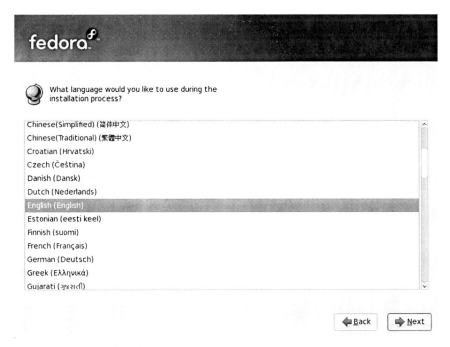

Figure 2-5: Language selection

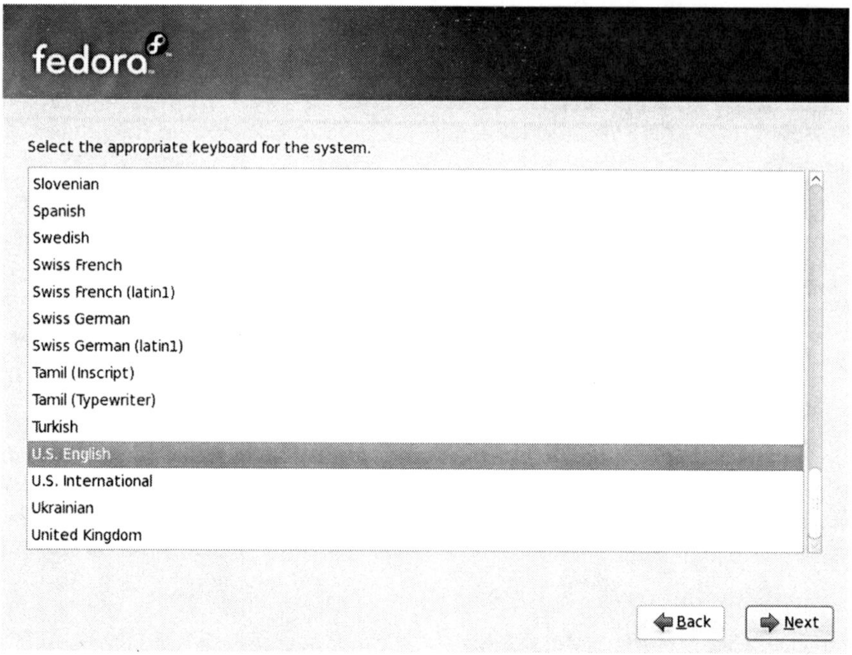

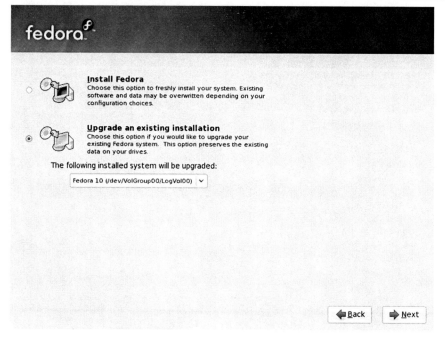

Figure 2-6: Keyboard selection

Figure 2-7: Install or Upgrade choice

System Configuration

You are then prompted to enter the host name for your computer, your computer name (see Figure 2-8). The default is **localhost.localdomain**.

"Please name this computer. The hostname identifies the computer on a network."

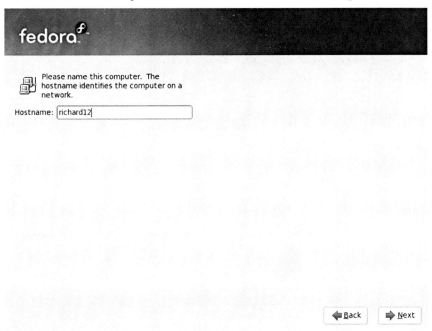

Figure 2-8: Hostname

On the Time Zone Configuration screen, you have the option of setting the time zone by using a map or pop-up menu to specify your location The Time Zone tool uses a new map feature that expands first to your region to let you easily select your Zone (see Figure 2-9). The selected city will appear as the pop-up menu selection. You can also select whether your system clock uses Universal Coordinated Time (UTC).

"Please select the nearest city in your time zone"

On the next screen, you can set the root password for the root account on your system (see Figure 2-10). This is the account used for system administration operations, such as installing software and managing users. After installation, a similar screen will let you also add an ordinary user account.

Enter the root password at the Root Password box, and then re-enter it in the Confirm box.

"The root account is used for administering the system. Enter the password for the root user"

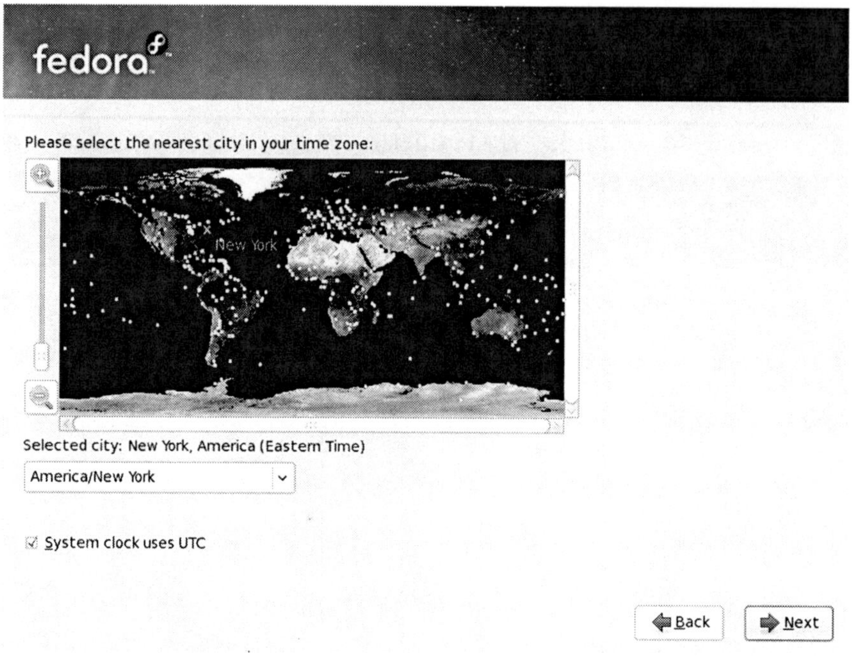

Figure 2-9: Time Zone selection

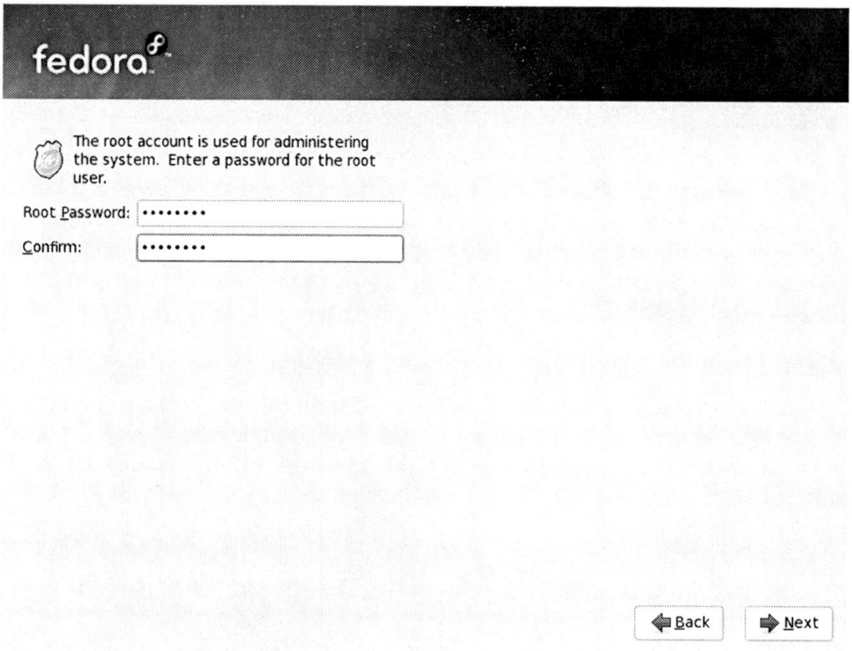

Figure 2-10: Root user password

Partitions, RAID, and Logical Volumes

Then you will be asked to designate the Linux partitions and hard disk configurations you want to use on your hard drives. Fedora provides automatic partitioning options if you just want to use available drives and free space for your Linux system. To manually configure your hard disks, Fedora uses a very detailed and graphic-oriented partitioning tool called Parted. With Parted, you can create specific partitions, or configure RAID devices, or set up logical volumes (LVM).

No partitions will be changed or formatted until you select your software packages later in the install process. You can opt out of the installation any time until that point, and your original partitions will remain untouched. A default layout used in the first three partition configurations, sets up a swap partition, a boot partition of type ext3 (Linux native) for the kernel, and an LVM partition that will hold all your apps and files.

Partition Layout

The partition layout screen will display a pop up menu with the automatic partition selections. The default setup is shown in Figure 2-11.

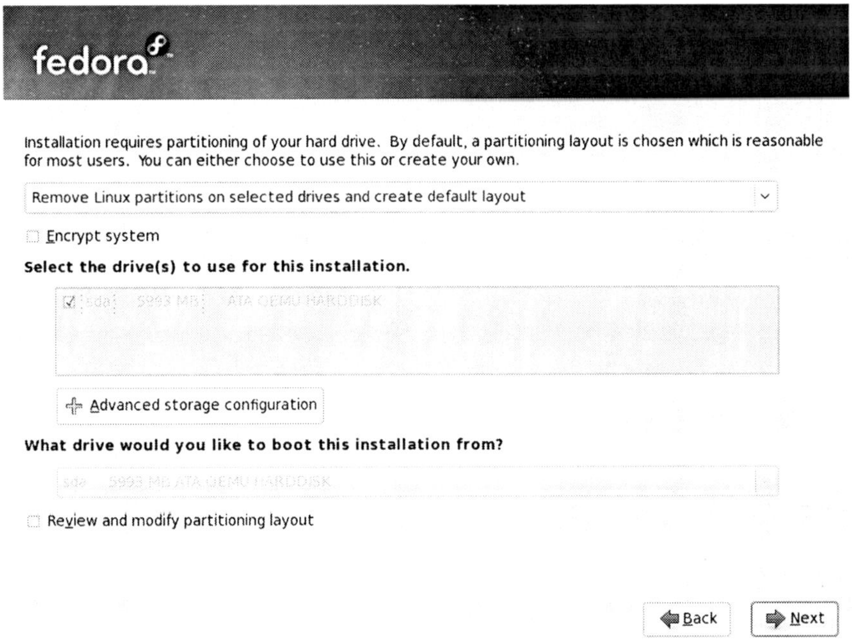

Installation requires partitioning of your hard drive. By default, a partitioning layout is chosen which is reasonable for most users. You can either choose to use this or create your own.

Remove Linux partitions on selected drives and create default layout

☐ Encrypt system

Select the drive(s) to use for this installation.

☑ sda   5993 MB   ATA QEMU HARDDISK

✛ Advanced storage configuration

What drive would you like to boot this installation from?

sda   5993 MB ATA QEMU HARDDISK

☐ Review and modify partitioning layout

⟵ Back   ⟶ Next

Figure 2-11: Default Partitions

Five partition options are supported, as shown in Figure 2-12. Remove all Partitions on selected drive, Remove Linux partitions on selected drive, Resize existing partitions and create default layout, Use Free Space on selected drive, and Create custom layout.

For the first three default partitions will be created   The Remove Linux Partitions option (2) is selected by default.

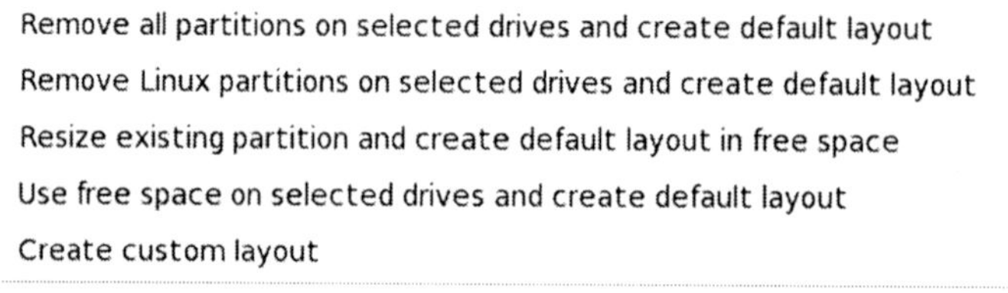

Remove all partitions on selected drives and create default layout

Remove Linux partitions on selected drives and create default layout

Resize existing partition and create default layout in free space

Use free space on selected drives and create default layout

Create custom layout

Figure 2-12: Partitions options

Remove Linux partitions on this selected drive and create default layout   This removes just Linux partitions that are already on your disks. Any Windows or other OS partitions will remain untouched.

Remove all partitions on this selected drive and create default layout   This removes all the partitions on the disk, effectively erasing it. You will lose any existing partitions, including Windows partitions.

Resize existing partitions and crate default layout in free space   This option will detect free space on existing partitions, and then resize them to open free space on the disk where new Linux partitions can be created. This is new with Fedora 10.

Use existing free space on this selected drive and create default layout   This is for disks that might be partially used, such as a partition for Windows that uses only part of the hard disk. This assumes that there is a significant amount of free space already on the disk.

Create custom layout This option open Parted directly and lets you create your own partitions or manually select current ones. This option provides the most control, but you need to know how partitions work and how they are implemented on a hard drive.

In a pane below the options is a list of all the hard drives on your system. You can select the one you want Linux installed on. If you have only one, it will be selected for you (see Figure 2-13).

"Select the drives to use for this installation"

"What drive would you like to boot this installation from"

An option at the bottom of the screen lets you review all your partitions in Parted, letting you modify them if you need to. This will not be checked by default. Check this to see exactly how Parted will be partitioning your system. You can also make changes if needed.

Review and modify the partitioning layout.

This allows you to make changes manually to the partitions as well as see exactly what partitions will be created on your drives. Like the Create custom layout option you are place in the Parted partition manager where you can modify you partitions as you wish.

If you want to organize your data using several partitions, such as **/home**, **/**, and **/var**, as well as boot, you will have to manually configure them. Automatic partitioning will set up a boot partition and an LVM Linux partition only.

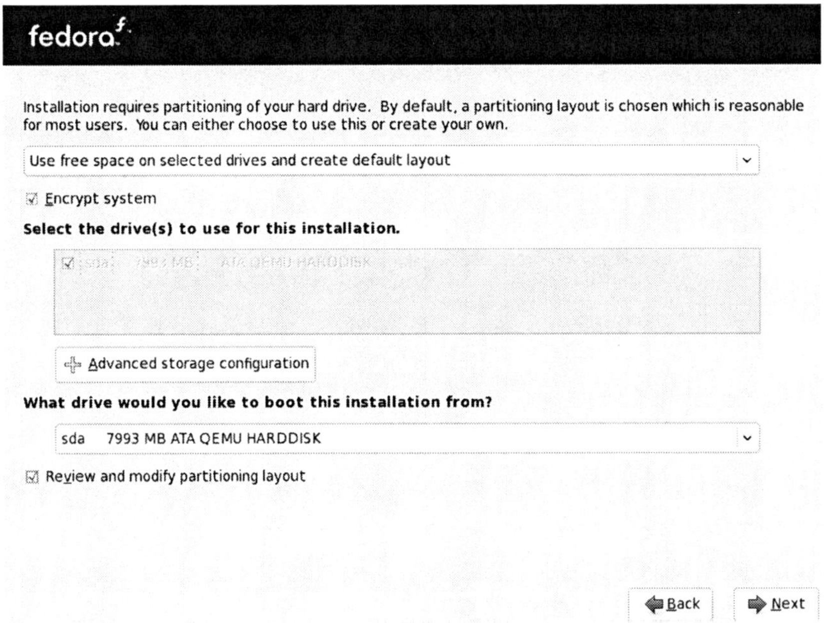

Figure 2-13: Partitions using free space with encryptions selected

The Advanced Storage Configuration button lets you either select an iSCSI device or disable your motherboard RAID device controller (**dmraid**).

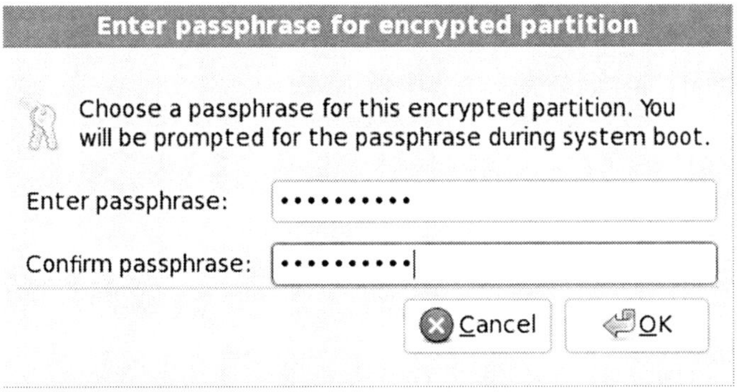

Figure 2-14: Prompt for encrypted partition passphrase

You also have the option to encrypt your disks. Click the "Encrypt System" check box. You are then prompted to enter a passphrase for your encrypted system (see Figure 2-14). When you start up your system, you wall be prompted to enter this passphrase for each partition you set up during the install process (usually a swap and root partition, within an LVM partition). The boot partition is not encrypted.

Encryption is performed using LUKS (Linux Unified Key Setup). Prompts for entry your passphrase will use the term LUKS.

A popular configuration uses free space to set up a Linux partition as shown in Figure 2-16. Notice also that the partitions will be encrypted.

If you have selected Custom Layout or checked "Review and modify", the partitioner will be started up and you can create or modify your partitions as described in the next section. If not, then you are first prompted to accept the partitioning, giving you the option to back out before any changes are made (see Figure 2-15). At this point you can click Go Back and nothing will have happened to your hard disk.

Figure 2-15: Confirm partitions

Custom and Review Partitioning

If you choose the "Create custom layout" option or checked the "Review and modify" option, the Disk Setup screen is displayed, placing you into the Parted partition configuration. Here, you can manually create Linux partitions or select the one where you want to install Fedora.

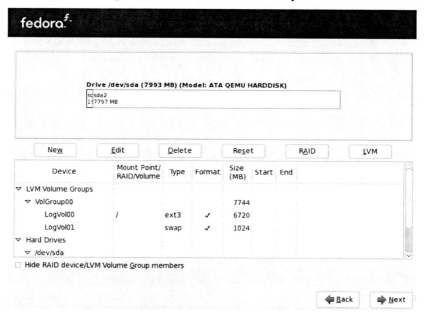

Figure 2-16: Custom partition configuration

The top pane lists the hard drives with their partitions on your computer (many computers will have only one hard drive), and the lower pane lists the partitions. Selecting a hard drive will list its partitions. The buttons above the partitions pane enables you to create, edit, and delete partitions. The Partitions screen is actually an interactive interface where you configure partitions as well as create new ones (see Figure 2-16).

If you are reviewing after default partitioning, then the hard disk partitions set up for you, will be displayed. The panel will show the specific partitions that will be created for your system.

Scrolling down you will see the hard drive partitions displayed. A lock icon will be shown for encrypted disks (see Figure 2-17). Notice that the boot partition is not encrypted, whereas the LVM partition is.

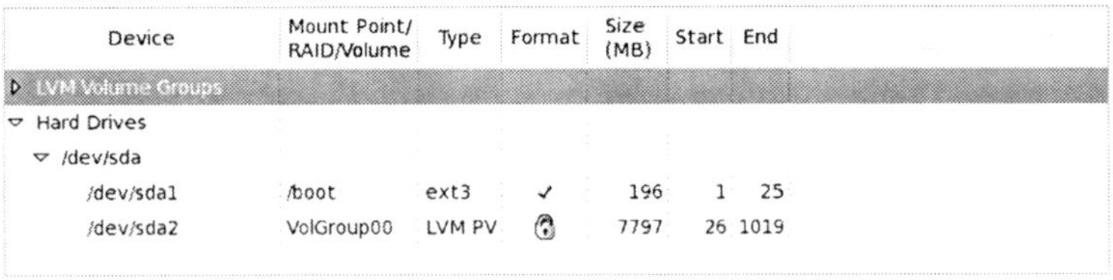

Device	Mount Point/ RAID/Volume	Type	Format	Size (MB)	Start	End
▷ LVM Volume Groups						
▽ Hard Drives						
▽ /dev/sda						
/dev/sda1	/boot	ext3	✓	196	1	25
/dev/sda2	VolGroup00	LVM PV	🔒	7797	26	1019

Figure 2-17: Hard disks partitions

If you are formatting any old Linux partitions that still have data on them, then, when you press the Next button, a screen will appear listing them and asking you to confirm that you want to format them (new Linux partitions that you created will automatically be formatted). If you already have a Linux system, you will most likely have several Linux partitions already. Some of these may be used for just the system software, such as the boot and root partitions. These should be formatted. Others may have extensive user files, such as a **/home** partition that normally holds user home directories and all the files they have created. You should *not* format such partitions.

Recommended Partitions

If you are manually creating your partitions, you are required to set up at least two Linux partitions: a swap partition and a root partition. The *root partition* is where the Linux system and application files are installed. In addition, it is recommended that you also set up a **boot** partition that would contain just your Linux kernel (**/boot** directory), and a **/home** partition that would hold all user files. Separating system files on the root and boot partitions from the user files on the home partition allows you to replace the system files should they ever become corrupt without touching the user files. Similarly, if just your kernel becomes corrupt, you would have to replace only the kernel files on your boot partition, leaving the system files on the root partition untouched.

If you are using LVM partitions, as the default setup does, then you would need at least two physical partitions, one for the **boot** partition and the other for the LVM physical partition. The **/boot** directory needs its own partition because you cannot boot from an LVM partition. The **/boot** partition will hold the kernel. An LVM partition works something like a Windows extended partition in which you can then set up several logical partitions, called logical volumes. In the default set up, two logical volumes (partitions), one for the **root** and the other for the **swap**, are set up on a single physical LVM partition (pv). In Figure 2-16, the LVM Volume Groups entry shows the default root and swap logical volumes.

This strategy of separating system directories into different partitions can be carried further to ensure a more robust system. For example, the **/var** directory, which now holds Web and FTP server files, can be assigned its own partition, physically separating the servers from the rest of your system. The **/usr** directory, which holds most user applications, can be placed in its own partition and then be shared and mounted by other systems. One drawback to this strategy is that you would need to know ahead of time the maximum space you would want to use for each partition. For system and kernel files, this can be easily determined, but for directories whose disk usage can change dramatically, like **/home**, **/var**, and even **/usr**, this can be difficult to determine. As an alternative to creating separate physical partitions for each directory, you could use logical volumes (described later). A basic partition configuration is shown here:

Swap partition   No mount point

/   Root partition for system files (and all other files if the only partition)

/boot   Boot partition holding the Linux kernel (approximately 200MB)

/home   User home directories and files

Except for the swap partition, when setting up a Linux partition, you must specify a mountpoint. A *mountpoint* is a directory where the files on that partition are connected to the overall Linux file structure for your system. The mountpoint for your root partition is the root directory, represented by a single slash (/). The mountpoint for your boot partition is the path **/boot**. For a user's partition, it would be **/home**.

The size of the swap partition should be the same size as your RAM memory, with a recommended minimum size of 64MB. With 512MB of RAM, you could use a 512MB swap partition. If your disk space is limited, you should make your swap size at least 64MB.

Creating Partitions

To create the new partition, click the New button to display a dialog box where you can enter the mountpoint, the size (in megabytes), the partition type, and the hard disk on which you want to create the partition (see Figure 2-18). By default you can select a fixed size, specifying the megabytes to use. You can also select a "Fill to maximum allowable size" option to have the partition automatically expand to the size of the remaining free space on the disk. You can have this option selected for more than one partition. In that case, the partition size will be taken as a required minimum and the remaining free space will be shared equally among the partitions. For partition type, select ext3 for standard Linux partitions and select the Linux swap type for your swap partition. You can even use Parted to create Windows vfat partitions (16 bit). There are five kinds of partitions supported during installation, ext2, ext3, swap, physical volume, software RAID, and vfat. The ext2 partition is an older form of the Linux standard partition type, ext3. You would use software RAID if you are setting up RAID arrays using the Linux RAID software instead of your motherboard RAID device support. Physical volumes are used to set up Logical volumes. If you choose to set up default partitions, you will see that a physical volume has already been created (LVM pv), with a corresponding Logical group and its volumes on which your swap and root partitions reside.

Figure 2-18: Adding a new partition

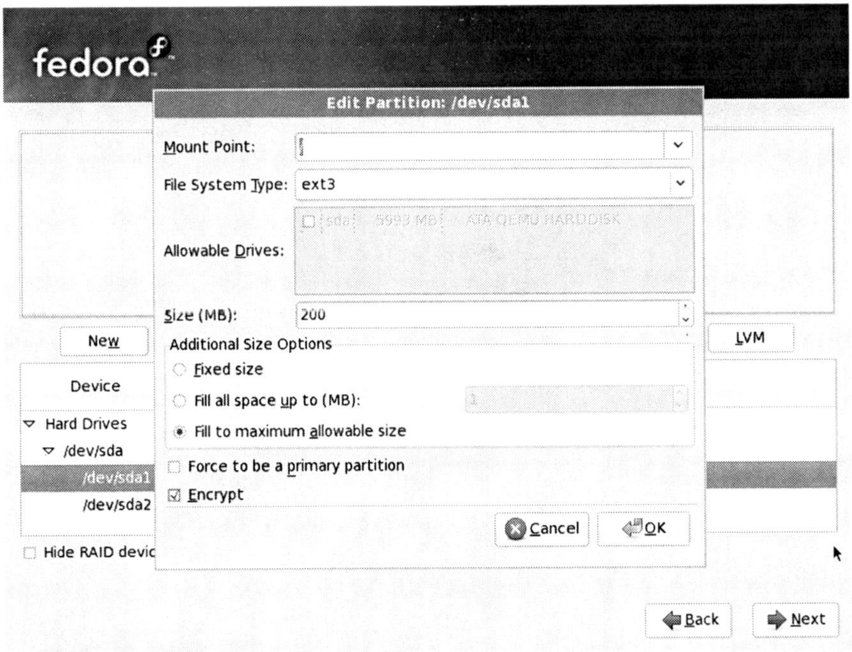

Figure 2-19: Editing a partition

To make any changes later, you can edit a partition by selecting it and clicking the Edit button (see Figure 2-19). Entries for the Add Partition and Edit Partition windows are the same, except that the Edit Partition window will use your previously specified values.

Logical Volumes

Fedora also supports Logical Volume Management (LVM), letting you create *logical volumes,* which you can use instead of using hard disk partitions directly. Logical volumes are implemented by Logical Volume Management (LVM). They provide a more flexible and powerful way of dealing with disk storage, organizing physical partitions into logical volumes in which memory can be managed easily. Disk storage for a logical volume is treated as one pool of memory, though the volume may in fact contain several hard disk partitions spread across different hard disks. There is one restriction. The boot partition cannot be a logical volume. You still have to create a separate hard disk partition as your boot partition with the **/boot** mountpoint in which your kernel will be installed. If you selected default partitioning, the **/boot** partition will have already been set up for you, along with an LVM volume partition for the rest of the system.

If you choose to let the install program set up a default partition layout for your, a logical group will be set up with volumes for both the swap and root partitions. The logical group will be labeled Logical0 by default and the logical volumes as Logical00, Logical01, and so on. You can elect to change these names either by editing the logical group and volumes during installation, or performing the task later by editing their properties with logical volume manager, **system-config-lvm** (System | Administration | Logical Volume Management). Figure 2-20 show the Edit Logical Volume window, accessed from the Edit Logical Group window. Here you can change the Logical Volume name entry, Logical00, to one you would prefer.

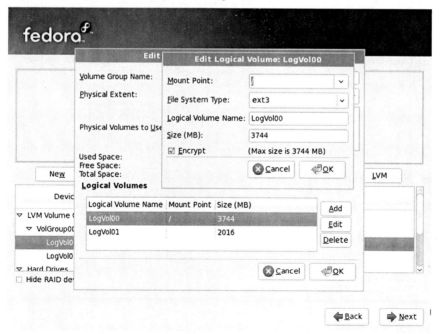

Figure 2-20: Editing a logical volume in an LVM group

Creating logical volumes involves several steps. First you create physical LVM partitions, then the volume groups you place these partitions in, and then from the volume groups you create the logical volumes, for which you then specify mount points and file system types. To create your physical LVM partitions, click New and select Physical Volume (LVM) for the File System Type. Create an LVM physical partition for each partition you want on your hard disks (you will normally only need one). Once you have created LVM physical partitions, you click the LVM button to create your logical volumes. You first need to assign the LVM physical partitions to volume groups. Volume groups are essentially logical hard drives. You could assign LVM physical partitions from different hard disks to the same volume group, letting the volume group span different hard drives. Once the volume groups are created, you are ready to create your logical volumes. You can create several logical volumes within each group. The logical volumes function like partitions. You will have to specify a file system type and a mountpoint for each logical volume you create. In a default configuration, two logical volumes have already been set up for the root and swap partitions.

RAID Disks

You also have the option of creating Linux software RAID disks. Such disks are for use with the Linux software RAID service, and are not used for your motherboard or computer's RAID devices. If you have already decided to use the motherboard RAID support, you do not need Linux software RAID. Linux supports both motherboard/computer RAID devices (dmraid) as well as its own Linux software RAID.

To create Linux software RAID device, first create partitions and select as their type Software RAID. Once you have created your partitions, you can create a RAID disk. Click the RAID button and then select the partitions you previously created that you want to make up the RAID disk, choosing also the type of RAID disk. RAID disks are used primarily for servers or for systems with several hard disks that can make use of RAID's recovery capabilities.

Write Partitions to disk

Once finished with your partitioning, click Next.

You are then prompted to write the changes to the disk. You can still back out at this time, and no changes will be made.

Boot Loader

Once your partitions are prepared, you install the boot loader. Fedora uses the Grand Unified Bootloader (GRUB). You use a boot loader to start Linux from your hard drive (see Figure 2-21).

At the top of the screen you are given to the option to install or not install the boot loader. The install option will be selected by default. Clicking the Change Device button lets you choose what partition to install the boot loader on. You have two choices for where to install the boot loader: the Master Boot Record (MBR) or the root partition. The recommended place is the MBR and will be selected by default.

The screen will display the partition to boot by default, listing all partitions with different operating systems installed on them, for instance, with a check box to select the default. The list is displayed in the **"Boot loader operating system list"** pane. Your Windows system will simply be labeled as Other. The Add button to the side will let you add a new entry, specifying its label, the partition it uses, and whether it should be the default. By selecting a current entry and clicking the Edit button, you can change any of these features, such as changing the Other entry name to Windows (see Figure 2-22).

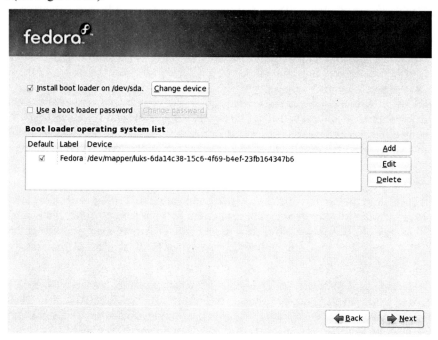

Figure 2-21: Boot Loader

You can also specify general kernel parameters, kernel options to be used when booting.

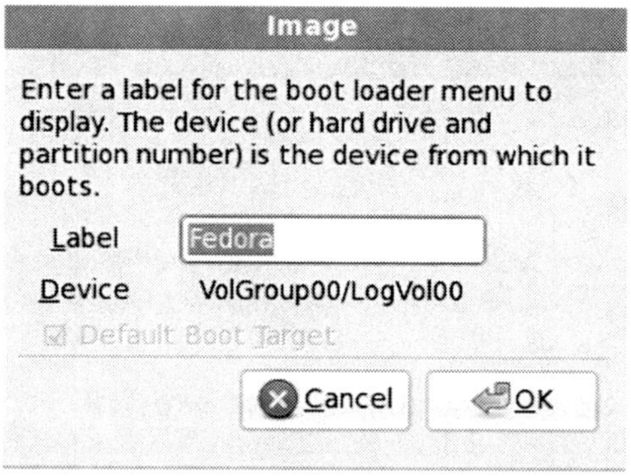

Figure 2-22: Boot Loader Label

You can also set a boot loader password. Without a password, anyone who boots up the system could change the boot loader options on the GRUB menu. A password would prevent anyone but authorized persons booting up your system from changing these options. When you click the checkbox labeled "Use a boot loader password", a dialog opens prompting you to enter the password. Before moving to the next screen, you can click the Change password button to change it.

Software Installation

The next screen will display three install options. You will also have the option to **Customize Now** and select the particular packages you want (see Figure 2-23).

Office and Productivity Home or desktop systems

Software Development. Includes software development

Web server

Web Server includes the Apache Web server. You can also install FTP servers, Samba and NFS file servers. The categories provide a quick install, using a standard selection of software packages. The **Customize Now** button will let you select the packages you want, including all packages, as well as give you more control over configuring your partitions.

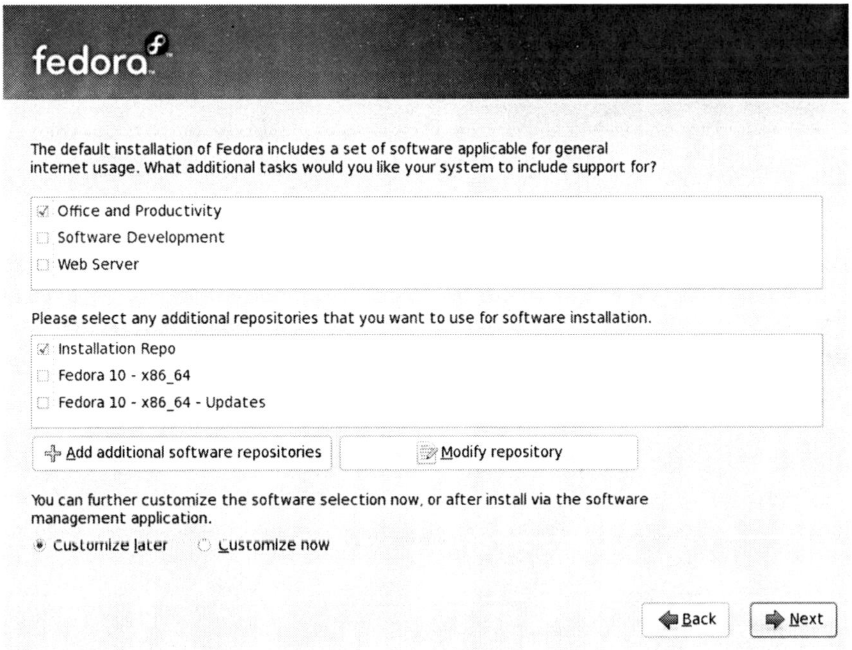

Figure 2-23: Software selection access configuration Screen

In addition you can choose to install software during installation from your installation and online software repositories, either from the install source, Fedora repository, or third party repositories you may want to add.

Initially this section will hold the entry "Installation repository", which will be selected already. For the DVD/CD install, this is the entire DVD/CD collection of software.

There will be addition entries for the Fedora repository and the Fedora Update repository. They will not be selected. These are the online Fedora repositories. Their names will differ depending on the whether you are installing the i386 or x86_64 version. The x86_64 version will have the name **Fedora 10 - x85_64** and **Fedora 10 - x86_64 - Updates**. The Updates repository will provide the latest updated software packages, so you do not have to perform a large update after installation. Both, of course, require a stable and fast Internet connection. If one is not available, you should not choose these options.

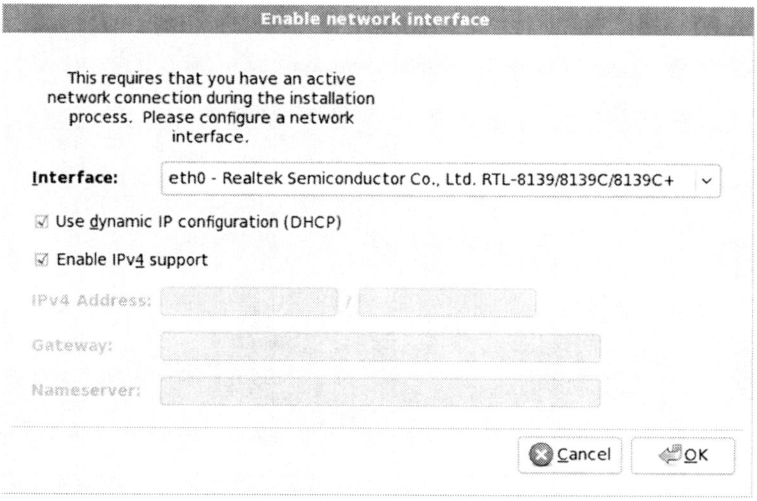

Figure 2-24: Additional Repositories Internet connection

The Fedora online repository entry, like **Fedora 10 -x86_64**, lets you access the entire Fedora software repository online (see Figure 2-25). The DVD or CD only holds a relatively small subset of Fedora software. Selecting these entries lets you access the entire repository and updates during installation.

When you click a Fedora online repository entry, you will first be prompted to confirm an Internet connection listing the network interface device to use (see Figure 2-24). Your connection will then be detected and configured. Installation information like package lists will be retrieved. You have to have a working network connection during installation for this to work, so you can access the repository. A dialog will appear to automatically configure and test this connection. The default network connection will be selected along with the connection type, like DHCP. You can also choose instead to enter specific network configuration information like the IP address. Your connection is then tested, and, if it works, you return to the install screen with the Additional Fedora Software entry selected.

Third party repositories can include software for critical software like proprietary graphics drivers from Nvidia or AMD, as well as multimedia support like MP3 or DVD which is not included with software repositories. Your company or institution may also run its own repository that holds a collection of customized software. The recommended repository for third party software is RPM Fusion, which integrates the Livna, Freshrpms, and Dribble repositories used for previous releases into one access point. RPM Fusion has both free and nonfree repositories. Software like Mplayer is in the free repository, but proprietary graphics card drivers from Nvidia and ATI are in the nonfree repository because they are proprietary, even though they can be legally distributed at no cost. For example, to be able to install Mplayer during installation, you would add a repository entry for the RPM Fusion Free repository. To install the vendor proprietary Nvidia or ATI graphics drivers, you would add an RPM Fusion Nonfree repository entry. You cannot use the nonfree repository entry alone. You first have to have set up access to the free repository. So to install the vendor graphics drivers during installation, you have to have two additional entries, one for the RPM Fusion Free repository and another for the RPM Fusion Nonfree repository.

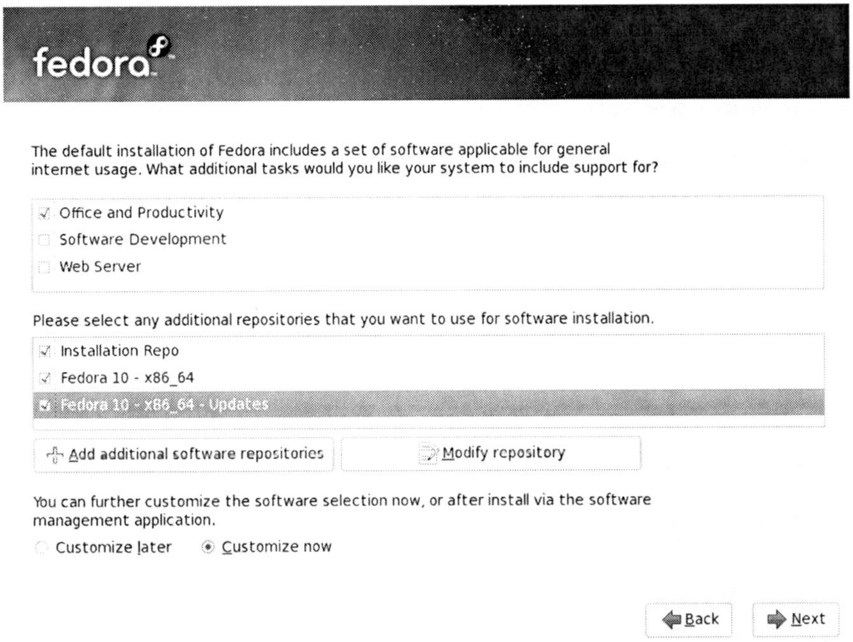

Figure 2-25: Fedora online repository access

To add a third party repository, click on the **Add Additional Software Repositories** button. If you have not done so already, you will again be asked to confirm your network connection. Then a dialog opens where you can enter the repository name and it's URL. The URL will have to be very specific. For RPM Fusion you will have to specify the release and the architecture, as in **/releases/10/Everything/x86_64/os/.** In this example, the release directory is 10 and the architecture is 64 bit, x86_64 (see Figure 2-26). Be sure the URL entry is exact. You can edit the line with your mouse, arrow keys, and backspace key. If not, you will be notified that the repository could not be accessed.

The RPM Fusion Free repository URL for an x86_64 install is:

```
http://download1.rpmfusion.org/free/fedora/releases/10/Everything/x86_64/os/
```

The RPM Fusion Nonfree repository URL for an x86_64 install is:

```
http://download1.rpmfusion.org/nonfree/fedora/releases/10/Everything/x86_64/os/
```

The RPM Fusion repositories will then appear on your install window (see Figure 2-27).

If you are downloading and installing from online repositories, be sure to **click the Customize now button** (not customize later) If you do not, you will not be given the opportunity to select packages from the online repositories. On the following "Begin Install" page, you can press the Back key to return and let you select Customize now. This option is not selected by default.

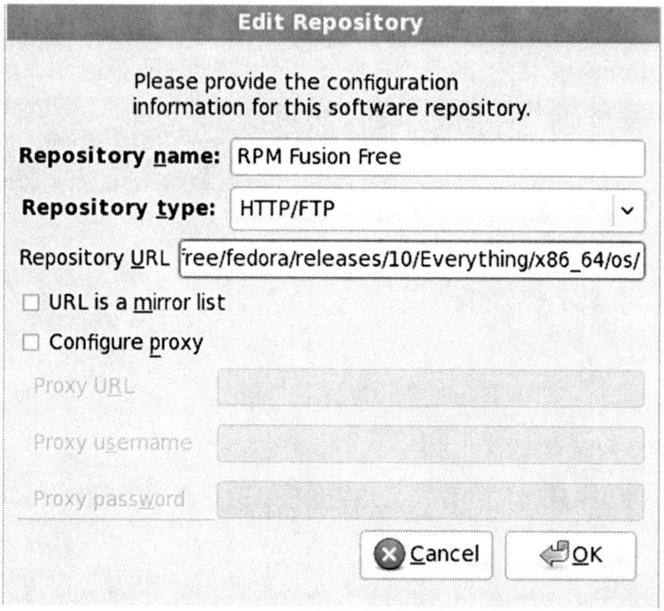

Figure 2-26: RPM Fusion repository configuration

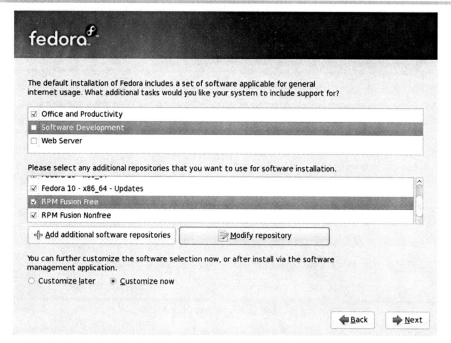

Figure 2-27: Fedora and RPM Fusion repositories configured for access

WARNING: If you want to choose additional software packages to install during installation, be sure to check the **Customize Now** button (customize later is checked by default).

Depending on the kind of install you choose, Fedora will select a set of predetermined software collections tailored to Customize Later (the default) or to Customize Now. If you customize now you can add packages to be installed from the CD/DVD-ROM as well as any online repositories you set up access to.

Tip: If you are installing well after the distribution release date, and you have a strong Internet connection, you should set up access to the Fedora - Updates repository. That way updated software will be downloaded and used instead of the older software on yoru disc. Alternatively, you may want to install as little software as possible. Much of the software may need updating, requiring a download from the online Fedora repository anyway. You can download the updated version directly, after you set up your system.

One important selection you may want to make is the Servers | Windows File Server. This is the Samba server used to set up access to any Windows systems on your network.

Figure 2-28: Selecting a software category

If you choose the Customize now option, you will be placed in the Pirut which is still used for the install process Software Manager (Add/Remove Software). A base selection is automatically made. You can then choose to add optional software packages or remove those selected. The Package Manger first displays two panes, one for a small set of major software categories like Desktops and Applications, and the other for subcategories depending on the major category selected (see Figure 2-28). The subcategories will have checkboxes for software selected. Within each sub-category an optional panel will list specific packages you can add or remove. The major categories are Desktop Environments, Applications, Development, Base System, Servers, and Languages. Desktop Environments will have only subcategories, GNOME and KDE of which only GNOME will be selected by default. Servers will list all the servers, most of which will not be selected. The Base System will hold your Administration and System Tools entries as well as Java. Applications have a several subcategories including Graphical Internet, Office/Productivity, and Sound and Video. To see what packages are actually selected for installation, as well as to add or remove others, select a subcategory and then click the "Optional packages" button. This opens a new window listing all the packages that can be installed for this subcategory, each with a checkbox next to its entry (see Figure 2-29). Checkboxes with checkmarks in them will be installed, those that are empty will not. Click on the checkbox to toggle between the two.

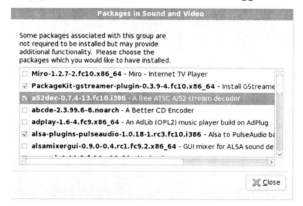

Figure 2-29: Selecting software to add from Optional Packages

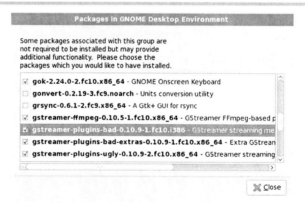

Figure 2-30: Selecting software to add from Optional Packages with integrated RPM Fusion packages

If you installed the RPM Fusion repository, the RPM Fusion packages will be integrated into the collection on the optional screens. To select an RPM Fusion package, click on a category and then click Optional packages. You will find the packages there. There will be nothing to distinguish them from packages on the Fedora repository. Figures 2-31 shows how you would select the Nvidia Linux graphics drivers provided by Nvidia. Choose Base System | Hardware

Support, and then click the checkbox for the xorg-x11-drv--nvidia package. (X.org also provides its own open source graphics drivers by default, but without many of the features that the vendor drivers provide). Selecting the Vendor graphics drivers from RPM Fusion during installation allows you to skip having to do it after installation.

For certain codec you, like the a52dec for High Definition audio streams, you would choose Applications | Sound & Video, click Optional packages, and then click the checkbox for a52dec (see Figure 2-29). Other packages include MythTV, Xine, x264 encoder, gstreamer-ugly, tvtime, and vlc (VideoLan).

Certain packages that you may think would logically appear in one category will actually be in another related one. For example, the gstreamer-bad and gstreamer-ffmpeg packages are actually in the Desktop Environments | GNOME Desktop Environment category, not in Applications | Sound & Video. In the Desktop Environments | GNOME Desktop Environment listing you will also find Seahorse (key ring manager) and gnome-applet-sensors (see Figure 30).

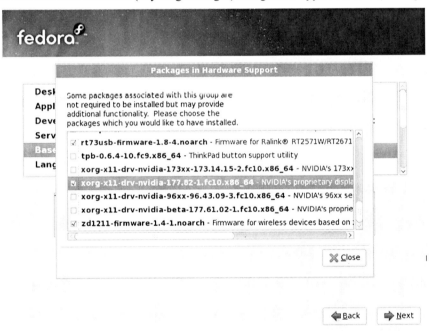

Figure 2-31: RPM Fusion nonfree Vendor graphics driver, Base System | Hardware Support, Optional packages

Many software packages require that other software packages also be installed. This is called a dependency. If you don't have these already selected for installation, they will be selected for you.

A dialog will open with a message first saying checking for dependencies, and the "Starting the install process, this may take several minutes". Package lists from online repositories will be downloaded along with update information, and the sequence of package installation will be determined.

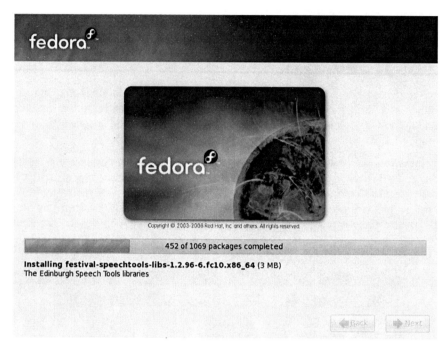

Figure 2-32: Installation of Software Packages

The packages are then installed; showing each package as it is installed and the progress of the installation (see Figure 2-32). Packages from online repositories will be downloaded.

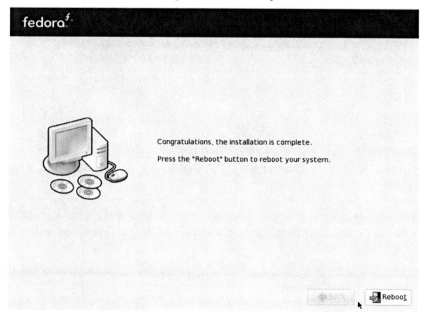

Figure 2-33: Finished and Reboot

Finishing Installation

The Reboot screen will be displayed with a Reboot button in the lower right. Be sure to remove your DVD/CD-ROM disk (see Figure 2-33).

"Congratulations, the installation is complete"

"Press the "Reboot" button to reboot your system"

You then click the Reboot button to reboot. Be sure to remove the install or boot DVD/CD-ROM. If you booted from a CD, your CD will be ejected before rebooting. If you booted directly from the CD-ROM, you may want to change your boot sequence in your BIOS back to your original settings.

GRUB on Restart

When you reboot, a GRUB boot loader will briefly display a start up message saying which operating system on your disk will be started. The default is usually your Linux system.

Start up messages are then displayed. If you have encrypted your hard disk partitions, you are then prompted to enter the LUKS passphrase for them. A standard installation will prompt for the same passphrase for your swap and root partitions on your LVM file system (see Figure 2-34). The prompt will use the physical partition name used for the LVM group, in this example /dev/sda2. There are two prompts, though, one for the LVM volume for the root file system, and one for the LVM volume swap file system.

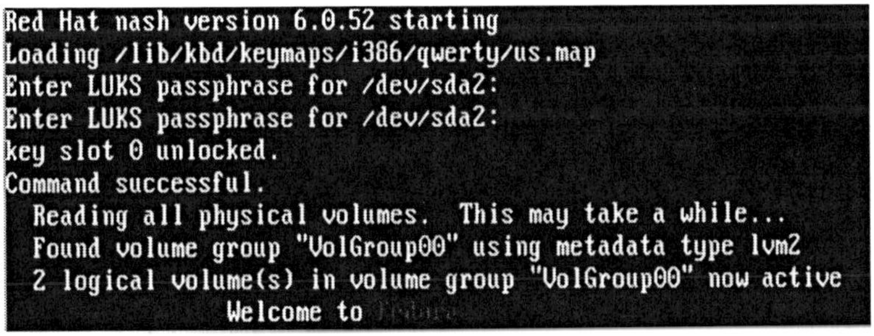

```
Red Hat nash version 6.0.52 starting
Loading /lib/kbd/keymaps/i386/qwerty/us.map
Enter LUKS passphrase for /dev/sda2:
Enter LUKS passphrase for /dev/sda2:
key slot 0 unlocked.
Command successful.
    Reading all physical volumes.  This may take a while...
    Found volume group "VolGroup00" using metadata type lvm2
    2 logical volume(s) in volume group "VolGroup00" now active
                Welcome to
```

Figure 2-34: Prompt for encrypted hard disk partitions

The Boot screen is then displayed showing the progress of your boot procedures. If your graphics card supports Kernel Modesettings, then the Plymouth boot up screen will be displayed, otherwise a simple progress bar is shown.

Setup

The first time you start up Fedora, the Setup Agent is run (see Figure 2-35). This agent will help you perform basic configuration of your system, letting you set the date and time, configure your firewall, and set up user accounts. The different steps will be listed on a side pane, with an arrow progressing through each one as you complete a task. Click the Forward button to continue on to the next screen. For Fedora, you will be initially asked to approve the GNU General Public License for this distribution. The steps are listed here:

Welcome

License Information

Create User

Date and time

Hardware Profile

Figure 2-35: Fedora first time setup

Create User

The Create User panel then lets you create a normal user account (see Figure 2-36). You should have at least one, other than root. A dialog box is displayed with entries for the username, the user's full name, the password, and the password confirmation. Once you have entered the information and clicked Forward, the new user will be created.

You can also select LDAP, Windbind, Hesiod, or NIS to configure a user's network login process. Click the Use Network Login button. Here you can configure the servers. This starts up system-config-authentication. Use this also if your network supports the authentication server. Three panels are displayed: User Information, Authentication, and Options. On the User Information panel, you can enable and configure LDAP, Kerberos, Windbind, and SMB (Samba) authentication. On the Authentication panel, you can enable and configure support for each, specifying NIS, LDAP, Smart Card, Kerberos, or SMB servers that your network may use. The options panel lists support for password authentication.

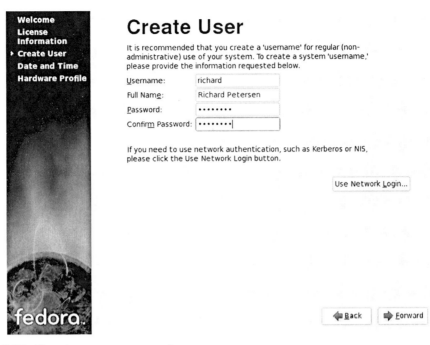

Figure 2-36: Create a user account

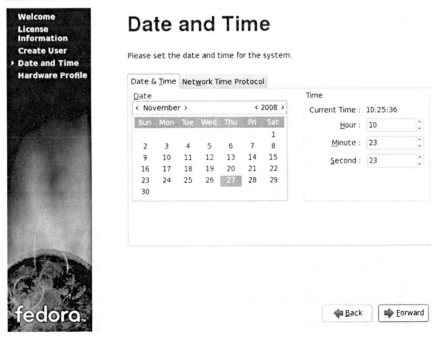

Figure 2-37: Date and Time

Date and Time

The Date and Time is detected and displayed. You can then adjust it as needed (see Figure 2-37). You also have the options to use the Network Time Protocol from a Time server.

Hardware Profile

You then have the option of sending your hardware profile (See Figure 2-38).

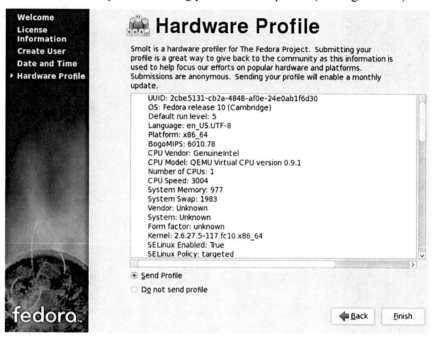

Figure 2-38: Hardware Profile

Login

The Setup Agent then concludes and your login screen is displayed. The login prompt or the login screen will appear. A graphical install will use the login screen. You can then log into your Linux system using a login name and a password for any of the users you have set up.

You cannot login as the **root** user from the login window. This is to deny running as the root user from a graphical desktop. For root user access you need to use the **su** command from a terminal window after you have logged in. If, instead, you wish to return to the login window, click Cancel.

On the login screen, users are listed in a graphical user list (see Figure 2-39), with Suspend, Restart, and Shut Down buttons. The Host name is displayed below the Fedora logo. A bottom panel shows the date on the right and next to it a button for a dialog with accessibility options. Clicking on the accessibility icon to the right open a dialog with accessibility options like the onscreen keyboard, reader, and magnifier.

Figure 2-39: Login screen with user list and Other user

Figure 2-40: User login

To login, select a user from the list, or select other to enter a user name. Once you select the user to login to, a login dialog is displayed with the user name and a text box for entering the password (see Figure 2-40). Once you select a user, three pop-up menus are displayed on the bottom panel: one for Sessions, one for keyboard, and the other for Language. The Sessions menu lets you choose what desktop graphical interface to use, such as KDE or GNOME (see Figure 2-40).

After entering the password, click Log In button to login to your account, or just press the ENTER key.

If you selected Other from the user listing, you will first be prompted to enter the user name in the text box, followed by the password.

Shutdown

To shutdown the system, you can click the Shut Down button on the login window dialog. Use the Restart button to restart, and Suspend to suspend. If you log out from either GNOME or KDE and return to the login screen, you can click the Shutdown button.

You can also shut down as a logged in user. If you are using a command line interface, use the command `halt`. From GNOME, KDE, and most other desktop, you can choose to shut down directly.

If the system should freeze on you for any reason, you can hold down the CTRL and ALT keys and press DEL (CTRL-ALT-DEL) to safely restart it. Never just turn it off. You can also use CTRL-ALT-F3 to shift to a command line prompt and login to check out your system, shutting down with the `halt` command.

GRUB Start Menu and boot problems

When you boot up again, the GRUB screen will be displayed for a few seconds before the boot procedure begins. Should you want to start up a different OS or add options to your start up, you will need to display the GRUB start up menu (see Figure 2-41). Do this by pressing any key on your keyboard. The GRUB menu will be displayed listing Linux and other operating systems you specified, such as Windows. Your Linux system should be selected by default. If not, use the arrow keys to move to the Linux entry, if it is not already highlighted, and press ENTER.

For graphical installations, some displays may have difficulty running the graphical start up display known as the Plymouth boot tool. This tool replaces the Red Hat Graphical Boot tool, but still uses the command **rhgb** for systems that do not fully support Plymouth. Currently only ATI supports Plymouth. If you have this problem, you can edit your Linux GRUB entry and remove the **rhgb quiet** terms at the end of the Grub start up line. Press the **e** key to edit a Grub Linux entry (see Figure 2-42).

Then move the cursor to the **kernel** line and press the **e** key again. This will let you edit the kernel boot line. You will be positioned at the end of the line (see Figure 2-41). Use the backspace key to delete the **rhgb quiet** entries one then press the ENTER key to confirm your edits. You will be placed back to the GRUB edit window as shown in Figure 2-43. The press the **b** key to boot the edited GRUB entry.

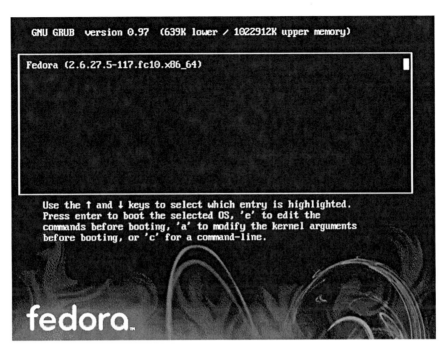

Figure 2-41: GRUB Menu

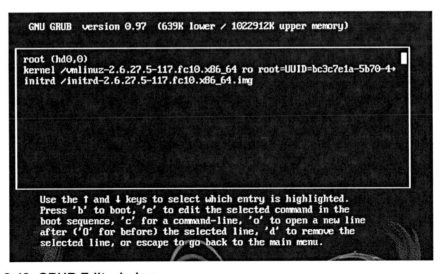

Figure 2-42: GRUB Edit window

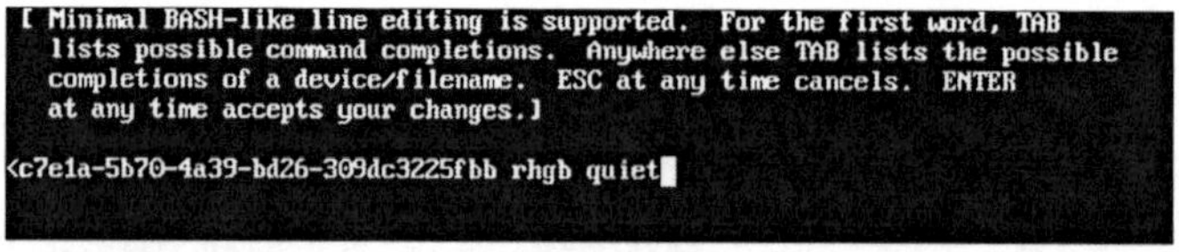

Figure 2-43: Edit a GRUB line

Your system will start up initially using text display for all the start up tasks, then shift to the graphical login. The Linux GRUB kernel line will look something like this, with the UUID used to identify the hard drive.

```
kernel /vmlinuz-2.6.27.5-117.fc10.x86_64 ro root=UUID-0fb2aac7-4aa8-4fd3-a109
rhgb quiet 3
```

Should you have difficulty displaying your graphical interface, you can, instead, choose to boot up the command line interface (see Chapter 3 and 11). From the command line interface, you can then make any needed configuration changes. To boot to the command line interface from GRUB, you edit the kernel line of the Linux GRUB entries, and add a 3 to the end of the line. The 3 indicates runlevel 3, which is the command line interface (the graphical interface is runlevel 5, the default).

Boot Disks

You can use **mkbootdisk** to create boot CD-ROM. Use the **--iso** option and the **--device** option with the name of an ISO image file to create. You then use CD-ROM-burning software to create the CD-ROM from the image file. The following example creates a CD-ROM image file called **mybootcd.iso** that can be used as a boot CD-ROM.

```
mkbootdisk --iso --device mybootcd.iso 2.6.27.5-117.fc10.x86_64
```

Rescue

If for some reason you are not able to boot or access your system, it may be due to conflicting configurations, libraries, or applications. In this case, you can boot your Linux system in a rescue mode and then edit configuration files with a text editor such as Vi, remove the suspect libraries, or reinstall damaged software with RPM. To enter the rescue mode, CD-ROM or the DVD-ROM boot disk, select **Rescue Installed System** on the initial menu.

You will boot into the command line mode with your system's files mounted at **/mnt/sysimage**. You will be notified that you can use the **chroot** command to set your system to the / directory as the root directory. Issue the following command at the command line prompt:

```
chroot /mnt/sysimage
```

Use the **cd** command to move between directories. Check **/etc** and **/etc/sysconfig** for your configuration files. You can use Vi to edit your files and the **less** command to view them. To reinstall files, use the **rpm** command. When you are finished, enter the **exit** command.

If you have a command line system, at the boot prompt, enter

```
linux rescue
```

You can also download and create the Linux rescue CD. Just download the Linux rescue CD iso from the Fedora repository and boot with this disk.

Re-installing the boot loader

If you have a dual-boot system, where you are running both Windows and Linux on the same machine, you may run into a situation where you have to re-install your GRUB boot loader. This problem occurs if your Windows system completely crashes beyond repair and you have to install a new version of Windows, or you are adding Windows to your machine after having installed Linux. Windows will automatically overwrite your boot loader (alternatively, you could install your boot loader on your Linux partition instead of the MBR). You will no longer be able to access your Linux system.

All you need to do is to reinstall your boot loader. First boot from your Linux DVD/CD-ROM installation disk, and at the menu select **Rescue Installed System**.

As noted in the preceding section, this boots your system in rescue mode. Then use `grub-install` and the device name of your first partition to install the boot loader. Windows normally wants to be on the first partition with the MBR, the master boot record. You would specify this partition. At the prompt enter

```
grub-install /dev/sda1
```

This will re-install your current GRUB boot loader, assuming that Windows is included in the GRUB configuration. You can then reboot, and the GRUB boot loader will start up. If you are adding Windows for the first time, you will have to add an entry for it in the **/boot/grub/grub.conf** file to have it accessible from the boot loader.

Tip: If even your Linux rescue discs are unable to access your system, you could use a Fedora Live CD to start up Fedora, and then manually mount your Fedora partitions. You will need to know your partition device names (use GParted). Once mounted, you can access the system files on the mounted partition and make any needed changes.

FirstAidKit

Fedora has introduced FirstAidKit which is designed to automatically detect and fix certain common problems. FirstAidKit is still under development. You will need to install FirstAidKit and its plugins. There are plugins for different problem areas, such as an xserver plugin for display problems, or passwd for password file corruption, and mdadm_conf for RAID file system issues. Currently under development are bootloader, partitions, RPM, and file system plugins. Use the **--list** option to list available plugins.

```
firstaidkit --list
```

See the following sites for more information.

```
https://fedorahosted.org/firstaidkit/
http://fedoraproject.org/wiki/Features/FirstAidKit
```

Plugins are different recovery processes, such as a recover process for the password file or a recover process for the Xserver (display). Within each recover process you can have certain recover task, like resetting the root password or using a different Xserver driver. FirstAidKit also support flows. These are ways to structure certain tasks in a recover process. You can think of them as different kinds of tasks to perform. The passwd plugin (recovery process) supports a **resetRoot** flow, to reset the root password. The xserver plugin supports a **diagnose**, **fix**, and **force** flow to just diagnose problems, fix them, or to force a fix. The RAID plugin supports only a **diagnose** and **fix** flow. Figure 2-45 shows the flow for the current plugins. To find out the flows for a specific plugin, as well as other information about the plugin, you can use the **firstaidkit** command with the **--info** option. The following displays detailed information about the xserver plugin.

```
firstaidkit --info xserver
```

If you want to use FirstAidKit in a rescue mode, first start up the Rescue mode from the Install DVD as described in the previous section, Rescue. Then you can use the **firstaidkit** command with the **-a** option to perform a general diagnostic.

```
firstaidkit -a
```

To fix a problem add the **fix** option.

```
firstaidkit -a fix
```

To perform a flow on a particular plugin use the -f option with the plugin and the flow specified. The following will perform a diagnostic on the xserver.

```
firstaidkit -f xserver diagnose
```

This command will reset the root user password. It will generate a random password. Be sure to copy it down, or change your root user password immediately to something you can remember.

```
firstaidkit -f passwd resetRoot
```

Also available is the FirstAidKit GNOME interface which you can run with the following command. Login as the root user first with the **su** command in a terminal window.

```
firstaidkit -g -gtk
```

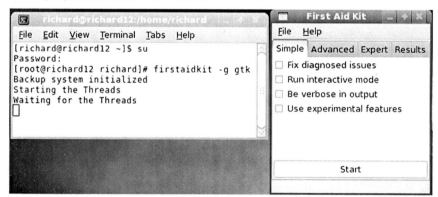

Figure 2-44: FirstAidKit GTK interface

The FirstAidKit gtk interface will open displaying four tabs: Simple, Advanced, Expert, and Results (see Figure 2-43). The Simple screen lets you run a diagnostic with supported plugins. You can set options like fixing issues or display detailed results.

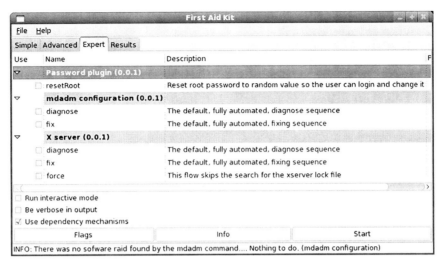

Figure 2-45: FirstAidKit GTK interface Expert tab

The Advanced tab has a drop-down menu that list different flows. The currently supported ones are listed: diagnose, fix. force, and resetRoot. You can only pick one. The Expert tab will let you choose several for specific plugins. It also lists several options: interactive, verbose output, experimental features, and dependency mechanism. The dependency mechanism is on by default and checks for dependencies between plugins.

The Expert tab lets you specify flows by plugin, and the Results tab display results of the diagnostic and fix operations (see Figures 2-45 and 2-46).

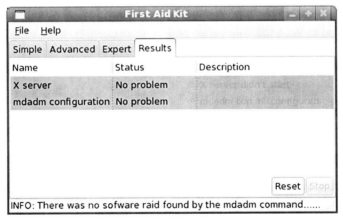

Figure 2-46: FirstAidKit GTK interface Results tab

3. Usage Basics: Login, Desktop, and Help

User Accounts

Accessing Your Linux System

Desktops

The GNOME Desktop

Desktop Operations

Installing Multimedia Support

Command Line Interface

Running Windows Software on Linux: Wine

Help Resources

Using Linux has become an almost intuitive process, with easy-to-use interfaces, including graphical logins and graphical user interfaces (GUIs) like GNOME and KDE. Even the standard Linux command line interface has become more user-friendly with editable commands, history lists, and cursor-based tools. To start using Fedora, you have to know how to access your Fedora system and, once you are on the system, how to execute commands and run applications. Access is supported through either the default graphical login or a command line login. For the graphical login, a simple window appears with menus for selecting login options and text boxes for entering your username and password. Once you access your system, you can then interact with it using either a command line interface or a graphical user interface (GUI). With GUI interfaces like GNOME and KDE, you can use windows, menus, and icons to interact with your system.

Linux is noted for providing easy access to extensive help documentation. It's easy to obtain information quickly about any Linux command and utility while logged in to the system. You can access an online manual that describes each command or obtain help that provides more detailed explanations of different Linux features. A complete set of manuals provided by the Linux Documentation Project is on your system and available for you to browse through or print. Both the GNOME and KDE desktops provide help systems that give you easy access to desktop, system, and application help files.

User Accounts

User access to the system is provided through *accounts.* UNIX, which Linux is based on, was first used on large minicomputers and mainframes that could accommodate hundreds of users at the same time. Using one of many terminals connected to the computer, users could log in to the UNIX system using their usernames and passwords. To gain access to the system, you need to have a user account set up for you. A system administrator creates the account, assigning a username and password for it. You then use your account to log in and use the system.

You can, create other new user accounts using special system administration tools like system-config-users. You can access these tools from any user account provided you supply the administrative password. When you installed your system, you had to provide a root user password. This is the administrative password required to access any administrative tool like the one for manage user accounts. Alternatively you can log in as the root user sung the user name **root** and the root user password. The *root user* is a special user account reserved for system administration tasks, such as creating users and installing new software.

Accessing Your Linux System

If you have installed the boot loader GRUB, when you turn on or reboot your computer, the boot loader first decides what operating system to load and run. Fore a few seconds, GRUB will display a short message telling the operating system it will start up. This is usually Fedora Linux by default.

If, instead, you press any key on your keyboard, the boot loader displays a menu listing all the operating systems installed on your system, with the default highlighted. If a Windows system is listed, you can choose to start that instead.

There are both command line login prompts and graphical login windows. Fedora will use a graphical interface by default, presenting you with a graphical login window at which you enter your username and password. If you choose not to use the graphical interface, you are presented with a simple command line prompt to enter your username.

The Display Manager: GDM

With the graphical login, your graphical interface starts up immediately and displays a login window with user listing. Upon selecting a user and then entry your password, default desktop starts up. On Fedora, this is GNOME by default (see Figure 3-1).

For Fedora, graphical logins are handled by the GNOME Display Manager (GDM). The GDM manages the login interface along with authenticating a user password and username, and then starting up a selected desktop. If problems ever occur using the graphical interface, you can force an exit of the GUI with the CTRL-ALT-BACKSPACE keys, returning to the Login screen. Also, from the GDM, you can shift to the command line interface with the CTRL-ALT-F6 keys, and then shift back to the GUI with the CTRL-ALT-F1 keys.

Figure 3-1: The Fedora GDM user listing

When the GDM starts up, it shows a login window with a scrollable listing of users that you can login as (see Figure 3-1). Currently GDM configuration is not supported. Just below the user listing are buttons for Shut Down and Restart. There is also a bottom panel, whose elements change when a user login is selected. Initially it will show a menu button on the left for accessibility options and the clock with the date and time on the right.

All normal users will be listed. Use the arrow keys to scroll through the listing. The Other user adds a text box where you type the user name in addition to the password. You can use it to just login to any user by typing the user name, instead of scrolling through the list to find it.

To select a user to login as, click on that user entry in the user listing. The user listing will be replaced by a dialog which will list the user name and a text box where you enter the password (see Figure 3-2). At the same time, the bottom panel will now display menus for menus for Language and Sessions. You can use the Sessions menu to select the desktop to use from those installed on your system, like Gnome, KDE, or XFce. The Language menu will open a window listing all the languages you can use.

Once you enter your password, click the Log In button. You will then be logged in as that user. You can click Cancel to not login and then return to the user listing.

When you log out from the desktop, you return to the GDM login window. To shut down your Linux system, click the Shutdown button below the user listing. To restart, click Restart.

Figure 3-2: GDM login

Alternatively, you can also shut down from GNOME. From the System menu, select the Shutdown entry. GNOME will display a dialog screen with the buttons Suspend, Hibernate, Restart, Cancel, and Shutdown (see Figure 3-3). Shutdown is the default and will occur automatically after a few seconds. A count down will commence in the dialog showing how much time you have left. Selecting Restart will shut down and restart your system. (You can also open a terminal window and enter the `halt` or `reboot` command; `halt` will log out and shut down your system.)

Figure 3-3: GNOME Shut Down dialog, GNOME Desktop

The User Switcher

The User Switcher lets you switch to another user, without having to log out or end your current user session. The User Switcher is installed automatically as part of your basic Gnome desktop configuration. The switcher will appear on the right side of the top panel as the name of the currently logged in user. If you left-click the name, a list of all the users also logged in will be displayed. Your current user name will also be listed, but grayed out. To switch a user, select the user from this menu. To switch to a user not already logged in, select the Other entry at the bottom of the list. The login manager (GDM) will appear and you can enter that user's password. If the user is already logged in, then the login window for the lock screen will appear (you can disable the lock screen). Just enter the user's password. The user's original session will continue with the same open windows and applications running when the user switched off. You can easily switch back and forth between logged-in users, with all users retaining their session from where they left off. When you switch off from a user, that user's running programs will continue in the background. The following illustration shows two other users logged in, Robert and George. You can use Other to login as yet another user.

Important Laptop Features

For working on a laptop, you will need two important operations: power management and support for multiple network connection, including wireless and LAN. Both are configured automatically.

For power management, Fedora uses the GNOME Power Manager (later in this chapter), gnome-power-manager, which is configured with the Power Management Preferences window (gnome-power-preferences), accessible from System | Preferences | System | Power Management. On a Laptop, the battery icon displayed on the panel will show how much power you have left, as well as when the battery become critical. It will also indicate an AC connection, as well as when the battery has recharged.

For network connections, Fedora uses Network Manager and system-config-network (see Chapter 14). Network Manager will automatically detect available network connections. They will be shown in the upper panel to the left as a pop-up menu. You can then choose the one you wan to use. Right-click and select configure to set up passphrase and encryption information.

Desktops

Two alternative desktop GUI interfaces, GNOME and the K Desktop (KDE), can be installed on Fedora. Each has its own style and appearance. GNOME uses the Nodoka theme for its interface with the Fedora screen background and menu icon as its default.

It is important to keep in mind that though the GNOME and KDE interfaces appear similar, they are really two very different desktop interfaces with separate tools for selecting preferences. The Preferences menus on GNOME and KDE display a very different selection of desktop configuration tools. These are discussed in Chapters 9 and 10.

GNOME also includes a window manager called compiz that provides 3-D effects. To use compiz, select System | Preferences | Look And Feel | Desktop Effects, and then click Enable Desktop Effects. You can select Windows wobble and Workspace cubes. When you log in to GNOME again, compiz will be used with your desktop effects enabled.

Fedora Desktop

Fedora features a Fedora desktop look and feel with a Fedora logo, as well as default Fedora screen background. The logo depicts an F encased in a blue circle. On the main panel you will now see the blue Fedora logo as the icon for the Applications menu, instead of Red Hat's hat. There are several Fedora backgrounds, including the Fedora Bubbles, Fedora DNA, Fedora Flying High, and Fedora Infinity. The logos even have their own package, fedora-logos.

The default theme is Nodoka with the Fedora icons (the Fedora theme). Numerous other themes are available from the theme manager (Theme panel on Appearances tool, System | Preferences | Look and Feel | Appearances).

KDE

The K Desktop Environment (KDE) displays a panel at the bottom of the screen that looks very similar to one displayed on the top of the GNOME desktop. The file manager appears slightly different but operates much the same way as the GNOME file manager. There is a Control Center entry in the main menu that opens the KDE control center, from which you can configure every aspect of the KDE environment, such as themes, panels, peripherals like printers and keyboards (already handled by Fedora system tools), even the KDE file manager's Web browsing capabilities.

XFce4 and LXDE

The XFce4 and LXDE desktops are lightweight desktop designed to run fast without the kind of overhead seen in full-featured desktops like KDE and GNOME. They use their own file manager and panel, but the emphasis is on modularity and simplicity. The desktop consists of a collection of modules, including the file manager, the panel, and the window manager. In keeping with its focus on simplicity, its small scale makes it appropriate for laptops or dedicated systems that have no need for the complex overhead found in other desktops.

GNOME

The Gnome desktop provides easy to use panels and menus, along with a flexible file manager and desktop. You can change its look and feel, changing themes, adding panels, using different file views, as well as adding panel applets of your own choosing.

Gnome panels and menus

The Fedora GNOME desktop display, shown in Figure 3-4, initially displays two panels at the top and bottom of the screen, as well as any file manager folder icons for your home directory and for the system. The top panel is used for menus, application icons, and notification tasks like your clock. There are three menus:

Applications   With category entries like Office and Internet, these submenus will list the applications installed on your system. Use this menu to start your applications.

Places   This menu lets you easily access commonly used locations like your home directory, the desktop folder for any files on your desktop, and the Computer window through which you can access devices, shared file systems, and all the directories on your local system. It also has entries for searching for files (Search For Files), accessing recently used documents, and logging into remote servers, like NFS and FTP servers. The menu is divided into four segments: the first listing your user folders; the second showing your computer storage devices like accessible file systems, DVD/CD-ROMs, and USB drives; the third showing entries to access network connections and serves, and the last showing file access tools like listing recent documents or searching for files and directories.

System   This includes a Preferences and Administration menu. The Preferences menu is used for configuring your GNOME settings, such as the appearance of your desktop and the behavior of your mouse. The Administration menu holds all the Fedora system configuration tools used to perform administrative tasks like adding users, setting up printers, configuring network connections, and managing network services like a Web server or Samba Windows access. This menu also hold entries for accessing the help system (Help), obtaining information about Fedora and Gnome projects and online resources, locking the screen (Lock Screen), logging out of the system (Logout of), and shutting down the system (Shutdown).

Next to the menus are application icons for the Firefox Web browser (the Mouse Fox and World logo) and the Evolution mail utility. Click one to start that application. You can also start other applications using the Applications menu. On the right you will see icons for the date/time, the sound volume control, the switch user tool, a notification area, and a note tool. The notification area will show update and security icons when updates are needed or security issues arise.

The bottom panel is used for interactive tasks like selecting workspaces and docking applications. The workspace switcher for virtual desktops appears as four squares in the lower-left corner. Clicking a square moves you to that area.

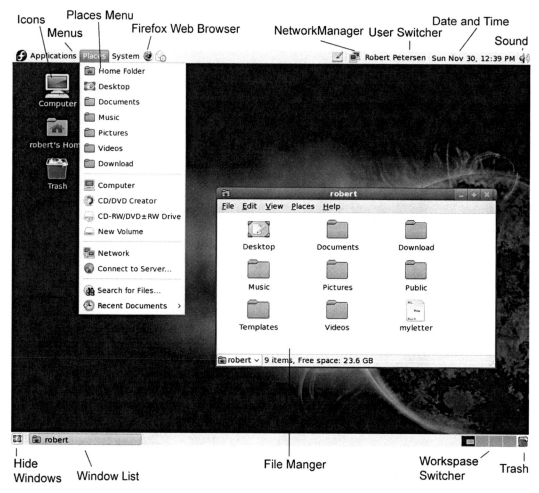

Figure 3-4: The Fedora GNOME desktop

Gnome file manager

When you click the folder for your home directory on your desktop, a file manager window opens showing your home directory. The file manager uses a spatial design by default, opening a new window for each subdirectory or parent directory you open. A directory window will show only the menus for managing files and the icons. The menu entries provide the full range of tasks involved in managing your files. On the lower-left bar of the window is a pop-up menu to access parent directories. The name of the currently displayed directory is shown.

Tip: If your desktop becomes too cluttered with open windows and you want to clear it by just minimizing all the windows, you can click on the Show Desktop Button at the left side of the lower panel.

Your home directory will already have default directories created for commonly used files. These include Pictures, Documents, Music, and Videos. Your office applications will automatically save files to the Documents directory by default. A Download directory functions as your automatic download directory. The Desktop folder will hold all files and directories saved to your desktop.

The file manager also supports a browser view that has more displayed components, including a browser toolbar, location box, and sidebar commonly found on most traditional file managers. To use the browser view, right-click on the folder's icon to display a pop-up menu, and then select Browse Folder. This will open that folder with the enhanced format. Also, from within a special window, you can select a folder and then select Browse Folder from the File menu to open it. When you open a new directory from a Browse Folder window, the same window is used to display it, and you can use the forward and back arrows to move through previously opened directories. In the location window, you can enter the pathname for a directory to move directly to it. Figure 3-5 shows both the spatial and browser views for the file manager windows.

Note: For both GNOME and KDE, the file manager is Internet-aware. You can use it to access remote FTP directories and to display or download their files; though in KDE the file manager is also a fully functional Web browser.

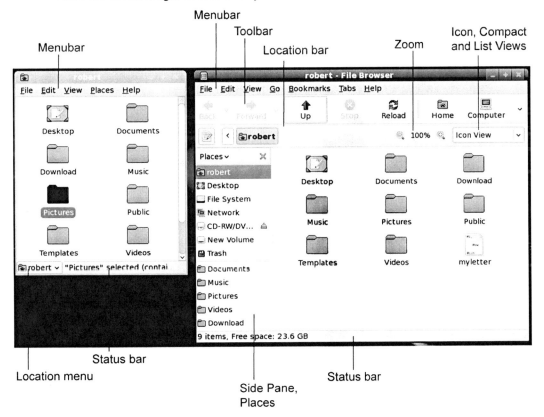

Figure 3-5: File manager, spatial and browser views

To move a window, left-click and drag its title bar. Each window supports Maximize, Minimize, and Close buttons. Double-clicking the title bar will maximize the window. Each window will have a corresponding button on the bottom panel. You can use this button to minimize and restore the window. The desktop supports full drag-and-drop capabilities. You can drag folders, icons, and applications to the desktop or other file manager windows open to other folders. The move operation is the default drag operation (you can also press the SHIFT key while dragging). To copy files, press the CTRL key and then click and drag before releasing the mouse button. To create a link, hold both the CTRL and SHIFT keys while dragging the icon to where you want the link, such as the desktop.

Exiting GNOME

To exit the GNOME desktop, select the Log Out entry from the System menu. This displays a dialog that include buttons for Logout, Switch User, Restart, and Shut Down (see Figure 3-3). Click the Shut Down button to shut down the system. Click Log Out to return to the login screen where you login again as a different user. Switch User will keep you logged in while you login to another user. Your active programs will continue to run in the background. The Restart button will shut down and the restart the system

GNOME Applets

GNOME applets are small programs that operate off your panel. It is very easy to add applets. Right-click the panel and select the Add to Panel entry. This lists all available applets. Some helpful applets are dictionary lookup, the system monitor which shows your CPU usage, the CPU Frequency Scaling Monitor, Search, and Run commands, as well as Lock, Shutdown, and Logout buttons. Some of these, including find, lock, and logout, are already on the Places menu. You could drag these directly from the menu to the panel to add the applet. Figure 3-6 shows some of the more common applets. You have, from left to right: the Hardware Sensor Monitor for CPU and hard drive temperatures, the CPU scaling monitor, Run applications, Search for files, System monitor, Fish (fortune teller), Eyes that follow your mouse around, dictionary lookup, Tomboy note taker, User Switcher, Network connection monitor, Notification area with update icon, Date and Time, and the sound applet.

Figure 3-6: GNOME applets

GNOME Configuration

You can configure different parts of your GNOME interface using tools listed the Preferences menu in the System menu. This menu will display entries for the primary GNOME preferences organized into submenu categories like Hardware and Personal, along with preferences listing task-specific tools, like that for the Palm Pilot or Desktop Switcher. Selecting one will open a window labeled with the tool name, like mouse preferences.

Your GNOME system has combined several desktop configuration tasks into one tool, Appearance. This tool is accessible from System | Preferences | Look and Feel | Appearance. As noted in Chapter 3 (Figures 9-12 and 9-13), the Appearance tool includes Theme, Background image, Fonts, and Interface configuration. You use the Background panel to select a background color or image, the Screensaver to select the screen saver images and wait time, and the Theme panel to choose a theme (see Figure 9-12). To configure your screen saver, you select the screensaver applet at System | Preferences | Look and Feel | Screensaver.

Sound, mouse, and keyboard configuration tools are found in the System | Preferences | Hardware menu. For the sound configuration, the Sound applet lets you select sound files to play for events in different GNOME applications. For your keyboard, you can set the repeat sensitivity and click sound with the Keyboard applet. You can configure mouse buttons for your right or left hand, and adjust the mouse motion.

Configuring your personal information

To set up your personal information, including the icon to be used for your graphical login, you use the About Me preferences tool. On the Fedora GNOME desktop, select the About Me entry in the System | Preferences menu (System | Preferences | About Me). The About Me preferences dialog lets you set up personal information to be used with your desktop applications, as well as change your password (see Figure 3-7). Each user can set up their own About Me personal information, including the icon or image they want to use to represent them.

Figure 3-7: About Me info: System | Preferences | About Me

Note: You can also open a window listing all the preferences as icons by entering the URL **preferences:** in the Nautilus file manager. Either select Open Location from the File menu and enter **preferences:** or open a Nautilus window in the Browse Folder mode and enter **preferences:** in the Location box. Be sure to include the trailing colon, **preferences:**.

Clicking on the image icon in the top left corner opens a browser where you can select a personal image. The Faces directory is selected by default displaying possible images. The selected image is displayed to the right on the browser. For a personal photograph you can select the Picture folder. This is the Pictures folder on your home directory. Should you place a photograph or image there, you could then select if for your personal image. The image will be use in the login screen when showing your user entry.

Should you want to change your password, you can click on the Change password button at the top right.

There are three panels: Contact, Addresses, and Personal Info. The Contact panel you enter email (home and work), telephone, and instant messaging addresses. On the Address panel you enter your home and work addresses, and on the Person Info panel you list your Web addresses and work information.

Figure 3-8: Desktop Background on Appearance Preference tool

Desktop Background

You use the Background panel on the Appearance tool to select or customize background image (see Figure 3-8). To open this tool, you can either right click anywhere on the desktop background and select Change Desktop Background from the pop-up menu, or from the panel menus select System | Preferences | Look and Feel | Appearance and then click on the Background panel. Installed backgrounds are displayed in a Wallpaper scroll box, with the current one selected. To add your own image, either drag and drop the image file to the Background Wallpaper box, or click on the Add button to locate and select the image file. To remove an image, select it and click the Remove button. To make an image the default for the entire system, click on the Make Default button. You will be prompted for the root user password. The image would then become the default background, replacing the current one (like the Fedora 10 Solar background).

The style menu lets you choose different display options like centered, scaled, or tiled. A centered or scaled image will preserve the image proportions. Fill screen may distort it. Any space not filled, such as with a centered or scaled images, will be filled in with the desktop color. You can change the color if you wish, as well as make it a horizontal or vertical gradient (Colors menu). Colors are selected from a color wheel providing an extensive selection of possible colors.

Tip: If you are downloading from **art.gnome.org**, you can just drag and drop the download icon from the Web page directly to the Theme panel, or download first and drop the theme package directly to the Theme preferences window to install.

GNOME International Clock: Time, Date, and Weather

The international clock applet is located on the top panel to the right. It displays the current time and date for your region, but can be modified to display the weather, as well as the time, date, and weather of any location in the world.

Figure 3-9: Selecting a location on the international clock

To add a location, right-click on the time and select Preferences from the pop-up menu. The Clock Preferences window will display three panels: General, Location, and Weather. To add a new location, click on the Add button on the Location panel (see Figure 3-9). This opens a box where you can enter the name, timezone, and coordinates of the location. It is easier to just click the Find button and open an expandable tree of locations, starting with continent, then to region, country, and city.

On the Weather panel, you can specify the temperature and wind measures to use. The General panel you can set the clocks display options for the locations, whether to show weather, temperature, date and seconds.

Once you set the location for your own location, you will see a weather icon appear next to the time on the panel, showing you your current weather (see Figure 3-10).

73 °F Sun Nov 30, 1:38 PM

Figure 3-10: International clock with weather icon

To see the locations you have selected, click on the time displayed on the top panel (see Figure 3-11). This opens a calendar, with Location label with an expandable arrow at the bottom.

Figure 3-11: International clock, full display

Click this arrow to display all your locations, their time and weather. You home location will have a house icon next to it. A world map will show all your locations as red dots, with a blue house icon for your current home location. When you click on a location entry, its corresponding dot will blink for a few seconds. Each location will have a small globe weather icon, indicating the general weather, like sun or clouds. To see weather details, move your mouse over the weather icon. A pop-up dialog will display the current weather, temperature, wind speed, and time for sunrise and sunset. The clock icons for each location will be dark, grey, or bright depending on the time of day at that location.

You can easily change your home location, by click the Set button to the right the location you want made your home. You will see the home icon shift to the new location. This is helpful when traveling. Each location has a set button which will be hidden until you move your mouse over it, on the right side of the clock display

To make any changes, you can click the Edit button next to the Locations label. This opens the Clock Preferences window where you can configure the display or add and remove locations.

The calendar will show the current date, but you can move to different months and years using the month and year scroll arrows at the top of the calendar.

To set the time manually, right-click on the time and select Adjust Date & Time (also from the General panel of the Clock Preferences window, click the Time Settings button). This opens a Time Settings window where you can enter the time and set the date (see Figure 1-12). Use the month and year arrows on the calendar to change the month and year. To set the time for the entire system, click the Set System Time button

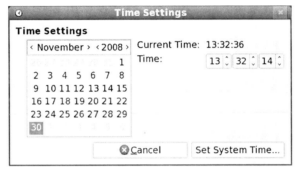

Figure 3-12: Manually setting the clock

Window Display Preferences

On you desktop you configure certain window display capabilities. The Window Preferences tool lets you enable three different features.

Window selection: Instead of clicking on a window to select it, you can just move the mouse over it. A delay lets you quickly pass over windows without selecting them, until you reach the one you want.

Title bar Action: For the title bar you can enable Roll Up. This means that double clicking the title bar will rollup the window to just its title bar. The default is full screen.

Movement Key: For moving a window, you can change the keyboard key used. By default this is the Alt key, but you can change it to the Control or Windows key.

Tip: The Keyboard Shortcuts tool (System | Preferences | Personal | Keyboard Shortcuts) lets you select a shortcut key for common tasks, like launching a Web browser. Some key will already be assigned.

GNOME Screensaver

With the GNOME Screensaver Preferences you can control when the computer is considered idle and what screen saver to use if any (see Figure 3-13). You can also control whether to lock the screen or not, when idle. Access the Screensaver Preferences from System | Preferences

| Look and Feel | Screensaver. To turn off the Screensaver by un-checking the "Activate screensaver when computer is idle" box.

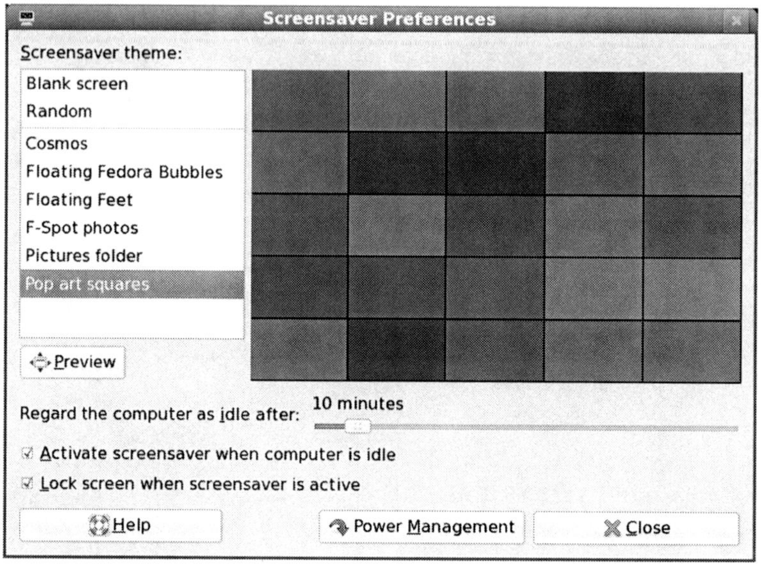

Figure 3-13: Gnome Screen Saver

Gnome Power Management

For power management, Fedora uses the GNOME Power Manager, gnome-power-manager, which makes use of ACPI support provided by a computer to manage power use. The GNOME Power manager is configured with the Power Management Preferences window (gnome-power-preferences), accessible from System | Preferences | System | Power Management. Power management can be used to configure both a desktop and a laptop. For a laptop there are only two panels, On AC Power and General.

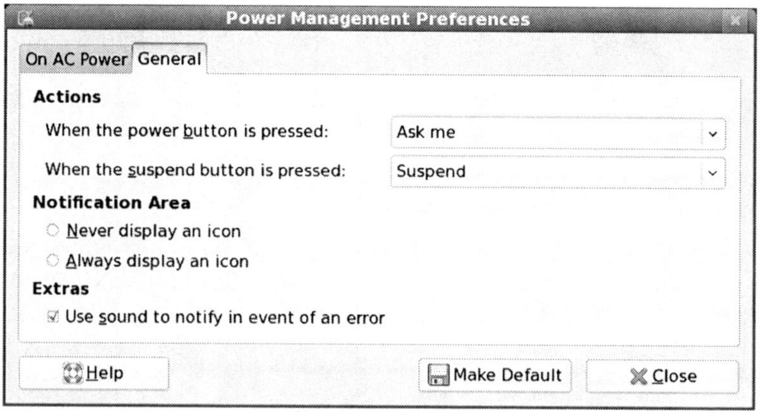

Figure 3-14: Power Management Preferences

On the On AC Power window you have two sleep options, one for the computer and one for the screen. You can put each to sleep after a specified interval of inactivity. On the General panel you set desktop features like actions to take when pressing the power button or whether to display the power icon (see Figure 3-14). The AC power icon will show a plug image for desktops and a battery for laptops. The icon is displayed on the top panel.

On a Laptop, the battery icon displayed on the panel will show how much power you have left, as well as when the battery become critical. It will also indicate an AC connection, as well as when the battery has recharged.

To see how your laptop or desktop is performing with power, you can use Power statistics, Applications | System Tools.

Desktop Operations

There are several desktop operations that you may want to take advantage of when first setting up your desktop. These include setting your font sizes larger for high resolution monitors, burning CD/DVD disks, searching your desktop for files, and using removable media like USB drives, along with access to remote host.

Searching files

There are two search tools available for your Linux desktop, "Search for Files" and Beagle. "Search for Files" is installed by default and will be accessible from Places | Search, and the desktop menu. You can choose to install the Beagle desktop, which will actually index your files making access more efficient. The GNOME file manager also provides its own search tool for quickly finding files.

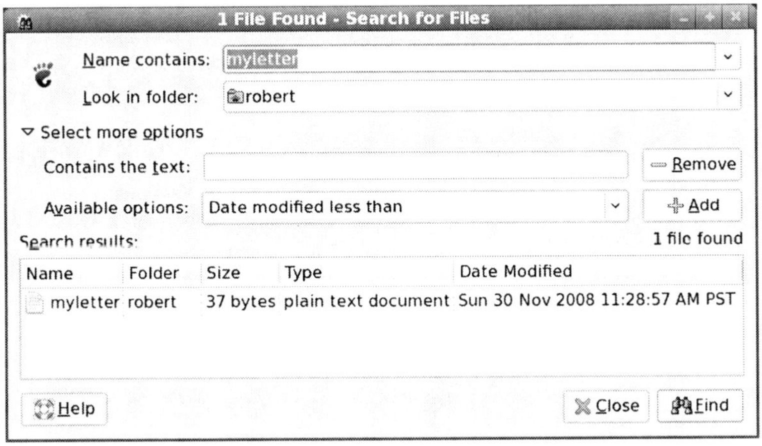

Figure 3-15: Search for Files

Search for Files and GNOME File Manager Search

Basic file searching is performed by a GNOME front end for the Linux grep, find, and locate tools (see Figure 3-15). Select Search for Files from the Places menu and enter the pattern to search for. File matching characters (wildcards) will help, like * for file name completion or [] to specify a range of possible characters or numbers.

Enter the pattern to search in the Name contains box, and then select the folder or file system to search from the Look in Folder pop up menu. The user home folder is selected by default. You can then elect to specify advanced options like the Contain text option for searching the contents of text files (grep), or additional file characteristics like the file date, size, or owner type (find). You can also use a regular expression to search file names.

The GNOME file manager uses a different search tool, with the similar features. You enter a pattern to search, but you can also specify file types. Search begins from the folder opened, but you can specify other folder to search (Location option). Click the + button to add additional location and file type search parameters. In the browser mode, you can click on the Search button on the toolbar to make the URL box a Search box. Popup menus for location and file type will appear in the folder window, with + and - button to add or remove location and file type search parameters.

Beagle

Alternatively, you can use Beagle as your desktop search tool (**beaglewiki.org**). You will have to download and install it (use Add/Remove Software, search on beagle). To start Beagle, select Search from the Places menu. Beagle will search all the files on your system, including images, e-mails, media files, and program source code. When you install Beagle, it will replace the search tool as the Search entry for the Places menu. The application name for Beagle is **beagle-search**.

On Fedora, to index files so that they can be searched, Beagle uses extended attributes for file systems, an option specified automatically for **ext3** file systems by HAL (user_xatter option). Beagle runs as the daemon **beagled**, which you can start or stop using system-config-services or the `beagled` services script. Keep in mind that Beagle does not run on the root user account, only on ordinary user accounts.

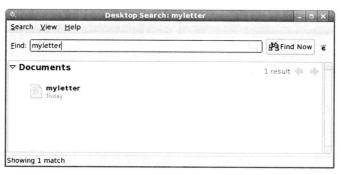

Figure 3-16: Beagle search

By default Beagle performs indexing automatically in the background. Your home directory is indexed by default. To set desktop index and search options use the Search Preferences tool accessible from System | Preferences | System | Searching & Indexing. Use the Indexing panel in the Search Preferences tool to add other directories, as well as specify which directories to exclude (see Figure 3-16). The `beagle-info` tool with the `--status` and `--index-info` options provide information about Beagle's current indexing state. Beagle also allows you to do static indexing of directories that do not change often, instead of constantly performing live background indexing.

For specific kinds of application data like Evolution address books, or Firefox accessed Web sites, you can install supporting backends and extensions to let Beagle extract indexing information from them. Fedora includes Beagle support packages for Firefox and Epiphany browsers, as well as the Thunderbird and Evolution mailers.

Using Removable Devices and Media

Removable media such as CD and DVD discs, USB storage disks, digital cameras, and floppy disks will be displayed as icons on your desktop. These icons will not appear until you place the disks into their devices. To open a disk, double-click it to display a file manager window and the files on it.

Fedora now supports removable devices and media like digital cameras, PDAs, card readers, and even USB printers. These devices are handled automatically with an appropriate device interface set up on the fly when needed. Such hotplugged devices are identified, and where appropriate, their icons will appear in the file manager window. For example, when you connect a USB drive to your system, it will be detected and displayed as storage device with its own file system. If you copied any files to the disk, be sure to unmount it first before removing it (right-click and select Unmount Volume).

Accessing File Systems, Devices, and Remote Shared Resources (Windows)

Removable media such as CD and DVD discs, USB storage disks, digital cameras, and floppy disks will be displayed as icons on your desktop. These icons will not appear until you place the disks into their devices. To open a disk, double-click it to display a file manager window and the files on it.

The desktop will also display a Computer folder (also accessible from the Places menu). Opening this folder will also list your removable devices, along with icons for your file system and network connections (see Figure 3-17). The file system icon can be used to access the entire file system on your computer, starting from the root directory. Regular users will have only read access to many of these directories, whereas the root user will have full read and write access.

Opening Network will list any hosts on your system with shared directories, like Windows systems accessible with Samba (also accessible as the Network entry in the Places menu). GNOME uses DNS-based service discovery to automatically detect these hosts. Opening a host's icons will list the shared directories available on that system. When opening a shared directory, you will be asked for a user and password, like the user and password for a directory owned by a Windows user. The first time you access a shared directory, you will also be asked to save this user and password in a key ring, which itself can be password protected. This allows repeated access without have to always enter the password.

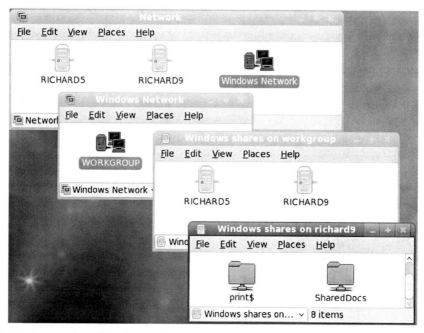

Figure 3-17: Accessing Windows file systems, Samba

To access shared folders and printers on Windows computers, you will have to first set up Samba using both the Samba, Firewall, and Services configuration tools on the System | Administration menu. Chapter 14 details how to set up Samba to enable access to Windows systems. The Samba tool specifies the Windows network to use, the Firewall tool allows access through Samba by that network, and the Services tool will automatically start Samba, providing Windows access whenever you system starts up.

Once configured you can then browse Windows shared folders from your desktop. Click on the Computer icon and then the Network icon, or select Network from the Places menu. All your networked computers will be displayed. Click on the one you know is the Windows host you want (see Figure 3-17), or click on Windows network to see just the Windows networks you are connected to (usually there will only be one).. Then select the Windows computer you want to access. Accessible shared folders will then be displayed (see Figure 3-17).

Using Removable Devices and Media

Fedora supports removable devices and media like DVD/CD discs, USB drives, digital cameras, PDAs, card readers, and even USB printers (see Figure 3-18). These devices are handled automatically with an appropriate device interface set up on the fly when needed. Such hot plugged devices are identified, and where appropriate, their icons will appear in the file manager window. For example, when you connect a USB drive to your system, it will be detected and displayed as storage device with its own file system. If you copied any files to the disk, be sure to unmount it first before removing it (right-click and select Unmount Volume).

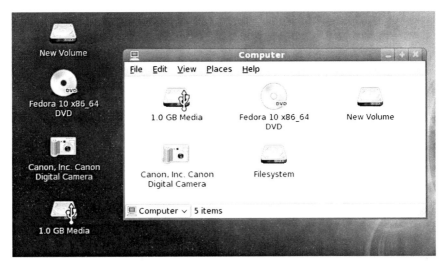

Figure 3-18: Removable devices and Computer folder

Tip: Fedora cannot play MP3, DVD, or DivX files as installed. You need to download and install supporting tools and libraries from RPM Fusion. PackageKit will let you automatically download and installed needed decoders.

DVD and CD discs are also treated like removable devices, with an icon for a disc automatically displayed when your put one in your CD/DVD drive. You can then double-click the CD/DVD disc icon to open a file manager window for it, displaying its contents. For media discs, such as music CDs, your system is configured to play the appropriate application. Music CDs will start up the CD player, which will let you play the music. For Video DVDs, however, you will need to download and install supporting video codecs, libraries, and applications from **fluendo.com** or RPM Fusion. (RPM Fusion, **http://rpmfusion.org**, can be configured for YUM and with packages installed directly with PackageKit).

Keep in mind that Totem will not play commercial DVD Videos. You would have to install a DVD Video-enabled player for commercial discs or the MPlayer, Xine, or Totem-zine players. Once you have installed your DVD Video player, you can then use the Drives and Removable Media tool to have the DVD movie automatically start up in your selected player.

Associated applications for most media, like music CDs, digital cameras or DVD/CDs with images, or DVD video, are now handled directly by the GNOME file manager (Nautilus). Use the File Management tool to configure which application to run automatically for a certain kinds of media (System | Preferences | Personal | File Management). You can choose applications for CD Audio, DVD Video, Music Player, Photos, and Software, and even Bluray discs.

Note: The GNOME Volume Manager can also be installed to associate applications for .digital cameras, scanners, PDAs, and Input devices. Most associations though are now handled by Nautilus. The GNOME Volume Manager is useful should you need specialize applications for digital video cameras or scanners. Install the **gnome-volume-manager** package and set the preferences on the Removable Drives and Media Preferences tool, accessible with the "Removable Drives And Media" entry in the System | Preferences | Hardware menu. This displays the

"Removable Drives And Media Preferences window with four panels: cameras, PDAs, Printers and Scanners, and Input devices

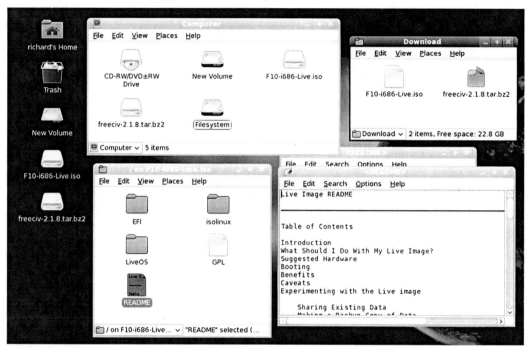

Figure 3-19: Archive Mounter for archives, packages, and CD/DVD disk images

Accessing archives, packages, and disk images from GNOME: Archive Mounter

With Archive Mounter, GNOME can now mount any archive, including software packages and CD/DVD ISO image files, directly (see Figure 3-19). It is an easy way to see what files are on a disc image or archive, and even read text files or extract specific files.

To mount an archive or package, right-click on the archive or package file and select Archive Mounter click. The archive is mounted as if it where a file system. A disk icon for the archive will appear on the desktop and in the Computer folder. To close the archive, right-click and select Unmount Volume. To extract a file from the archive, double click on its icon to open a window for it. You can then browse its contents, select items, and drag them to another folder on your system. The archive is mounted as read only. You cannot add files to the archive.

Fedora also supports using Archive Mounter to mount CD/DVD disk images as archives. You can then extract files directly from the ISO image by dragging them to another folder. To mount the ISO image as an archive, simply double-click on a disk image file (.iso extension) and the image is automatically mounted as an archive. A disk icon for the CD/DVD will appear on the desktop. It will be read only. You can also right-click on the disk image file and select Archive Mounter (usually the first option). Figure 3-19 shows the Fedora DVD disk image mounted as a virtual disk. The disk will appear in the Computer folder as a valid disk. To unmount the disk image, right-click and select Unmount Volume.

Burning DVD/CDs with Gnome

With GNOME, burning data to a DVD or CD is a simple matter of dragging files to an open blank CD or DVD and clicking the Write To Disk button. When you insert a blank DVD/CD disc, a window will open labeled CD/DVD Creator (see Figure 3-20).

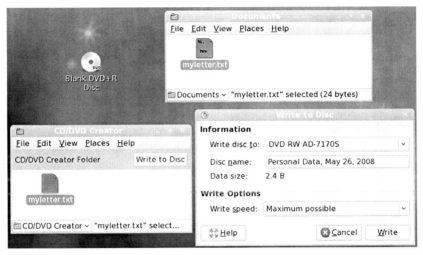

Figure 3-20. Burning DVD/CDs on Gnome

To burn files, just drag them to that window. All Read/Write discs, even if they are not blank, are also recognized as writable discs and opened up in a DVD/CD Creator window. Click Write To Disk when ready to burn a DVD/CD. A dialog will open. You can specify write speed, the DVD/CD writer to use (if you have more than one), and the disc label.

When you click Write, a dialog opens showing the write progress. Once finished, you can then eject the disk, and then make another copy if you wish.

GNOME also supports burning ISO images. Just double-click the ISO image file or right-click the file and select Open With CD/DVD Creator. This opens the CD/DVD Creator dialog, which prompts you to burn the image. Be sure to first insert a blank CD or DVD into your CD/DVD burner. You can also burn DVD-Video disks.

For more complex DVD/CD burning you can use the Brasero DVD/CD burner, Brasero (see Figure 3-21). This is included with Fedora and is a GNOME project. Brasero supports drag and drop operations for creating Audio CDs. In particular, it can handle CD/DVD read/write discs, erasing discs. It also supports multi-session burns, adding data to DVD/CD disc. Initially Brasero will display a dialog with buttons for the type of project you want to do. You have the choice of creating a data or audio project, as well as copying a DVD/CD or burning a DVD/CD image file.

GNOME also supports burning ISO images. Just double-click the ISO image file or right-click the file and select Open With CD/DVD Creator. This opens the CD/DVD Creator dialog, which prompts you to burn the image. Be sure to first insert a blank CD or DVD into your CD/DVD burner.

Figure 3-21: Burning DVD/CDs with Brasero

Display Resolution Preferences: RandR

The X display drivers for Linux used on Fedora now support user level resolution and orientation changes. Any user can specify their own resolution or orientation without affecting the settings of other users. The gnome-display-properties tool provides a simple interface for setting rotation, resolution, and selecting added monitors, allowing for cloned or extended displays across several connected monitors.

Figure 3-22: Screen Resolution, RandR

Open the Monitor Resolution Settings window by selecting Administration | Preferences | Screen Resolution (see Figure 3-22). This is a feature provided by GNOME. From pop-up menus you can set the resolution, refresh rate, and rotation, as well as detect attached displays. After you select a resolution, click Apply. The new resolution is displayed with a dialog with button that asks you whether to keep the new resolution or return to the previous one.

Multimedia Support: MP3, DVD Video, and DivX

Due to licensing and other restrictions, the Fedora distribution does not include MP3, DVD Video, or DivX media support. You cannot play MP3 files, DVD Video discs, or DivX files after installing Fedora. RPM Fusion (**http://rpmfusion.org**) provides needed libraries and support files for these media formats. All packages are RPM packages that you can install with YUM, after first downloading and installing their YUM repository configuration files.

The commercial DVD-Video codec (DVDCSS) is available only from Livna or Freshrpms, not RPM Fusion. See **rpm.livna.org** to configure access and download the libdvdcss package.ALso **www.fluendo.com** will provide DVD Video and MP3 codecs.The MP3 coded is free.

DivX support can be obtained from **http://labs.divx.com/DivXLinuxCodec**. The open source version of DivX, Xvid (xvid-core), can be downloaded from **http://rpmfusion.org**. It will play most DivX files.

Check **www.fedoraproject.org/wiki/Multimedia** for more information. There are many forbidden items that cannot be included with Fedora due to licensing restrictions, including MP3 support, Adobe reader, and Nvidia vendor provided drivers. Check **www.fedoraproject.org/wiki/ForbiddenItems** for details.

Command Line Interface

When using the command line interface, you are given a simple prompt at which you type in your command. Even with a GUI, you sometimes need to execute commands on a command line. The terminal window is no longer available on the Gnome desktop menu. You now have to access it from the Applications | System Tools menu. If you use terminal windows frequently you may want to just drag the menu entry to the desktop to create a desktop icon for the terminal window. Just click to open.

Linux commands make extensive use of options and arguments. Be careful to place your arguments and options in their correct order on the command line. The format for a Linux command is the command name followed by options, and then by arguments, as shown here:

```
$ command-name    options    arguments
```

An *option* is a one-letter code preceded by one or two hyphens, which modifies the type of action the command takes. Options and arguments may or may not be optional, depending on the command. For example, the `ls` command can take an option, `-s`. The `ls` command displays a listing of files in your directory, and the `-s` option adds the size of each file in blocks. You enter the command and its option on the command line as follows:

```
$ ls -s
```

An *argument* is data the command may need to execute its task. In many cases, this is a filename. An argument is entered as a word on the command line after any options. For example, to display the contents of a file, you can use the **more** command with the file's name as its argument. The **less** or **more** command used with the filename **mydata** would be entered on the command line as follows:

```
$ less  mydata
```

The command line is actually a buffer of text you can edit. Before you press ENTER, you can perform editing commands on the existing text. The editing capabilities provide a way to correct mistakes you may make when typing in a command and its options. The BACKSPACE and DEL keys let you erase the character you just typed in. With this character-erasing capability, you can BACKSPACE over the entire line if you want, erasing what you entered. CTRL-U erases the whole line and enables you to start over again at the prompt.

Tip: You can use the UP ARROW key to redisplay your last-executed command. You can then re-execute that command, or you can edit it and execute the modified command. This is helpful when you have to repeat certain operations over and over, such as editing the same file. This is also helpful when you've already executed a command you entered incorrectly.

Accessing Linux from the Command Line Interface

For the command line interface, you are initially given a login prompt. The system is now running and waiting for a user to log in and use it. You can enter your username and password to use the system. The login prompt is preceded by the hostname you gave your system. In this example, the hostname is **turtle**. When you finish using Linux, you first log out. Linux then displays exactly the same login prompt, waiting for you or another user to log in again. This is the equivalent of the login window provided by the GDM. You can then log into another account.

```
Fedora release 10 (Cambridge)
Kernel 2.6 on an x86_64

turtle login:
```

Logging in to your Linux account involves two steps: entering your username and then entering your password. Type in the user name for your user account. If you make a mistake, you can erase characters with the BACKSPACE key. In the next example, the user enters the username **richlp** and is then prompted to enter the password:

```
Fedora release 10 (Cambridge)
Kernel 2.6 on an x86_64

turtle login: richlp
Password:
```

When you type in your password, it does not appear on the screen. This is to protect your password from being seen by others. If you enter either the username or the password incorrectly, the system will respond with the error message "Login incorrect" and will ask for your username again, starting the login process over. You can then reenter your username and password.

Once you enter your username and password correctly, you are logged in to the system. Your command line prompt is displayed, waiting for you to enter a command. Notice the command line prompt is a dollar sign ($), not a number sign (#). The $ is the prompt for regular users, whereas the # is the prompt solely for the root user. In this version of Fedora, your prompt is preceded by the hostname and the directory you are in. Both are bounded by a set of brackets.

```
[turtle /home/richlp]$
```

To end your session, issue the **logout** or **exit** command. This returns you to the login prompt, and Linux waits for another user to log in.

```
[turtle /home/richlp]$ logout
```

Shutting Down Linux from the Command Line

If you want to turn off your computer, you must first shut down Linux. If you don't shut down Linux, you could require Linux to perform a lengthy systems check when it starts up again. You shut down your system in either of two ways. First, log in to an account and then enter the **halt** command. This command will log you out and shut down the system.

```
$ halt
```

Alternatively, you can use the **shutdown** command with the -h option. With the -r option, it shuts down the system and then reboots it. In the next example, the system is shut down after five minutes. To shut down the system immediately, you can use +0 or the word **now**.

```
# shutdown -h now
```

Tip: Shutting down involves a series of important actions, such as unmounting file systems and shutting down any servers. You should never simply turn off the computer, though it can normally recover.

You can also force your system to reboot at the login prompt, by holding down the CTRL and ALT keys and then pressing the DEL key (CTRL-ALT-DEL). Your system will go through the standard shutdown procedure and then reboot your computer.

Starting a GUI from the Command Line

Once logged into the system using the command line interface, you also have the option of starting an X Window System GUI, such as GNOME or KDE, and using it to interact with your Linux system. In Linux, the command **startx** starts the X Window System along with a GUI, which then enables you to interact with the system using windows, menus, and icons. The **startx** command starts the GUI desktop by default. Once you shut down the GUI interface, you will return to your command line interface, still logged in.

```
$ startx
```

Running Windows Software on Linux: Wine

In many cases, certain accommodations need to be made for Windows systems. Most Linux systems are part of networks that also run Windows systems. Using Linux Samba servers, your Linux and Windows systems can share directories and printers. In addition you may also need to run Windows applications directly on your Linux system. Though there is an enormous amount of Linux software available, in some cases you many need or prefer to run a Windows application. The Wine compatibility layer allows you to do just that, for many Windows applications (not all).

Wine is a Windows compatibility layer that will allow you to run many Windows applications natively on Linux. Though you could run the Windows OS on it, the actual Windows operating system is not required. Windows applications will run as if they were Linux applications, able to access the entire Linux file system and use Linux-connected devices. Applications that are heavily driver dependent, like graphic intensive games, most likely will not run. Others, like newreaders that do not rely on any specialized drivers may run very well. For some applications, you may also need to copy over specific Windows DLLs from a working Windows system to your Wine Windows system32 or system directory.

To install Wine on your system, search for **wine** on Add/Remove Software. You will see several packages listed. You will need to select only the Wine package. Others will be selected by YUM as dependent packages, including wine-twain and wine-tools. Some are already included with the Wine package but are presented as separate packages, such as wine-arts, in case you do not want to install everything.

Tip: Alternatively, you can use the commercial Windows compatibility layer called Crossover Office. This is a commercial product tested to run certain applications like Microsoft Office. Check **www.codeweavers.com** for more details.

Once installed, a Wine menu will appear in the Applications menu. The Wine menu holds entries for Wine configuration, the Wine software uninstaller, and Wine file browser, as well as a regedit registry editor, a notepad, and a Wine help tool.

To set up Wine, a user starts the Wine Configuration tool. This opens a window with panels for Applications, Libraries (DLL selection), Audio (sound drivers), Drives, Desktop Integration, and Graphics. On the Applications window you can select which version of Windows an application is designed for. The Drives panel will list your detected partitions, as well as your Windows-emulated drives, such as drive C. The C: drive is really just a directory, **.wine/drive_c**, not a partition of a fixed size. Your actual Linux file system will be listed as the Z drive.

Once configured, Wine will set up a **.wine** directory on the user's home directory (the directory is hidden, so enable Show Hidden Files in the file browser View menu to display it). Within that directory will be the **drive_c** directory, which functions as the C: drive holding your Windows system files and program files in the Windows and Program File subdirectories. The System and System32 directories are located in the Windows directory. Here is where you would place any needed DLL files. The Program Files directory will hold your installed Windows programs, just as they would be installed on a Windows Program Files directory.

To install a Windows application with Wine, you can either use the Wine configuration tool or just open a terminal window and run the **wine** command with the Windows application as an argument. The following example installs the popular newsbin program:

```
$ wine newsbin.exe
```

To install applications with the Windows Configuration tool, select the Applications panel and then click Add.

Some applications like newsbin will also require that you use certain DLL files from a working Windows operating system. The DLL files are normally copied to the user's **.wine/drive_c/Windows/system32** directory.

Icons for installed Windows software will appear on your desktop. Just double-click an icon to start up the application. It will run normally within a Linux window as would any Linux application.

Installing Windows fonts on Wine is a simple matter of copying fonts from a Windows font directory to your Wine **.wine/drive_c/Windows/fonts** directory. You can just copy any Windows **.ttf** file to this directory to install a font.

Wine will use a stripped down window style for features like buttons and titlebar. If you want to use the XP style, download and install the Royal theme from Microsoft. Keep in mind though that supporting this theme is very resource intensive and will likely slow down your system.

To install applications that have the **.msi** extension you use the msiexec command with the **/a** option. The following installs the Mobipocket Ebook Reader.

```
msiexec /a mobireadersetup.msi
```

Help Resources

A great deal of support documentation is already installed on your system, as well as accessible from online sources. Table 3-1 lists Help tools and resources accessible on your Fedora Linux system. Both the GNOME and KDE desktops feature Help systems that use a browser-like interface to display help files. To start the GNOME or KDE Help browser, select the Help entry in the main menu. You can then choose from the respective desktop user guides, including the KDE manual, Linux Man pages, and GNU info pages. The GNOME Help Browser also accesses documents for GNOME applications such as the File Roller archive tool and Evolution mail client. The GNOME Help browser and the KDE Help Center also incorporate browser capabilities, including bookmarks and history lists for documents you view.

Context-Sensitive Help

Both GNOME and KDE, along with other applications, also provide context-sensitive help. Each KDE and GNOME application features detailed manuals that are displayed using their respective Help browsers. Also, system administrative tools feature detailed explanations for each task.

Application Documentation

On your system, the **/usr/share/doc** directory contains documentation files installed by each application. Within each directory, you can usually find HOW-TO, README, and INSTALL documents for that application.

The Man Pages

You can also access the Man pages, which are manuals for Linux commands available from the command line interface, using the `man` command. Enter `man` with the command on which you want information. The following example asks for information on the `ls` command:

```
$ man ls
```

Pressing the SPACEBAR key advances you to the next page. Pressing the B key moves you back a page. When you finish, press the Q key to quit the Man utility and return to the command line. You activate a search by pressing either the slash (/) or question mark (?). The / searches forward, and the ? searches backward. When you press the /, a line opens at the bottom of your screen, and you then enter a word to search for. Press ENTER to activate the search. You can repeat the same search by pressing the N key. You needn't reenter the pattern.

Resource	Description
KDE Help Center	KDE Help tool, GUI interface for documentation on KDE desktop and applications, Man pages, and info documents
GNOME Help Browser	GNOME Help tool, GUI interface for accessing documentation for the GNOME desktop and applications, Man pages, and info documents
/usr/share/doc	Location of application documentation
man *command*	Linux Man pages, detailed information on Linux commands, including syntax and options
info *application*	GNU info pages, documentation on GNU applications
www.fedoraproject.org	Fedora Project site, with numerous Documentation, FAQ, and Help resources and links, with links to forums, newsgroups, and community Web sites.
http://docs.fedoraproject.org	Online documentation, guides, HOWTOs, and FAQs for Fedora Linux
www.redhat.com	Red Hat Enterprise documentation, guides, HOWTOs, and FAQs. Located under "Support and Documentation," much of the Red Hat Linux documentation may be helpful
http://library.gnome.org	Gnome documentation site
www.fedoraforum.org	End user discussion support forum, endorsed by the Fedora Project. Includes FAQs and news links.
www.fedorafaq.org	Unofficial FAQ with quick help topics
fedoranews.org	Collects the latest news and developments on Fedora, as well as articles and blogs about recent changes.
http://fcp.homelinux.org	Fedora Community Portal: Fedora forums, FAQs, questions, and news
www.fedorasolved.org	Solutions to common problems

Table 3-1: Fedora Linux Help Resources

The Info Pages

Online documentation for GNU applications, such as the gcc compiler and the Emacs editor, also exist as *info* pages accessible from the GNOME and KDE Help Centers. You can also access this documentation by entering the command **info**. This brings up a special screen listing different GNU applications.

The info interface has its own set of commands. You can learn more about it by entering `info info`. Typing m opens a line at the bottom of the screen where you can enter the first few letters of the application. Pressing ENTER brings up the info file on that application.

Tip: You can also use either the GNOME or KDE Help system to display Man and info pages.

Web Resources

You can obtain documentation for Fedora at the Fedora and Red Hat Web sites. Some of the Red Hat documentation is still applicable to Fedora. Most Linux applications are covered by the Linux Documentation Project. The GNOME and KDE Web sites also contain extensive documentation showing you how to use the desktop and taking you through a detailed explanation of Linux applications. Several dedicated Fedora support sites are also available.

Part 2: Applications

Installing and Updating Software
Office Applications and Editors
Multimedia and Graphics
Mail and News
Web, Java, FTP, IM, and VoIP

4. Installing and Updating Software: YUM, PackageKit, and RPM

Updating Fedora

Managing Packages with PackageKit

Fedora Software Repositories

RPM Fusion

YUM configuration

Software Package Types

RPM Software Packages

Managing software with rpm command

Source code applications

Fedora software has grown so large and undergoes such frequent updates that it no longer makes sense to use discs as the primary means of distribution. Instead distribution is effected using an online Fedora software repository. This repository contains an extensive collection of Fedora-compliant software, merging the Fedora Core and Fedora Extras used in previous releases into one large repository.

For Fedora, you can add software to your system by accessing software repositories supporting YUM (Yellowdog Update, Modified). In addition many software applications, particularly multimedia ones, have potential licensing conflicts. By leaving such software in third party repositories, Fedora avoids possible legal issues. Many of the popular multimedia application such as video and digital music support can be obtained from third party repositories using the same simple YUM commands you would use for Fedora sponsored software.

This approach heralds a move from thinking of most Linux software included on a few disks, to viewing the disk as just a core from which you can expand your installed software as you like from online repositories. Most software is now located on the Internet connected repositories. With the integration of YUM into your Fedora system, you can now think of that software as an easily installed extension of your current collection. Relying on disk media for your software becomes, in a sense, obsolete. You can find out more about how YUM is used on Fedora in Managing Software with YUM, located on the Fedora documentation page:

`http://docs.fedoraproject.org/yum/en/`

Updating Fedora: Update System (PackageKit)

New versions of Fedora are released every six months or so. In the meantime, new updates are continually being prepared for particular software packages. These are posted as updates you can download from software repositories and install on your system. These include new versions of applications, servers, and even the kernel. Such updates may range from single software packages to whole components—for instance, all the core, application, and development packages issued when a new release of GNOME, KDE, or X11 is made available.

TIP: If you are installing or updating several months after the official Fedora release, it may be easier to use a Fedora Re-Spin disk. This is disk with the latest updates. This way you avoid having to download numerous updates to the original packages from online repositories. Fedora Re-Spins are issued every three months by the Fedora Unity project. Fedora Re-Spins disks can be downloaded using Jigdo from **www.fedoraunity.org**.

Updating your Linux system has become a very simple procedure, using the automatic update tools. For Fedora, you can update your system by accessing software repositories supporting the YUM (Yellowdog Updater, Modified) update methods. YUM uses RPM headers to determine which packages need to be updated. To update your packages, you now use the Update System (PackageKit), labeled as Update System in the System | Administration menu. Update System is a graphical update interface for YUM, which now performs all updates. With Update System (PackageKit) you no longer have to update using a **yum** update command entered in a terminal window.

Update System makes use of the Update System applet on your GNOME panel, which will automatically check for updates whenever you log in. If updates are detected, Update System will display an update icon on the panel and display a message in the lower right panel telling you that updates are available and how many there are (see Figure 4-1). The message has buttons to install updates and a button to not show the message again. If you **do not** choose to install immediately, you can close the window and then later choose to install using the update menu accessible from the update system icon. Click the update system **icon to** opens a menu (see Figure 4-1) where you can select either to perform all updates directly (**Update** system Now), or to review and possibly choose updates to perform (Show Updates). If you **choose** to Update System Now, a small progress bar is displayed under the applet as the downloads **and updates** are performed.

The update icon image shown varies on whether the **update includes** security, bug, or software enhancement updates. All three could be included in **an update,** but for the icon display, security takes precedent, followed by bugs, and then enhancement. **If the** update includes any security fixes, the red star security icon is shown. If there are no security updates, but there are bug fixed, then the orange star with a bug image is used. For just enhancements, then the orange star is displayed.

Figure 4-1: Update System (PackageKit) notification message and update menu

The Show Updates option will start up the gpk-update-viewer tool to display your updates. You can also select Update System manually from its Update System entry in the System | Administration menu. Initially the Update Overview window is displayed (see Figure 4-2).

Figure 4-2: Update System with available updates, Overview window

The number of updates is shown for each category: security, bugs, and enhancements. The last refresh and the time of the previous update are also displayed. There are buttons to update the system or review the packages to update, "Update System" and "Review". To simply perform the updates, click the Update System button. If you want review the updates, and, perhaps deselect certain updates, you click the Review button.

Tip: After a new install, if Update System fails to run or function, you may need to first update using the **yum** command. Enter the **yum update** command in a terminal window (Applications | System Tools). Enter y at the prompts. This initial update should fix problems with Update System, which should then function.

On the Review window, all needed updates will be selected automatically when Update System starts up. The check boxes for each entry let you deselect any particular packages you may not want to update (see Figure 4-3).. Should you want to see details about a particular package, click on the package entry in the package listing. The window is then divided into two panes, a package listing and package description.Information about the package will display on the lower pane (see Figure 4-4). Information includes features like the version and repository. Bug fixes will show Bugzilla entries for bugs that have been fixed.

Figure 4-3: Package Updater listing packages to be updated, Review window

Software updates will show information about the update, including a description of new features.

Click the Apply Updates button to start updating. You will be first asked by policykit to enter your root password, allowing the updates to be performed (see Figure 4-5).

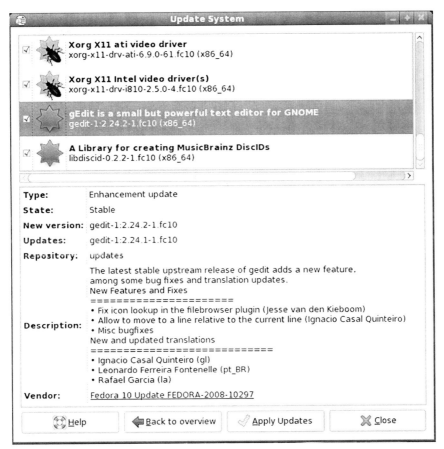

Figure 4-4: Package Updater selected package with displayed description

Figure 4-5: Package Updater authorization

During the update, a status window will open displaying the different update stages, beginning with dependency checks, then download, followed by testing, and ending with update, installation, and cleanup (see Figure 4-6). You can click the Cancel button during dependency and downloading to cancel the update. The Close button will close the window, but continue with the updating. The Help button opens the PackageKit manual.

Figure 4-6: Update progress window

If, during update, Packagekit has to access a new repository for the first time, you will be prompted to accept the repository's key (see Figure 4-6). Click the Yes button to approve access to that repository. You will then be prompted to authenticate the action by entering the root user (administrative) password.

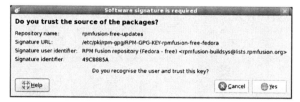

Figure 4-6: New repository key acceptance prompt

Should a new kernel be installed, when you boot you will then be using the new kernel. Your old kernel will remain as a GRUB option should you have difficulties with the new kernel. To choose the old kernel, you will have to select it from the GRUB boot screen. To make the old kernel the default again, you can either select it with the Bootloader configuration screen (System | Administration | Bootloader) or set the default option in the **/etc/grub/grub.conf** file to 1 (the new kernel will be 0).

Tip: To upgrade to a new Fedora release, you can download Fedora DVD install ISO image through **http://fedoraproject.org/get-fedora**. You can then burn the ISO image and upgrade from that install DVD. Alternatively, you can use the **yum** command with the **upgrade** option in any terminal window. This will perform a package by package online upgrade.

Manual Update

You can also manually perform updates instead of waiting for a notification icon. Select Update System from the System | Administration menu. This opens the Update System Overview window with a notice showing how many updates are available, along with the time since the last refresh and the last update (see Figure 4-2)

To perform your package updates, you can just click the Update System button.

A refresh downloads the update package listings from repositories showing packages to update. A refresh will occur automatically at scheduled times. You can manually perform a refresh by press the Refresh button. If it has been more than several hours or days since your last refresh, you should perform one before updating.

To see a listing of updates, click the review button. This displays the Update System review window, as shown in Figure 4-3), with a listing of packages to update. You can deselect those you do not want updated. You can then click the Update System button to perform the updates. The overview button returns you to the Overview window (Figure 4-2), showing the number of updates and the times of the last refresh and update.

Update Preferences

You configure when checks are mad for updating as well as whether to perform the updates automatically. Use the Update Preferences window to set your update options. Select System | Preferences | Software Updates. This opens the Software Update Preferences window where you can set the intervals for checking for updates and major upgrades as well as whether to enable automatic updating (see figure 4-7). You can also specify when the Update icon will be displayed on the top panel.

Initially, updates will be checked daily and no action will be taken. The user will have to apply the updates. On the Check for update pop up menu you can select hourly, daily, weekly, or never. Daily is selected and is the option normally used. The never option would require that the user manually check for updates.

The Automatically install pop up menu will have options for All updates, Only security updates, or Nothing. If you want all software and security updates to be performed automatically for you, select All updates. Should you want to be selective as to what applications you update, you could select Only security updates.

On the "Check for major upgrades" pop up menu you select Daily, Weekly, or Never.

The Display Notification section has options for notifying you when updates are available, and when long tasks are completes. If you selected All updates for the Automatically install setting, then the When updates are available option in the Display Notification section will be grayed out.

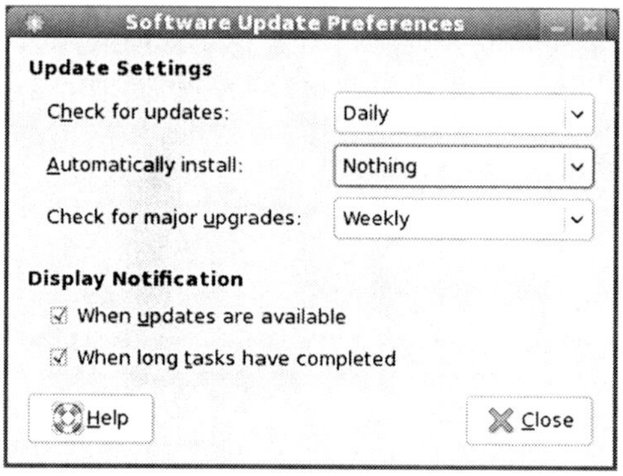

Figure 4-7: Software Update Preferences

Update with the yum command

Alternatively you can update using the **yum** command with the **update** option. The following would update an already installed **Gnumeric** package.

```
yum update  gnumeric
```

You can use the **check-update** option to see what packages need to be updated.

```
yum check-update
```

To perform a complete update of all your installed packages, you just use the update option. This would have the same effect of updating with Update System.

```
yum update
```

In some cases, when you first install a new system from your CD/DVD, there may be incompatibilities or bugs that prevent you from using Update System to update to the latest system fixes on the Fedora repository. In this case you can open a terminal window and update directly with the **yum** command.

```
yum update
```

This can also happen if your display fails and you cannot access your desktop. You could then boot into the command line interface (runlevel 3), and, after login in, enter the yum update command.

A manual update may also become necessary if you have broken dependencies. If, among a set of packages to be updated, just one or more have broken dependencies, then the entire set will not be updated by PackageKit. PackageKit does not always inform you of the packages causing trouble. Otherwise you could just deselect them from the package listing in Update System. To exclude a package you can open a terminal window and run **yum update** with the **--exclude** option. To select several packages with the same prefix, add a * file matching operator to the package name. You can add as many exclude options as you want. The following updates all packages except the Perl packages.

```
yum update --exclude=perl*
```

Automatic YUM Update with cron

The **yum-cron** package installs cron configuration file for YUM. These include a **yum.cron** files in the **/etc/cron.daily** and **/etc/cron.weekly** directories, which will automatically update your system. The cron entry will first update the YUM software if needed and then proceed to download and install any updates for your installed packages. It runs **yum** with the **update** option.

The automatic update will run only if it detects a YUM lock file in the **/var/lock/subsys** directory. By default, this is missing. You can add it using the **yum-cron** service script. The **start** option creates the lock file, enabling the cron-supported updates, and the **stop** option removes the file, disabling the automatic update.

```
/etc/init.d/yum-cron start
```

Installing Software Packages

Installing software is an administrative function performed by a user with administrative access. Unless you chose to install all your packages during your installation, only some of the many applications and utilities available for users on Linux were installed on your system. On Fedora, you can easily install or remove software from your system with either the PackageKit software manager (Add/Remove Software) or the **rpm** command. Alternatively, you can install software by downloading and compiling its source code. The procedure for installing software using its source code has been simplified to just a few commands, though you have a great deal of flexibility in tailoring an application to your specific system.

An RPM software package operates like its own installation program for a software application. A Linux software application often consists of several files that must be installed in different directories. The program itself is most likely placed in a directory called **/usr/bin**, online manual files go in another directory, and library files go in yet another directory. In addition, the installation may require modification of certain configuration files on your system. The RPM software packages perform all these tasks for you. Also, if you later decide you don't want a specific application, you can uninstall packages to remove all the files and configuration information from your system.

The software packages on your DVD/CD-ROMs, as extensive as they are, represent only some of the software packages available for Fedora Linux. Most reside on the Fedora Software repository, a repository whose packages are available for automatic download using Add/Remove Software application. Many multimedia applications and support libraries can be found at the RPM Fusion repository (**http://rpmfusion.org**), and, once configured, downloaded directly with YUM and PackageKit.   Table 4-1 lists several Fedora software sites. Fedora and RPM Fusion are all YUM supported, meaning that a simple YUM configuration enables you to directly download and install software from those sites using the **yum** command or the PackageKit software manager. Fedora is already installed, and RPM Fusion provides its own YUM configuration file.

Fedora provides only open source applications in its own repository. For proprietary applications like NVIDIA's own graphics drivers or multimedia application that may have patent issues, you need to use third-party repositories like RPM Fusion. The list of forbidden items for the official Fedora repository can be found at **www.fedoraproject.org/wiki/ForbiddenItems**. These include items like the NVIDIA and ATI graphics drivers (those you can obtain from **http://rpmfusion.org**).

You can download additional software from online software sites such as GNOME's **www.gnomefiles.org**, KDE's **www.kde-apps.org**, and **www.sourceforge.net**. The **www.sourceforge.net** site not only distributes software but also serves as the primary development site for a massive number of open source software projects. You can also locate many of the newest Linux applications from **www.freshmeat.net** or **www.rpmfind.net**. Check first, though, to see if they are already available on the Fedora Software repository, most are.

Internet Sites	Description
`http://fedoraproject.org/wiki/Distribution/Download`	Fedora download instructions and distribution information
`http://fedoraproject.org/get-fedora`	Fedora distribution disks, download links for all formats
`http://torrents.fedoraproject.org`	Fedora BitTorrent files for ISO and DVD disks
`http://download.fedoraproject.org`	Fedora Software repository, mirror link
`http://download1.rpmfusion.org` `http://rpmfusion.org`	RPM Fusion repository for third-party multimedia and driver Fedora compliant software (Fedora Project extension)
`http://fedoraproject.org/wiki/ForbiddenItems`	Packages not included in the main Fedora software repository.
`http://fedoraproject.org/wiki/Multimedia`	Information on multimedia packages available for Fedora

Table 4-1: Fedora Software Sites

Installing with YUM

Downloading Fedora software or software from any configured Fedora YUM repository is a simple matter of using Add/Remove Software (PackageKit), which provides a GUI interface for YUM. YUM by default stops the entire install process if there is any configuration or dependency problem with any one repository or package. Check http://fedoraproject.org/Wiki/Tools/yum for tips on using yum, including a script to let you perform partial installs.

Alternatively, you can enter the yum command with the **install** option and the name of the package in a terminal window. YUM will detect the software and any dependencies, and it will prompt you to download and install it. For example, the following command will install Abiword:

```
yum install abiword
```

Installing individual packages with your browser

Alternatively, you can download an individual package directly using your browser. You would use this method only for packages not already available from YUM supported repositories. You will also have to manually install any needed dependent packages, as well as check system compatibility (x86_64, i38c, ppc). Your Fedora Web browsers will let you perform both a download and install in one simple operation. On a GNOME desktop already-downloaded packages can be installed with a simple right-click and install selection, invoking PackageKit to perform the installation (**gpk-install-file**).

PackageKit, Add/Remove Software

PackageKit is the new software management front end for YUM introduced with Fedora 10. The PackageKit Package Manager is Internet based, installing from online repositories, using YUM to download and install. It is designed to be a cross-distribution package manager that can be used on any YUM supported Linux distribution.

PackageKit provides a variety of applications for different software tasks, including installation, removal; updating, repository management, logs, and software install of a package file (see Table 4-2). The primary PackageKit application is **gpk-application**, access as Add/Remove Software on the System | Administration menu. The **gpk-update-viewer** lets you examine and select updates. The **gpk-log** (Applications | System Tools | Software Log) display a list of all your previous install, removal, and update operation, including major updates and individual package installs.

To use PackageKit you select the Add/Remove Software entry from the System | Administration menu. PackageKit will start up by gathering information on all your packages. An Add/Remove Software window opens with a sidebar for searching and a category list. Before you install packages, it is advisable to first refresh your software lists. This is the listings of software packages available on your enabled repositories. Select Refresh applications lists from the System menu.

Application	Description
gpk-application	Add/Remove Software
gpk-update-viewer	Update you system, Update System
gpk-prefs	Configure update preferences, Preferences	System	Software Updates.
gpk-repo	Manage software repositories
gpk-log	history of updates, Administration	System Tools
gpk-install-file	Install local software packages
gpkupdate-icon	display update icon

Table 4-1: PackageKit applications

PackageKit Browsing

You can find packages by category by selecting a category on the sidebar. All the packages in that category will be listed. Uninstalled packages will be gray. Figure 4-8 shows the packages for the Gnome desktop category.

Using categories is similar to the Browse panel in the Pirut Add/Remove Software utility used in previous Fedora releases. Categories let you browse through your software, seeing what is available for different kinds of tasks or features, like Multimedia applications or applications designed for the GNOME desktop.

Figure 4-8: Add/Remove Software, PackageKit

To install several packages at once, click on their checkboxes, and then click the Apply button. The status bar at the bottom will show tasks being performed, starting with downloading, then installing, and finally finished. A progress bar will show the install tasks progress. The PackageKit notification icon in the top panel will also show a download image as the package is downloaded. Once installed, the package icon color will changed from gray to brown.

PackageKit Selected Package Actions and Information

To see information about a particular package, select it. This open a pane at the bottom with tabs panels for Description and the Project home page (see Figure 4-9). A Selection menu will appear on the menubar between the Filters and Help menu buttons (see Figure 4-10). Click on the Selection button to display a menu with several action and information choices. The "Project homepage" entry will open your browser to the package home page where you can find more detailed information about it. The "Run program" entry lets you run an installed package directly.

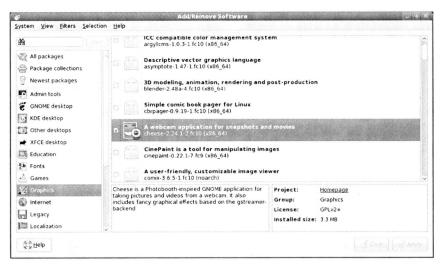

Figure 4-9: Package information

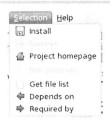

Figure 4-10: Package Selection Menu

You can also install or remove a selected package. Just click on the package and then, from the Selection menu, choose Install or Remove. For an uninstalled package, choosing Install from the Selection menu will place a checkmark for you on the selected package's checkbox. To actually perform the install, you then click the Apply button. An installed package will only allow removal, and an uninstalled package allows only installation. For installed packages, choosing Remove will uncheck the package's checkbox. Clicking Apply will then remove the package. Before you click Apply, you can always change your mind, checking or unchecking the package's checkbox as you wish.

The "Get file list", Depends on, and Required by entries will open a separate window listing those files and packages. The "Get file list" entry opens a window that lists all the actual files the package will install, or has installed (see Figure 4-11). This can be helpful for tracking down the actual command names and location of configurations files.

Figure 4-11: Package Selection, "Get file list"

The Depends on and Required entries open windows that show the package's dependencies, those that depend in it as well as those it, in turn, depends on (see Figure 4-12).

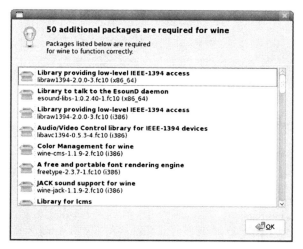

Figure 4-12: Package Selection, "Depends on"

PackageKit Searching

Instead of tracking down a package through categories, you can just search for it using its package name. Just enter a pattern to search for in the Search box, located at the top of the category sidebar, and press ENTER or click the Find button. The results will be listed as shown in Figure 4-13. Here the pattern searched for is **win**, listing all the Fedora packages beginning with *win*, including the wine packages. Select a package to then install it, showing its information panels and Install button. The status bar will show download and install tasks with a progress bar as they are performed.

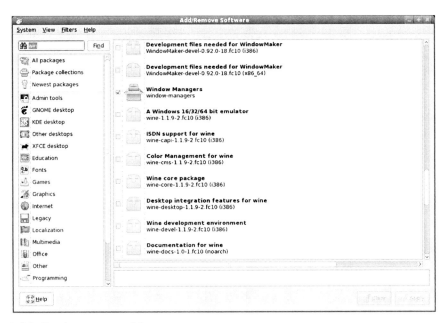

Figure 4-14: Package searching

If you enter a complete package name, like wine, that package will be selected and displayed (see Figure 4-15).

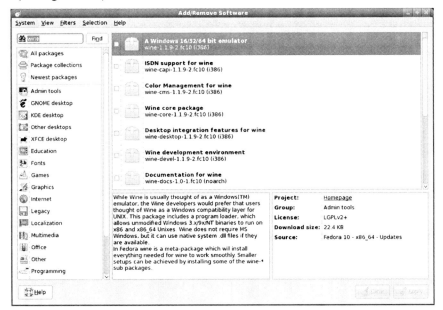

Figure 4-15: Package searching with exact match

PackageKit Filtering

Instead of showing all your available packages, both installed and uninstalled, you can filter the package listing. Several filters are available from the Filters menu (see Figure 4-16). You can filter by Installed, Development, Graphical, and Free packages. The Installed option lets you display only installed or uninstalled packages (available). Graphical is for packages that operate on a GUI desktop. The Free option will let you choose only open source free packages, instead of any licensed or restricted proprietary packages. Restricted packages like graphic drivers, could still be freely available, but not open source, and in that sense not free. If you are looking for software you know is not free, you can select the "Only non free" option.

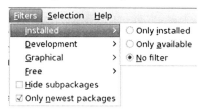

Figure 4-16: Package Filters

Managing Repositories

YUM is the primary install packages tool. When you install a package, YUM will be invoked and it will automatically select and download the package from the appropriate repository. After having installed your system, when you then want to install additional packages, PackageKit will use YUM to install from a repository. This will include all active YUM online repositories you may have configured such as sites like **http://rpmfusion.org**, not just the Fedora and update repositories configured for you during installation.

Figure 4-17: Software Sources: Configured Software Repositories

You can also install from the Fedora Install DVD, should you have it. You can enable or disable your configured YUM repositories using the Repository Viewer (**gpk-viewer**). On the Add/Remove Software window, select Software Sources from the System menu. You can also select Software Sources from the System | Administration menu. This opens the Repository Viewer window listing all your configured repositories (see Figure 4-17).

The repository viewer will lists all configured repositories. These are repositories that have YUM configuration files in the **/etc/yum.repos.d** directory, holding information like URLs, GPG keys, and descriptions. Those that are enabled will be checked. You can disable a repository by un-checking it. The Fedora repository names will include the release number and the platform, like x86_64 for the 64 bit version.

Add/Remove Software will list the packages available from all the active repositories. If you should want to see just the package from one or the other repository, you could deactivate the others. For example, if just wanted to see what was on the RPM Fusion repository, you could deactivate all others, including Fedora. Then the only packages on the RPM Fusion repository would be shown. You can later reactivate the other repositories.

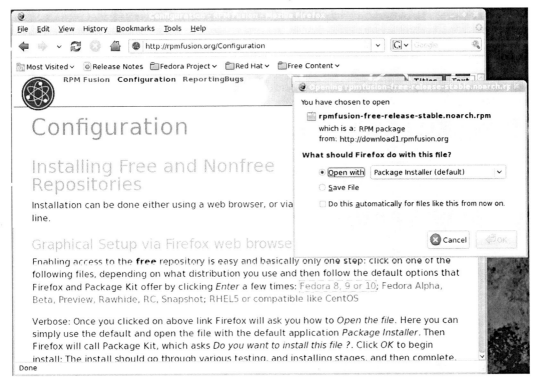

Figure 4-18: RPM Fusion repository configuration file downloaded from http://rpmfusion.org

Repositories also have specialized repositories for development, debugging, and source code files. Here you have find applications under development that may be useful, and well as the latest revisions. Some will have testing repositories for applications not yet completely validated for the current release. These applications may or may not work well. Source, Test, and Debug repositories will normally be disabled. Rawhide is the development repository for a future release currently under development. Fedora and Fedora Update repositories will usually be enabled. The source repositories hold source code packages, and the test repositories are for packages still in the testing stages.

Note: To remove packages with PackageKit, just locate and select its entry, and then click the Uninstall button.

Using the RPM Fusion repository with PackageKit

The RPM Fusion repository (**http://rpmfusion.org**) holds most of the third party drivers and codec most users expect. These include the vendor graphics drivers for Linux, such as those provided by Nvidia and ATI/AMD. The RPM Fusion packages are configured for Fedora. Also included on the repository are multimedia codecs with licensing issues like MP3, AC3, and MPEG2 codecs, as well ad MPEG4 and DivX (Xvid).

To access the RPM Fusion repository, you first have to download and install both its YUM configuration file and its GPG authentication key. These are both included in RPM Fusion's **rpmfusion-free** package. Simply download and install this package using your Web browser. The package is located at **http://rpmfusion.org** (see Figure 4-18). Click on the Configuration link at the top of the page to go to the Configuration page. On the section titled "Graphical Setup via Firefox web browser", click on the links labeled "Fedora 8, 9, or 10. There are free and nonfree packages, with links for each. Be sure to install the free package first. The nonfree package is optional. When you click the link, Fedora detects that it is a software package and opens a dialog with the option to install it directly (see Figure 4-18).

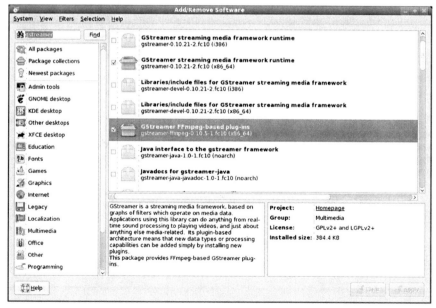

Figure 4-19: Software package accessible from RPM Fusion repository

Perform the installation. You will be warned that there is no authentication key for the package. Install anyway. The key is not yet installed, but will be as part of the package.

The page also tells you how to perform an installation of both free and nonfree RPM Fusion YUM configuration packages from the command line using the **rpm** command.

Once installed, you can open Software Sources to check that the RPM Fusion repository is enabled (see Figure 4-17), System | Administration | Software Sources.

With RPM Fusion repository now enabled, you can use PackageKit to search, select, and install any packages on its repository. Both RPM Fusion and the Fedora repositories will have their packages intertwined in the PackageKit display (see Figure 4-19).

Note: It is still possible to use the atrpms repository (**http://atrpms.net**), though most of its packages, including MythTV, are now available from the RPM Fusion repository. There are potential conflicts between atrpms packages and RPM Fusion packages. Most packages are duplicated on the repositories. As a rule, you should only use RPM Fusion packages not on the atrpms repository.

YUM Extender: yumex

The YUM Extender is an alternative GUI interface for managing software packages on your YUM repositories (see Figure 4-18). Yumex is included with Fedora. The YUM Extender provides more flexibility than PackageKit. It provides detailed package information, as well as allowing you to turn repositories on an off directly, without having to edit repo files. Click Open Add/Remove Software, and on the Browse panel select Base System, then Administration Tools, and then click the Optional Packages to see yumex listed. Check to install. You can also just search for **yumex** on the Search panel or use the following command in a terminal window:

```
yum install yumex
```

You can then access **yumex** with the YUM Extender entry in the Applications | System Tools menu. The YUM Extender screen has five panels, each accessed by view icons on the left column, as shown in Figure 4-20. You can select package using either the Package or the Groups button. The Package button will list all possible packages, whereas the Groups panel shows the categories. Uninstalled packages are shown in red.

The Package panel features ways to narrow your displayed packages. You can choose to display updates, installed packages, or uninstalled packages only. You can further specify categories, like repositories, displaying only packages from a certain repository. Clicking a package will display detailed information about it on the panel below, where you can select the description, files included with the package, and the change log if available.

To select a package, just check the one you want to install. Once selected, the package is added to the Process Queue panel.

Once you have added packages to the Queue, click the Queue icon to see the list of packages you want to install. From this panel you can choose to delete items or just save the list for later installation. To perform the installation, click the Process Queue button. All dependent packages will also be displayed. The install process will be shown on the Output panel.

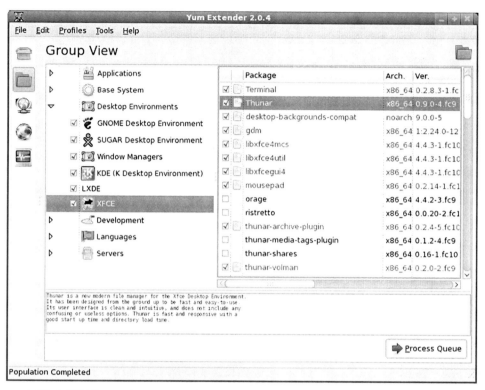

Figure 4-20: YUM Extender group view

The Repos panel operates as a repository manager, listing all your configured repositories. From this panel you can enable or disable any repositories. For example, if you need to temporarily enable the RPM Fusion repository, you can select it on this panel, and then install software from that repository. Once finished, you could then disable the repository using the Repos panel.

Installing Packages with the yum command

You can also use the `yum` command in a terminal window or command line interface, to access Fedora repositories, downloading new software. To use the **yum** command, enter the **yum** command with the **install** option on a command line. The package will be detected, along with any dependent software, and you will be asked to confirm installation. The download and installation will be automatic. You can check the download repository online, as well as the repodata directories to display the available packages on a Web page. The page will include easy access features such as package groups and an index links based on the first letters of package names.

The following example installs the Xine video player:

```
yum install xine
```

You can also remove packages, as well as search for packages and list packages by different criteria, such as those for update, those on the repository not yet installed, and those already installed. The following example lists all installed packages:

```
yum list installed
```

The available option shows uninstalled packages.

```
yum list available
```

To search for a particular package you can use the search option.

```
yum search xine
```

Tip: You can use Third Party Fedora YUM software repositories like **http://rpmfusion.org** to download additional software. Their configuration files will be in **/etc/yum.repos.d**.

Recovering packages with the yum command

There is a bug in Add/Remove Software which will falsely identify far more packages as dependent than should be, and mark them for removal when installing certain software. If there are dependencies, you will be notified first. Be sure to always check this dependency list and make sure a larger number of packages are not being marked for removal. In some cases, the entire GNOME desktop along with the GDM and PackageKit (Add/Remove Software) could be removed. If this is the case you could re-install GNOME, GDM, and PackageKit with **yum** commands in a terminal window or the command line interface. You might also have to reinstall graphics drivers. You can use **groupinstall** to install the entire GNOME desktop. **grouplist** display groups.

```
yum groupinstall gnome-desktop
yum install gdm
yum install PackageKit
```

Installing some popular third-party packages

Before installing certain third-party multimedia packages, you will first need to install the YUM configuration file for a repository that carries them. Once configured, installation is a simple matter using Add/Remove Software to search for and install packages. YUM downloads the package, performing the installation. It will also be careful to select the package for your architecture, like x86_64 for 64 bit or i686 for 32 bit. YUM will first ask for confirmation before installing, listing any dependent packages that will also have to be installed.

Tip: Make sure during both installation and removal, that a large number of unrelated packages are not being removed. This can happen, possibly removing all of GNOME along with PackageKit. If you find an extensive set of unrelated packages marked for removal as dependencies, you may want to cancel the installation. Click the Cancel button on the Dependencies dialog.

Multimedia packages

For your third-party packages, you could use RPM Fusion which carries collections of multimedia packages, including GStreamer and MPlayer. DVD/MPEG Video players you may want are Xine, MPlayer, and VideoLAN. All support DVD, DVB, HDTV, H264, and MP3 provided the needed codecs are installed.

> Xine   Media player

> MPlayer   Media player

> VideoLAN   Media and network stream player

> MythTV   TV and DVR

For DVR capability you may want to download and install MythTV from the RPM Fusion repository.

TIP: For information on multimedia applications available for Fedora see **http://fedoraproject.org/wiki/Multimedia**.

Many of the following packages are automatically selected and installed for you as dependents when you install either Xine or MPlayer. It may be simpler to just install one of these, than try to install all the added packages separately.

For audio you may want HDTV audio, DVD/MPEG2 audio support, DTS, and MP3. Search for the following RPM Fusion packages using Add/Remove software.

> a52dec   HDTV audio (ATSC A/52, AC3)

> faad2   MPEG2/ 4 AAC audio decoding, high quality

> faac   MPEG2/ 4 AAC sound encoding and decoding

> libdca   DTS Coherent Acoustics playback capability

> lame   MPEG1 and MPEG2 audio decoding

For Video you may want DVD Video capability, MPEG and MPEG2 playback, DVB/HDTV playback, and H264 (HD media) decoding capability.

> libdvbpsi   MPEG TS stream (DVB and PSI) decoding and encoding.

> vlc-core   DVD video playback capability, VideoLAN project.

> libdvdnav   DVD video menu navigation

> libdvdcss   DVD video commercial decoding, Livna repository, **rpm.livna.org**.

x264   H264/AVC decoding and encoding (high definition media)

For all GStreamer supported applications you will want the bad and ugly packages.

> gstreamer-plugins-bad   not fully reliable codecs and tools for GStreamer, some with possible licensing issues.

> gstreamer-plugins-ugly   reliable video and audio codecs for GStreamer that may have licensing issues

Vendor Video Driver support

You can obtain the Nvidia and ATI vendor graphics drivers from RPM Fusion (**nonfree** repository). These you can download and install with YUM. RPM Fusion, which now includes all the former Livna repository drivers, is the best repository for specialized kernel drivers and modules. Keep in mind though, that due to recent open sourcing of much of both the Nvidia and ATI vendor drivers, the Xorg open source versions are becoming almost as effective, especially for 2D display support. For normal usage you may not need vendor driver support.

The graphic drivers use two packages, one for the supporting software and another for the kernel. The kernel modules are specific to the kernel you are using. Once RPM Fusion is configured for PackageKit, a search on nvidia or fglrx will list the ATI and Nvidia modules for each kernel version. Each time you update to a new kernel, you will need a new graphics kernel module created specifically for that kernel. This will be automatically downloaded and installed for you as a dependent package when you update your kernel (the RPM Fusion repository will have to be active).

Note: The Nvidia and ATI vendor drives will be provided by the RPM Fusion repository as they become available for Fedora 10.

```
xorg-nvidia-x11-drv-nvidia-177
kmod-nvidia-177

xorg-x11-drv-fglrx
kmod-ati
```

The name of the ATI kernel module is **fglrx**, when available. The Xorg will be labeled **ati**, **xorg-x11-drv-ati**.

The Nvidia driver for GEForce 8 and above is **177**. There are also Nvidia driver package for **173** (Geforce 5-7), **legacy**, and **96xx** divers used for older Nvidia video cards. These cards also have their own Nvidia configuration tools. The Xorg open source drivers will be labeled **nv**, **xorg-x11-drv-nv**.

```
xorg-nvidia-x11-drv-nvidia-96xx
kmod-nvidia-96xx
xorg-nvidia-x11-drv-nvidia-legacy
kmod-nvidia-legacy
```

With RPM Fusion activated, you can download and install the graphics card driver using PackageKit, with Update System providing automatic updates. Use the Search box to search for either fglrx (ATI) or NVIDIA. You only need to use the initial unique term, **kmod-fgrlx**. YUM will detect the rest of the package name, selecting the package appropriate for your kernel. For Nvidia you would use **kmod-nvidia** in either PackageKit (Add/Remove Software), or in a **yum** command. YUM will detect and select **xorg-x11-drv-nvidia**, the Nvidia driver software.

Alternatively you could use a **yum** command entered in a terminal window.

```
yum install kmod-nvidia
```

Using repositories

A few repositories provide much of the software you will normally need. The main Fedora software repository will most likely contain the software you want. Always check this repository first, before trying a third-party repository. Some specialized applications like vendor-supplied graphics drivers, as well as third-party multimedia support, can be located at **http://rpmfusion.org.** Java applications are located at **http://jpackage.org**, though some are already in the Fedora repository. Together these repositories make up a set of software sites you can use to provide most of the functionality users expect from a desktop system. All are YUM compliant, with YUM configuration files designed for specific Fedora releases. The sites and their repository files are shown here.

`http://download.fedoraproject.org`	The Fedora Repository, mirror link: Fedora-compliant software. **fedora.repo**
`http://download.fedora.redhat.com` `/pub/fedora/linux/releases`	The Fedora Repository: Fedora-compliant software. **fedora.repo**
`http://download1.rpmfusion.org`	RPM Fusion: Repository for driver, multimedia, and other RPM packages, **rpmfusion-free.repo** and **rpmfusion-nonfree.repo**
`http://jpackage.org`	Java applications. **jpackage.repo**

To see what packages are available, you can use your Web browser to access the sites. Fedora and RPM Fusion provide **repodata** directories for detailed listings.

To use YUM on a software repository, YUM has to be configured to access them. This is a simple matter of listing the site's URL, both its Web address and directory location. Configurations for repositories are placed in **repo** files located in the **/etc/yum.repos.d** directory on your Linux system. The repo files for Fedora are already installed. You will have to add repo files for RPM Fusion before you can access them with YUM. However, RPM Fusion provides an RPM packages or free and non-free collections, named **rpmfusion-free-release-stable.noarch.rpm** and rpmfusion-**nonfree-release-stable.noarch.rpm** on their Web site, that, when installed, automatically sets up the needed YUM configuration files. For RPM fusion these are **rpmfusion-free.repo** and **rpmfusion-nonfree.repo**, with corresponding updates and development files.

Repository repo package files

To install packages, use PackageKit, yumex, or the `yum` command. All will automatically use the repo files to check your enabled repositories. One important exception to this rule is the initial install of the repository configuration files from third party repositories. These configuration files (repo files) are usually contained in their own RPM packages. You would download and install a repo package directly from the repository Web site using your Web browser. For example, the repo package for the RPM Fusion third party Fedora YUM repository **rpmfusion-free-release-stable.noarch.rpm**. You would download and install this package directly using a Web browser, being sure to select the prompted install option for the download.

Fedora Repository

The Fedora repository is already configured for use by YUM. To download any Fedora package, simply use the PackageKit program manager (System | Administration | Add/Remove Software), or enter the `yum` command with the **install** options on a command line. The package will be detected, along with any dependent software, and you will be asked to confirm installation. The download and installation will be automatic. Check the **repodata** files on the Fedora repository to list the available Fedora files. There will be one in the **os** directory for respective version, **i386**, **x86_64** for 64-bit, and **ppc** for PowerPC versions. You can then click a particular package to display its RPM package data, showing version information and links to download the package, as well as to the package development Web site. Though you could download the package, it is preferable to use YUM or a YUM interface like PackageKit.

The **repodata** directory page features several ways to browse the very extensive collection of Fedora packages. The page first lists recent additions and updates, and then provides groups for different packages. The groups are also listed at links in the left-hand pane. Should you know the beginning letter of a package, you can use the Jump to Letter index at the top right, displaying pages with packages beginning with just that letter.

The first time you install a package from the Fedora repository, you will be prompted to install the Fedora GPG key, used to authenticate the packages. Just click Yes to install the key.

To download a Fedora package, you should use either PackageKit (System | Administration | Add/Remove Software), yumex (Applications | System Tools | YUM Extender), or the **yum** command. On PackageKit, you can access all the packages using its Find box, not just the categories listed in the sidebar. Alternatively, you can use a **yum** command in a terminal window with the **install** option as shown here. The following command installs Gnumeric:

```
yum install gnumeric
```

The following command installs KOffice from the Fedora repository:

```
yum install koffice
```

The Fedora repo file shown here lists several repository options. The name is Fedora, with **releaserver** and **basearch** used to determine the release and architecture parts of the name. The **mirrorlist** option is used instead of **baseurl**, which is commented out. Again, the **releaserver** is used to specify the release. The **gpgkey** used, RPM-GPG-KEY-fedora, is already installed in **/etc/pki/rpm-gpg** directory.

```
[fedora]
name=Fedora $releasever - $basearch
failovermethod=priority
#baseurl=http://download.fedoraproject.org/pub/fedora/linux/releases/$releasever/Everything/b
asearch/os/
mirrorlist=http://mirrors.fedoraproject.org/mirrorlist?repo=fedora-$releasever&arch=$basearch
enabled=1
gpgcheck=1
gpgkey=file:///etc/pki/rpm-gpg/RPM-GPG-KEY-fedora-$basearch
```

RPM Fusion

The **http://rpmfusion.org** site provides access to popular software for many software applications, including multimedia applications like MPlayer, as well as those not included with Fedora due to licensing issues. Several of the more popular packages include the vendor ATI and NVIDIA graphics drivers. RPM Fusion specializes in configuring sometimes difficult drivers for compatibility with Fedora. For example, you can download the NVIDIA Linux driver directly from the NVIDIA Web site and try to install it on your Fedora system. But there can be complications and the driver could require additional configuration. As an alternative, RPM Fusion provides a version of the driver that has already been configured for Fedora. A safer and more reliable approach is to simply install the RPM Fusion package for the NVIDIA driver. RPM Fusion also provides ATI driver packages (**fglrx**).

To configure YUM on your system to access **http://rpmfusion.org**, just install the **rpmfusion-free-release** and **rpmfusion-nonfree-release** packages. These will install the **rpmfusion-free.repo** and **rpmfusion-nonfree.repo** configuration files in the **/etc/yum.repos.d** directory, as well as download the RPM Fusion GPG key. You can install the GPG manually or just wait until you first install a package from RPM Fusion, in which case YUM will install it for you, after prompting for your approval. Check the RPM Fusion configuration page at **http://rpmfusion.org** for details. The name of the package will be something like

```
rpmfusion-free-release
```

You can download and install the package directly with **rpm** command from within a terminal window. Login as root with **su** first. The RPM Fusion site's configuration page provides a detailed example.

```
rpm -ivh http://download1.rpmfusion.org/free/fedora/rpmfusion-free-release-
stable.noarch.rpm
rpm -ivh http://download1.rpmfusion.org/nonfree/fedora/rpmfusion-nonfree-release-
stable.noarch.rpm
```

Alternatively, you can install directly from your browser by selecting Open With "Software Installer", or download it, right-click it, and select Open With "Software Installer". The package will be listed in the RPM Fusion category for the RPM Fusion Web display of the Fedora release.

You could also install it later with the **rpm** command as shown here:

```
rpm -ivh rpmfusion-free-release-stable.noarch.rpm
rpm -ivh rpmfusion-nonfree-release-stable.noarch.rpm
```

Once the repository is installed, all packages will be accessible with YUM.

The GPG keys are in included in the packages and installed automatically. They are named:

```
RPM-GPG-Key-rpmfusion-free-fedora
RPM-GPG-Key-rpmfusion-nonfree-fedora
```

They will be installed to the **/etc/pki/rpm-gpg** directory.

To install manually, you could extract them with the Archive Manger and then use rpm with the **--import** command.

```
rpm --import RPM-GPG-Key-rpmfusion-free-fedora
```

To see what packages are available on RPM Fusion, use your Web browser to go to **http://download1.rpmfusion.org**. Here you will find a listing of directories for each supported release. Selecting your release directory, you then choose your architecture, such as i386 (32 bit) or x86_64 (64 bit). Here you will see a simple file listing of all available packages.

Part of the **rpmfusion-free.repo** configuration file installed by the **rpmfusion-free-release** package is shown here. The configuration specifies several baseurl sites, instead of a mirror list. The failover method option indicates what sequence to use in choosing a site. It can be either priority, in sequence, or round robin, random. The file also holds a testing configuration to let you access very new untested packages.

```
[rpmfusion-free]
name=RPM Fusion for Fedora $releasever - Free
#baseurl=http://download1.rpmfusion.org/free/fedora/releases/$releasever/Everything/$basearch
/os/
mirrorlist=http://mirrors.rpmfusion.org/mirrorlist?repo=free-fedora
$releasever&arch=$basearch
enabled=1
gpgcheck=1
gpgkey=file:///etc/pki/rpm-gpg/RPM-GPG-KEY-rpmfusion-free-fedora
```

The corresponding part of the **rpmfusion-nonfree.repo** configuration file installed by the **rpmfusion-nonfree-release** package is shown here.

```
[rpmfusion-nonfree]
name=RPM Fusion for Fedora $releasever - Nonfree
#baseurl=http://download1.rpmfusion.org/nonfree/fedora/releases/$releasever/Everything/$basea
rch/os/
mirrorlist=http://mirrors.rpmfusion.org/mirrorlist?repo=nonfree-fedora
$releasever&arch=$basearch
enabled=1
gpgcheck=1
gpgkey=file:///etc/pki/rpm-gpg/RPM-GPG-KEY-rpmfusion-nonfree-fedora
```

Note: Livna, Freshrpms, and Dribble are now integrated with RPM Fusion.

Additional Java Applications: jpackage.org

Though Fedora already includes an extensive collection of Java software, you can download additional Java applications from **http://jpackage.org**. Simply use their YUM repository for Java packages. Keep in mind that **http://jpackage.org** does not provide the JRE. This you will have to download and install from Sun. Also, development packages on **http://jpackage.org** are commercial.

First download and install the **jpackage.repo**. Place **jpackage.repo** in the **/etc/yum.repos.d** directory. Check first to see if the repository has been set up for your particular version of Fedora. If not, you will have to use the generic version. Use the **enabled** option to activate or deactivate a version. Generic will be set by default.

The packages will show up in PackageKit (List or Search views). They will have the identifier **jpp**.

Jpackage repo file configurations for different Linux distributions are displayed at **www.jpackage.org/yum.php**. Here you will find a listing for the latest Fedora distribution. You can also download the generic version which will let you enable Fedora. A sample **jpackage.repo** file is listed here. Like Fedora, it uses a mirrorlist. The gpgkey is located online at **http://www.jpackage.org/jpackage.asc**. Due to licensing restrictions, Jpackage cannot freely distribute development tools like the JDK. These you will have to purchase from Jpackage commercially. The JRE is also part of the non-free Java package.

If you download the generic jpackage.repo file you will find repository listing for Fedora. You will also have generic configurations for free and non-free repositories, also enabled. Disable the one that do not apply to your distribution. The **mirrorlist** used in the generic configuration for Fedora is shown in the previous Fedora example, though commented out.

YUM Configuration

YUM options are configured in the **/etc/yum.conf** file, and the **/etc/yum.repos.d** directory holds repository (repo) files that list accessible YUM repositories. The repository files have the extension **.repo**. Check the **yum.conf** Man page for a listing of the different YUM options along with entry formats. The **yum.conf** file consists of different segments separated by bracket-encased headers, the first of which is always the main segment. Segments for different YUM server repositories can follow, beginning with the repository label encased in brackets. On Fedora, however, these are currently placed in separate repository files in the **/etc/yum.repos.d** directory.

In addition to yum.conf, YUM also supports a **/etc/yum** directory that can hold additional configuration information. On Fedora, this directory has a **pluginconf.d** subdirectory with configuration for YUM plugins. These include blacklist, whiteout, and refresh-packagekit. The blacklist and whiteout plugins are disabled, but the refresh-packagekit are enabled.

/etc/yum.conf

The **yum.conf** file will just have the main segment with settings for YUM options. There are general YUM options like `logfile`, which lists the location of YUM logs, and `distroverpkg`, which is used to determine which release to use. Packages will be downloaded to the directory specified with the `cachdir` option, in this case **/var/cache/yum**. You can elect to keep the downloaded packages or have them removed after they are installed. The `tolerant` option allows for package install errors, and the **retries** option specifies the number of times to try to access a package. Both `exactarch` and `obsoletes` apply to YUM updating procedures, invoked with the YUM `update` command. The `tolerant` option will allow package list errors such as those for already installed software, enabling installation of other packages in the list to continue. The `obsoletes` option is used for distribution level updates, and `exactarch` will only update packages in your specific architecture, such as i386 instead of i686. `gpgcheck` is a repository option that is set here globally for the **repo** files. It checks for GPG software signatures.

```
[main]
cachedir=/var/cache/yum
keepcache=0
debuglevel=2
logfile=/var/log/yum.log
tolerant=1
exactarch=1
obsoletes=1
gpgcheck=1
plugins=1
installonly_limit=3

#metadata_expire=90m

# PUT YOUR REPOS HERE OR IN separate files named file.repo
# in /etc/yum.repos.d
```

A commented entry for metadata shows the default. Making this bigger avoids more frequent package metadata downloading from the YUM repository, but runs the risk of not retrieving the latest updated package information.

Repository Files: /etc/yum.repos.d

The repository entries in the repo files begin with a bracket-enclosed server ID, a single-word unique name. Repository-specific options govern the access of software repositories. These include **gpgcheck**, which checks for GPG software signatures, **gpgkey**, which specifies the location of the signature, and **mirrorlist**, which references a URL holding mirror sites. The repository-specific **name** option provides a name for the repository. The URL reference is then assigned to the **baseurl** option. There should be only one **baseurl** option, but you can list several URLs for it, each on its own line. With the **mirrorlist** option you can just list a URL for a list of mirrors, instead of listing each mirror separately in the **baseurl** option. The URL entries often make use of special variables, **releaserver** and **basearch**. The **releaserver** obtains the release information from the **distroverpkg** option set in the main segment. The **basearch** variable specifies the architecture you are using as determined by YUM, such as i386. The enabled option actually turns on access to the repository. By setting it to 0, you choose not to access a specific repository. The **gpgcheck** option specifies that you should perform a GPG authentication check to make sure the download is intact. The **enabled** option will enable a repository, allowing YUM to use it. You can set the enable bit to 0 or 1 to turn off or on access to the repository.

The **gpgkey** option provides an authentication check on the package to make sure you have downloaded the appropriate version. Sometimes downloads can be intercepted and viruses inserted. The GPG key check protects against such attacks. It can also check to make sure the download is not corrupt or incomplete. The Fedora public GPG key may already be installed on your system. If you have already used YUM, you will have already downloaded it. The Fedora GPG key allows you to access Fedora packages. The RPM Fusion free and non-free repositories use their own public keys, referenced with the **gpgkey** option in their repos files. The keys for all these repositories will be installed in **/etc/pki/rpmgpg** directory.

Project-based repositories

Some software projects are electing to distribute updates through YUM and Apt, instead of providing RPMs directly. The K3b KDE burner does this, providing the following entry for YUM:

```
[xcyb-stable]
name=Fedora 10 ( xcyborg / stable
baseurl=http://rpms.xcyb.org/fedora/10/stable/
```

Creating Local YUM Repositories

For local networks where you may have several Fedora systems, each of which may need to update using YUM, you could set up a local repository instead of having each system update from Internet sites directly. In cases where local systems share a single Internet connection, this may significantly reduce download speeds. You can also control what packages can be installed. In effect, you download those packages on a YUM repository you want, and then create from those packages a local repository on one of your local systems. Your local systems them use the local repository to update install and update packages. You will have to manually keep the local repository updated. Use the **createrepo** command to create a repository from a directory holding the packages you want in it. Then it is a simple matter of providing a configuration file for it, specifying its location.

Managing YUM Caches

With the keepcache option enabled, YUM will keep its downloaded packages in the **/var/cache/yum** directory. Should you want to save or copy any particular packages, you can locate them there. Caching lets you easily uninstall and reinstall packages without having to download them again. The package is retained in the cache. If caching is disabled, then packages are automatically deleted after they are installed.

The size of your cache can increase rapidly, so you may want to clean it out on occasion. If you just want to deleted these packages, as they are already installed, you can use the clean packages option.

```
yum clean packages
```

Yom also maintains a list of package headers with information on all packages downloaded. The headers are used to update your system, showing what has already been installed. You can opt to remove the headers with the **clean headers** option.

If you want YUM to just access packages in the cache, you use the **-C** option. The following lists just packages in the cache.

```
yum -C list
```

Manually Installing Packages with rpm

If you are installing a package that is not part of a YUM repository, and you do not have access to the desktop or you prefer to work from the command line interface, you can use the **rpm** command to manage and install software packages (you can also open a terminal window by selecting the Terminal entry in the Applications | System Tools menu). In most cases you will not need to use the **rpm** command. Most software now resides on YUM-supported, Fedora-compliant repositories. You would just use the **yum** command or the PackageKit (Add/Remove Software) front end, to install your package. YUM has the advantage of automatically installing any dependent packages, whereas the **rpm** command, though it will detect needed packages, will not install them. You will have to separately install any dependent packages in the correct order.

RPM has undergone a major upgrade with a complete rewrite with version 4.6. The actual command interface and options have not changed. The under package management has been made much more reliable and efficient. The rpm commands used remain the same.

For packages that are not part of any YUM-supported repository, such as custom-made packages and that have few or no dependent packages, you can use the **rpm** command directly. You could also use the **rpm** command to bypass YUM, forcing installation of a particular package instead of from YUM repositories (YUM's **localinstall** option will achieve the same purpose, or selecting only the Install DVD in the PackageKit repository manager).

The **rpm** command performs installation, removal, and verification of software packages. Each software package is actually an RPM package, consisting of an archive of software files and information about how to install those files. Each archive resides as a single file with a name that ends with **.rpm**, indicating it is a software package that can be installed by the Red Hat Package Manager.

You can use the `rpm` command to either install or uninstall a package. The `rpm` command uses a set of options to determine what action to take. The `-i` option installs the specified software package, and the `-U` option updates a package. With an `-e` option, `rpm` uninstalls the package. A `q` placed before an `i` (`-qi`) queries the system to see if a software package is already installed and displays information about the software (`-qpi` queries an uninstalled package file). The `rpm` command with no options provides a complete list of `rpm` options. A set of commonly used options is shown in the following table.

Option	Action
-U	Updates package
-i	Installs package
-e	Removes package
-qi	Displays information for an installed package
-ql	Displays file list for installed package
-qpi	Displays information from an RPM package file (used for uninstalled packages)
-qpl	Displays file list from an RPM package file (used for uninstalled packages)
-K	Authenticates and performs integrity check on a package

The software package name is usually quite lengthy, including information about the version and release date in its name. All end with **.rpm**. In the next example, the user installs the xvidcore package using the `rpm` command. Notice that the full filename is entered. To list the full name, you can use the `ls` command with the first few characters and an asterisk. The following examples use the DivX xvidcore RPM packages downloaded using http:**//rpmfusion.org**.

```
ls xvid*
```

You can also use the `*` to match the remainder of the name, as in the following:

```
ls xvidccore-1*.rpm
```

In most cases, you are installing packages with the `-U` option, for update. Even if the package is not already installed, `-U` still installs it.

```
$ rpm -Uvh xvidcore--1.1.3-4.fc10.x86_64.rpm
```

When RPM performs an installation, it first checks for any dependent packages. These are other software packages with programs the application you are installing needs to use. If other dependent packages must be installed first, RPM cancels the installation and lists those packages. You can install those packages and then repeat the installation of the application. To determine if a package is already installed, use the `-qi` option with `rpm`. The `-q` stands for query. To obtain a list of all the files the package has installed, as well as the directories it installed to, use the `-ql` option. To query package files, add the `p` option. The `-qpi` option displays information about a package, and `-qpl` lists the files in it. The following example lists all the files in the xvidcore package:

```
$ rpm -qpl xvidcore-1.1.3-4.fc10.x86_64.rpm
```

To remove a software package from your system, first use `rpm -qi` to make sure it is actually installed, and then use the `-e` option to uninstall it. As with the `-qi` option, you needn't use the full name of the installed file. You only need the name of the application. In the next example, the user removes the DivX xvidcore from the system:

```
$ rpm -e xvidcore
```

Package Security Check

If you download a software package, you may want to check its integrity and authentication, making sure the package was not tampered with and that it was obtained from a valid source. YUM is configured to automatically perform this check on all software downloaded from your Fedora-compliant repositories. Each repository configuration file in the **/etc/yum.repos.d** directory will have its `gpgcheck` option set to 1. Should you want to turn off this check for a particular repository, you can set its `gpgcheck` option to 0.

To authenticate a package, you check its digital signature. Packages are signed with encrypted digital keys that can be decrypted using the public key provided by the author of the package. This public key has to first be downloaded and installed on the encryption tool used on your system. Fedora, along with most Linux distributions, uses the GNU Privacy Guard (GPG) encryption tool. To use a public key to authenticate an RPM package, you first have to install it in the RPM key database. For all RPM packages that are part of the Fedora distribution, you can use the Fedora public key, placed during installation in the **/etc/pki/rpm-gpg/RPM-GPG-KEY-fedora** file. Here you will also find the RPM GPG keys for all your configured repositories, including RPM Fusion. There will also be GPG keys for the Fedora test and rawhide repositories, **RPM-GPG-KEY-fedora-test** and **RPM-GPG-KEY-fedora-rawhide.**

You need to import the key to the RPM database before you can check Fedora RPM packages. The first time you use PackageKit to install a package you will be prompted to import the GPG key. Once imported, you need not import it again. Alternatively, you can manually import the key as shown here:

```
rpm --import /etc/pki/rpm-gpg/RPM-GPG-KEY-fedora
```

If you have downloaded an RPM package from another site, you can also download and install its public key, with which you can authenticate that package. For example there are public keys for both the RPM Fusion free and nonfree Fedora YUM repositories. These are included in the RPM Fusion YUM configuration files which you can download and install, like **rpmfusion-free-release-stable.noarch.rpm** for Livna. The keys will be automatically installed along with the configuration.

Once the public key is installed, you can check the package authentication using the `rpm` command with the `-K` option.

```
$ rpm -K xvidcore-1.1.3-4.fc10.x86_64.rpm
```

To see a list of all the keys you have imported, you can use the `-qa` option and match on the gpg-pubkey* pattern. Using `rpm` with the `-qi` option and the public key, you can display detailed information about the key. The following example shows the Fedora public key:

```
$ rpm -qa gpg-pubkey*
gpg-pubkey-4f2a6fd2-3f9d9d3b
gpg-pubkey-db42a60e-37ea5438
```

You can manually check just a package's integrity with the **rpm** command with the **-K** and the **--nosignature** options. A value called the MD5 digest measures the contents of a package. If the value is incorrect, the package has been tampered with. Some packages provide just digest values, allowing only integrity checks. In the next example, the user checks whether the xvidcore package has been tampered with. The **--nosignature** option says not to perform authentication, doing the integrity check only.

```
$ rpm -K --nosignature xvidcore-1.1.3-4.fc10.x86_64.rpm
```

Installing Source Code Applications

Many programs are available for Linux in source code format. These programs are stored in a compressed archive that you need to decompress and then extract. The resulting source code can then be configured, compiled, and installed on your system. The process has been simplified to the extent that it involves not much more than installing an RPM package. The following example shows the common method to extract, compile, and install software, in this case the freeciv program, a linux game. Always check the included README and INSTALL files that come with the source code to check the appropriate method for creating and installing that software.

Tip: Be sure that you have installed all development packages onto your system. Development packages contain the key components such as the compiler, GNOME and KDE headers and libraries, and preprocessors. You cannot compile source code software without them.

First you locate the software—in this case, from **www.linuxgames.com**—and then you download it to your system. freeciv is downloaded in a file named - **freeciv-2.1.8.tar.bz2**. Then decompress and extract the file either with the Archive Manager on the desktop, or with the **tar** command in a terminal window.

Extracting the Archive: Archive Manager (File Roller)

The easiest way to extract compressed archives is to use the Archive Manager (Applications | Accessories | Archive Manager) on GNOME (Archive Manager is the fileroller application). Either double-click the compressed archive file, or right-click and select Open With "Archive Manager". This displays the top-level contents of the archive, which you can browse if you wish, even reading text files like README and INSTALL files. You can also see what files will actually be installed. Use the button to navigate and double-click a directory to open it. Nothing is extracted at this point. To extract the archive, click Extract. You will be able to select what directory to extract to, the default will be a subdirectory in the current one (see Figure 4-21).

Archive Manager will let you actually read text files in the archive directly. Just select and double click the text file from its listing in the Archive manager window. Archive Manager will extract the file on the fly and display it in window (see Figure 4-22). The file is not actually extracted anywhere at this point.

You can also use Archive manager to create your own archives, creating an archive with the New button and then selecting files and folders for it with the Add File and Add Folder buttons.

Alternatively, on a command line, you can use the **tar** command to extract archives. To use the **tar** command, first open a terminal window (right-click on the desktop and select Open

Terminal). At the prompt, enter the **tar** command with the **xvjf** options (**j** for **bz2** and **z** for **gz**), as shown here:

```
tar xvjf freeciv-2.1.8.tar.bz2
```

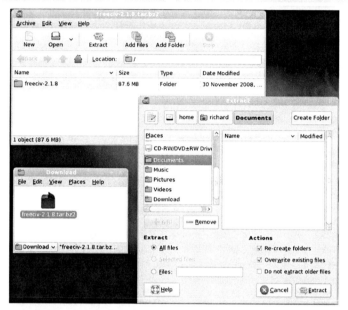

Figure 4-21: Archive Manager (File Roller) to exact software archive.

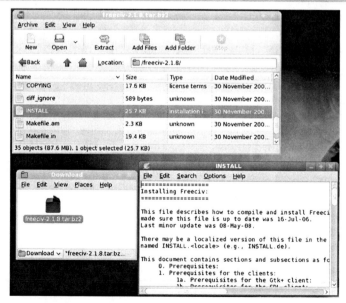

Figure 4-22: Archive Manager displaying archive text file.

Configure, Compile, and Install

Extracting the archive will create a directory with the name of the software, in this case **freeciv-2.1-4**. Once it is extracted, you have to configure, compile, and install the software. This usually needs to be done from a terminal window.

Change to the software directory with the **cd** command:

```
cd freeciv-2.1-4
```

Issue the command **./configure**. This generates a compiler configuration for your particular system.

```
./configure
```

Compile the software with the **make** command:

```
make
```

Then install the program with the **make install** command:

```
make install
```

Most KDE and GNOME software will also place an entry for the program in the appropriate menus—for example, a freeciv entry will be placed in the KDE Applications menu. You can then run freeciv from the menu entry. You could also open a terminal window and enter the program's name.

5. Office Applications and Editors

Running Microsoft Office on Linux: CrossOver

OpenOffice.org

KOffice

GNOME Office

Document Viewers (PostScript, PDF, and DVI)

PDA Access

Editors

Database Management Systems

A variety of office suites are now available for Linux (see Table 5-1). These include professional-level word processors, presentation managers, drawing tools, and spreadsheets. The freely available versions are described in this chapter. Sun has initiated development of an Open Source Office suite using StarOffice code. The applications, known as OpenOffice, provide Office applications integrated with GNOME. OpenOffice is currently the primary office application supported by Fedora. KOffice is an entirely free office suite designed for use with KDE. The GNOME Office suite integrates GNOME applications into a productivity suite that is freely available. CodeWeavers CrossOver Office provides reliable support for running MS Office Windows applications directly on Linux, integrating with them with KDE and GNOME.

Web Site	Description
`www.openoffice.org`	OpenOffice open source office suite based on StarOffice
`www.koffice.org`	KOffice Suite, for KDE
`www.gnome.org/gnome-office`	GNOME Office, for GNOME
`www.sun.com/staroffice`	StarOffice Suite
`www.codeweavers.com`	CrossOver Office (MS Office support)
`www.scribus.net`	Scribus desktop publishing tool.

Table 5-1: Linux Office Suites

You can also purchase commercial office suites such as StarOffice from Sun. For desktop publishing, especially PDF generation, you can use Scribus, a cross-platform tool available from the Fedora repository. A variety of database management systems are also available for Linux. These include high-powered, commercial-level database management systems, such as Oracle, IBM's DB2, and Sybase. Most of the database management systems available for Linux are designed to support large relational databases. Fedora includes both MySQL and PostgreSQL databases in its distribution. For small personal databases, you can use the desktop database management systems being developed for KDE and GNOME. In addition, some software is available for databases accessed with the Xbase database programming language. These are smaller databases using formats originally developed for dBase on the PC. Various database management systems available to run under Linux are listed in Table 5-8 later in this chapter.

Fedora also provides several text editors that range from simple text editors for simple notes to editors with more complex features such as spell-checkers, buffers, or pattern matching. All generate character text files and can be used to edit any Linux text files. Text editors are often used in system administration tasks to change or add entries in Linux configuration files found in the **/etc** directory or a user's initialization or application dot files located in a user's home directory. You can use any text editor to work on source code files for any of the programming languages or shell program scripts.

Running Microsoft Office on Linux: CrossOver

One of the primary concerns for new Linux users is what kind of access they will have to their Microsoft Office files, particularly Word files. The Linux operating system and many applications for it are designed to provide seamless access to MS Office files. The major Linux Office suites, including KOffice, OpenOffice, and StarOffice, all read and manage any Microsoft

Office files. In addition, these office suites are fast approaching the same level of features and support for office tasks as found in Microsoft Office.

If you want to use any Windows application on Linux, three important alternatives are the Wine virtual windows API support, VMware virtual platform technology, and the CrossOver Office by CodeWeavers. VMware and CrossOver are commercial packages.

Wine allows you to run many Windows applications directly, using a supporting virtual windows API. See the Wine Web site for a list of supported applications, **www.winehq.com**. Well written applications may run directly from Wine, like the newsbin newsreader. Often you will have to have a working Windows system from which to copy system DLLs needed by particular applications. You can also import your Windows fonts by directly copying them to the Wine font directory. Each user can install their own version of Wine with its own simulated C: partition on which Windows applications are installed. The simulated drive is installed as **drive_c** in your **.wine** directory. The **.wine** directory is a hidden directory. It is not normally displayed with the `ls` command or the GNOME file manager. You can also use any of your Linux directories for your Windows application data files instead of your simulated C: drive. These are referenced by Windows applications as the **z:** drive.

In a terminal window, using the `wine` command with an install program will automatically install that Windows application on the simulated C: drive. The following example installs Microsoft Office. Though there may be difficulties with latest Microsoft Office versions, earlier versions like 2003 should work fine. When you insert the Microsoft Office CD, it will be mounted to the /media directory using as its folder the disk label. Check the /media folder (Filesystem) to see what the actual name is. You want to run the setup.exe program for Office with wine. Depending on the version of Office you have, there may be further subfolders for the actual Office setup.exe program. The following example assumes that the label for Office is OFFICE and that the setup.exe program for Office is on the top level directory of that CD.

```
$ wine /media/OFFICE/setup.exe
```

The install program will start up and you will be prompted to enter your product key. Be sure to use uppercase. In the Wine menu in the Applications menu, you will also find entries for Microsoft Word (Applications | Wine | Programs | Microsoft Office). The application will start up normally. If you right-click on the menu entry, like the one for Microsoft Word, you can select the Add Launcher to Desktop entry to add an icon for the application on your desktop. The application is referenced by Wine on the user's simulated C drive, like the following for Word.

```
wine  "C:\Program Files\Microsoft Office\OFFICE11\WINWORD.EXE"
```

The Windows My Documents folder is set up by Wine to be the user's home directory. There you will find any files saved to My Documents.

Wine is constantly being updated to accommodate the latest versions of Windows applications. However, for some applications you may need to copy DLL files from a working Windows system to the Wine Windows folder, **.wine/drive_c/windows**, usually to the **system** or **system32** directories. Though effective, Wine support will not be as stable as Crossover.

CrossOver Office also lets you install and run most Microsoft Office applications. CrossOver Office was developed by CodeWeavers, which also supports Windows Web browser plug-ins as well as several popular Windows applications like Adobe Photoshop. CrossOver features both standard and professional versions, providing reliable application support. You can find out more about CrossOver Office at **www.codeweavers.com**. You can also try CrossOver for unsupported applications. They may or may not run.

CrossOver can be installed either for private multi-user mode or managed multi-user mode. In private multi-user mode, each user installs his or her own Windows software, such as full versions of Office. In managed multi-user mode, the Windows software is installed once and all users share it. When you install new software, you first open the CrossOver startup tool, and then on the Add/Remove panel you will see a list of supported software. This will include Office applications as well as some Adobe applications, including earlier versions of Photoshop. An Install Software panel will then let you select whether to install from a CD-ROM or an .exe file. For Office on a CD-ROM, select CD-ROM, place the Windows CD-ROM in your CD-ROM drive, and then click Next. The Windows Office installer will start up in a Linux window and will proceed as if you were on a Windows system. When the install requires a restart of the system, CrossOver will simulate it for you. Once the software is installed, you will see a Windows Applications menu on the main menu, from which you can start your installed Windows software. The applications will run within a Linux window, just as if they were running in Windows.

With VMware, you can run Windows under Linux, allowing you to run Windows applications, including Microsoft Office, on your Linux system. For more information, check the VMware Web site at **www.vmware.com**.

OpenOffice.org

OpenOffice.org (OO) is a fully integrated suite of office applications developed as an open source project and freely distributed to all. It is included as the primary office suite for Fedora, accessible from the Office menu. It includes word processing, spreadsheet, presentation, and drawing applications (see Table 5-2). Versions of OpenOffice exist for Linux, Windows, and Mac OS. You can obtain information such as online manuals and FAQs as well as current versions from the OpenOffice.org Web site at **www.openoffice.org**.

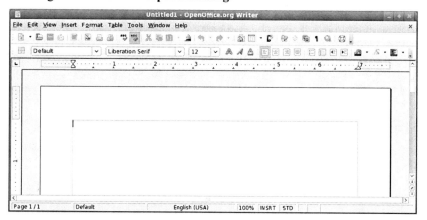

Figure 5-1: OpenOffice.org Writer word processor

OpenOffice is an integrated suite of applications. You can open the writer, spreadsheet, or presentation application directly. Also, in most OpenOffice applications, you can select New from the File menu and select a different application if you wish. The Writer word processor supports standard word processing features, such as cut and paste, spell-checker, and text formatting, as well as paragraph styles (see Figure 5-1). You can embed objects within documents, such as using Draw to create figures that you can then drag and drop to the Writer document. You can find out more about each component at their respective produce pages listed at, `www.openoffice.org/product`.

Calc is a professional-level spreadsheet. With Math, you can create formulas that you can then embed in a text document. With the presentation manager (Impress), you can create images for presentations, such as circles, rectangles, and connecting elements like arrows, as well as vector-based illustrations. Impress supports advanced features such as morphing objects, grouping objects, and defining gradients. Draw is a sophisticated drawing tool that includes 3-D modeling tools. You can create simple or complex images, including animation text aligned on curves. OpenOffice also includes a printer setup tool with which you can select printers, fonts, paper sizes, and page formats.

Note: StarOffice is a fully integrated and Microsoft Office–compatible suite of office applications developed and supported by Sun Microsystems, **www.sun.com/staroffice**. Sun provides StarOffice as a commercial product, though educational use is free.

Application	Description
Calc	OpenOffice spreadsheet
Draw	OpenOffice drawing application
Writer	OpenOffice word processor
Math	OpenOffice mathematical formula composer
Impress	OpenOffice presentation manager
Base	Database front end for accessing and managing a variety of different databases.

Table 5-2: OpenOffice.org Applications

OpenOffice also provides access to many database files. File types supported include ODBC 3.0 (Open Database Connectivity), JDBC (Java), ADO, MySQL, dBase, CSV, PostgreSQL, and MDB (Microsoft Access) database files. You can also create your own simple databases. Check the OpenOffice.org – Base page and Project page (**http://dba.openoffice.org**) for detailed information on drivers and supported databases.

OpenOffice features an underlying component model that can be programmed to develop customized applications. Check the OpenOffice API project for more details (**http://api.openoffice.org**). The OpenOffice Software Development Kit (SDK) provides support for using OpenOffice components in applications written in C++ or Java. The Unified Network Objects (UNO) model is the component model for OpenOffice, providing interaction between programming languages, other object models, and network connections.

Also for use on GNOME is Scribus, the desktop publishing tool (see Figure 5-2). (**www.scribus.net**)

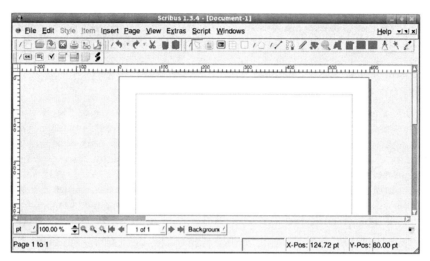

Figure 5-2: Scribus desktop publisher

KOffice

KOffice is an integrated office suite for the KDE (K Desktop Environment) consisting of several office applications, including a word processor, a spreadsheet, and graphic applications. KOffice is part of the Fedora. You can download it using PackageKit/YUM (Add/Remove Software). All applications are written for the KOM component model, which allows components from any one application to be used in another. This means you can embed a spreadsheet from KSpread or diagrams from Karbon14 in a KWord document. You can obtain more information about KOffice from the KOffice Web site at **www.koffice.org**.

Tip: KOffice applications have import and export filters that allow them to import or export files from popular applications like Abiword, OpenOffice.org applications, MS Word, and even Palm documents. The reliability of these filters varies, and you should check the KOffice Filters Web page for a listing of the different filters and their stability.

KOffice Applications

Currently, KOffice includes KSpread, KPresenter, KWord, Karbon14, KFormula, KChart, Kugar, Krita, and Kivio (see Table 5-3). The contact application, Kontact, has been spun off as a separate project. Kontact is an integrated contact application including Kmail, Korganizer, Kaddressbook, and Knotes. KSpread is a spreadsheet, KPresenter is a presentation application, Karbon14 is a vector graphics program, KWord is a Publisher-like word processor, KFormula is a formula editor, and KChart generates charts and diagrams. Kugar is a report generator, Krita is a bitmap image editor, and Kivio creates flow charts. Kexi provides database integration with KOffice applications, currently supporting PostgreSQL and MySQL.

KSpread is the spreadsheet application, which incorporates the basic operations found in most spreadsheets, with formulas similar to those used in Excel. You can also embed charts, pictures, or formulas using KChart, Krita, Karbon14, or KFormula.

With KChart, you can create different kinds of charts, such as bar graphs, pie charts, and line graphs, as well as create diagrams. To generate a chart, you can use data in KSpread to enter your data. With KPresenter, you can create presentations consisting of text and graphics modeled using different fonts, orientations, and attributes such as colors. You can add such elements as speech bubbles, arrows, and clip art, as well as embed any KOffice component. Karbon14 is a vector-based graphics program, much like Adobe Illustrator and OpenOffice Draw. It supports the standard graphic operations such as rotating, scaling, and aligning objects.

Application	Description
KSpread	Spreadsheet
KPresenter	Presentation program
Kontour	Vector drawing program
Karbon14	Vector graphics program
KWord	Word processor (desktop publisher)
KFormula	Mathematical formula editor
KChart	Tool for drawing charts and diagrams
Kugar	Report generator
Krita	Paint and image manipulation program
Kivio	Flow chart generator and editor (similar to Vivio)
Kexi	Database integration
KPlato	Project management and planning
Kontact (separate project)	Contact application including mail, address book, and organizer

Table 5-3: KOffice Applications

KWord can best be described as a desktop publisher, with many of the features found in publishing applications like Microsoft Publisher and FrameMaker. Although it is also a fully functional word processor, KWord is not page-based like Word or WordPerfect. Instead, text is set up in frames that are placed on the page like objects. Frames, like objects in a drawing program, can be moved, resized, and even reoriented. You can organize frames into a frame set, having text flow from one to the other.

GNOME Office

The GNOME Office project supports three office applications: AbiWord, Gnumeric, and GNOME-DB. Former members of GNOME Office still provide certain Office tasks, like Novell's Evolution e-mail and contact client. Many former members are still GNOME projects, with information listed for them at **www.gnome.org/projects**. The GNOME Office applications, as well as other GNOME-based Office applications, are part of Fedora and can be downloaded with Add/Remove Software (YUM). You can find out more from the GNOME Office site at **www.gnome.org/gnome-office**. A current listing for common GNOME Office applications, including those not part of the GNOME Office suite is shown in Table 5-4. All implement the

CORBA model for embedding components, ensuring drag-and-drop capability throughout the GNOME interface.

AbiWord is a word processor, Gnumeric is a spreadsheet, and GNOME-DB provides database connectivity. Gnumeric is a GNOME spreadsheet, a professional-level program meant to replace commercial spreadsheets. Like GNOME, Gnumeric is freely available under the GNU Public License. Gnumeric is included with the GNOME release, and you will find it installed with GNOME on any distribution that supports GNOME. You can download current versions from **www.gnome.org/projects/gnumeric**. Gnumeric supports standard GUI spreadsheet features, including auto filling and cell formatting, and it provides an extensive number of formats. It supports drag-and-drop operations, enabling you to select and then move or copy cells to another location. Gnumeric also supports plug-ins, making it possible to extend and customize its capabilities easily.

AbiWord is an open source word processor that aims to be a complete cross-platform solution, running on Mac, UNIX, and Windows, as well as Linux. It is part of a set of desktop productivity applications being developed by the AbiSource project (**www.abisource.com**).

The GNOME-DB project provides a GNOME Data Access (GDA) library supporting several kinds of databases, such as PostgreSQL, MySQL, Microsoft Access, and unixODBC. It provides an API to which databases can plug in. These back-end connections are based on CORBA. Through this API, GNOME applications can then access a database. You can find out more about GNOME-DB at **www.gnome-db.org**.

Application	Description
GNOME Office	**Description**
AbiWord	Cross-platform word processor
Gnumeric	Spreadsheet
GNOME-DB	Database connectivity
Other GNOME Office Apps	**Description**
Evolution	Integrated e-mail, calendar, and personal organizer (Novell)
Dia	Diagram and flow chart editor (GNOME project)
GnuCash	Personal finance manager (GNOME project)
Balsa	E-mail client (GNOME project)
GnuCash	Personal finance manager (GNOME project)
Planner	Project manager (GNOME project)
OpenOffice	OpenOffice office suite

Table 5-4: GNOME Office and Other Office Applications for GNOME

Dia is a drawing program designed to create diagrams (GNOME project). You can select different kinds of diagrams to create, such as database, circuit object, flow chart, and network diagrams. You can easily create elements along with lines and arcs with different types of endpoints such as arrows or diamonds. Data can be saved in XML format, making it easily transportable to other applications.

GnuCash (**www.gnucash.org**) is a personal finance application for managing accounts, stocks, and expenses (GNOME project). It includes support for home banking with the OpenHBCI interface. OpenHBCI is the open source home banking computer interface (**openhbci.sourceforge.net**).

Document Viewers (PostScript, PDF, and DVI)

Though located under Graphic submenu in the Applications menu, PostScript, PDF, and DVI viewers are more commonly used with Office applications (see Table 5-5). Evince and Ghostview can display both PostScript (.ps) and PDF (.pdf) files. Its X Window System front end is gv. KPDF and Xpdf are PDF viewers. KPDF includes many of the standard Adobe reader features such as zoom, two-page display, and full-screen mode. Alternatively, you can download Acrobat reader for Linux from Adobe to display PDF files. All these viewers also have the ability to print documents. To generate PDF documents you can use Scribus desktop publisher (**www.scribus.net**), and to edit PDF documents you can use **pdfedit**.

Linux also features a professional-level typesetting tool, called TeX, commonly used to compose complex mathematical formulas. TeX generates a DVI document that can then be displayed by DVI viewers, of which there are several for Linux. DVI files generated by the TeX document application can be viewed by KDVI, which is a plug-in to the KViewShell tool. KViewShell can display and print any kind of document for which it has a plug-in.

Viewer	Description
Evince	Document Viewer for PostScript and PDF files
KPDF	KDE tool for displaying PDF files
KGhostView	KDE interface for displaying PostScript and PDF files
xpdf	X Window System tool for displaying PDF files only
KDVI	KDE tool for displaying TeX DVI files
Acrobat Reader for Linux	Adobe PDF and PostScript display application
Scribus	Desktop publisher for generating PDF documents
gv	X Window System viewer for ghostscript files.
pdfedit	Edit PDF documents

Table 5-5: PostScript, PDF, and DVI viewers

PDA Access

For many PDAs you can use the pilot tools to access your handheld, transferring information between it and your system. The **pilot-link** package holds the tools you use access your PDA. Check **www.pilot-link.org** for detailed documentation and useful links. The tool name usually begins with "pilot"; for instance, **pilot-addresses** read addresses from an address book. Other tools whose names begin with "read" allow you to convert Palm data for access by other applications; **read-expenses**, for instance, outputs expense data as standard text. One of the more useful tools is **pilot-xfer**, used to back up your Palm.

Instead of using command line commands directly, you can use the J-Pilot, KPilot, and GnomePilot applications to access your PDA. To use your PDA on GNOME, you can use the gnome-pilot applet from your GNOME panel to configure your connection. In the gnome-pilot applet's Preferences windows (right-click on applet), the Conduits panel lets you enable several hot sync operations to perform automatically, including e-mail, memos, and installing files. Click the Help button for a detailed manual.

J-Pilot provides a GUI interface that lets you perform basic tasks such as synchronizing address book and writing memos. J-Pilot is accessible from the Office menu and is part of Fedora. KPilot is included with the **kpim** package installed as part of the KDE Desktop. On Fedora you need to open a terminal window and enter the `kpilot` command to run it. It will first let you automatically sync with your PDA. You then have the option to use either Evolution or Kontact with your PDA, or just perform backups. You can then perform operations like hot syncs, viewing addresses, and installing files. For text and Palm format conversions, you can use KPalmDoc. This tool will convert text files to Palm files, and Palm files to text files.

Editors

Traditionally, most Linux distributions, including Fedora, install the cursor-based editors Vim and Emacs. *Vim* is an enhanced version of the Vi text editor used on the UNIX system. These editors use simple, cursor-based operations to give you a full-screen format. You can start these editors from the shell command line without any kind of X Window System support. In this mode, their cursor-based operations do not have the ease of use normally found in window-based editors. There are no menus, scroll bars, or mouse-click features.

The K Desktop	Description
KEdit	Text editor
Kate	Text and program editor
Notetaker	Notebook editor
KWord	Desktop publisher, part of KOffice
GNOME	
Gedit	Text editor
AbiWord	Word processor
X Window System	
GNU Emacs	Emacs editor with X Window System support
XEmacs	X Window System version of Emacs editor
gvim	Vim version with X Window System support
OpenWriter	OpenOffice word processor that can edit text files

Table 5-6: Desktop Editors

The K Desktop and GNOME do support powerful GUI text editors with all these features. These editors operate much more like those found on Macintosh and Windows systems. They have full mouse support, scroll bars, and menus. You may find them much easier to use than the Vi and

Emacs editors. These editors operate from their respective desktops, requiring you first have either KDE or GNOME installed, though the editors can run on either desktop. Vi and Emacs have powerful editing features that have been refined over the years. Emacs, in particular, is extensible to a full-development environment for programming new applications. Newer versions of Emacs, such as GNU Emacs and XEmacs, provide X Window System support with mouse, menu, and window operations. They can run on any window manager or desktop. In addition, the gvim version of the Vim editor also provides basic window operations. You can access it on both GNOME and KDE desktops. Table 5-6 lists several GUI-based editors for Linux.

Note: Fedora Linux includes a fully functional word processor, Writer (OpenOffice). AbiWord is now part of Fedora, along with Kword, which is part of KOffice. You can find out more on AbiWord at **www.abiword.com**.

GNOME Text Editor: Gedit

The Gedit editor is a basic text editor for the GNOME desktop. It provides full mouse support, implementing standard GUI operations, such as cut and paste to move text, and click and drag to select text. It supports standard text editing operations such as Find and Replace. You can use Gedit to create and modify your text files, including configuration files. Gedit also provides more advanced features such as print preview and configurable levels of undo/redo operations, and it can read data from pipes. It features a plug-in menu that provides added functionality, and it includes plug-ins for spell-checking, encryption, e-mail, and text-based Web page display.

K Desktop Editors: Kate and KEdit

All the K Desktop editors provide full mouse support, implementing standard GUI operations, such as cut and paste to move text, and click and drag to select text. The K Desktop editors are accessible from the Utilities | Editors menu on the K Desktop (you have to log in using the K-Desktop, check KDE entry in login screen's Options | Select Session menu), though you can start any of them up from GNOME using the terminal window and the command name. Kate is an advanced editor, with such features as spell-checking, font selection, and highlighting. Most commands can be selected using menus. A toolbar of icons for common operations is displayed across the top of the Kate window. A sidebar displays panels for a file selector and a file list. With the file selector, you can navigate through the file system selecting files to work on. Kate also supports multiple views of a document, letting you display segments in their own windows, vertically or horizontally. You can also open several documents at the same time, moving between them with the file list. Kate is designed to be a program editor for editing software programming/development-related source code files. Although Kate does not have all the features of Emacs or Vi, it can handle most major tasks. Kate can format the syntax for different programming languages, such as C, Perl, Java, and XML. In addition, Kate has the capability to access and edit files on an FTP or Web site.

KEdit is an older simple text editor meant for editing simple text files such as configuration files. A toolbar of buttons at the top of the KEdit window enables you to execute common editing commands easily using just a mouse click. With KEdit, you can also mail files you are editing over a network. The entry for KEdit in the K menu is listed simply as Text Editor.

The Emacs Editor

Emacs can best be described as a working environment featuring an editor, a mailer, a newsreader, and a Lisp interpreter. The editor is tailored for program development, enabling you to format source code according to the programming language you use. Many versions of Emacs are currently available for use on UNIX and Linux systems. The versions usually included with Linux distributions are either GNU Emacs or XEmacs. The current version for GNU Emacs is X Window System–capable, enabling GUI features such as menus, scroll bars, and mouse-based editing operations. Check the update FTP sites for your distribution for new versions as they come out, and also check the GNU Web site at **www.gnu.org** and the Emacs Web site at **www.emacs.org**. You can find out more information about XEmacs at its Web site, **www.xemacs.org**.

Emacs derives much of its power and flexibility from its capability to manipulate buffers. Emacs can be described as a buffer-oriented editor. Whenever you edit a file in any editor, the file is copied into a work buffer, and editing operations are made on the work buffer. Emacs can manage many work buffers at once, enabling you to edit several files at the same time. You can edit buffers that hold deleted or copied text. You can even create buffers of your own; fill them with text, and later save them to a file. Emacs extends the concept of buffers to cover any task. When you compose mail, you open a mail buffer; when you read news, you open a news buffer. Switching from one task to another is simply a matter of switching to another buffer.

The Emacs editor operates much like a standard word processor. The keys on your keyboard represent input characters. Commands are implemented with special keys, such as control (CTRL) keys and alternate (ALT) keys. There is no special input mode, as in Vi. You type in your text, and if you need to execute an editing command, such as moving the cursor or saving text, you use a CTRL key. Such an organization makes the Emacs editor easy to use. However, Emacs is anything but simple—it is a sophisticated and flexible editor with several hundred commands. Emacs also has special features, such as multiple windows. You can display two windows for text at the same time. You can also open and work on more than one file at a time, displaying each on the screen in its own window. You invoke the Emacs editor with the command **emacs**. You can enter the name of the file you want to edit, and if the file does not exist, it is created. In the next example, the user prepares to edit the file **mydata** with Emacs:

```
$ emacs mydata
```

The GNU Emacs editor now supports an X Window System graphical user interface. To enable X support, start Emacs within an X Window System environment, such as a KDE, GNOME, or XFce desktop. The basic GUI editing operations are supported: selection of text with click-and-drag mouse operations; cut, copy, and paste; and a scroll bar for moving through text. The Mode line and Echo areas are displayed at the bottom of the window, where you can enter keyboard commands. The scroll bar is located on the left side. To move the scroll bar down, click it with the left mouse button. To move the scroll bar up, click it with the right mouse button.

Note: XEmacs is the complete Emacs editor with a graphical user interface and Internet applications, including a Web browser, a mail utility, and a newsreader. XEmacs is available on the Fedora repository.

The Vi Editor: Vim and Gvim

The Vim editor included with most Linux distributions is an enhanced version of the Vi editor. It includes all the commands and features of the Vi editor. Vi, which stands for *visual,* remains one of the most widely used editors in Linux. Keyboard-based editors like Vim and Emacs use a keyboard for two different operations: to specify editing commands and to receive character input. Used for editing commands, certain keys perform deletions, some execute changes, and others perform cursor movement. Used for character input, keys represent characters that can be entered into the file being edited. Usually, these two different functions are divided among different keys on the keyboard. Alphabetic keys are reserved for character input, while function keys and control keys specify editing commands, such as deleting text or moving the cursor. Such editors can rely on the existence of an extended keyboard that includes function and control keys. Editors in UNIX, however, were designed to assume a minimal keyboard with alphanumeric characters and some control characters, as well as the ESC and ENTER keys. Instead of dividing the command and input functions among different keys, the Vi editor has three separate modes of operation for the keyboard: command and input modes, and a line editing mode. In *command* mode, all the keys on the keyboard become editing commands; in the *input* mode, the keys on the keyboard become input characters. Some of the editing commands, such as **a** or **i**, enter the input mode. On typing **i**, you leave the command mode and enter the input mode. Each key now represents a character to be input to the text. Pressing ESC automatically returns you to the command mode, and the keys once again become editor commands. As you edit text, you are constantly moving from the command mode to the input mode and back again. With Vim, you can use the CTRL-O command to jump quickly to the command mode and enter a command, and then automatically return to the input mode. Table 5-7 lists a very basic set of Vi commands to get you started.

Although the Vi command mode handles most editing operations, it cannot perform some, such as file saving and global substitutions. For such operations, you need to execute line editing commands. You enter the line editing mode using the Vi colon command. The colon is a special command that enables you to perform a one-line editing operation. When you type the colon, a line opens up at the bottom of the screen with the cursor placed at the beginning of the line. You are now in the line editing mode. In this mode, you enter an editing command on a line, press ENTER, and the command is executed. Entry into this mode is usually only temporary. Upon pressing ENTER, you are automatically returned to the Vi command mode, and the cursor returns to its previous position on the screen.

Although you can create, save, close, and quit files with the Vi editor, the commands for each are not all that similar. Saving and quitting a file involves the use of special line editing commands, whereas closing a file is a Vi editing command. Creation of a file is usually specified on the same shell command line that invokes the Vi editor. To edit a file, type **vi** or **vim** and the name of a file on the shell command line. If a file by that name does not exist, the system creates it. In effect, giving the name of a file that does not yet exist instructs the Vi editor to create that file. The following command invokes the Vi editor, working on the file **booklist**. If **booklist** does not yet exist, the Vi editor creates it.

```
$ vim  booklist
```

After executing the **vim** command, you enter Vi's command mode. Each key becomes a Vi editing command, and the screen becomes a window onto the text file. Text is displayed screen by screen. The first screen of text is displayed, and the cursor is positioned in the upper-left corner. With a newly created file, there is no text to display. This fact is indicated by a column of tildes at the left side of the screen. The tildes represent the part of a screen that is not part of the file.

Command	Cursor Movement
h	Moves the cursor left one character.
l	Moves the cursor right one character.
k	Moves the cursor up one line.
j	Moves the cursor down one line.
CTRL-F	Moves forward by a screen of text; the next screen of text is displayed.
CTRL-B	Moves backward by a screen of text; the previous screen of text is displayed.
Input	*(All input commands place the user in input; the user leaves input with ESC.)*
a	Enters input after the cursor.
i	Enters input before the cursor.
o	Enters input below the line the cursor is on; inserts a new empty line below the one the cursor is currently on.
Text Selection (Vim)	**Cursor Movement**
v	Visual mode; move the cursor to expand selected text by character. Once selected, press key to execute action: **c** change, **d** delete, **y** copy, **:** line editing command, **J** join lines, **U** uppercase, **u** lowercase.
V	Visual mode; move cursor to expand selected text by line.
Delete	**Effect**
x	Deletes the character the cursor is on.
dd	Deletes the line the cursor is on.
Change	*(Except for the replace command, r, all change commands place the user into input after deleting text.)*
cw	Deletes the word the cursor is on and places the user into the input mode.
r	Replaces the character the cursor is on. After pressing **r**, the user enters the replacement character. The change is made without entering input; the user remains in the Vi command mode.
R	First places into input mode, and then overwrites character by character. Appears as an overwrite mode on the screen but actually is in input mode.
Move	Moves text by first deleting it, moving the cursor to desired place of insertion, and then pressing the **p** command. (When text is deleted, it is automatically held in a special buffer.)
p	Inserts deleted or copied text after the character or line the cursor is on.
P	Inserts deleted or copied text before the character or line the cursor is on.
dw p	Deletes a word, and then moves it to the place you indicate with the cursor (press **p** to insert the word *after* the word the cursor is on).

yy or **Y p**	Copies the line the cursor is on.
Search	The two search commands open up a line at the bottom of the screen and enable the user to enter a pattern to be searched for; press ENTER after typing in the pattern.
/pattern	Searches forward in the text for a pattern.
?pattern	Searches backward in the text for a pattern.
n	Repeats the previous search, whether it was forward or backward.
Line Editing Commands	**Effect**
w	Saves file.
q	Quits editor; **q!** quits without saving.

Table 5-7: Editor Commands

When you first enter the Vi editor, you are in the command mode. To enter text, you need to enter the input mode. In the command mode, **a** is the editor command for appending text. Pressing this key places you in the input mode. Now the keyboard operates like a typewriter and you can input text to the file. If you press ENTER, you merely start a new line of text. With Vim, you can use the arrow keys to move from one part of the entered text to another and work on different parts of the text. After entering text, you can leave the input mode and return to the command mode by pressing ESC. Once finished with the editing session, you exit Vi by typing two capital Zs, **zz**. Hold down the SHIFT key and press **z** twice. This sequence first saves the file and then exits the Vi editor, returning you to the Linux shell. To save a file while editing, you use the line editing command **w**, which writes a file to the disk; **w** is equivalent to the Save command found in other word processors. You first type a colon to access the line editing mode, and then type **w** and press ENTER.

You can use the **:q** command to quit an editing session. Unlike the **zz** command, the **:q** command does not perform any save operation before it quits. In this respect, it has one major constraint. If any modifications have been made to your file since the last save operation, the **:q** command will fail and you will not leave the editor. However, you can override this restriction by placing a **!** qualifier after the **:q** command. The command **:q!** will quit the Vi editor without saving any modifications made to the file in that session since the last save (the combination **:wq** is the same as **zz**).

To obtain online help, enter the **:help** command. This is a line editing command. Type a colon, enter the word **help** on the line that opens at the bottom of the screen, and then press ENTER. You can add the name of a specific command after the word **help**. The F1 key also brings up online help.

As an alternative to using Vim in a command line interface, you can use gvim, which provides X Window System–based menus for basic file, editing, and window operations. Gvim is installed as the **vim-x11** package, which includes several links to Gvim such as **evim**, **gview**, and **gex** (open Ex editor line). To use Gvim, you can select it from the Programming menu as VIM Improved, or enter the **gvim** command at an X Window System terminal prompt. You can also right-click a text file and select VIM Improved from the list under Open With Other Application. After selecting it once, it will always appear as a possible option when you right-click a text file.

The standard Vi interface is displayed, but with several menu buttons displayed across the top along with a toolbar with button for common commands like searches and file saves. All the standard Vi commands work just as described previously. However, you can use your mouse to select items on these menus. You can open and close a file, or open several files using split windows or different windows. The editing menu enables you to cut, copy, and paste text as well as undo or redo operations. In the editing mode, you can select text with your mouse with a click-and-drag operation, or use the Editing menu to cut or copy and then paste the selected text. Text entry, however, is still performed using the **a**, **i**, or **o** command to enter the input mode. Searches and replacements are supported through a dialog window. There are also buttons on the toolbar for finding next and previous instances. Gview also features programming support, with color coding for programming syntax, for both shell scripts and C++ programs. There is even a Make button for running Make files.

You can also split the view into different windows to display parts of the same file or different files. Use the **:split** command to open a window, and **:hide** to close the current one. Use Ctrl-w with the up and down arrow keys to move between them. On Gvim, you use entries in the Windows menu to manage windows. Configuration preferences can be placed in the user's **.vimrc** file.

Database Management Systems

Database software can be generally organized into three categories: SQL, Xbase, and desktop databases. *SQL-based databases* are professional-level relational databases whose files are managed by a central database server program. Applications that use the database do not access the files directly. Instead, they send requests to the database server, which then performs the actual access. *SQL* is the query language used on these industrial-strength databases. Fedora includes both MySQL and PostgreSQL databases. Both are open source projects freely available for your use. Table 5-8 lists database management systems currently available for Linux.

SQL Databases (RDBMS)

SQL databases are relational database management systems (RDBMSs) designed for extensive database management tasks. Many of the major SQL databases now have Linux versions, including Oracle, Informix, Sybase, and IBM (but not, of course, Microsoft). These are commercial and professional database management systems of the highest order. Linux has proved itself capable of supporting complex and demanding database management tasks. In addition, many free SQL databases are available for Linux that offer much the same functionality. Most commercial databases also provide free personal versions, as do Oracle, Adabas D, and MySQL.

OpenOffice.org Base

OpenOffice provides a basic data base application, OpenOffice.org Base that can access many database files. You can set up and operate a simple database, as well as access and manage files from other database applications. When you start up OpenOffice.org Base, you will be prompted to either start a new database or connect to an existing one. File types supported include ODBC 3.0 (Open Database Connectivity), JDBC (Java), ADO, MySQL, dBase, CSV, PostgreSQL, and MDB (Microsoft Access) database files (install the **unixodbc** and **java-libmysql** packages).

You can also create your own simple databases. Check the OpenOffice.org – Base page and Project page (**http://dba.openoffice.org**) for detailed information on drivers and supported databases.

System	Site
OpenOffice.org	OpenOffice.org database: **www.openoffice.org**
PostgreSQL	The PostgreSQL database: **www.postgresql.org**
MySQL	MySQL database: **www.mysql.com**
Oracle	Oracle database: **www.oracle.com**
Sybase	Sybase database: **www.sybase.com**
DB2	IBM database: **www.software.ibm.com/data/db2/linux**
Informix	Informix database: **www.informix.com/linux**
MaxDB	SAP database: **www.sdn.sap.com/irj/sdn/maxdb**
GNU SQL	The GNU SQL database: **www.ispras.ru/~kml/gss**

Table 5-8: Database Management Systems for Linux

PostgreSQL

PostgreSQL is based on the POSTGRESQL database management system, though it uses SQL as its query language. POSTGRESQL is a next-generation research prototype developed at the University of California, Berkeley. Linux versions of PostgreSQL are included in most distributions, including the Red Hat, Fedora, Debian, and Mandrake distributions. You can find more information on it from the PostgreSQL Web site at **www.postgresql.org**. PostgreSQL is an open source project, developed under the GPL license.

MySQL

MySQL, included with Fedora, is a true multi-user, multithreaded SQL database server, supported by MySQL AB. MySQL is an open source product available free under the GPL license. You can obtain current information on it from its Web site, **www.mysql.com**. The site includes detailed documentation, including manuals and FAQs.

6. Graphics and Multimedia

Graphics Applications

Multimedia

GStreamer

Sound Drivers and Interfaces

Music Applications

CD Burners

Video Applications

Fedora includes a wide range of both graphic and multimedia applications and tool, including simple image viewers like GwenView, sophisticated image manipulation programs like GIMP, music and CD players like Rhythmbox, and TV viewers like Totem. Graphics tools available for use under Linux are listed in later Table 6-2. Additionally, there is strong support for multimedia tasks from video and DVD to sound and music editing (see Tables 6-5 and 6-6). Thousands of multimedia and graphic projects, as well as standard projects, are under development or currently available from **www.sourceforge.net** and **http://rpmfusion.org**. For information on graphics hardware and drivers, check **www.phoronix.com**.

Projects and Sites	Description
Fedora repository `http://fedoraprojet.org`	Fedora Repository which includes most GNU licensed multimedia applications.
`http://rpmfusion.org`	Repository for drivers and multimedia applications and libraries, that are not included with Fedora. This is an official extension of the Fedora project
`ftp://ftp.infradead.org/pub/spins/`	Omega 10 Desktop, Fedora 10 multimedia spin
SourceForge	This site holds many development projects for multimedia software for Linux: **www.sourceforge.net**
KDE multimedia applications	KDE supports an extensive set of multimedia software applications: **www.kde-apps.org**
GNOME multimedia applications	Many multimedia applications have been developed for GNOME: **www.gnomefiles.org**
Sound & MIDI Software for Linux	Lists a wide range of multimedia and sound software. **linux-sound.org**
Advanced Linux Sound Architecture (ALSA)	The Advanced Linux Sound Architecture (ALSA) project for current sound drivers: **www.alsa-project.org**
Open Sound System	Open Sound System, drives for older devices: **www.opensound.com**
PulseAudio	PulseAudio sound interface, now the default for Fedora. **www.pulseaudio.org**

Table 6-1: Linux Multimedia Sites

Support for many popular multimedia operations, specifically MP3, DVD, and DivX, are not included with the Fedora distribution, because of licensing and other restrictions. To play MP3, DVD, or DivX files, you will have to download and install support packages manually. Precompiled RPM binary packages for many popular media applications and libraries, such as MPlayer and XviD, are available on the RPM Fusion repository (see **http://rpmfusion.org**). These include many that are not part of the Fedora distribution. RPM Fusion is an official Fedora repository that provides RPM Fedora-compatible packages for many multimedia and other applications that cannot be included with the Fedora distribution. These include MP3 support, and DVD and DivX codecs. Current multimedia sites are listed in Table 6-1.

For those who want to install a multimedia system, like that for an HTPC, you can use the Omega spin of Fedora 10. The Omega 10 Desktop includes Fedora 10 as well as many free and non-free multimedia codecs and applications available from the RPM Fusion repository.

Graphics Tools

GNOME, KDE, and the X Window System support an impressive number of graphics tools, including image viewers, window grabbers, image editors, and paint tools. On the KDE and GNOME desktops, these tools can be found under either a Graphics submenu.

Photo Management Tools: F-Spot and Cheese

The F-Spot Photo Manager provides a simple and powerful way to manage, display, and import your photos and images (**www.f-spot.org**). Photos can be organized by different categories such as events, people, and places. You can perform standard display operations like rotation or full-screen viewing, along with slide shows. Image editing support is provided. Selected photos can be directly burned to a CD (uses Nautilus burning capabilities).

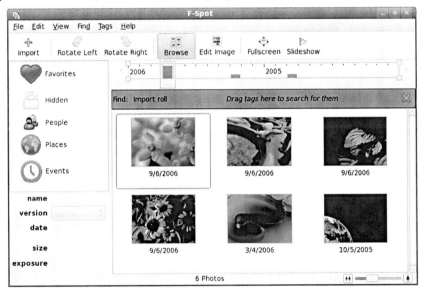

Figure 6-1: F-spot Photo Management

Features include a simple and easy-to-use interface. A timeline feature lets you see photos as they were taken. You can also display photos in full-screen mode or as slide shows. F-Spot includes a photo editor that provides basic adjustments and changes like rotation, red eye correction, and standard color settings including temperature and saturation (see Figure 6-1). You can tag photos placing them in groups, making them easier to access. With a tag you can label a collection of photos. Then use the tag to instantly access them. The tag itself can be a user-selected icon, including one that the user can create with the included Tag icon editor. F-Spot provides several ways to upload photos to a Web site using a Flickr account (**www.flickr.com**)

Cheese is a Web cam picture taking and video recording tool (**www.gnome.org/projects/cheese**). With Cheese you can snap pictures from your Web cam and apply simple effects (see Figure 6-2). Click the Photo button to manage photos and the Video button to record video. Icons of photos and video will appear on the bottom panel, letting you select ones for effects or removal. The effects panel will show effects that can be turned on or off for the current image. To save a photo, right click on its icon on the lower panel and select Save to from the pop-up menu. You can also export the selected photo or video to F-Spot, as well as email it as an attachment. You can also use the pop-up menu on particular icons to remove a photo. The Edit menu has a "Move all to trash" option for removing all items.

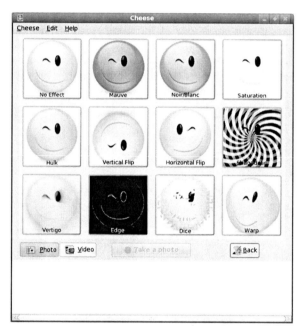

Figure 6-2: Cheese Web cam photo/video manager

KDE Graphics Tools

GwenView is a simple image viewer for image files. The KSnapshot program is a simple screen grabber for KDE, which currently supports only a few image formats. KFourier is an image-processing tool that uses the Fourier transform to apply several filters to an image at once. KuickShow is an easy-to-use, comfortable image browser and viewer supporting slide shows and numerous image formats. KolourPaint is a simple paint program with brushes, shapes, and color effects; it supports numerous image formats. Krita is the KOffice professional image paint and editing application, with a wide range of features, such as creating Web images and modifying photographs (formerly known as Krayon and KImageShop).

GNOME Graphics Tools

GNOME features several powerful and easy-to-use graphic tools. Some are installed with Fedora, whereas you can download others, such as GView and gtKam, from **www.gnomefiles.org**. Also, many of the KDE tools work just as effectively in GNOME and are accessible from the GNOME desktop.

The gThumb application is a thumbnail image viewer that lets you browse images using thumbnails, display them, and organize them into catalogs or easy reference. GPicView is an image viewer similar to Windows Picture Viewer with a simple resize and browsing interface.

Tools	Description
F-Spot	GNOME digital camera application and image library manager (**f-spot.org**)
Cheese	GNOME Web cam application for taking pictures and videos
KDE	
GwenView	Simple image viewer for image files
ShowFoto	Simple image viewer, works with digiKam (**www.digikam.org**)
KSnapshot	Screen grabber
KuickShow	Image browser and viewer
KolourPaint	Paint program
Krita	Image editor (**www.koffice.org/krita**)
GNOME	
gThumb	Image browser, viewer, and cataloger (**gthumb.sourceforge.net**)
GPicView	Image browser, similar to Windows Picture Viewer.
GIMP	GNU Image Manipulation Program (**www.gimp.org**)
Inkscape	GNOME Vector graphics application (**www.inkscape.org**)
Eye of Gnome	GNOME Image Viewer
gpaint	GNOME paint program
OpenOffice Draw	OpenOffice Draw application
X Window System	
Xpaint	Paint program
Xfig	Drawing program
ImageMagick	Image format conversion and editing tool

Table 6-2: Graphics Tools for Linux

GIMP is the GNU Image Manipulation Program, a sophisticated image application much like Adobe Photoshop. You can use GIMP for such tasks as photo retouching, image composition, and image authoring. It supports features such as layers, channels, blends, and gradients. GIMP makes particular use of the GTK+ widget set. You can find out more about GIMP and download the newest versions from its Web site at **www.gimp.org**. GIMP is freely distributed under the GNU Public License.

Inkscape is a Gnome based vector graphics application for SVG (scalable vector graphics) images. It features capabilities similar to professional level vector graphics applications like Adobe Illustrator. The SVG format allows easy generation of images for Web use as well as complex art. Though its native format is SVG, it can also export to PNG format. It features layers and easy object creation, including stars and spirals. A color bar lets you quickly change color fills.

The gPhoto project provides software for accessing digital cameras (**www.gphoto.org**). Several front-end interfaces are provided for a core library, called libgphoto2, consisting of drivers and tools that can access numerous digital cameras.

Tip: The Windows version of Photoshop is now supported by Wine. You can install Photoshop CS on Fedora using Wine and then access it through the Wine Windows support tool. Once started, Photoshop will operate like any Linux desktop application.

X Window System Graphic Programs

X Window System–based applications run directly on the underlying X Window System, which supports the more complex desktops like GNOME and KDE. These applications tend to be simpler, lacking the desktop functionality found in GNOME or KDE applications. Xpaint is a paint program, much like MacPaint. You can load graphics or photographs, and then create shapes, add text, and add colors. You can use brush tools with various sizes and colors. Xfig is a drawing program. ImageMagick lets you convert images from one format to another; you can, for instance, change a TIFF image to a JPEG image. Table 6-2 lists some popular graphics tools for Linux.

Multimedia

Many applications are available for both video and sound, including sound editors, MP3 players, and video players (see Tables 6-5 and 6-6). Linux sound applications include mixers, digital audio tools, CD audio writers, MP3 players, and network audio support. There are literally thousands of projects currently under development.

Note: Linux has become a platform of choice for many professional-level multimedia tasks such as generating computer-generated images (CGI), using such demanding software as Maya and Softimage. Linux graphic libraries include those for OpenGL, MESA, and SGI.

Many applications designed specifically for the GNOME or KDE user interface can be found at their respective software sites (**www.gnomefiles.org** and **www.kde-apps.org**). Precompiled binary RPM packages for most applications are at the Fedora repository, or in third party repositories like RPM Fusion.

Omega Fedora Spin

For those who want to install a multimedia system, like that for an HTPC, you can use the Omega spin of Fedora 10. The Omega 10 Desktop includes Fedora 10 as well as many free and non-free multimedia codecs and applications available from the RPM Fusion repository. It also includes the DVDCSS codec for commercial DVD Video playback from the Livna repository (**libdvdcss**). The spin installs a very basic Fedora GNOME desktop with an extensive set of multimedia packages, but with minimal packages for other categories like Office and Graphics. Most applications are to be found in the Applications | Sound and Video menu (see Figure 6-3).

You can download the Omega spin from:

```
ftp://ftp.infradead.org/pub/spins/
```

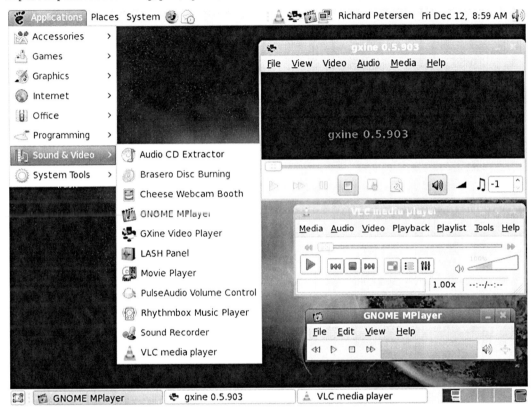

Figure 6-3: Omega desktop

Certain specialized multimedia applications like MythTV for video recording are not installed. The advantage of installing Omega is that all your multimedia codecs are automatically installed during installation. As you install more multimedia applications, the codecs they require will already be available. Figure 6-4 shows that Omega has installed both the **libdvdcss** package from the Livna repositories, as well as other supporting DVD packages from the RPM Fusion repository.

Codec Support with PackageKit

PackageKit is designed to work with GStreamer to detect and install needed codecs. Whenever you try to run a media file using a GStreamer supported application like the Totem Movie player, and the codec is missing, PackageKit is run to check for a supporting codec packages and let you install them.

If you have RPM Fusion support installed for YUM, PackageKit will find and install multimedia codecs not included with the official Fedora release. For MP3, you will be able to download the MP3 codec directly, including the free licensed Fluendo version, and have PackageKit install it. There are also several multimedia codecs such as MPEG2 (DVD video), MPEG4 (DivX), Dolby AC3 audio, and MPEG video playback.

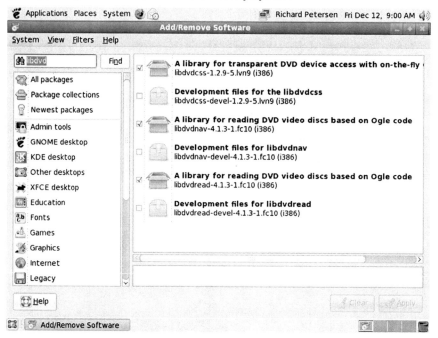

Figure 6-4: Omega installed codec and support

Codeina, the Codec Installation helper used in Fedora 9, has been replaced by PackageKit support.

For Fedora, you can also purchase third party commercial and fully licensed codecs like Window media or Dolby codecs from Fluendo (**www.fluendo.com**). Fluendo provides many licensed codecs, most for a small fee. Currently Fluendo provides a free MP3 licensed codec for playing MP3 music files, already integrated into RPM Fusion.

Third Party multimedia codecs with license issues

Fedora does not include any codecs or applications that may have licensing restrictions of any kind. These include multimedia codecs like the DVD Video decoder and the MP3 music decoder, as well as proprietary vendor graphics drivers like NVIDIA's own graphics driver. A list of forbidden items is located at:

http:// www.fedoraproject.org/wiki/ForbiddenItems

Many of these codecs are available from RPM Fusion, http:**//rpmfusion.org**. A listing of popular multimedia codecs available at these sites is shown in Table 6-3. Of particular interest may be the a52dec, faad2, and lame codecs for sound decoding, as well as the xvidcore, x264, and libdvbpsi for video decoding. For GStreamer supported applications like the Totem movie player, you will need a special set of packages called gstreamer-plugins-bad and gstreamer-plugins-ugly. The packages labeled freeworld provide open source solutions for added capability, like DVD support for Xine and MP3 support for Audacious. For extensive video and DVD support, you can install VLC media player (**vlc-core** package). The commercial DVD-Video codec DVDCSS is only available from the Livna repository directly, **rpm-livna.org**, not from RPM Fusion. The **libdvdcss** package is the only package on Livna, all other having been moved to RPM Fusion.

Obtaining the DVDCSS DVD-Video codec from Livna and Freshrpms

There is one exception. The **dvdcss** decryption coded used to playback commercial DVD-Video discs, is not included in the RPM-Fusion repositories, free or nonfree. Due to licensing issues, the dcss codec could not be included in the RPM-Fusion repository. Instead this codec remain the only software package still available on the Freshrpms.net and Livna repositories. All other packages from Freshrpms and Livna have been transferred to RPM-Fusion and are no longer available on the Freshrpms and Livna repositories. In effect these repositories currently have only one package, the **dvdcss** DVD-Video decryption package. The package is same in either repository. You only need to access one or the other.

To obtain the **dvdcss** decryption package you can either download it directly from Livna or Freshrpms and install it, or you can install the Livna repository YUM configuration package, and then use PackageKit to install the dcss package from Livna. The Livna Web site is at **http://rpm.livna.org**. You could instead install the Freshrpms YUM configuration package. You only need one. Both have the same **libdvdcss** package.

For Livna, to insure installation of the correct Livna YUM repository package, open a terminal window and enter the following command. You will prompt to enter your root user password. The **su** command logins as the root user, and the **-c** option indicates a command to run. The command to run is an **rpm** command to install (**ivh**) the **livna-release.rpm** package, which will be downloaded by **rpm** from **http://rpm.livna.org**.

```
su -c "rpm -ivh http://rpm.livna.org/livna-release.rpm"
```

Once installed, you can search for the **libdvdcss** package on PackageKit, which will then install the correct version for your system.

The actual Livna **libdvdcss** package is located at:

```
http://rpm.livna.org/fedora/10/
```

There will be x86_64 and i386 directories.

Should you want to use Freshrpms instead, the Freshrpms YUM configuration package is:

```
freshrpms-release-1.2-1.noarch.rpm
```

The Freshrpms YUM configuration package is located here:

```
http://ftp.freshrpms.net/pub/freshrpms/fedora/linux/10/freshrpms-release/
```

The Freshrpms **libdvdcss** package is located at:

```
http://ftp.freshrpms.net/pub/freshrpms/fedora/linux/10/libdvdcss/
```

Package	Description
a52dec	HDTV audio (ATSC A/52, AC3)
faad2	MPEG2/4 AAC audio decoding, high quality
faac	MPEG2/4 AAC sound encoding and decoding
ffmpeg, ffmpeg-libs	Play, record, convert, stream audio and video. Includes digital streaming server, conversion tool, and media player.
gstreamer-ffmpeg	ffmpeg plug-in for GStreamer
gstreamer-plugins-bad	Not fully reliable codecs and tools for GStreamer, some with possible licensing issues.
gstreamer-plugins-ugly	reliable video and audio codecs for GStreamer that may have licensing issues
audacious-plugins-freeworld-mp3, -aac, -wma	MP3, AAC, and WMA plugin packages for Audacious
lame	MP3 playback capability, not an official MP3 decoder
libdca	DTS Coherent Acoustics playback capability
libdvbpsi	MPEG TS stream (DVB and PSI) decoding and encoding capability, VideoLAN project.
libdvdnav	DVD video menu navigation
fame, libfame	Fast Assembly MPEG video encoding
libmad	MPEG1 and MPEG2 audio decoding
libmpeg3	MPEG video audio decoding (MPEG1/2 audio and video, AC3, IFO, and VOB)
libquicktime	Quicktime playback
libopendaap	Itunes support
mpeg2dec	MPEG2 and MPEG1 playback
twolame	MPEG audio layer 2, MP2 encoding
x264	H264/AVC decoding and encoding (high definition media)
xvidcore	OpenDivx codec (DivX and Xvid playback)
smpeg	Smpeg MPEG video and audio decoder for SPLAY
swfdec	FLASH animation decoding
totem-xine	Totem movie player using Xine libraries instead of gstreamer
vlc-core	DVD video playback capability, VideoLan project.
xine-lib-extras-freeworld	Added video and audio playback capability for Xine

`libdvdcss`	DVD-Video codec for commercial DVDs. Available only from Livna or Freshrpms repositories or Web sites: http://rpm.livna.org. Not available from RPM-Fusion.

Table 6-3: Multimedia third-party codecs

Tip: Both the Livna (**http://rpm.livna.org**) and the Freshrpms (**http://freshrpms.net**) repositories still maintain packages for earlier Fedora releases. Livna locates theirs in its archive directory. With Fedora 10, they no longer provide packages, except for the **libdvdcss** DVD-Video package.

As noted in Chapter 4, there are also several third party multimedia applications you may want. Three of the major applications with their recommended sites for Fedora are shown here. All are available through RPM Fusion.

Xine	Xine multimedia player
MPlayer	MPlayer multimedia player
MythTV	Home media center
VLC	VideoLAN network/media, **vlc-core**

GStreamer

Many of the GNOME-based applications make use of GStreamer. GStreamer is a streaming media framework based on graphs and filters. Using a plug-in structure, GStreamer applications can accommodate a wide variety of media types. You can download modules and plug-ins from **gstreamer.freedesktop.org**. Fedora includes several GStreamer applications:

➢ The Totem video player uses GStreamer to play DVDs, VCDs, and MPEG media.

➢ Rhythmbox provides integrated music management; it is similar to the Apple iTunes music player.

➢ Sound Juicer is an audio CD ripper.

➢ A CD player, a sound recorder, and a volume control are all provided as part of the GStreamer GNOME Media package.

GStreamer Multimedia System Selector

GStreamer can be configured to use different input and output sound and video drivers and servers. You can make these selections using the GStreamer properties tool. To open this tool from the Desktop menu, first select Preferences, then More Preferences, and then the Multimedia Systems Selector entry. You can also enter `gstreamer-properties` in a terminal window. The properties window displays two tabbed panels, one for sound and the other for video. The output drivers and servers are labeled Default Sink, and the input divers are labeled Default Source. There are pop-up menus for each listing the available sound or video drivers or servers. For example the sound server used is ALSA, but you can change that to OSS.

GStreamer Plug-ins: the Good, the Bad, and the Ugly

Many GNOME multimedia applications like Totem use GStreamer to provide multimedia support. To use such features as DVD Video and MP3, you have to install GStreamer extra plug-ins. You can find out more information about GStreamer and its supporting packages at **gstreamer.freedesktop.org**.

The supporting packages can be confusing. For version 1.0 and above, GStreamer establishes four different support packages called the base, the good, the bad, and the ugly. The base package is a set of useful and reliable plug-ins. These are in Fedora the repository. The good package is a set of supported and tested plug-ins that meets all licensing requirements. This is also part of the Fedora repository. The bad is a set of unsupported plug-ins whose performance is not guaranteed and may crash, but still meet licensing requirements. The ugly package contains plug-ins that work fine, but may not meet licensing requirements, like DVD support. These you can obtain from the RPM Fusion repositories.

> **The base**   Reliable commonly used plug-ins

> **The good**   Reliable additional and useful plug-ins

> **The ugly**   Reliable but not fully licensed plug-ins (DVD/MP3 support)

> **The bad**   Possibly unreliable but useful plug-ins (possible crashes)

Another plug-in for GStreamer that you may want include is ffmpeg, **gstreamer-ffmpeg** (RPM Fusion repositories). ffmpeg provides several popular codecs, including ogg and .264. For Pulse (sound server) and Farsight (video conferencing) support, use their respective gstreamer plugins on the Fedora repository.

PackageKit will automatically detect the codec you will need to use for your GStreamer application. For commercial codecs like MP3 or AAC, PackageKit will select the appropriate RPM Fusion package (with RPM Fusion enabled). For commercial DVD-Video, you can install the libdvdcss package from the Livna repository (**rpm.livna.org**). You can also purchase and download the codec plugins from Fluendo (**www.fluendo.com**).

To download and install the GStreamer plug-in packages, just search for **gstreamer** on Add/Remove Software. If you have enabled RPM Fusion or repository, you will also see entries for the ugly and bad packages. Alternatively, you could use the following YUM command to install all plug-ins at once. Be sure to include the asterisk to match on all the plug-in packages. Your architecture (i586, i686, or x86_64) will automatically be detected.

```
yum install gstreamer-plugins*
```

GStreamer MP3 Compatibility

To play MP3 song files as well as songs from your iPod and other MP3 devices to work with GNOME applications like Rhythmbox, you will need to install MP3 support for GStreamer. MP3 support is not included with Fedora distributions because of licensing issues. You can, however, download and install the GStreamer **gstreamer-plugins-ugly** package which contains most multimedia support codecs and applications that are not included with the distribution. You can install the package from **http://rpmfusion.org**. Just be sure that the RPM Fusion repository is configured for your system. The package will then appear in PackageKit, which you can then use to install it.

IPod

To play songs from your IPod, Fedora provides the **libgpod** library for GNOME and **libipoddevice** for HAL. These allow player applications like Rythmbox and Amarok to use your iPod. Gstreamer MP3 support is provided by the **gstreamer-plugins-ugly** package.

To sync, import, or extract from your iPod, you can use iPod management software such as GUI for iPod, **gtkpod**, and **ipod-sharp** for higher level features. Several tools are currently available for iPod access; they include gpixpod, gpodder, and CastPodder.

Sound Drivers and Interfaces

Sound devices on Linux are supported by hardware sound drivers. With the current Fedora kernel, hardware support is implemented by the Advanced Linux Sound Architecture (ALSA) system. ALSA replaces the free version of the Open Sound System used in previous releases, as well as the original built-in sound drivers. You can find more about ALSA at **www.alsa-project.org**. See Table 6-4 for a listing of sound device and interface tools.

Your sound cards are automatically detected for you when you start up your system. Your sound cards should all be detected for you. Your sound devices are automatically detected by ALSA, which is invoked by udev when your system starts up. Removable devices, like USB sound devices, will also be detected.

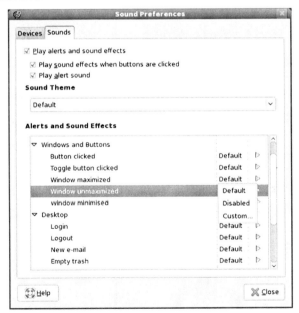

Figure 6-5: Sound Preferences

You select preferences for your sounds using the GNOME sound preferences. On GNOME choose System | Preferences | Hardware | Sound. This opens the Sound Preferences window, which has two panels: Devices and Sounds (see Figure 6-5). On the Devices panel you can select the sound interface to use for Sound Events, Music and Movies, and Audio

Conferencing, as well as for Default Mixer Tracks. Normally the ALSA interface is selected. You can use PulseAudio instead.

The Sounds panel lets you select a sound theme, enabling system sounds for particular tasks like check boxes or logouts. The Sound effects lets you use visual sounds like flashes on the desktop for your system sounds. Sound themes can be selected from the pop-up menu under the Sound Themes label. The Alerts and Sound Effects pane then lists the sound and effects supported by the theme. You can click on the Default entry for a sound to open a pop-up menu with entries for Disable, Default, and Custom. Disable to turn off that particular alert or effect. Custom will open a window with sound files where you can select your own sound to use, located in **/usr/share/sounds**. (see Figure 6-6). Sound themes are implemented according to the Freedesktop.org Sound Theme and Naming Specification.

Figure 6-6: Selecting custom sounds

Connection Configuration: GNOME Volume Control

Various output and input connections are then activated and configured during automatic configuration. The standard connections are activated, but others, like SPDIF digital connections, may not. You can mute and un-mute, as well as control the volume of different connection with either GNOME Volume Control or KDE KMix. KMix will provide a complete display of every connection on your system, whereas GNOME Volume Control will show only those selected for display. KMix will show SPDIF connections, but GNOME Volume Control may not.

As an alternative to either GNOME Volume Control or KMix, you can also use the command-line ALSA control tool, **alsamixer**. This will display all connections and allow you to use keyboard command to select (arrow keys), mute (m key), or set sound levels (Page Up and Down). Use Escape to exit. The **amixer** command lets you perform the same tasks for different sound connections from the command line. To actually play and record from the command-line, you can use the **play** are **rec** commands.

Sound tool	Description
GNOME Volume Control	GNOME sound connection configuration and volume tool
KMix	KDE sound connection configuration and volume tool
alsamixer	ALSA sound connection configuration and volume tool
amixer	ALSA command for sound connection configuration
play	Command to play sound
rec	Command to record sound
Sound Preferences	GNOME Sound Preferences, used to select sound interface like ALSA or PulseAudio (System | Preferences | Hardware | Sound)
PulseAudio	PulseAudio sound interface, selected in Sound Preferences, www.pulseaudio.org
PulseAudio Volume Control	PulseAudio Volume Control (Applications | Sound and Video menu), controls stream input, output, and playback, pavucontrol package.
PulseAudio Volume Meter	Volume Meter (Applications | Sound and Video menu), displays active sound levels, pavumeter package
PulseAudio Manager	Manager for information and managing PulseAudio, pman package (Applications | Sound and Video menu)
PulseAudio Device Chooser	Device selection, padevchooser (Applications | Sound and Video menu)
PulseAudio Preferences	Options for network access and virtual output, papref. (System | Preferences menu)

Table 6-4: Sound device and interface tools

You can access GNOME Volume Control tool either from the sound applet your top panel, or from System | Preferences | Hardware | Volume Control menu entry (see Figure 6-6). Depending upon the kinds of devices displayed, there may be as many as four tabs: Playback, Recording, Switches, and Options, depending on the sound playback and recording sources selected. If recording devices (capture) are selected, then the recording tab is displayed showing those devices. The Switches tab usually has just an entry for headphones. If capture devices are displayed, the Options tab would show a pop-up menu for streams like PCM. In Figure 6-7, the digital playback sources are selected. This will display a Recording tab for digital capture and an Options panel for selecting a digital playback source.

On the Playback tab you can set the sound levels for different connections, both right or left, locking them together, or muting the connection altogether. Only a few commonly used connections are displayed. To display others, you need to configure the Volume Control properties.

To set the default sound device, select the device from the drop down menu labeled Device at the top of the Volume Control window. These are the same devices listed in the Sound Preferences Device pop-up menu. You can easily switch between defaults using just the Volume Control.

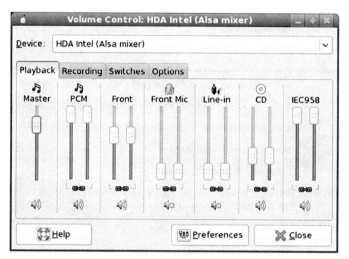

Figure 6-6: GNOME Volume Control

Figure 6-7: Volume Control Preferences, SPDIF selection

Configuring digital output for SPDIF (digital) connectors can be confusing. The digital output may be muted by default. You will have to first configure GNOME Volume Control Preferences to display the SPDIF digital connection. To display the Preferences window, either right-click on the sound applet and select Preferences, or select Preferences from Edit menu. The Preferences window will list all possible connections (tracks) on your system, with checks for those that will be displayed (see Figure 6-7). From the list of tracks find the device name of the optical output and click its checkbox. This will make it show up on the Volume control window. Once your digital output is selected, you can then un-mute it by clicking on the Volume control applet and then clicking on the digital output sound segment's sound icon. The red x should disappear.

The name of the SPDIF output is not always obvious. You may need to run **aplay -L** in a terminal window to see what the name of the digital output device is on your system. It will be the entry with Digital in it. On an Intel chip system this could be something like IEC958 for Intel HDA sound devices found on many computer motherboards.

PulseAudio and sound interfaces

In addition to hardware drivers, sound system also use sound interfaces to direct encoded sound streams from an application to the hardware drivers and devices. There are a multitude of sound interfaces. ALSA and OSS have their own. Some operate as daemons like the Enlightened Sound Daemon (ESD) used for Gstreamer applications. The JACK server can share audio streams between applications.

Figure 6-8: PulseAudio selected in Sound Preferences, System | Preferences | Hardware | Sound

This multitude of sound interfaces, though still available, has been superseded on Fedora the PulseAudio server. PulseAudio aims to combine and consolidate all sound interfaces into a simple, flexible, and powerful server. The ALSA hardware drivers are still used, but the application interface is handled by PulseAudio.

PulseAudio provides packages for interfacing with Gstreamer, MPlayer, ALSA, and xmms, and Xine, replacing those sound interfaces with PulseAudio. The KDE aRts interface is not supported as aRts also performs its own synthesizing.

PulseAudio is cross-platform sound server, allowing you to modify the sound level for different audio streams separately. See **www.pulseaudio.org** for documentation and help. PulseAudio offers complete control over all your sound streams, letting you combine sound devices and direct the stream anywhere on your network. PulseAudio is not confined to a single system. It is network capable, letting you direct sound from one PC to another. Installed with Pulse Audio are the Pulse Audio tools. These are command line tools for managing Pulse Audio and playing sound files. The **paplay** and **pacat** will play a sound files, **pactl** will let you control the sound server and **pacmd** lets you reconfigure it.

Pulse audio is installed as the default set up for Fedora. Each user can choose to use Pulse Audio or not. Activation is performed from GNOME or KDE desktop preferences (see Figure 6-8). On GNOME choose System | Preferences | Hardware | Sound. Then on the Devices Panel, you can select Pulse Audio from the various pop-up menus.

For full easy configuration be sure to install all the Pulse Audio GUI tools. Most begin with the prefix **pa** in the package name. To select all of them for installation, search for and install either **paman** or **padevchooser**.

padevchooser

The **padevchooser** tool is a gnome applet that can be used to start up all the other pulseaudio tools. Except for PulseAudio Preferences and PulseAudio Device Chooser, menu entries are not set up for these tools. You would use the PulseAudio Device Chooser applet (**padevchooser**) to run them. Should you not want to run the applet, you can open a terminal window and enter their commands, starting them directly. They will then run as GUI GNOME applications. For example, you can open a terminal window and enter the command **paman** to run the PulseAudio Manager. The PulseAudio tools and their command names are shown here.

```
PulseAudio Volume Control, pavucontrol
PulseAudio Volume Meter, pavumeter
PulseAudio Manager, paman
PulseAudio Device Chooser, pavdevchooser
PulseAudio Preferences, papref
```

The PulseAudio tools and the Device Chooser are shown in Figure 6-7.

To run the PulseAudio Device Chooser applet select its entry in the Applications | Sound & Video menu. The PulseAudio Device Chooser applet will appear in the top panel to the right. The applet's Preferences dialog has an option for starting the Pulse Audio Device Chooser automatically. To select a PulseAudio tool, left-click on the PulseAudio Device Chooser icon and select the tool from the pop-up menu (see Figure 6-9). There are entries for Manager (PulseAudio Manager), Volume Control, Volume Meter (Playback and Recording), and Configure Local Sound Server (PulseAudio Preferences, **papref**). You can also use the Device Chooser to select the default server, sink (output device), and source (input device) should there be more than one. Passing the mouse over an entry will display detailed information about the interface, device, or server.

PulseAudio could be running on different hosts and configured by different users on a given host. You can choose which one to use.

Figure 6-9: PulseAudio Device Chooser menu and applet icon, Applications | Sound & Video | PulseAudio Device Chooser

Once PulseAudio is activated, you can use the PulseAudio Volume Control tool to set the sound levels for different playback applications and sound devices (select Volume Control on the PulseAudio Device Chooser applet, choose Applications | Sound & Video | PulseAudio Volume Control, or enter **pavucontrol** in a terminal window). The PulseAudio Volume Control applications will show three panels: Playback, Output Devices, and Input Devices (see Figure 6-10). The Playback panel shows all the applications currently use PulseAudio. You can adjust the volume for each application separately.

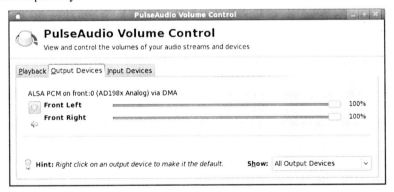

Figure 6-10: PulseAudio Volume Control, Applications | Sound & Video | PulseAudio Volume Control

You can also use the Output devices panel to set the volume control at the source. Input devices are for capture or microphone input, and can also be adjusted.

You can also use the PulseAudio Volume control to direct different applications (streams) to different outputs (devices). For example you could have two sound sources running, one for video and another for music. The video could be directed through one device to headphones and the music through another device to the speakers, or even to another PC. To redirect an application to a different device, right-click on it in the Playback panel. A pop-up menu will list the available devices and let you select the one you want to use.

The PulseAudio Volume Meter will show the actual volume of your devices Volume Meter, see Figure 6-11 (select Volume Meter, Playback or Recording, on the PulseAudio Device Chooser applet menu, or enter **pavumeter** in a terminal window).

Figure 6-11: PulseAudio Volume Meter

The PulseAudio Manager will show information about your PulseAudio configuration (select Manager on the PulseAudio Device Chooser applet menu; choose Applications | Sound & Video | PulseAudio Manager, or enter **paman** in a terminal window). Devices panel shows the currently active sinks (outputs or directed receivers) and sources (see Figure 6-12). The Clients panel will show all the applications currently using PulseAudio for sound

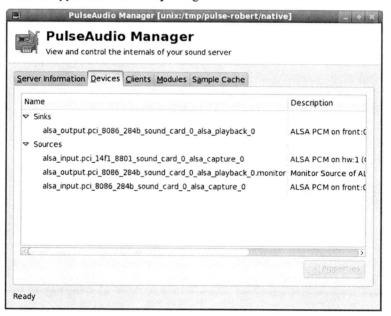

Figure 6-12: PulseAudio Manager Devices panel

To configure network access, you use the PulseAudio Configuration tool (choose System | Preferences | PulseAudio Configuration, or select Configure Local Sound Server on the PulseAudio Device Chooser applet menu). Here you can permit network access (see Figure 6-13). You can also enable multicast and simultaneous output. Simultaneous output creates a virtual output device to the same hardware device. This lets you channel two sources onto the same output. With PulseAudio Volume Control you could then channel playback streams to the same output device, but using a virtual device as the output for one. This lets you change the output volume for each stream independently. You could have music and voice directed to the same hardware device, using a virtual device for music and the standard device for voice. You can then reduce the music stream, or raise the voice stream.

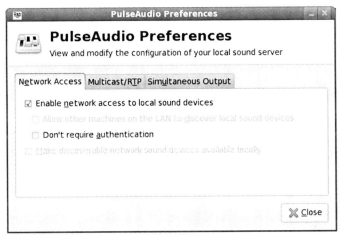

Figure 6-13: PulseAudio Preferences selected in System | Preferences | PulseAudio Preferences

Note: To enable the sound on ATI HDMI capable HD graphics cards, you will need ALSA release. Be sure to upgrade.

Music Applications

Many music applications are currently available for GNOME, including sound editors, MP3 players, and audio players (see Table 6-5). You can use the Rhythmbox and Sound Juicer to play music from different sources, and the GNOME Sound Recorder to record sound sources. A variety of applications are also available for KDE, including the media players Amarok, a mixer (KMix), and a CD player (Kscd).

GNOME includes sound applications like the XMMS2 multimedia player, GNOME CD Player, Sound Juicer (Audio CD Extractor), and Rhythmbox in the Sound And Video menu. Rhythmbox is the default sound multimedia player, supporting music files, radio streams, and podcasts. KDE applications include Amarok and Juk. Amarok is the primary multimedia player for KDE4. JuK (Music Jukebox) is the KDE4 music player for managing music collections. Linux systems also support HelixPlayer, the open source project used for RealPlayer.

Application	Description
Xine	Multimedia player for video, DVD, and audio
Rhythmbox	Music management (GStreamer), default CD player with iPod support.
Sound Juicer	GNOME CD audio ripper (GStreamer)
Grip	CD audio ripper
Amarok	KDE4 multimedia player
Kscd	Music CD player
Juk	KDE4 Music player (jukebox) for managing music collections
GNOME CD Player	CD player
GNOME Sound Recorder	Sound recorder
XMMS	CD player
Xplaycd	Music CD player
RealPlayer	RealMedia and RealAudio streaming media (**www.real.com**)
HelixPlayer	Open source version of Real Player (**www.real.com**)

Table 6-5: Music Players and Rippers Applications

MP3 with Lame

LAME originally stood for **L**ame **A**in't an **Mp3 E**ncoder, but it has long since evolved into a full MP3 encoder whose software is available under the LPGL license. It is included with VideoLAN and FFmpeg, and YUM will download from RPM Fusion in support of MPlayer or Xine.

Due to licensing and patent issues, Fedora does not include support for MP3 files, though RPM Fusion does. MP3 playback capability has been removed from multimedia players like XMMS and Noatun. As an alternative to MP3, you can use Ogg Vorbis compression for music files (**www.vorbis.com**).

CD Burners

Several CD ripper and writer programs that can be used for CD music and MP3 writing (burners and rippers). These include Sound Juicer, Brasero (see Chapter 3), K3b, and Grip (See Table 6-6). GNOME also features two CD audio rippers installed with Fedora, Grip and Sound Juicer. For burning DVD/CD data discs, you can use Brasero and the Nautilus CD/DVD burner. The Nautilus CD/DVD burner is integrated into the Nautilus file manager, the default file manager for the GNOME desktop. For KDE you can use K3b

Qdvdauthor, dvdauthor, Brasero, and K3b can all be used to create DVD Video discs. All use mkisofs, cdrecord, and cdda2wav DVD/CD writing programs, which are installed as part of your distribution. DVD Video and CD music rippers may require addition codecs installed, which the codec wizard will prompt you for

Application	Description
Brasero	Full service CD/DVD burner, for music, video, and data discs.
Sound Juicer	GNOME music player and CD burner and ripper
Serpentine	GNOME music CD burner and ripper.
ogmrip	DVD transcoding with DivX support
K3b	KDE CD writing interface
dvdauthor	Tools for creating DVDs (**http://dvdauthor.sourceforge.net**).
Qdvdauthor	KDE front end for dvdauthor (**www.kde-apps.org**)

Table 6-6: DVD Burners

Video Applications

Several projects provide TV, video, DivX, DVD, and DTV support for Linux (see Table 6-7). Many of these applications are not on the Fedora Software repository. In some cases, the most recent versions will be in source code format on the original site. For these you will have to download the source code, which you will then need to compile and install. Most applications, though, are already available in binary RPM packages on the RPM Fusion repository (**http://rpmfusion.org**). Use one of the other. You should not mix the two. It is recommended that you install the RPM Fusion YUM configuration file first, and then use either PackageKit (System | Administration | Add/Remove Software), Yumex (Applications | System Tools), or the **yum** command on a command line (Terminal window) to install the applications.

Video and DVD Players

Several popular video and DVD players are listed here.

➢ The VideoLAN project (**www.videolan.org**) offers network streaming support for most media formats, including MPEG-4, x264, and MPEG-2. It includes a cross-platform multimedia player, VLC.

➢ MPlayer is one of the most popular and capable multimedia/DVD players in use. It is a cross-platform open source alternative to RealPlayer and Windows Media Player. MPlayer includes support for DivX. You can download MPlayer from **www.mplayerhq.hu**. MPlayer uses an extensive set of supporting libraries and supporting applications like **lirc**, **lame**, **lzo**, and **aalib**. If you have trouble displaying video, be sure to check the preferences for different Video devices, selecting one that works best.

➢ Xine is a multipurpose video player for Linux/Unix systems that can play video, DVD, and audio discs. See **http://xinehq.de** for more information. Xine is available in source code form, which you will have to compile and install, though you can download an RPM binary from **http://rpmfusion.org**.

➢ Totem, installed with Fedora, is a GNOME movie player based on Xine that uses GStreamer. To expand Totem capabilities, you need to install added GStreamer plug-ins (see Figure 6-14). Totem now features plugins for DVB, MythTV, and YouTube search.

214 Part 2: Applications

> Dragon Player is a KDE4 multimedia player, installed with KDE4 desktop (see Figure 6-15)

> Kaffeine, installed with KDE, is a KDE multimedia player numerous formats, including DVD, DVB, and Music CDs.

> KMPlayer is a KDE movie player (older movie player)

> kdtv KDE television viewer

> tvtime TV viewer

> Additions codec support is supplied by ffmpeg and x264. The x264 codec is an open source version, developed by VideoLAN, of the high definition H.264 codec.

Projects and Players	Sites
LinuxTV.org	Links to video, TV, and DVD sites: **www.linuxtv.org**
Xine	Xine video player: **www.xinehq.de**
Totem	Totem video and DVD player for GNOME based on Xine and using GStreamer, includes plugins for DVB, YouTube, nd MythTV: **www.xinehq.de**
VideoLAN	Network multimedia streaming, includes x264 high definition support. **www.videolan.org**
MPlayer	MPlayer DVD/multimedia player **www.mplayerhq.hu**
MythTV	Home media center with DVD, DVR, and TV capabilities **www.mythtv.org** (package included with RPM Fusion)
kdetv	KDE TV viewer
tvtime	TV viewer, **http://tvtime.sourceforge.net**
DivX for Linux	**http://labs.divx.com/DivXLinuxCodec** (requires direct download)
XviD	Open Source DivX, **www.xvid.org**
Dragon Player	Dragon Player video and DVD player for KDE4

Table 6-7: Video and DVD Projects and Applications

None of the open source software on the Fedora Software repository performs CSS decryption of commercial DVDs. You could, however, download and install the **libdvdcss** library from the Livna repository (**http://rpm.livna.org**), which works around CSS decryption by treating the DVD as a block device, allowing you to use any of the DVD players to run commercial DVDs. It is also provides region-free access. Bear in mind that this may be not be legal in certain countries that require CSS licenses for DVD players. See the previous section "Obtaining the DVDCSS DVD-Video codec from Livna and Freshrpms".

Originally, many of these players did not support DVD menus. With the **libdvdnav** and **libdvdplay** libraries, these players now feature full DVD menu support. The **libdvdread** library provides basic DVD interface support such as reading IFO files. You can download RPM binaries for these packages from the RPM Fusion repository using PackageKit.

Figure 6-14: Totem Movie player

TV Players

The site **www.linuxtv.org** provides detailed links to DVD, digital video broadcasting (DVB), and multicasting. The site also provides downloads of many Linux video applications.

The primary TV player on Fedora is tvtime, which works with many common video capture cards, relying on drivers developed for TV tuner chips on those cards like the Conexant chips. It can only display a TV image. It has no recording or file playback capabilities. Check **http://tvtime.sourceforge.net** for more information.

Dragon Player, Kaffiene, and Kdetvare KDE multimedia players that will also play TV.

MythTV, popular video recording and playback application on Linux systems. (RPM Fusion repository). See **www.mythbuntu.org** for more information.

For KDE and GNOME, several video applications are available or currently under development. Check **www.kde-apps.org** for KDE player, for GNOME players check **www.gnomefiles.org**. Most are available on the Fedora repositories.

Tip: Many graphics cards do not provide support for HDTV (H264) hard ware acceleration in Linux, though that is rapidly changing. Software acceleration with the x264 codec is adequate.

Figure 6-15: KDE4 Dragon Player

DVB and HDTV support

For DVB and HDTV reception you can use most DVB cards as well as many HDTV cars like the PCHDTV video card (**www.pdhdtv.com**). For the latest PCHDTV card, you can use the c88-dvb drivers included with Fedora. For earlier versions you would have to download, compile, and install a separate driver. The DVB kernel driver is installed by default.

Many DVB capable applications like Kaffeine already have DVB accessibility installed. The GNOME Movie Player (Totem) now also has a DVB plugin for viewing DVB channels. You can also use the dvb-tools to manage access. The DVB tools can also be used to record HDTV and DVB broadcasts to TS (transport stream) files. The transport stream (**.ts** or **.tp**) file can then be viewed with an HDTV capable viewer, such as the HDTV versions of Xine or Videolan VLC media player. You can use MythTV and vdr (video disk recorder) to view and record. Check the MythTV site for details (**www.mythtv.org**).

Be sure appropriate decoders are installed like mpeg2, FFmpeg, and A52 (ac3). For DVB broadcasts, many DVB capable players and tools like Kaffeine and Klear, as well as vdr will tune and record DVB broadcasts in t, s, and c formats. The dvb-tools package holds sample configurations.

For the PCHDTV card and related cards using the connextant c88 chips like FusionTV, the c88x DVB kernel module will automatically be detected and loaded. You can then use the PCHDTV atsc tools to access and record programs. From the PCHDTV site, download the **atsc-dvb-tools**. These are source code programs you will have to compile. Uzip the archive file to a directory. In a terminal window change to that directory issue the **make** and **make install** commands. Be sure you have already downloaded and installed the kernel development packages.

```
make
make install
```

You can then use the **getatsc** and **dtvsignal** commands, among others to check and record HDTV receptions. The following records a channel to a file.

```
getatsc 12 > my.ts
```

This is an open ended process that will continue until you kill the process. To stop the recording you could do the following which uses the **ps** command to obtain the process id (pid) for the **getatsc** process. These getatsc and kill operations can be set up with cron tasks (GNOME Schedule) to implement automatic recording like a DVR or VCR.

```
kill `ps -C getatsc -o pid=`
```

You could then use any application like VideoLAN or a DVB enabled Totem movie player (**a52dec** and **libdvbpsi**) to play back the file.

You can also use the **dvb-apps** packages available on the Fedora repository to manage viewing. The dvb-tools include a **scandvb** for scanning your channels and the **azap** tool for accessing the signal directly. You will first need to create a channels configuration file using scandvb. This tool makes use of channel frequencies kept in the **/usr/share/dvb-tools/atsc** directory. There are files for ATSC broadcast as well as cable. Redirect the results into a channels configuration file like **channels.conf** which you can then use to tune and record using applications like Xine, MythTV, or MPlayer.

DivX and Xvid on Linux

MPEG-4 compressed files for provide DVD-quality video with relatively small file sizes. They have become popular for distributing high quality video files over the Internet. When you first try to play an MPEG-4, the codec wizard will prompt you to install the needed codec packages to play it. Many multimedia applications like VLC already support Mpeg4 files.

DivX is a commercial video version of MPEG-4 compress video files, free for personal use. You can download the Linux version of DivX for free from **http://labs.divx.com/DivXLinuxCodec**. You have to manually install the package, following the instructions. Keep in mind that most multimedia software like VideoLan and MPlayer will include support for playing DivX files.

An alternative, you can use the open source version of DivX known as Xvid (**xvidcore** package on RPM Fusion repository). Most DivX files can be run using XviD. XviD is an entirely independent open source project, but it's compatible with DivX files (**http://xvid.org**).

To convert DVD Video files to an MPEG-4/DivX format you can use **transcode** or **ffmpeg**. Many DVD burners can these to convert DVD video files to DivX/Xvid files.

7. Mail and News

Your Linux system supports a wide range of both electronic mail and news clients. Mail clients enable you to send and receive messages with other users on your system or accessible from your network. News clients let you read articles and messages posted in a newsgroups, which are open to access by all users. This chapter reviews mail and news clients installed with Fedora Linux.

Mail Clients

You can send and receive e-mail messages in a variety of ways, depending on the type of mail client you use. Although all electronic mail utilities perform the same basic tasks of receiving and sending messages, they tend to have different interfaces. Some mail clients operate on a desktop, such as KDE or GNOME. Others run on any X Window System managers. Several popular mail clients were designed to use a screen-based interface and can be started only from the command line. Other traditional mail clients were developed for just the command line interface, which requires you to type your commands on a single command line. Most mail clients described here are included in standard Linux distributions and come in a standard RPM package for easy installation. For Web-based Internet mail services, such as Hotmail, GMail, and Yahoo, you use a Web browser instead of a mail client to access mail accounts provided by those services. Table 7-1 lists several popular Linux mail clients. Mail is transported to and from destinations using mail transport agents. Sendmail, Exim, and Smail send and receive mail from destinations on the Internet or at other sites on a network. To send mail over the Internet, they use the Simple Mail Transport Protocol (SMTP). Most Linux distributions, including Fedora, automatically install and locally configure Sendmail for you. On starting up your system, having configured your network connections, you can send and receive messages over the Internet.

Mail Client	Description
Kontact (KMail, KAddressbook, KOrganizer)	Includes the K Desktop mail client, KMail; integrated mail, address book, and scheduler
Evolution	E-mail client
Thunderbird	Mozilla group stand-alone mail client and newsreader
Sylpheed	Gtk mail and news client
Claws-mail	Extended version of sylpheed Email client
GNUEmacs and XEmacs	Emacs mail clients
Mutt	Screen-based mail client
Mail	Original Unix-based command line mail client
Squirrel Mail	Web-based mail client

Table 7-1: Linux Mail Clients

You can sign your e-mail message with the same standard signature information, such as your name, Internet address or addresses, or farewell phrase. Having your signature information automatically added to your messages is helpful. To do so, you need to create a signature file in your home directory and enter your signature information in it. A *signature file* is a standard text file you can edit using any text editor. Mail clients such as KMail enable you to specify a file to function as your signature file. Others, such as Mail, expect the signature file to be named **.signature**.

MIME

MIME (the term stands for *Multipurpose Internet Mail Extensions*) is used to enable mail clients to send and receive multimedia files and files using different character sets such as those for different languages. Multimedia files can be images, sound clips, or even video. Mail clients that support MIME can send binary files automatically as attachments to messages. MIME-capable mail clients maintain a file called **mailcap** that maps different types of MIME messages to applications on your system that can view or display them. For example, an image file will be mapped to an application that can display images. Your mail clients can then run that program to display the image message. A sound file will be mapped to an application that can play sound files on your speakers. Most mail clients have MIME capabilities built in and use their own version of the **mailcap** file. Others use a program called metamail that adds MIME support. MIME is not only used in mail clients. Both the KDE and GNOME file managers use MIME to map a file to a particular application so that you can launch the application directly from the file.

Though you can create your own MIME types, a standard set already is in use. The types text, image, audio, video, application, multipart, and message, along with their subtypes, have already been defined for your system. You will find that commonly used file extensions such as **.tif** and **.jpg** for TIFF and JPEG image files are already associated with a MIME type and an application. Though you can easily change the associated application, it is best to keep the MIME types already installed. The current official MIME types are listed at the IANA Web site (**www.iana.org**) under the name Media Types, provided as part of their Assignment Services. You can access the media types file directly on their site.

S/MIME and OpenPGP/MIME are authentication protocols for signing and encrypting mail messages. S/MIME was originally developed by the RSA Data Security. OpenPGP is an open standard based on the PGP/MIME protocol developed by the PGP (Pretty Good Privacy) group. Clients like KMail and Evolution can use OpenPGP/MIME to authenticate messages. Check the Internet Mail Consortium for more information, **www.imc.org**.

Evolution

Evolution is the primary mail client for the GNOME desktop. It is installed by default along with OpenOffice. Though designed for GNOME, it will work equally well on KDE. Evolution is an integrated mail client, calendar, and address book, currently being developed by Novell and now known as the Novell Evolution. The Evolution mailer is a powerful tool with support for numerous protocols (SMTP, POP, and IMAP), multiple mail accounts, and encryption. With Evolution, you can create multiple mail accounts on different servers, including those that use different protocols such as POP or IMAP. You can also decrypt PGP- or GPG-encrypted messages.

The Evolution mailer provides a simple GUI interface, with a toolbar for commonly used commands and a sidebar for shortcuts. A menu of Evolution commands allows access to other operations. The main panel is divided into two panes, one for listing the mail headers and the other for displaying the currently selected message. You can click any header title to sort your headers by that category. Evolution also supports the use of virtual folders. These are folders created by the user to hold mail that meets specified criteria. Incoming mail can be automatically distributed to their particular virtual folder.

To configure Evolution, select Preferences from the Edit menu. On the Evolution Preferences window, a sidebar holds icons for main accounts, auto-completion, mail preferences, composition preference, calendar and task and certificates. The main accounts entry displays a list of current accounts. An Add button lets you add new ones, and the Edit button allows you to change current accounts. When editing an account, you have Account Editor Displays panels for Identity, Receiving email (your incoming mail server), sending email (outgoing mail server), and security (encryption and digital signatures). The Mail Preferences entry is where you configure how Evolution displays and manages messages. In the Compose Preferences entry lets you set up composition features like signatures, formatting, and spell-checking. The Automatic Contact panel in Mail Preferences is where you can specify that addresses of mail you reply to should be automatically added to the Evolution address book. To see and manage the contacts in your address book, click on the Contacts button on the left lower sidebar.

With evolution you can also create search folders to organize access to your messages. A search folder is not an actual folder. It simply collects links to messages based on certain search criteria. Using search folders, you can quickly display messages on a given topic, subject, or from a specific user. In effect, it performs an automatic search on messages as they arrive. To set up a search folder, select Search Folders in the Edit menu and click Add to open the Add Rule window. Here you can add criteria for searches and the folders to search. You can also right-click a message header that meets criteria you want searched and select Create Rule from Message, and then one of the Search Rule entries.

To extend Evolution's capabilities, numerous plugins are available. Most are installed and enabled for you automatically, including the SpamAssasin plugin for handling junk mail. To manage your plugins, select the Plugin entry in the Edit menu. This opens the Plugin Manger, with plugins listed in a left side scroll window and configuration panels located for a selected plugin on the right side.

Evolution also supports filters. You can use filters to automatically direct some messages to certain folders, instead of having all incoming messages placed in the inbox folder. To create a filter, you can select the Message Filters entry in the Edit menu and click Add to open the Add Rule message. You can also right-click on the header of a message whose head meets your criteria, like a subject or sender, and select Create Rule from Message and select a Filter entry for sender, subject, or recipient. On the Add Rule window you can add other criteria and also specify the action to take, like moving the message to a certain folder. You can also add other actions like assigning a score, changing the color, copying the message, or just deleting it.

Note: Other GNOME mail clients include sylpheed and Claws-mail. Sylpheed is a mail and news client with an interface similar to Windows mail clients. Claws-mail is an extended version of Sylpheed with many additional features (**www.claws-mail.org**).

Thunderbird

Thunderbird is a full-featured stand-alone e-mail client provided by the Mozilla project (**www.mozilla.org**). It is designed to be easy to use, highly customized, and heavily secure. It features advanced intelligent spam filtering, as well as security features like encryption, digital signatures, and S/MIME. To protect against viruses, e-mail attachments can be examined without being run. Thunderbird supports both Internet Message Access Protocol (IMAP) and the Post Office Protocol (POP), as well as functioning as a newsreader. It also features a built-in RSS reader. Thunderbird also supports the use of Lightweight Directory Access Protocol (LDAP) address books. Thunderbird is an extensible application, allowing customized modules to be added to enhance its capabilities. You can download extensions such as dictionary search and contact sidebars from its Web site. GPG encryption can be supported with the enigmail extension.

The interface uses a standard three-pane format, with a side pane for listing mail accounts and their boxes. The top pane lists main entries, and the bottom pane shows text. Command can be run using the toolbar, menus, or keyboard shortcuts. You can even change the appearance using different themes. Thunderbird also supports HTML mail, displaying Web components like URLs in mail messages.

The message list pane will show several fields by which you can sort your messages. Some use just symbols like the Threads, Attachments, and Read icons. Clicking Threads will gather the messages into respective threads with replies grouped together. The last icon in the message list fields is a pop-up menu letting you choose which fields to display. Thunderbird provides a variety of customizable display filters, such as People I Know, which displays only messages from those in your address book, and Attachments, which displays messages with attached files. You can even create your own display filters. Search and sorting capabilities also include filters that can match selected patterns in any field, including subject, date, or the message body.

When you first start up Thunderbird, you will be prompted to create an e-mail account. You can add more e-mail accounts or modify your current ones by selecting Account Settings from the Edit menu. Then click Add Account to open a dialog with four options, one of which is an e-mail account. Upon selecting the Email option, you are prompted to enter your e-mail address and name. In the next panel you specify either the POP or IMAP protocol and enter the name of the incoming e-mail server, such as **smtp.myemailserver.com**. You then specify an incoming user name, the user name given you by your e-mail service. Then you enter an account name label to identify the account on Thunderbird. A final verification screen lets you confirm your entries. In the Account Settings window you will see an entry for your news server, with panels for Server Settings, Copies & Folders, Composition & Addressing, Offline & Disk Space, Return Receipt, and Security. The Server Settings panel has entries for your server name, port, user name, and connection and task configurations such as automatically downloading new messages. The Security panel opens the Certificate Manager, where you can select security certificates to use to digitally sign or encrypt messages.

Thunderbird provides an address book where you can enter complete contact information, including e-mail addresses, street addresses, phone numbers, and notes. Select Address Book from the Tools menu to open the Address Book window. There are three panes, one for the address books available, one listing the address entries with field entries like name, e-mail, and organization, and one for displaying address information. You can sort the entries by these fields. Clicking an entry will display the address information, including e-mail address, street addresses, and phone. Only fields with values are displayed. To create a new entry in an address book, click New Card to open a window with panels for Contact and Address information. To create mailing lists from the address book entries, you click the New List button, specify the name of the list, and enter the e-mail addresses.

Once you have your address book set up, you can use its addresses when creating mail messages easily. On the Compose window, click the Contacts button to open a Contacts pane. Your address book entries will be listed using the contact's name. Just click the name to add it to the address box of your e-mail message. Alternatively, you can open the address book and drag and drop addresses to an address box on your message window.

A user's e-mail messages, addresses, and configuration information are kept in files located in the **.thunderbird** directory within the user's home directory. Backing up this information is as simple as making a copy of that directory. Messages for the different mail boxes are kept in a **Mail** subdirectory. If you are migrating to a new system, you can just copy the directory from the older system. To back up the mail for any given mail account, just copy the **Mail** subdirectory for that account. Though the default address books, **abook.mab** and **history.mab**, can be interchangeably copied, non-default address books need to be exported to an LDIF format and then imported to the new Thunderbird application. It is advisable to regularly export your address books to LDAP Data Interchange Format (LDIF) files as backups.

GNOME Mail Clients: Evolution, Sylpheed, and Others

Several GNOME-based mail clients are now available (see Table 7-2). These include Evolution, and Sylpheed (Evolution is included with Fedora). Check **www.gnomefiles.org** for more mail clients as they come out. Many are based on the GNOME mail client libraries (camel), which provides support for standard mail operations. As noted previously, Evolution is an integrated mail client, calendar, and contact manager from Novell. Sylpheed is a mail and news client with an interface similar to Windows mail clients. Claws-mail is an extended version of Sylpheed with many additional features (**www.claws-mail.org**).

Application	Description
Evolution	Integrated mail client, calendar, and contact manager
Sylpheed	Mail and news client similar to Windows clients
gnubiff	E-mail checker and notification tool
Mail Notification	E-mail checker and notification that works with numerous mail clients, including MH, Sylpheed, Gmail, Evolution, and Mail
Claws-mail	Extended version of sylpheed

Table 7-2: GNOME Mail Clients

The K Desktop Mail Client

The: KMail K Desktop mail client, KMail, provides a full-featured GUI interface for composing, sending, and receiving mail messages. KMail is now part of the KDE Personal Information Management suite, KDE-PIM, which also includes an address book (KAddressBook), an organizer and scheduler (KOrganizer), and a note writer (KNotes). All these components are also directly integrated on the desktop into Kontact. To start up KMail, you start the Kontact application. The KMail window displays three panes for folders, headers, and messages. The upper-left pane displays your mail folders. You have an inbox folder for received mail, an outbox folder for mail you have composed but have not sent yet, and a sent-mail folder for messages you have previously sent. You can create your own mail folders and save selected messages in them, if you wish. The top-right pane displays mail headers for the currently selected mail folder. To display a message, click its header. The message is then displayed in the large pane below the header list. You can also send and receive attachments, including binary files. Pictures and movies that are received are displayed using the appropriate K Desktop utility. If you right-click the message, a pop-up menu displays options for actions you may want to perform on it. You can move or copy it to another folder, or simply delete it. You can also compose a reply or forward the message. KMail, along with Kontact, KOrganizer, and KaddressBook, is accessible from the KDE Desktop, Office, and Internet menus.

To set up KMail for use with your mail accounts, you must enter account information. Select the Configure entry in the Settings menu. Several panels are available on the Settings window, which you can display by clicking their icons in the left column. For accounts, you select the Network panel. You may have more than one mail account on mail servers maintained by your ISP or LAN. A configure window is displayed where you can enter login, password, and host information. For secure access, KMail now supports the Secure Sockets Layer (SSL), provided OpenSSL is installed. Messages can now be encrypted and decoded by users. It also supports IMAP in addition to POP and SMTP protocols.

SquirrelMail

You Web Mail Client use the SquirrelMail Web mail tool to access mail on a Linux system using your Web browser. It will display a login screen for mail users. It features an inbox list and message reader, support for editing and sending new messages, and a plug-in structure for adding new features. You can find out more about SquirrelMail at **www.squirrelmail.org**. The Apache configuration file is **/etc/httpd/conf.d/squirrelmail.conf**, and SquirrelMail is installed in **/usr/share/squirrelmail**. Be sure that the IMAP mail server is also installed.

To configure SquirrelMail, you use the **config.pl** script in the **/usr/share/squirrelmail/config** directory. This displays a simple text-based menu where you can configure settings like the server to use, folder defaults, general options, and organizational preferences.

```
./config.pl
```

To access SquirrelMail, use the Web server address with the **/squirrelmail** extension, as in **localhost/squirrelmail** for users on the local system, or **www.mytrek.com/squirrelmail** for remote users.

Emacs

The Emacs mail clients are integrated into the Emacs environment, of which the Emacs editor is the primary application. They are, however, fully functional mail clients. The GNU version of Emacs includes a mail client along with other components, such as a newsreader and editor. GNU Emacs is included on Fedora distributions. Check the Emacs Web site at **www.gnu.org/software/emacs** for more information. When you start up GNU Emacs, menu buttons are displayed across the top of the screen. If you are running Emacs in an X Window System environment, you have full GUI capabilities and can select menus using your mouse. To access the Emacs mail client, select from the mail entries in the Tools menu. To compose and send messages, just select the Send Mail item in the Tools menu. This opens a screen with prompts for To and Subject header entries. You then type the message below them, using any of the Emacs editing capabilities. GNU Emacs is a working environment within which you can perform a variety of tasks, with each task having its own buffer. When you read mail, a buffer is opened to hold the header list, and when you read a message, another buffer will hold the contents. When you compose a message, yet another buffer holds the text you wrote. The buffers you have opened for mail, news, or editing notes or files are listed in the Buffers menu. You can use this menu to switch among them.

XEmacs is another version of Emacs, designed to operate solely with a GUI interface. The Internet applications, which you can easily access from the main XEmacs button bar, include a Web browser, a mail utility, and a newsreader. When composing a message, you have full use of the Emacs editor with all its features, including the spell-checker and search/replace.

Command Line Mail Clients

Several mail clients use a simple command line interface. They can be run without any other kind of support, such as the X Window System, desktops, or cursor support. They are simple and easy to use but include an extensive set of features and options. Two of the more widely used mail clients of this type are Mail and Mutt. Mail is the mailx mail client that was developed for the UNIX system. It is considered a kind of default mail client that can be found on all UNIX and Linux systems. Mutt is a cursor-based client that can be run from the command line.

Note: You can also use the Emacs mail client from the command line, as described in the previous section.

Mutt

Mutt has an easy-to-use screen-based interface. Mutt has an extensive set of features, such as MIME support. You can find more information about Mutt from the Mutt Web site, **www.mutt.org**. Here you can download recent versions of Mutt and access online manuals and help resources. On most distributions, the Mutt manual is located in the **/usr/doc** directory under Mutt. The Mutt newsgroup is **comp.mail.mutt**, where you can post queries and discuss recent Mutt developments.

Mail

What is known now as the Mail utility was originally created for BSD Unix and called, simply, mail. Later versions of Unix System V adopted the BSD mail utility and renamed it mailx. Now, it is simply referred to as Mail. Mail functions as a de facto default mail client on UNIX and Linux systems. All systems have the mail client called Mail, whereas they may not have other mail clients.

To send a message with Mail, type `mail` along with the address of the person to whom you are sending the message. Press ENTER and you are prompted for a subject. Enter the subject of the message and press ENTER again. At this point, you are placed in input mode. Anything typed in is taken as the contents of the message. Pressing ENTER adds a new line to the text. When you finish typing your message, press CTRL-D on a line of its own to end the message. You will then be prompted to enter a user to whom to send a carbon copy of the message (Cc). If you do not want to send a carbon copy, just press ENTER. You will then see *EOT (end-of-transmission)* displayed after you press CTRL-D

You can send a message to several users at the same time by listing those users' addresses as arguments on the command line following the `mail` command. In the next example, the user sends the same message to both **chris** and **aleina**.

```
$ mail chris aleina
```

To receive mail, you enter only the `mail` command and press ENTER. This invokes a Mail shell with its own prompt and mail commands. A list of message headers is displayed. Header information is arranged into fields beginning with the status of the message and the message number. The status of a message is indicated by a single uppercase letter, usually N for *new* or U for *unread.* A message number, used for easy reference to your messages, follows the status field. The next field is the address of the sender, followed by the date and time the message was received, and then the number of lines and characters in the message. The last field contains the subject the sender gave for the message. After the headers, the Mail shell displays its prompt, an ampersand (**&**). At the Mail prompt, you enter commands that operate on the messages. An example of a Mail header and prompt follows:

```
$ mail
Mail version 8.1 6/6/93. Type ? for help.
"/var/spool/mail/larisa": 3 messages 2 unread
 1 chris@turtle.mytrek. Thu Jun 7 14:17 22/554 "trip"
>U 2 aleina@turtle.mytrek Thu Jun 7 14:18 22/525 "party"
 U 3 dylan@turtle.mytrek. Thu Jun 7 14:18 22/528 "newsletter"
& q
```

Mail references messages either through a message list or through the current message marker (>). The greater-than sign (>) is placed before a message considered the current message. The current message is referenced by default when no message number is included with a Mail command. You can also reference messages using a message list consisting of several message numbers. Given the messages in the preceding example, you can reference all three messages with **1-3**.

You use the **R** and **r** commands to reply to a message you have received. The **R** command entered with a message number generates a header for sending a message and then places you into the input mode to type in the message. The **q** command quits Mail. When you quit, messages you have already read are placed in a file called **mbox** in your home directory. Instead of saving messages in the **mbox** file, you can use the **s** command to save a message explicitly to a file of your choice. Mail has its own initialization file, called **.mailrc**, that is executed each time Mail is invoked, for either sending or receiving messages. Within it, you can define Mail options and create Mail aliases. You can set options that add different features to mail, such as changing the prompt or saving copies of messages you send. To define an alias, you enter the keyword **alias**, followed by the alias you have chosen and then the list of addresses it represents. In the next example, the alias **myclass** is defined in the **.mailrc** file.

```
alias myclass chris dylan aleina justin larisa
```

In the next example, the contents of the file **homework** are sent to all the users whose addresses are aliased by **myclass**.

```
$ mail myclass < homework
```

Notifications of Received Mail

As your mail messages are received, they are automatically placed in your mailbox file, but you are not automatically notified when you receive a message. You can use a mail client to retrieve any new messages, or you can use a mail monitor tool to tell you if you have any mail waiting. Several mail notification tools are also available, such as **gnubiff** and Mail Notification.

Mail Notification will support Gmail, as well as Evolution (for Evolution, install the separate plug-in package). When you first log in after Mail Notification has been installed, the Mail Notification configuration window is displayed. Here you can add new mail accounts to check, such as Gmail accounts, as well as set other features like summary pop-ups. When you receive mail, a mail icon will appear in the notification applet of your panel. Move your cursor over it to check for any new mail. Clicking it will display the Mail Notification configuration window, though you can configure this to go directly to your e-mail application. **gnubiff** will notify you of any POP3 or IMAP mail arrivals.

The KDE Desktop has a mail monitor utility called Korn that works in much the same way. Korn shows an empty inbox tray when there is no mail and a tray with slanted letters in it when mail arrives. If old mail is still in your mailbox, letters are displayed in a neat square. You can set these icons as any image you want. You can also specify the mail client to use and the polling interval for checking for new mail. If you have several mail accounts, you can set up a Korn profile for each one. Different icons can appear for each account, telling you when mail arrives in one of them.

For command line interfaces, you can use the biff utility. The biff utility notifies you immediately when a message is received. This is helpful when you are expecting a message and want to know as soon as it arrives. Then biff automatically displays the header and beginning lines of messages as they are received. To turn on biff, you enter `biff y` on the command line. To turn it off, you enter `biff n`. To find out if biff is turned on, enter `biff` alone.

You can temporarily block biff by using the `mesg n` command to prevent any message displays on your screen. The `mesg n` command not only stops any Write and Talk messages, it also stops biff and Notify messages. Later, you can unblock biff with a `mesg y` command. A `mesg n` command comes in handy if you don't want to be disturbed while working on some project.

Accessing Mail on Remote POP Mail Servers

Most new mail clients are equipped to access mail accounts on remote servers. For such mail clients, you can specify a separate mail account with its own mailbox. For example, if you are using an ISP, most likely you will use that ISP's mail server to receive mail. You will have set up a mail account with a username and password for accessing your mail. Your e-mail address is usually your username and the ISP's domain name. For example, a username of **justin** for an ISP domain named **mynet.com** would have the address **justin@mynet.com**. The username would be **justin**. The address of the actual mail server could be something like **mail.mynet.com**. The user **justin** would log in to the **mail.mynet.com** server using the username **justin** and password to access mail sent to the address **justin@mynet.com**. Mail clients, such as Evolution, KMail, Sylpheed, and Thunderbird, enable you to set up a mailbox for such an account and access your ISP's mail server to check for and download received mail. You must specify what protocol a mail server uses. This is usually either the Post Office Protocol (POP) or the IMAP protocol (IMAP). This procedure is used for any remote mail server. Using a mail server address, you can access your account with your username and password.

Should you have several remote e-mail accounts, instead of creating separate mailboxes for each in a mail client, you can arrange to have mail from those accounts sent directly to the inbox maintained by your Linux system for your Linux account. All your mail, whether from other users on your Linux system or from remote mail accounts, will appear in your local inbox. Such a feature is helpful if you are using a mail client, such as Mail, that does not have the capability to access mail on your ISP's mail server. You can implement such a feature with Fetchmail. Fetchmail checks for mail on remote mail servers and downloads it to your local inbox, where it appears as newly received mail (you will have to be connected to the Internet or the remote mail server's network).

To use Fetchmail, you have to know a remote mail server's Internet address and mail protocol. Most remote mail servers use the POP3 protocol, but others may use the IMAP or POP2 protocols. Enter `fetchmail` on the command line with the mail server address and any needed options. The mail protocol is indicated with the `-p` option and the mail server type, usually POP3. If your e-mail username is different from your Linux login name, you use the `-u` option and the e-mail name. Once you execute the `fetchmail` command, you are prompted for a password. The syntax for the `fetchmail` command for a POP3 mail server follows:

```
fetchmail -p POP3 -u username mail-server
```

Connect to your ISP and then enter the `fetchmail` command with the options and the POP server name on the command line. You will see messages telling you if mail is there and, if so, how many messages are being downloaded. You can then use a mail client to read the messages from your inbox. You can run Fetchmail in daemon mode to have it automatically check for mail. You have to include an option specifying the interval in seconds for checking mail.

```
fetchmail -d 1200
```

You can specify options such as the server type, username, and password in a **.fetchmailrc** file in your home directory. You can also have entries for other mail servers and accounts you may have. Once it is configured, you can enter `fetchmail` with no arguments; it will read entries from your **.fetchmailrc** file. You can also make entries directly in the **.fetchmailrc** file. An entry in the **.fetchmailrc** file for a particular mail account consists of several fields and their values: poll, protocol, username, and password. *Poll* is used to specify the mail server name, and *protocol,* the type of protocol used. Notice you can also specify your password, instead of having to enter it each time Fetchmail accesses the mail server.

Mailing Lists

As an alternative to newsgroups, you can subscribe to mailing lists. Users on mailing lists automatically receive messages and articles sent to the lists. Mailing lists work much like a mail alias, broadcasting messages to all users on the list. Mailing lists were designed to serve small, specialized groups of people. Instead of posting articles for anyone to see, only those who subscribe receive them. Numerous mailing lists, as well as other subjects, are available for Linux. For example, at the **www.gnome.org** site, you can subscribe to any of several mailing lists on GNOME topics, such as **gnome-themes-list@gnome.org**, which deals with GNOME desktop themes. You can do the same at **lists.kde.org** for KDE topics. At **www.liszt.com**, you can search for mailing lists on various topics. By convention, to subscribe to a list, you send a request to the mailing list address with a **–request** term added to its username. For example, to subscribe to **gnome-themes-list@gnome.org**, you send a request to **gnome-themes-list-request@gnome.org**. At **www.linux.org**, on the Documentation page you can access a listing of mailing lists and submit subscriptions. Lists exist for such topics as the Linux kernel, administration, security, and different distributions. For example, **linux-admin** covers administration topics, and **linux-apps** discuses software applications; **vger.kernel.org** provides mailing list services for Linux kernel developers.

Note: You can use the Mailman and Majordomo programs to automatically manage your mailing lists. Mailman is the GNU mailing list manager, included with Fedora (**www.list.org**). You can find out more about Majordomo at **www.greatcircle.com/majordomo**, and about Mailman at **sourceforge.net**.

Usenet News

Usenet is an open mail system on which users post messages that include news, discussions, and opinions. It operates like a mailbox that any user on your Linux system can read or send messages to. Users' messages are incorporated into Usenet files, which are distributed to any system signed up to receive them. Each system that receives Usenet files is referred to as a *site*. Certain sites perform organizational and distribution operations for Usenet, receiving messages from other sites and organizing them into Usenet files, which are then broadcast to many other sites. Such sites are called *backbone sites,* and they operate like publishers, receiving articles and organizing them into different groups.

To access Usenet news, you need access to a news server. A news server receives the daily Usenet newsfeeds and makes them accessible to other systems. Your network may have a system that operates as a news server. If you are using an Internet service provider (ISP), a news server is probably maintained by your ISP for your use. To read Usenet articles, you use a *newsreader*—a client program that connects to a news server and accesses the articles. On the Internet and in TCP/IP networks, news servers communicate with newsreaders using the Network News Transfer Protocol (NNTP) and are often referred to as NNTP news servers. Or you could also create your own news server on your Linux system to run a local Usenet news service or to download and maintain the full set of Usenet articles. Several Linux programs, called *news transport agents,* can be used to create such a server. This chapter focuses on the variety of newsreaders available for the Linux platform.

Usenet files were originally designed to function like journals. Messages contained in the files are referred to as *articles.* A user could write an article, post it in Usenet, and have it immediately distributed to other systems around the world. Someone could then read the article on Usenet, instead of waiting for a journal publication. Usenet files themselves were organized as journal publications. Because journals are designed to address specific groups, Usenet files were organized according to groups called *newsgroups.* When a user posts an article, it is assigned to a specific newsgroup. If another user wants to read that article, he or she looks at the articles in that newsgroup. You can think of each newsgroup as a constantly updated magazine. For example, to read articles on the Linux operating system, you would access the Usenet newsgroup on Linux. Usenet files are also used as bulletin boards on which people carry on debates. Again, such files are classified into newsgroups, though their articles read more like conversations than journal articles. You can also create articles of your own, which you can then add to a newsgroup for others to read. Adding an article to a newsgroup is called *posting* the article.

Note: The Google Web site maintains online access to Usenet newsgroups. It has the added capability of letting you search extensive newsgroup archives. You can easily locate articles on similar topics that may reside in different newsgroups. Other sites such as Yahoo maintain their own groups that operate much like Usenet newsgroups, but with more supervision.

Linux has newsgroups on various topics. Some are for discussion, and others are sources of information about recent developments. On some, you can ask for help for specific problems. A selection of some of the popular Linux newsgroups is provided here:

Newsgroup	Topic
comp.os.linux.announce	Announcements of Linux developments
comp.os.linux.admin	System administration questions
comp.os.linux.misc	Special questions and issues
comp.os.linux.setup	Installation problems
comp.os.linux.help	Questions and answers for particular problems
linux.help	Obtain help for Linux problems

Newsreaders

You read Usenet articles with a newsreader, such as KNode, Pan, Mozilla, trn, or tin, which enables you to first select a specific newsgroup and then read the articles in it. A newsreader operates like a user interface, enabling you to browse through and select available articles for reading, saving, or printing. Most newsreaders employ a sophisticated retrieval feature called *threads* that pulls together articles on the same discussion or topic. Newsreaders are designed to operate using certain kinds of interfaces. For example, KNode is a KDE newsreader that has a KDE interface and is designed for the KDE desktop. Pan has a GNOME interface and is designed to operate on the GNOME desktop. Pine is a cursor-based newsreader, meaning that it provides a full-screen interface that you can work with using a simple screen-based cursor that you can move with arrow keys. It does not support a mouse or any other GUI feature. The **tin** program uses a simple command line interface with limited cursor support. Most commands you type in and press ENTER to execute. Several popular newsreaders are listed in Table 7-3.

Newsreader	Description
Pan	GNOME Desktop newsreader
KNode	KDE Desktop newsreader
Thunderbird	Mail client with newsreader capabilities (X based)
Sylpheed	GNOME Windows-like newsreader
Slrn	Newsreader (cursor based)
Emacs	Emacs editor, mail client, and newsreader (cursor based)
trn	Newsreader (command line interface)
NewsBin	Newsreader (Windows version works under Wine)

Table 7-3: Linux Newsreaders

Note: Numerous newsreaders currently are under development for both GNOME and KDE. You can check for KDE newsreaders on the software list on the K Desktop Web site at **www.kde-apps.org**. For GNOME newsreaders, check Internet tools on the software map on the GNOME Web site at **www.gnome-files.org**.

Most newsreaders can read Usenet news provided on remote news servers that use the NNTP. Many such remote news servers are available through the Internet. Desktop newsreaders, such as KNode and Pan, have you specify the Internet address for the remote news server in their own configuration settings. Several shell-based newsreaders, however, such as trn and tin, obtain the news server's Internet address from the **NNTPSERVER** shell variable. Before you can connect to a remote news server with such newsreaders, you first have to assign the Internet address of the news server to the **NNTPSERVER** shell variable, and then export that variable. You can place the assignment and export of **NNTPSERVER** in a login initialization file, such as **.bash_profile**, so that it is performed automatically whenever you log in. Administrators could place this entry in the **/etc/profile** file for a news server available to all users on the system.

```
$ NNTPSERVER=news.domain.com
$ export NNTPSERVER
```

Newsbin under Wine

There is as yet not good binary based newsreader, one that can convert text messages to binary equivalents, like those found in **alt.binaries** newsgroups. One solution is to use the Windows version of the popular NewsBin newsreader running under Wine (Windows compatibility layer for Linux). You need to install Wine first. The current version of Newsbin runs stable and fast with Wine (you may need to use the video hardware drives for your graphics card).

You can download and install Wine using the Synaptic Package Manager. Then download and install Newsbin. The current version of Newsbin works on Wine and Fedora with no modifications needed. Newsbin will be accessible directly from an icon on your desktop as you would any application. It is advisable to disable the Message of the Day (MOTD) feature on the Options Advanced panel. You can save files directly on any Linux file system, as well as newsgroup downloads. The Autorar feature works effectively for binary files. Your entire Linux files system along with any mounted files systems is accessible as the **z:** drive. To test Par2 files for binaries you will need to also download and install QuickPar, another windows program the works effectively on Wine (**www.quickpar.org.uk**). QuickPar will be accessible from Newsbin.

slrn

The **slrn** newsreader is screen-based. Commands are displayed across the top of the screen and can be executed using the listed keys. Different types of screens exist for the newsgroup list, article list, and article content, each with its own set of commands. An initial screen lists your subscribed newsgroups with commands for posting, listing, and subscribing to your newsgroups. When you start slrn for the first time, you may will have to create a **.jnewsrc** file in your home directory. Use the following command: **slrn -f .jnewsrc -create**. Also, you will have to set the **NNTPSERVER** variable and make sure it is exported.

The slrn newsreader features a new utility called **slrnpull** that you can use to automatically download articles in specified newsgroups. This allows you to view your selected newsgroups offline. The slrnpull utility was designed as a simple single-user version of Leafnode; it will access a news server and download its designated newsgroups, making them available through slrn whenever the user chooses to examine them. Newsgroup articles are downloaded to the **SLRNPULL_ROOT** directory. On Fedora, this is **/var/spool/srlnpull**. The selected newsgroups to be downloaded are entered in the **slrnpull.conf** configuration file placed in the **SLRNPULL_ROOT** directory. In this file, you can specify how many articles to download for each group and when they should expire. To use **slrn** with **slrnpull**, you will have to further configure the **.slrnrc** file to reference the **slrnpull** directories where newsgroup files are kept.

News Transport Agents

Usenet news is provided over the Internet as a daily newsfeed of articles and postings for thousands of newsgroups. This newsfeed is sent to sites that can then provide access to the news for other systems through newsreaders. These sites operate as news servers; the newsreaders used to access them are their clients. The news server software, called *news transport agents,* is what provides newsreaders with news, enabling you to read newsgroups and post articles. For Linux, three of the popular news transport agents are INN, Leafnode, and Cnews. Both Cnews and Leafnode are small and simple, and useful for small networks. INN is more powerful and complex, designed with large systems in mind (see **www.isc.org** for more details).

Daily newsfeeds on Usenet are often large and consume much of a news server's resources in both time and memory. For this reason, you may not want to set up your own Linux system to receive such newsfeeds. If you are operating in a network of Linux systems, you can designate one of them as the news server and install the news transport agent on it to receive and manage the Usenet newsfeeds. Users on other systems on your network can then access that news server with their own newsreaders.

If your network already has a news server, you needn't install a news transport agent at all. You only have to use your newsreaders to remotely access that server (see **NNTPSERVER** in the preceding section). In the case of an ISP, such providers often operate their own news servers, which you can also remotely access using your own newsreaders, such as KNode and Pan. Remember, though, that newsreaders must take the time to download the articles for selected newsgroups, as well as updated information on all the newsgroups.

You can also use news transport agents to run local versions of news for only the users on your system or your local network. To do this, install INN, Leafnode, slrnpull, or Cnews and configure them just to manage local newsgroups. Users on your system could then post articles and read local news.

8. Internet Applications: Web, FTP, Java, IM, VoIP, and Online Desktop

Web Browsers

Firefox

Epiphany

Java, OpenJDK

Network File Transfer: FTP

VoIP: Ekiga and Skype

Instant Messenger: Pidgin, Empathy, and Kopete

GNOME Online Desktop

Fedora provides powerful Web and FTP clients for accessing the Internet. Many are installed automatically and are ready to use when you first start up your Linux system. Linux also includes full Java development support, letting you run and construct Java applets. This chapter will cover some of the more popular Web, Java, and FTP clients available on Linux. Web and FTP clients connect to sites that run servers, using Web pages and FTP files to provide services to users. There are also network tools for setting up messaging connections, like Pidgin for Instant Messages (IM) and Ekiga for Voice over Internet Protocol (VoIP) connections.

Web Clients

The World Wide Web (WWW, or the Web) is a hypertext database of different types of information, distributed across many different sites on the Internet. A *hypertext database* consists of items linked to other items, which, in turn, may be linked to yet other items, and so on. Upon retrieving an item, you can use that item to retrieve any related items. For example, you could retrieve an article on the Amazon rain forest and then use it to retrieve a map or a picture of the rain forest. In this respect, a hypertext database is like a web of interconnected data you can trace from one data item to another. Information is displayed in pages known as *Web pages.* On a Web page, certain keywords or graphics are highlighted that form links to other Web pages or to items, such as pictures, articles, or files.

On your Linux system, you can choose from several Web browsers, including Firefox, Konqueror, Epiphany, and Lynx. Firefox, Konqueror, and Epiphany are X Window System–based browsers that provide full picture, sound, and video display capabilities. Most distributions also include the Lynx browser, a line-mode browser that displays only lines of text. The K Desktop incorporates Web browser capabilities into its file manager, letting a directory window operate as a Web browser. GNOME-based browsers, such as Express and Mnemonic, are also designed to be easily enhanced.

Web browsers and FTP clients are commonly used to conduct secure transactions such as logging in to remote sites, ordering items, or transferring files. Such operations are currently secured by encryption methods provided by the Secure Sockets Layer (SSL). If you use a browser for secure transactions, it should be SSL enabled. Most browsers such as Mozilla and ELinks include SSL support. For FTP operations, you can use the SSH version of ftp, **sftp**, or the Kerberos 5 version. Linux distributions include SSL as part of a standard installation.

URL Addresses

An Internet resource is accessed using a Universal Resource Locator (URL). A URL is composed of three elements: the transfer protocol, the hostname, and the pathname. The transfer protocol and the hostname are separated by a colon and two slashes, *://*. The *pathname* always begins with a single slash:

```
transfer-protocol://host-name/path-name
```

The *transfer protocol* is usually HTTP (Hypertext Transfer Protocol), indicating a Web page. Other possible values for transfer protocols are **ftp**, and **file**. As their names suggest, **ftp** initiates FTP sessions, whereas **file** displays a local file on your own system, such as a text or HTML file. Table 8-1 lists the various transfer protocols.

Protocol	Description
`http`	Uses Hypertext Transfer Protocol for Web site access.
`ftp`	Uses File Transfer Protocol for FTP connections.
`fish`	Uses File Transfer Protocol using SSH secure connection.
`telnet`	Makes a Telnet connection.
`news`	Reads Usenet news; uses Network News Transfer Protocol (NNTP).

Table 8-1: Web Protocols

The *hostname* is the computer on which a particular Web site is located. You can think of this as the address of the Web site. By convention, most hostnames begin with **www**. In the next example, the URL locates a Web page called **guides.html** on the **tldp.org** Web site:

```
http://tldp.org/guides.html
```

If you do not want to access a particular Web page, you can leave the file reference out, and then you automatically access the Web site's home page. To access a Web site directly, use its hostname. If no home page is specified for a Web site, the file **index.html** in the top directory is often used as the home page. In the next example, the user brings up the Red Hat home page:

```
http://www.redhat.com/
```

File Type	Description
`.html`	Web page document formatted using HTML, the Hypertext Markup Language
Graphics Files	
`.gif`	Graphics, using GIF compression
`.jpeg`	Graphics, using JPEG compression
`.png`	Graphics, using PNG compression (Portable Network Graphics)
Sound Files	
`.au`	Sun (Unix) sound file
`.wav`	Microsoft Windows sound file
`.aiff`	Macintosh sound file
Video Files	
`.QT`	QuickTime video file, multiplatform
`.mpeg`	Video file
`.avi`	Microsoft Windows video file

Table 8-2: Web File Types

The pathname specifies the directory where the resource can be found on the host system, as well as the name of the resource's file. For example, **/pub/Linux/newdat.html** references an HTML document called **newdat** located in the **/pub/Linux** directory.

The resource file's extension indicates the type of action to be taken on it. A picture has a **.gif** or **.jpeg** extension and is converted for display. A sound file has an **.au** or **.wav** extension and is played. The following URL references a **.gif** file. Instead of displaying a Web page, your browser invokes a graphics viewer to display the picture. Table 8-2 provides a list of the more common file extensions.

```
http://www.train.com/engine/engine1.gif
```

Enabling Flash plugin

Fedora includes two free and open source versions of Flash: swfdec and gnash. It is preferable that you try these before trying to use the version provided directly by Adobe. The swfdec version is newer.

For the Adobe Flash version, if you are not using Flash 10, you need to first install the **libflashsupport** package.

Adobe only provides a 32 bit version of Flash for Linux. To use the Adobe version of Flash on a 64 bit system you have to first install the 32bit **nspluginwrapper** packages for both **x86_64** and **i386** platforms, as well as the **libflashsupport** package for the **i386** platform. Be sure the **/usr/lib/mozilla/plugins** directory exits. Then install the Adobe plugin. You can then run the **mozilla-plugin-config -i -g -v** to register the plugin.

Web Browsers

Most Web browsers are designed to access several different kinds of information. Web browsers can access a Web page on a remote Web site or a file on your own system. Some browsers can also access a remote news server or an FTP site. The type of information for a site is specified by the keyword **http** for Web sites, **nntp** for news servers, **ftp** for FTP sites, or **file** for files on your own system. As noted previously, several popular browsers are available for Linux. Three distinctive ones are described here: Mozilla, Konqueror, and Lynx. Mozilla is an X Window System–based Web browser capable of displaying graphics, video, and sound, as well as operating as a newsreader and mailer. Konqueror is the K Desktop file manager. KDE has integrated full Web-browsing capability into the Konqueror file manager, letting you seamlessly access the Web and your file system with the same application. Lynx and ELinks are command line–based browsers with no graphics capabilities, but in every other respect they are fully functional Web browsers.

To search for files on FTP sites, you can use search engines provided by Web sites, such as Yahoo! or Google. These usually search for both Web pages and FTP files. To find a particular Web page you want on the Internet, you can use any of these search engines or perform searches from any number of Web portals. Web searches have become a standard service of most Web sites. Searches carried out on documents within a Web site may use local search indexes set up and maintained by indexing programs like ht:/Dig. Sites using ht:/Dig use a standard Web page search interface. Hypertext databases are designed to access any kind of data, whether it is text, graphics, sound, or even video. Whether you can actually access such data depends to a large extent on the type of browser you use.

Note: Fedora now includes a free open source Flash plugin from swfdec

The Mozilla Framework

The Mozilla project is an open source project based on the original Netscape browser code that provides a development framework for Web-based applications, primarily the Web browser and e-mail client. Originally, the aim of the Mozilla project was to provide an end-user Web browser called Mozilla. Its purpose has since changed to providing a development framework that anyone can use to create Web applications, though the project also provides its own. Table 8-3 lists some Mozilla resources.

Web Site	Description
`www.mozilla.org`	The Mozilla project
`www.mozdev.org`	Mozilla plug-ins and extensions
`www.oreillynet.com/mozilla`	Mozilla documentation and news
`www.mozillazine.org`	Mozilla news and articles
`www.mozillanews.org`	Mozilla news and articles

Table 8-3: Mozilla Resources

Currently the framework is used for Mozilla products like the Firefox Web browser and the Thunderbird mail client, as well for non-Mozilla products like the Netscape, Epiphany, and Galleon Web browsers. In addition, the framework is easily extensible, supporting numerous add-ons in the form of plug-ins and extensions. The Mozilla project site is **www.mozilla.org**, and the site commonly used for plug-in and extension development is **www.mozdev.org**.

The first-generation product of the Mozilla project was the Mozilla Web browser, which is still available. Like the original Netscape, it included a mail client and newsreader, all in one integrated interface. The second generation products have split this integrated package into separate stand-alone applications, the Firefox Web browser and the Thunderbird e-mail/newsreader client. Also under development is the Camino Web browser for Mac OS X and the Sunbird calendar application.

In 1998, Netscape made its source code freely available under the Netscape Public License (NPL). Mozilla is developed on an open source model much like Linux, KDE, and GNOME. Developers can submit modifications and additions over the Internet to the Mozilla Web site. Mozilla releases are referred to as Milestones. Mozilla products are currently released under both the NPL license for modifications of Mozilla code and the MPL license (Mozilla Public License) for new additions.

The Firefox Web Browser

Firefox is the next generation of browsers based on the Netscape core source code known as Mozilla (see Figure 8-1). In current releases, Fedora uses Firefox as its primary browser. Firefox is a streamlined browser featuring fast web access. Firefox is based on the Netscape core source code known as mozilla. Firefox is an X Window System application you can operate from any desktop, including GNOME, KDE, and XFce. Firefox is installed by default with both a menu entry in the Main menu's Internet menu and an icon on the different desktop panels. When opened, Firefox displays an area at the top of the screen for entering a URI address and a Navigation toolbar with series of buttons for various web page operations. Menus on the top menu bar provide access to such Firefox features as Tools, View, History, and Bookmarks. A status bar at the bottom shows the state of the current page.

To the right of the URI box is a search box where you can use different search engines for searching the Web, selected sites, or particular items. A pop-up menu lets you select a search engine. Currently included are Google, Yahoo, Amazon, and eBay, along with Dictionary.com for looking up word definitions. Firefox also features button links and tabbed pages. You can drag the URI from the URI box to the button link bar to create a button with which to quickly access the site. Use this for frequently accessed sites.

For easy browsing, Firefox features tabbed panels for displaying web pages. To open an empty tabbed panel, press CTRL-T or select New Tab from the File menu. To display a page in that panel, drag it's URL from the URL box or from the bookmark list to the panel. You can have several panels open at once, moving from one page to the next by clicking their tabs. You can elect to open all your link buttons as tabbed panels by right-clicking the link bar and selecting Open In Tabs.

Tip: Right-clicking on the Web page background displays a pop-up menu with options for most basic operations like page navigation, saving and sending pages,

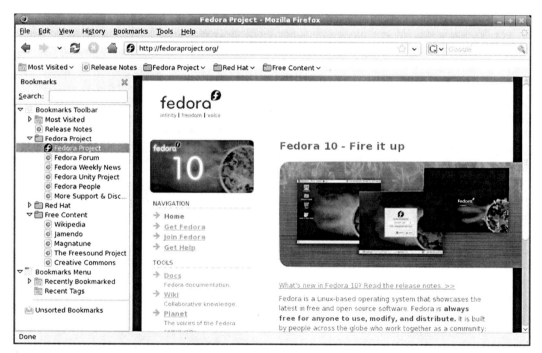

Figure 8-1: Firefox Web Browser

To search a current page for certain text, enter CTRL-F key. This opens a search toolbar at the bottom of Firefox where you can enter a search term. You have search options to highlight found entries or to match character case. Next and Previous buttons let you move to the next found pattern.

When you download a file using Firefox, the download is managed by the Download Manager. You can download several files at once. Progress can be displayed in the Download Manager window, accessible from the Tools menu. You can cancel a download at any time, or just pause a download, resuming it later. Right-clicking a download entry will display the site it was downloaded from as well as the directory you saved it in. To remove an entry, click Remove for the toolbar. To clear out the entire list, click Clean Up.

Firefox Bookmarks and History

Firefox refers to the URIs of web pages you want to keep as *bookmarks,* marking pages you want to access directly. The Bookmarks menu enables you add your favorite web pages. You can also press CTRL-T to add a bookmark. You can then view a list of your bookmarks and select one to view. You can also edit your list, adding new ones or removing old ones. When adding a bookmark an Add Bookmark window opens with a pop-up menus for folders and tags. The Folder menu is set to Bookmarks folder by default. You can also select the Bookmarks Toolbar or unfilled bookmarks.

History is a list of previous URIs you have accessed. The URI box also features a pop-up menu listing your previous history sites. Bookmarks and History can be viewed as sidebars, selectable from the View menu.

Firefox also features Bookmark toolbar. Use this for frequently accessed sites. The Bookmark toolbar is displayed just above the Web page. You can drag the URI from the URI box to the Bookmark toolbar to create a button with which to quickly access the site. Buttons can also be folders, containing button links for several pages. Clicking on a folder button will display the button links in a pop-up menu. You can also right-click on the Bookmark toolbar to display a pop-up menu with entries for adding a bookmark and creating a new folder. Entries include a "Open all in Tabs", letting you open a whole group of commonly used Web pages at once.

To manage your bookmarks, click on the Show all bookmarks entry in the Bookmarks menu. This opens the Library window with bookmark folders displayed in a sidebar. Bookmarks in a folder are shown in the upper right panel, and properties for a selected bookmark in that list is displayed in the lower right panel. The Organize menu has an option to create a new folder. The View menu lets you sort your bookmarks. The Import and Backup menu has options to save backups of your bookmark, as well as export your bookmark for use on other systems using Firefox. You can also import exported Firefox bookmarks from other systems.

Bookmarks also maintains a Smart Bookmarks folder that keeps a list of Most Visited, Recently Bookmarked, and Recent Tags. This lets you easily find sites you visit most often, or ones you consider important.

Firefox supports live bookmarks. A live bookmark connects to a site that provides a live RSS feed. This is a page that is constantly being updated, like a news site. Live bookmarks are indicated by a live bookmark icon to the right of its URI. Click on this icon or select Subscribe to this Page from the Bookmark menu, to subscribe to the site. A pop-up menu is displayed in the main window with the prompt "Subscribe to this feed using". Live Bookmarks is selected by default, but you can also choose MY Yahoo, Bloglines, or Google. You can also choose to Always use Live bookmarks for feeds. You can then click Subscribe Now to set up the live bookmark. This opens a dialog where you can choose to place the live bookmark, either in the Bookmark menu, or on the Bookmark toolbar. In the Bookmark toolbar, the live bookmark becomes a pop-up menu listing the active pages, with an entry at the end for the main site.

When you click on the live bookmark either in the Bookmark toolbar or the live bookmark icon in its URI entry, a list of active pages is displayed. An "Open all in Tabs" entry at the bottom of the listing lets you open all the active pages at once. News pages on a site are often RSS feeds that you can set up as a live bookmark. You can subscribe to the Fedora Weekly News (**www.fedoraproject.org/wiki/FWN**) as live bookmarks. When you select a subscribed site on the bookmark menu, a submenu of active pages is displayed that you can choose from.

Firefox Configuration

The Preferences menu (Edit | Preferences) in Firefox enables you to set several different options. There are preference panels for Main, Tabs, Content, Applications, Privacy, Security, and Advanced (see Figure 8-2). On the Main panel you can set you home page, download options, and access add-on management. Tabs control tab opening and closing behavior

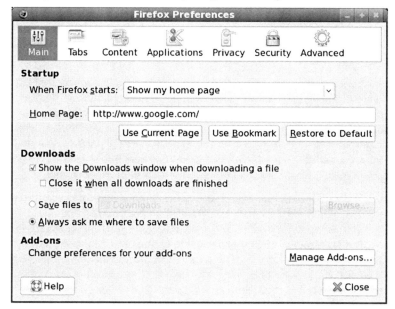

Figure 8-2: Firefox Preferences

Content sets you set the font and fond size, as well as color and language to use. You can also block pop-ups and enable java. Applications associate content with applications to run it, like video or mp3. Privacy controls history, cookies, and private data. Security is where you can remember passwords and set warning messages. The Advanced panel has several panels: General, Network, Update, and Encryption. The General panel provides features like spell checking, and keyboard navigation. The Network panel has a Setting button for the Connection feature which is where you set up your network connections such as the direct connection to the internet or proxy settings. Here you can also set up offline storage size. The encryption panel is where you can manage certificates, setting up validation methods, viewing, and revocation. If you are on a network that connects to the Internet through a firewall, you must use the Proxies screen to enter the address of your network's firewall gateway computer. A *firewall* is a computer that operates as a controlled gateway to the Internet for your network. Several types of firewalls exist. The most restrictive kinds of firewalls use programs called *proxies,* which receive Internet requests from users and then make those requests on their behalf. There is no direct connection to the Internet.

Figure 8-3: Firefox Add-ons Management

Firefox also support profiles. You can set up different Firefox configurations, each with preferences and bookmarks. This is useful for computers like laptops that may connect to different networks or used for different purposes. You can select and create Profiles by starting up the profile manager. Enter the firefox command in a terminal window with the -P option.

```
firefox -P
```

A default profile is already set up. You can create a new profile which runs the profile wizard to prompt you for the profile name and directory to use. Select a profile to use and click Start Firefox. The last profile you used will be used up the next time you start Firefox. You have the option to prompt for the profile to use at start up, otherwise run the **firefox -P** command again to change your profile.

Firefox Add-ons

Add-on Management button, on the Preferences Main panel, opens a window with panels for Extensions, Themes, and Plugins (see Figure 8-3). From the Add-ons window you can select the get Add-ons panel to link to the Add-ons sties and to load Firefox Extensions. The Extensions panel opens an Install/Remove Extension window listing available extension packages designed to work well with Fedora. Check the ones you want and click Apply Changes.

The K Desktop Web Browser: Konqueror

If you are using the K Desktop, you can use the Konqueror Web browser. It can display Web pages, including graphics and links. The K Desktop's file manager supports standard Web page operation, such as moving forward and backward through accessed pages. Clicking a link accesses and displays the Web page referenced. In this respect, the Web becomes seamlessly integrated into the K Desktop (see Chapter 10).

GNOME Web Browsers: Galeon and Epiphany

Several GNOME-based Web browsers are also available. Epiphany, Galeon, and Kazehakase support standard Web operations. Epiphany is a GNOME Web browser designed to be fast with a simple interface (see Figure 8-4). The Bookmarks menu will hold entries for Fedora, Red Hat, and Free Content sites like the Fedora Forum and Wikipedia. You can find out more about Epiphany at **http://epiphany.mozdev.org**. Epiphany is included with Fedora. Epiphany works well as a simple browser with a clean interface. It is also integrated with the desktop, featuring a download applet that will continue even after closing Epiphany. Epiphany also supports tabbed panels for multiple Web site access. Galeon is a fast, light browser also based on the Mozilla browser engine (Gecko). Kazehakase emphasizes a customizable interface with download boxes and RSS bookmarks.

For GNOME, you can also download numerous support tools, such as the RSSOwl to display news feeds and the GNOME Download Manager (Gwget) for controlling Web-based downloads.

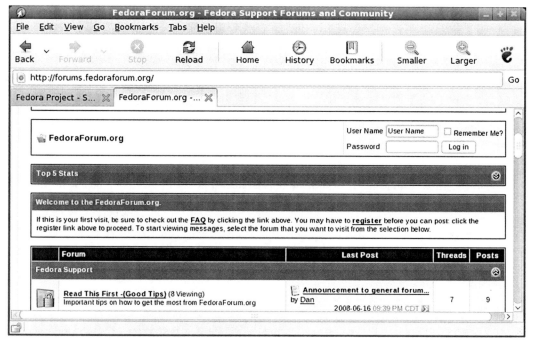

Figure 8-4: Epiphany Web browser

Lynx and ELinks: Line-Mode Browsers

Lynx is a line-mode browser you can use without the X Window System. A Web page is displayed as text only. A text page can contain links to other Internet resources but does not display any graphics, video, or sound. Except for the display limitations, Lynx is a fully functional Web browser. You can also use Lynx to download files or access local pages. All information on the Web is still accessible to you. Because it does not require much of the overhead that graphics-based browsers need, Lynx can operate much faster, quickly displaying Web page text. To start the Lynx browser, you enter **lynx** on the command line and press ENTER.

Another useful text-based browser shipped with most distributions is ELinks. ELinks is a powerful screen-based browser that includes features such as frame, form, and table support. It also supports SSL secure encryption. To start ELinks, enter the **elinks** command in a terminal window.

Note: To create your own Web site, you need access to a Web server. If you choose Web server during installation, the Apache Web server will be installed. You can also rent Web page space on a remote server—a service many ISPs provide, some for free. On Fedora systems, the directory set up by your Apache Web server for your Web site pages is **/var/httpd/html**.

Java for Linux

To develop Java applications, use Java tools, and run many Java products, you must install the Java 2 Software Development Kit (SDK) and the Java 2 Runtime Environment (JRE) on your system. The SDK is a superset of the JRE, adding development tools like compilers and debuggers. Together with other technologies like the Java API, they make up the Java 2 Platform, Standard Edition (J2SE).

Sun has open sourced Java as the OpenJDK. Sun supports and distributes Linux versions of this product. The JRE subset can be installed as OpenJRE. They are directly supported by Fedora as packages on the main repository. You can install them with the Synaptic Package Manager. On Fedora, the **java-1.6.0-openjdk** package installs the Java runtime environment (JRE). The package is labeled "OpenjDK Runtime Environment" on PackageKit. To install the SDK, you use the **java-1.6.0-openjdk-devel** package, named OpenjDK Development Environment. For browser plugins, the **java-1.6.0-openjdk-plugin** package will be installed for using Java with your Web browsers, including Firefox. Java packages and applications are listed in Table 8-4.

Note: On Firefox be sure Java support is enabled.

Sun now provides an open source development environment called Iced Tea designed for developing completely open source Java applications (OpenJDK). OpenJDK provides a Java development platform for entirely open source Java applications. Detailed descriptions of features can be found in the SDK documentation, **http://java.sun.com/docs**.

jpackage, Sun, and Java-like (java-gcj-compat)

Fedora includes numerous free Java applications and support, like Jakarta. Check the **www.fedoraproject.org/wiki/JavaFAQ** for information on how Java is implemented on Fedora. You should use the Fedora versions of Java packages, as they have been specially modified for use on Fedora. The main Java Runtime Environment and SDK are now supported directly by the **openjdk** packages.

Fedora still includes a Java-like collection of support packages that enable the use of Java Runtime operations. Keep in mind that the **openjdk** packages are now used for the JRE. There is no official name for this collection, though it is referred to as the Java Runtime compatibility layer, java-gci-compat, as well as Java-like. This collection provides a free and open source environment included with Fedora, consisting of three packages: GNU Java runtime (**libgcj**), the Eclipse Java compiler (**ecj**), and a set of wrappers and links (**java-gcj**). The **java-gcj** and **libgcj** packages are installed by default.

Application	Description
Java 2 Software Development Kit (SDK), OpenJDK	The open source Java development environment with a compiler, interpreters, debugger, and more, **www.openjdk.java.net**. Part of the Java 2 platform. Included as part of the Fedora 10 distribution as **java-1.6.0-openjdk-devel**
Java Runtime Environment, OpenJRE	The open source Java runtime environment (**www.java.com**), including the Java virtual machine Included as part of the Fedora 10 distribution as **java-1.6.0-openjdk**
Java compatibility layer	The Java-like Free and Open Environment, consisting of the GNU Java runtime (libgcj), the Eclipse Java compiler (ecj), and supporting wrappers and links (java-gcj-compat). Included with Fedora.
Java System Web Server	A Web server implemented with Java. Available at Java Web site at **http://java.sun.com**. (commercial).
GNU Java Compiler	GNU Public Licensed Java Compiler (GJC) to compile Java programs, **http://gcc.gnu.org/java**. Included with Fedora, libgjc.
Jakarta Project	Apache Software Foundation project for open source Java applications, **http://jakarta.apache.org**.
CACAO	A just-in-time (jit) compiler only implementation of the Java Virtual Machine (JVM).**www.cacaojvm.org**.
Classpath	GNU license Java open source libraries, **www.gnu.org/software/classpath**

Table 8-4: Java Packages and Java Web Applications

Java Applications

Numerous additional Java-based products and tools are currently adaptable for Linux. Tools include Java 3D, Java Media Framework (JEFF), and Java Advanced Imaging (JAI). Many of the products such as the Java Web server run directly as provided by Sun. You can download several directly from the Sun Java Web site at **http://java.sun.com**. The Jakarta project (**http://jakarta.apache.org**), part of the Apache Software Foundation, provides open source Java tools and applications, including libraries, server applications, and engines. Jakarta along with other packages are included with Fedora. These are derived from the JPackage Project at **jpackage.org**, which also includes some packages that are not in Fedora, which you can download and install. JPackage is a Fedora YUM—supported repository.

For those that want an entire open source and GNU licensed version of the Java libraries, you can install the classpath Java libraries, also available on Fedora, **www.gnu.org/software/classpath**.

BitTorrent Clients (transmission)

GNOME and KDE provide several very effective BitTorrent clients. With BitTorrent you can download very large files quickly in a shared distributed download operation where several users participate in downloading different parts of a file, sending their parts of the download to other participants, known as peers. Instead of everyone trying to access a few central servers, all peers participating in the BitTorrent operation become sources for the file being downloaded. Certain peers function as seeders, those who have already downloaded the file, but continue to send parts to those who need them.

Fedora will install and use the GNOME BitTorrent client, Transmission (Applications | Internet | Transmission BitTorrent Client). For KDE you can use the Ktorrent BitTorrent client. To perform a BitTorrent download you need the BitTorrent file for the file you want to download. The BitTorrent file for the Fedora 10 DVD iso image is **fedora-10-x86_64-dvd.torrent**. When you download the file from the Fedora torrents site (**torrents.fedoraproject.com**), you will be prompted to either open it directly with Transmission or save it to a file.

Transmission can handle several torrents at once. On the toolbar are buttons for starting, pausing, and remove a download. The Add button can be used to load a BitTorrent file (**.torrent**), setting up a download. When you first open a torrent file, the Torrent Options window opens where you can specify the destination folder and the priority. The option to start the download automatically will be selected by default. Figure 8-5 shows Transmission with two BitTorrent operations set up, one of which is active. A progress bar shows how much of the file has been downloaded.

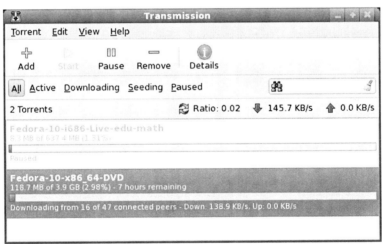

Figure 8-5: Transmission BitTorrent client

You could set up Transmission to manage several BitTorrents, of which only a few many be active, others paused, and still others that have finished but continue to functions as seeders. There are display buttons for All, Active, Downloading, Seeding, and Paused torrents.

To see more information about a torrent, select it and then click the Details button. This opens a Details window with tabs for Activity, Peers, Tracker, Information, Files, and Options. Activity shows statistics like the progress, times, and errors. Peers show all the peers participating in the download. Tracker displays the location of the tracker, the server that manages the torrent operation. Files shows the progress of the file download (a torrent could download more than one file). Information shows description, origin, and locations of the download folder and torrent file. The Options tab lets you set bandwidth and connection parameters, limiting the download or upload, and the number of peers.

FTP Clients

With FTP clients, you can connect to a corresponding FTP site and download files from it. FTP clients are commonly used to download software from public FTP sites that operate as software repositories. Most Linux software applications can be downloaded to your Linux system from such sites. These sites feature anonymous logins that let any user access their files. A distribution site like **ftp.redhat.com** is an example of one such FTP site, holding an extensive set of packaged Linux applications you can download using an FTP client and then easily install on your system. Basic FTP client capabilities are incorporated into the Konqueror (KDE) and Nautilus (GNOME) file managers. You can use a file manager window to access an FTP site and drag files to local directories to download them. Effective FTP clients are also now incorporated into most Web browsers, making Web browsers a primary downloading tool. Firefox in particular has strong FTP download capabilities.

Though file managers and Web browsers provide effective access to public (anonymous login) sites, to access private sites, you may need a stand-alone FTP client like curl, wget, gFTP or **ftp**. These clients let you enter user names and passwords with which you can access a private FTP site. The stand-alone clients are also useful for large downloads from public FTP sites, especially those with little or no Web display support. Popular Linux FTP clients are listed in Table 8-5.

FTP Clients	Description
Firefox	Mozilla Web and FTP browser
Konqueror	K Desktop file manager
Nautilus	GNOME file manager
gFTP	GNOME FTP client
ftp	Command line FTP client
lftp	Command line FTP client capable of multiple connections
NcFTP	Screen-based FTP client
curl	Internet transfer client (FTP and HTTP)

Table 8-5: Linux FTP Clients

Network File Transfer: FTP

With File Transfer Protocol (FTP) clients you can transfer extremely large files directly from one site to another. FTP can handle both text and binary files. This is one of the TCP/IP protocols, and it operates on systems connected to networks that use the TCP/IP protocols, such as the Internet. FTP performs a remote login to another account on another system connected to you on a network. Once logged in to that other system, you can transfer files to and from it. To log in, you need to know the login name and password for the account on the remote system. For example, if you have accounts at two different sites on the Internet, you can use FTP to transfer files from one to the other. Many sites on the Internet allow public access using FTP, however. Such sites serve as depositories for large files anyone can access and download. These sites are often referred to as *FTP sites,* and in many cases, their Internet addresses begin with the word *ftp,* such as **ftp.gnome.org** or **ftp.redhat.com**. These public sites allow anonymous FTP login from any user. For the login name, you use the word "anonymous," and for the password, you use your email address. You can then transfer files from that site to your own system.

You can perform FTP operations using any one of a number of FTP client programs. For Linux systems, you can choose from several FTP clients. Many now operate using GUI interfaces such as GNOME. Some, such as Firefox, have limited capabilities, whereas others, such as NcFTP, include an extensive set of enhancements. The original FTP client is just as effective, though not as easy to use. It operates using a simple command line interface and requires no GUI or cursor support, as do other clients.

The Internet has a great many sites open to public access. They contain files anyone can obtain using file transfer programs. Unless you already know where a file is located, however, finding it can be difficult. To search for files on FTP sites, you can use search engines provided by Web sites, such as Yahoo!, Google, or Lycos. For Linux software, you can check sites such as **www.freshmeat.net, www.sourceforge.net, www.rpmfind.net, http://dowload1.rpmfusion.org, apps.kde.com**, and **www.gnome.org**. These sites usually search for both Web pages and FTP files.

Web Browser–Based FTP: Firefox

You access an FTP site and download files from it with any Web browser. A Web browser is effective for checking out an FTP site to see what files are listed there. When you access an FTP site with a Web browser, the entire list of files in a directory is listed as a Web page. You can move to a subdirectory by clicking its entry. With Firefox, you can easily browse through an FTP site to download files. To download a file with Firefox, click the download link. This will start the transfer operation, opening a box for selecting your local directory and the name for the file. The default name is the same as on the remote system. You can manage your downloads with the download manager, which will let you cancel a download operation in progress or remove other downloads requested. The manager will show the time remaining, the speed, and the amount transferred for the current download. Browsers are useful for locating individual files, though not for downloading a large set of files, as is usually required for a system update.

The KDE File Managers: Konqueror and Dolphin

On the KDE desktop, the desktop file managers (Konqueror and dolphin) have built-in FTP capability. The FTP operation has been seamlessly integrated into standard desktop file operations. Downloading files from an FTP site is as simple as copying files by dragging them from one directory window to another, but one of the directories happens to be located on a remote FTP site. On KDE, you can use a file manager window to access a remote FTP site. Files in the remote directory are listed just as your local files are. To download files from an FTP site, you open a window to access that site, entering the URL for the FTP site in the window's location box. Use the **ftp://** protocol for FTP access. You can also use the **fish://** protocol for FTP access using SSH secure connections. Once connected, open the directory you want, and then open another window for the local directory to which you want the remote files copied. In the window showing the FTP files, select the ones you want to download. Then simply click and drag those files to the window for the local directory. A pop-up menu appears with choices for Copy, Link, or Move. Select Copy. The selected files are then downloaded. Another window then opens, showing the download progress and displaying the name of each file in turn, along with a bar indicating the percentage downloaded so far.

GNOME Desktop FTP: Nautilus

The easiest way to download files is to use the built-in FTP capabilities of the GNOME file manager, Nautilus. On GNOME, the desktop file manager—Nautilus—has a built-in FTP capability much like the KDE file manager. The FTP operation has been seamlessly integrated into standard desktop file operations. Downloading files from an FTP site is as simple as dragging files from one directory window to another, where one of the directories happens to be located on a remote FTP site. Use the GNOME file manager to access a remote FTP site, listing files in the remote directory, just as local files are. Just enter the FTP URL following the prefix **ftp://** and press ENTER. The top directory of the remote FTP site will be displayed. Simply use the file manager to progress through the remote FTP site's directory tree until you find the file you want. Then open another window for the local directory to which you want the remote files copied. In the window showing the FTP files, select those you want to download. Then CTRL-click and drag those files to the window for the local directory. CTRL-clicking performs a copy operation, not a move. As files are downloaded, a dialog window appears showing the progress.

gFTP

The gFTP program is a simpler GNOME FTP client designed to let you make standard FTP file transfers. The gFTP window consists of several panes (see figure 8-6). The top-left pane lists files in your local directory, and the top-right pane lists your remote directory. Subdirectories have folder icons preceding their names. The parent directory can be referenced by the double period entry (**..**) with an up arrow at the top of each list. Double-click a directory entry to access it. The pathnames for all directories are displayed in boxes above each pane. You can enter a new pathname for a different directory to change to it, if you want.

Two buttons between the panes are used for transferring files. The left arrow button, <-, downloads selected files in the remote directory, and the right arrow button, ->, uploads files from the local directory. To download a file, click it in the right-side pane and then click the left arrow button, <-. When the file is downloaded, its name appears in the left pane, your local directory. Menus across the top of the window can be used to manage your transfers. A connection manager enables you to enter login information about a specific site. You can specify whether to perform an anonymous login or to provide a username and password. Click Connect to connect to that site. A drop-down menu for sites enables you to choose the site you want. Interrupted downloads can be restarted easily.

wget

The wget tool lets you easily access Web and FTP sites for particular directories and files. Directories can be recursively downloaded, letting you copy an entire Web site. **wget** takes as its option the URL for the file or directory you want. Helpful options include -**q** for quiet, -**r** for recursive (directories), -**b** to download in the background, and -**c** to continue downloading an interrupted file. One of the drawbacks is that your URL reference can be very complex. You have to know the URL already. You cannot interactively locate an item as you would with an FTP client. The following would download the Fedora Live CD in the background.

```
wget -b
ftp://download.fedora.redhat.com/pub/fedora/linux/releases/9/Live/i686/iso/FC-9-
i686-Live.iso
```

TIP: With the Gnome Wget tool you can run wget downloads using a GUI interface. Select Applications | Internet | Download Manager to display Gnome Wget.

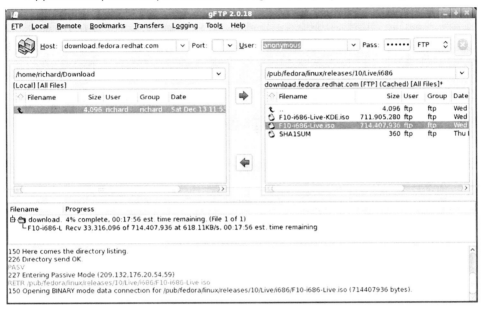

Figure 8-6: gFTP FTP client

curl

The **curl** Internet client operates much like wget, but with much more flexibility. With curl you can specify multiple URLs on its command line. You can also use braces to specify multiple matching URLs, like different Web sites with the same domain name. You can list the different Web site host names within braces, followed by their domain name (or visa versa). You can also use brackets to specify a range of multiple items. This can be very useful for downloading archived files that have the same root name with varying extensions, like different issues of the same magazine. curl can download using any protocol, and will try to intelligently guess the protocol to use if none is given. Check the curl man page for more information.

ftp

The name ftp designates the original FTP client used on UNIX and Linux systems. The ftp client uses a command line interface, and it has an extensive set of commands and options you can use to manage your FTP transfers. You start the ftp client by entering the command **ftp** at a shell prompt. If you have a specific site you want to connect to, you can include the name of that site on the command line after the ftp keyword. Otherwise, you need to connect to the remote system with the ftp command **open**. You are then prompted for the name of the remote system with the prompt "(to)". When you enter the remote system name, ftp connects you to the system and then prompts you for a login name. The prompt for the login name consists of the word "Name" and, in parentheses, the system name and your local login name. Sometimes the login name on the remote system is the same as the login name on your own system. If the names are the same, press ENTER at the prompt. If they are different, enter the remote system's login name. After entering the login name, you are prompted for the password. In the next example, the user connects to the remote system **garnet** and logs in to the **robert** account:

Command	Effect
`ftp`	Invokes the ftp program.
`open` *site-address*	Opens a connection to another system.
`close`	Closes connection to a system.
`quit` or `bye`	Ends ftp session.
`ls`	Lists the contents of a directory.
`dir`	Lists the contents of a directory in long form.
`get` *filename*	Sends file from remote system to local system.
`put` *filename*	Sends file from local system to remote system.
`mget` *regular-expression*	Enables you to download several files at once from a remote system. You can use special characters to specify the files.
`mput` *regular-expression*	Enables you to send several files at once to a remote system. You can use special characters to specify the files.
`reget` *filename*	Resumes transfer of an interrupted file from where you left off.
`binary`	Transfers files in binary mode.
`ascii`	Transfers files in ASCII mode.
`cd` *directory*	Changes directories on the remote system.
`lcd` *directory*	Changes directories on the local system.
`help` or `?`	Lists ftp commands.
`mkdir` *directory*	Creates a directory on the remote system.
`rmdir`	Deletes a remote directory.
`delete` *filename*	Deletes a file on the remote system.
`mdelete` *file-list*	Deletes several remote files at once.
`rename`	Renames a file on a remote system.
`hash`	Displays progressive hash signs during download.
`status`	Displays current status of ftp.

Table 8-6: The ftp Client Commands

```
$ ftp
ftp> open
(to) garnet
Connected to garnet.berkeley.edu.
220 garnet.berkeley.edu FTP server ready.
Name (garnet.berkeley.edu:root): robert
password required
Password:
user robert logged in
ftp>
```

Once logged in, you can execute Linux commands on either the remote system or your local system. You execute a command on your local system in ftp by preceding the command with an exclamation point. Any Linux commands without an exclamation point are executed on the remote system. One exception exists to this rule. Whereas you can change directories on the remote system with the **cd** command, to change directories on your local system, you need to use a special ftp command called **lcd** (local **cd**). In the next example, the first command lists files in the remote system, while the second command lists files in the local system:

```
ftp> ls
ftp> !ls
```

The ftp program provides a basic set of commands for managing files and directories on your remote site, provided you have the permission to do so (see Table 8-6). You can use **mkdir** to create a remote directory, and **rmdir** to remove one. Use the **delete** command to erase a remote file. With the **rename** command, you can change the names of files. You close your connection to a system with the **close** command. You can then open another connection if you want. To end the ftp session, use the **quit** or **bye** command.

```
ftp> close
ftp> bye
Good-bye
$
```

To transfer files to and from the remote system, use the **get** and **put** commands. The **get** command receives files from the remote system to your local system, and the **put** command sends files from your local system to the remote system. In a sense, your local system gets files *from* the remote and puts files *to* the remote. In the next example, the file **weather** is sent from the local system to the remote system using the **put** command:

```
ftp> put weather
PORT command successful.
ASCII data connection
ASCII Transfer complete.
ftp>
```

If a download is ever interrupted, you can resume the download with **reget**. This is helpful for an extremely large file. The download resumes from where it left off, so the whole file needn't be downloaded again. Also, be sure to download binary files in binary mode. For most FTP sites, the binary mode is the default, but some sites might have ASCII (text) as the default. The command **ascii** sets the character mode, and the command **binary** sets the binary mode. Most software packages available at Internet sites are archived and compressed files, which are binary files. In the next example, the transfer mode is set to binary, and the archived software package **mydata.tar.gz** is sent from the remote system to your local system using the `get` command:

```
ftp> binary
ftp> get mydata.tar.gz
PORT command successful.
Binary data connection
Binary Transfer complete.
ftp>
```

You may often want to send several files, specifying their names with wildcard characters. The `put` and `get` commands, however, operate only on a single file and do not work with special characters. To transfer several files at a time, you have to use two other commands, `mput` and `mget`. When you use `mput` or `mget`, you are prompted for a file list. You can then either enter the list of files or a file-list specification using special characters. For example, `*.c` specifies all the files with a **.c** extension, and `*` specifies all files in the current directory. In the case of `mget`, files are sent one by one from the remote system to your local system. Each time, you are prompted with the name of the file being sent. You can type `y` to send the file or `n` to cancel the transmission. You are then prompted for the next file. The `mput` command works in the same way, but it sends files from your local system to the remote system. In the next example, all files with a **.c** extension are sent to your local system using `mget`:

```
ftp> mget
(remote-files) *.c
mget calc.c? y
PORT command successful
ASCII data connection
ASCII transfer complete
mget main.c? y
PORT command successful
ASCII data connection
ASCII transfer complete
ftp>
```

Answering the prompt for each file can be a tedious prospect if you plan to download a large number of files, such as those for a system update. In this case, you can turn off the prompt with the `prompt` command, which toggles the interactive mode on and off. The `mget` operation then downloads all files it matches, one after the other.

```
ftp> prompt
Interactive mode off.
ftp> mget
(remote-files) *.c
 PORT command successful
ASCII data connection
ASCII transfer complete
PORT command successful
ASCII data connection
ASCII transfer complete
ftp>
```

Note: To access a public FTP site, you have to perform an anonymous login. Instead of a
login name, you enter the keyword **anonymous** (or **ftp**). Then, for the password,
you enter your email address. Once the ftp prompt is displayed, you are ready to
transfer files. You may need to change to the appropriate directory first or set the
transfer mode to binary.

lftp

The **lftp** program is an enhanced FTP client with advanced features such as the
capabilities to download mirror sites and to run several FTP operations in the background at the
same time. It uses a command set similar to that for the ftp client. You use `get` and `mget` commands
to download files, with the `-o` option to specify local locations for them. Use `lcd` and `cd` to change
local and remote directories.

To manage background commands, you use many of the same commands as for the shell.
The & placed at the end of a command puts it into the background. Use CTRL-Z to put a job already
running into the background. Commands can be grouped with parentheses and placed together into
the background. Use the `jobs` command to list your background jobs and the `wait` or `fg` command
to move jobs from the background to the foreground. When you exit lftp, the program will continue
to run any background jobs. In effect, lftp becomes a background job itself.

When you connect to a site, you can queue commands with the `queue` command, setting
up a list of FTP operations to perform. With this feature, you could queue several download
operations to a site. The queue can be reordered and entries deleted if you wish. You can also
connect to several sites and set up a queue for each one. The `mirror` command lets you maintain a
local version of a mirror site. You can download an entire site or just update newer files, as well as
removing files no longer present on the mirror.

You can tailor lftp with options set in the **.lftprc** file. System-wide settings are placed in
the **/etc/lftp.conf** file. Here, you can set features like the prompt to use and your anonymous
password. The **.lftp** directory holds support files for command history, logs, bookmarks, and startup
commands. The lftp program also supports the **.netrc** file, checking it for login information.

Tip: The NcFTP program runs as a command line operation similar to ftp with many of the
same commands. To start up NcFTP, you enter the `ncftp` command on the
command line. It also provides **ncftpput** and **ncftpget** for use in shell scripts.

VoIP and Messenger Clients

You may, at times, want to communicate directly with other users on your network. You
can do so with VoIP, ICQ, IM (Instant Messenger), and IRC utilities, provided the other user is also
logged in to a connected system at the same time (see Table 8-7). With Voice over the Internet
Protocol applications, you can speak over Internet connections, talking as if on a telephone.

ICQ (I Seek You) is an Internet tool that notifies you when other users are online and
enables you to communicate with them. ICQ works much like an instant messenger. With an
Internet Relay Chat utility (IRC), you can connect to a remote server where other users are also
connected and talk with them.

Clients	Description
Ekiga	VoIP application
Pidgin	Messenger interface for all instant messenger protocols including MSN, AIM, Yahoo, MySpaceIM, ICQ, XMPP, and IRC. Pidgin was formerly GAIM.
empathy	GNOME 2.24 new instant messenger client, replacing Pidgin
Kopete	KDE 4 instant messenger client
X-Chat	Internet Relay Chat (IRC) client, also has a GNOME version, **gnome-xchat**.
Konversation	KDE IRC client
Jabber	Jabber client (XMPP)
psi	Jabber client using QT (KDE), XMPP
Finch	Command line cursor-based IRC, ICQ, and AIM client
naim	Command line cursor-based IRC, ICQ, and AIM client

Table 8-7: Talk and Messenger Clients

Instant Messenger: Pidgin, Empathy, and Kopete

Instant messenger (IM) clients operate much the same way as ICQ, allowing users on the same IM system to communicate anywhere across the Internet. Currently some of the major IM systems are AIM (AOL), Microsoft Network (MSN), Yahoo, ICQ, and Jabber. Unlike the others, Jabber is an open source instant messenger service (**www.jabber.org**). It uses an XML protocol it developed called XMPP, Extensible Messaging and Presence Protocol (**www.xmpp.org**).

Fedora will install Pidgin as its standard interface for Instant Messaging (Pidgin was formerly GAIM). Pidgin is a multi-protocol IM client that works with most IM protocols including AIM, MSN, Jabber, Google Talk, ICQ, IRC, Yahoo, MySpaceIM, and more. Pidgin is accessible from Applications | Internet | Instant Messenger. To create a new account, select Manage from the Accounts menu. To configure your setup, select Preferences from the Tools menu. The Conversations panel lets you set the font, images, and smiley icons for your messages. The Network panel lets to configure your network connection, and the Logging panel lets you turn logging of your messages on or off. The Sounds panel allows you to choose sounds for different events. You can find out more about Pidgin at **http://pidgin.im**. Pidgin is a GNOME front end that used the libpurple library for is actual IM tasks (formerly libgaim). The libpurple library is used by many different IM applications such as Finch.

Note: An icon indicating your IM status, like a green circle for available or a red triangle for away, will be displayed on the top panel notification area (too the right) whenever you are running either Pidgin or Empathy.

Fedora also supports the new GNOME replacement for Pidgen, Empathy. You will have to install it. Pidgen is still used as the default. Empathy is based on the Telepathy framework, which is designed to provide IM support to any application that wants an IM capability. All major IM services are supported, including Google Talk, AIM, Bonjour, MSN Messenger, Jabber (XMPP), ICQ, and Yahoo. Use the accounts window to add new accounts. Then select a type and click the Create button. The appropriate entries will be provided for configuration. A drop down menu on the Contact List window lets your select your status, like Available, Busy, or Away. Empathy is still considered under development and not as stable as Pidgin. Telepathy provides IM support with connection managers, making IM services easy to maintain and add. Current connection managers include telepathy-gabble for Jabber/XMPP, telepathy-idle for IRC, telepathy-butterfly for MSN, telepathy-salut for local network (link-local) XMPP connections, telepathy-sofiasip for SIP, and telepathy-haze for Pidgin's Yahoo, AIM, and other support (llibpurple). (**http://telepathy.freedesktop.org**).

For KDE you can use Kopete, the KDE Instant Messenger client. Kopete features a simple interface with a Status menu for selecting your availability such as Online, Away, or Busy. You can also add a new status, giving it your own name and message. All the major services are supported, including XMPP, Google Talk, AIM, ICQ, and MSN Messenger. See the Kopete Handbook, accessible from the Help menu for detailed instructions.

Ekiga

Ekiga is GNOME's VoIP application providing Internet IP Telephone and video conferencing support (see Figure 8-7). It was formerly called GnomeMeeting, and its web site is still at **www.gnomemeeting.org**. Ekiga supports both the H.323 and SIP (Session Initiation Protocol) protocols. It is compatible with Microsoft's NetMeeting. H.323 is a comprehensive protocol that includes the digital broadcasting protocols like DVB and H.261 for video streaming, as well as the supporting protocols like the H.450 series for managing calls.

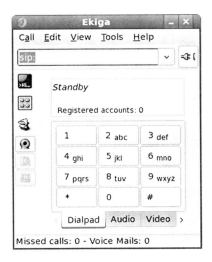

Figure 8-7: Ekiga VoIP

To use Ekiga you will need a SIP address. You can obtain a free one from **www.ekiga.net**. You will first have to subscribe to the service. When you first start Ekiga, you will be prompted to configure your connection. Here you can provide information like contact information, your connection method, sound driver, and video device. Use the address book to connect to another Ekiga user. A white pages directory lets you search for people who are also using Ekiga.

Skype

Skype provides a Fedora 7 i586 version. You can download the RPM package from the Skype site and then use the PackageKit **gpk-install-file** command to install it. This is an i586 version that is meant to run only on 32bit version of Fedora, though it will work on the 64bit, x86_64, version.

```
skype-2.0.0.72-fc5.i586.rpm
```

To install the package, either choose the install option when you download the package from the Skype Web site using your Web browser, or download the file and then double click on it. Both will use the **gpk-install-file** PackageKit install tool to install the package. You will be prompted to enter your root user password. You will also be notified that there is no authentication key, install anyway. On 64 bit versions you may also have to force the install.

Once installed, you can access Skype from the Applications | Internet menu. The interface is similar to the Windows version (see Figure 8-9). A Skype panel icon will appear on the panel, once you start Skype. You can use it to easily access Skype throughout your session.

Figure 8-9: Skype VoIP and panel icon

ICQ

The ICQ protocol enables you to communicate directly with other users online, like an instant messenger utility. Using an ICQ client, you can send users messages, chat with them, or send files. You can set up a contact list of users you may want to contact when they are online. You are then notified in real time when they connect, and you can communicate with them if you wish. Several modes of communication are supported. These include chat, message, e-mail, file transfer, and games. To use ICQ, you register with an ICQ server that provides you with an ICQ number, also known as a Universal Internet Number (UIN). You can find out more about the ICQ protocol at **www.icq.com**.

Internet Relay Chat (IRC) operates like a chat room, where you can enter channels and talk to other users already there. First, you select an IRC server to connect to. Various servers are available for different locales and topics. Once connected to a server, you can choose from a list of channels to enter. The interface works much like a chat room. When you connect to the server, you can choose a nickname by which you will be known. Several Internet Relay Chat clients are available for use on Linux systems. Most operate on either the X Window System, KDE, or GNOME platforms.

Several GNOME- and KDE-based ICQ and IRC clients are available for your use. Check the GNOME software listings at **www.gnomefiles.org** for new versions and recent updates. For KDE-based ICQ clients, check **www.kde-apps.org** (Network | Chat).

GNOME Online Desktop

Fedora provides a demo version of the GNOME Online Desktop. This is a desktop specially configured to take advantage of online resources such as Google mail, Flickr, and Mugshot. You, of course, have to separately set up accounts of your own for each service. The Online Desktop features a panel called BigBoard that displays button with which you can connect to services directly. Account names and passwords will be remembered for easy access. See **http://live.gnome.org/OnlineDesktop** for detailed information and documentation. The site has a link to the OnlineDesktop tour at the Red Hat Magazine, which provides a very detailed discussion of all the Online Desktop components with images.

The Online Desktop aims to take advantage of Cloud computing. With clouds, massive server farms provide services and applications that were originally provided by a local PC. The server farms form clouds of storages and services that anyone can hook into easily. Services are accessed over the Internet, and all storage and applications are kept on the clouds. For example, GMail (Google's mail service) operates entirely on the cloud, whereas Thunderbird is a local application on a PC. You can access your mail from any system using GMail, but with Thunderbird you have to have access to you own personal PC. Google calendar and Google docs provide access to online organization and office applications. The flickr and Mugshot services provide online image and photo storage. Soon, most of your computing may be done on the cloud, instead of a local PC. In effect, open source software has already moved onto the cloud in the form of repositories. Gone are the days when you needed a CD to install software. Now all you need is an Internet connection and access to a repository. Software is only a click away.

To install the GNOME Online Desktop, use the Search panel on Add/Remove Software and search for online-desktop. Several packages will be displayed. Select them (dependencies will be added), then install. The GNOME Online Desktop currently consists of the following packages:

```
online-desktop
online-desktop-gmail
online-desktop-flickr
online-desktop-google-reader
online-desktop-google-calendar
online-desktop-google-docs
bigboard
mugshot
```

The Online Desktop is currently still under development. The recommended way to use it is to create a new user that you would use for just the Online Desktop (System | Administration | Users and Groups, or the Switch User tool - right-click). This avoids any possible problems with the desktops of your current users.

Once installed, you can access the Online Desktop from the GDM session menu. Log out to the Login screen. Then click on the Sessions button to display the Sessions dialog. You will see listed an entry for the Online Desktop demo. Select it. Then when you login the Online Desktop interface with its specialized panel will be used. You can also use the User Switching tool, instead of logging out completely.

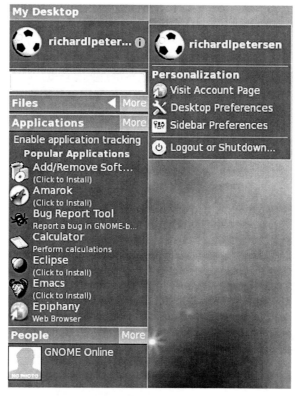

Figure 8-10: GNOME Online Desktop sidebar

When you login for the first time, you will need to set up an account at **online.gnome.org**. You have to submit an email address to which a message with a link for setting up your account is listed. Your browser will open to an account preferences page where you first have to accept the terms of use. Then you can set up your account. You can indicate GMail and IM access. You can also choose a personal image to use. The sidebar will use your browser's cookies for authentication and access.

The Online Desktop will display a desktop sidebar called bigboard on the left side of the screen (see Figure 8-0). This will contain widgets with links for your commonly used services. The sidebar initially has widgets for Files, Apps, and People. You can add a Calendar and Mugshot widget. At the top is a self area with the user icon and name, with a search box for searching your sidebar online links. Clicking on the user icon opens a menu with entries for the sidebar and desktop preferences, as well as a shutdown button. There is also a link to your **online.gnome.org** account page. See the Online Desktop Tour at Red Hat magazine for a detailed explanation of each component.

The widgets are designed to integrate online resources. The Files widget will holds both your recent locally used files as well as those you used on online services, linking directly to the page on that service (like files edited with Google Docs). The People widgets can hold links to people's web sites or home pages.

The sidebar itself can only display a few entries. To see a complete listing of resources, click the **more** button next to the section title (see Figure 8-11). The more button on the People section will open a window listing all the home pages you have links for. Files will list links to all your online files and documents. The Apps widget will list all your install applications. To add or remove an application from the Apps widget, select the application icon and then check or uncheck its Add to sidebar box.

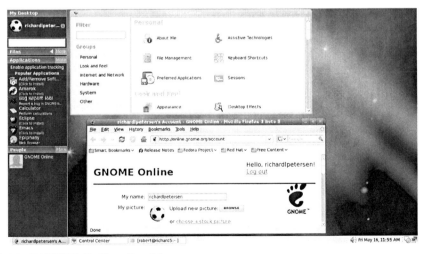

Figure 8-11: GNOME Online Desktop

To add or remove widgets, open the sidebar preferences window (see Figure 8-12). All available widgets will be shown. Select the one you want to add and click the Add to sidebar button.

You can have the sidebar minimized by first checking that option in the sidebar preferences window. A box will appear on the left side of the bottom panel. Click on it to minimize and then maximize the sidebar.

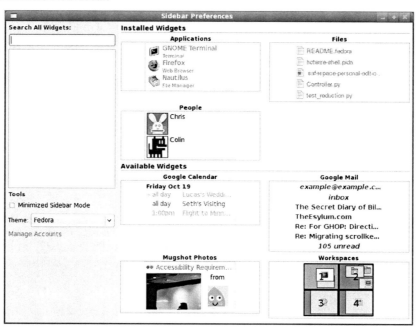

Figure 8-12: GNOME Online Desktop sidebar preferences

Part 3: Interfaces

GNOME

KDE

The Shell

9. GNOME

The GNU Network Object Model Environment, also known as *GNOME,* is a powerful and easy-to-use environment consisting primarily of a panel, a desktop, and a set of GUI tools with which program interfaces can be constructed. GNOME is designed to provide a flexible platform for the development of powerful applications. Currently, GNOME is supported by several distributions and is the primary interface for Fedora. GNOME is free and released under the GNU Public License. You can download the source code, as well as documentation and other GNOME software, directly from the GNOME Web site at **www.gnome.org**. Several companies have joined together to form the GNOME Foundation, an organization dedicated to coordinating the development of GNOME and GNOME software applications. These include such companies as Sun, IBM, and Hewlett-Packard as well as Linux distributors such as Mandrake, Fedora, and TurboLinux. Modeled on the Apache Software Foundation, which developed the Apache Web server, the GNOME Foundation will provide direction to GNOME development as well as organization, financial, and legal support.

The core components of the GNOME desktop consist of a panel for starting programs and desktop functionality. Other components normally found in a desktop, such as a file manager, Web browser, and window manager, are provided by GNOME-compliant applications. GNOME provides libraries of GNOME GUI tools that developers can use to create GNOME applications. Programs that use buttons, menus, and windows that adhere to a GNOME standard can be said to be GNOME-compliant. The official file manager for the GNOME desktop is Nautilus. The GNOME desktop does not have its own window manager as KDE does. Instead, it uses any GNOME-compliant window manager. The Metacity window manager is the one bundled with the GNOME distribution.

Support for component model interfaces is integrated into GNOME, allowing software components to interconnect regardless of the computer language in which they are implemented or the kind of machine on which they are running. The standard used in GNOME for such interfaces is the Common Object Request Broker Architecture (CORBA), developed by the Object Model Group for use on UNIX systems. GNOME uses the ORBit implementation of CORBA. With such a framework, GNOME applications and clients can directly communicate with each other, enabling you to use components of one application in another. With GNOME 2.0, GNOME officially adopted GConf and its libraries as the underlying method for configuring GNOME and its applications. GConf can configure independently coordinating programs such as those that make up the Nautilus file manager.

You can find out more about GNOME at its Web site, **www.gnome.org**. The Web site provides online documentation, such as the GNOME User's Guide and FAQs, and also maintains extensive mailing lists for GNOME projects to which you can subscribe. The **www.gnomefiles.org** site provides a detailed software listing of current GNOME applications and projects. For detailed documentation check the GNOME documentation site at **library.gnome.org**. Documentation is organized by Users, Administrators, and Developers. The Desktop Users Guide provides a complete tutorial on desktop use. For administrators, the GNOME Desktop System Administration Guide details how administrators can manage user desktops. The Desktop Administrators' Guide to GNOME Lockdown and Pre-configuration shows how administrators can control access to tasks like printing or saving files.

If you want to develop GNOME programs, check the Developers section at the GNOME documentation site as well as **developer.gnome.org**, which provides tutorials, programming guides, and development tools. Here you can links to extensive support tools such as tutorials and integrated development environments (IDEs). The GNOME documentation site includes detailed online documentation for the GTK+ library, GNOME widgets, and the GNOME desktop, as well as the complete API reference manual online. The Overview of the GNOME Platform provides a comprehensive description of all GNOME components. For offline developer help, install and use the DevHelp utility (part of the GNOME Developer's Tools release). Table 9-1 offers a listing of useful GNOME sites.

Web Sites	Descriptions
`www.gnome.org`	Official GNOME Web site
`http://library.gnome.org`	GNOME documentation Web site for Users, Administrators, and Developers
`http://art.gnome.org`	Desktop themes and background art
`http://www.gnomefiles.org`	GNOME Software applications, applets, and tools.
`www.gnome.org/gnome-office`	GNOME Office applications.
`http://developer.gnome.org`	Gnome developers site, see library.gnome.org for developer documentation.

Table 9-1: GNOME Resources

Fedora 10 Desktop Look and Feel

Fedora features a desktop look and feel with the Fedora logo, as well as default Fedora logo screen background. The logo depicts an F encased in a blue circle. On the main panel you will see the blue Fedora logo as the icon for the Applications menu, instead of Red Hat's hat. The logos even have their own package, fedora-logos. There are several Fedora background images to choose from, including the Fedora blue F logo encased in a bubble and surrounded by other rising bubbles, the Fedora double helix, and the Fedora hot air balloon image.

The default theme is Nadoka with Fedora icons. The desktop images are based on Cairo with more intuitive and user-friendly icons. Buttons and windows are easier to use and appear more pleasing to the eye. The Cairo images theme is compliant with the TANGO style guidelines. TANGO is an open source standard for desktop images, providing the same image style across all open source desktops. See **http://tango.freedesktop.org** for more information. In addition, GNOME also adheres to the freedesktop.org standard naming specifications. KDE, GNOME, and XFce all adhere to the same naming specifications, using the same standard names for icons on their desktops.

Tip: You can download and add the icons manually using the Appearances Theme panel (System | Preferences | Look and Feel | Appearances). Select a theme, then click Customize and select the Icons panel. There you will find an entry for the downloaded icons.

The GNOME Control Center provides an intuitive organization and access for your desktop configuration. This is integrated into Fedora as submenus in the System | Preferences menu. Preferences are organized into Personal, Look and Feel, Internet and Network, Hardware, and System categories. The GNOME Control Center is also implemented as a GUI interface that will display a dialog with icons on the left for the different categories like Personal and Hardware, and a continuous display of preferences on the right. Selecting a category moves to and highlights the appropriate preferences. You can invoke the control center GUI by entering **gnome-control-center** in a terminal window.

Tip: There are three menus with the name System in it: the main System menu with its own button listed next to Applications and Places, the System Tools submenu in the Applications main menu (used for specialized system tools like the Disk Usage Analyzer, the Terminal window, and Update System), and finally the System submenu in the Preferences main menu used for GNOME configuration tools, like the GNOME Power Management tool.

GNOME 2 Features

Check **www.gnome.org** for a detailed description of GNOME features and enhancements, with screen shots and references. GNOME releases new revisions on a frequent schedule. Several versions since the 2.0 release have added many new capabilities. GNOME now has efficiencies in load time and memory use, making for a faster response time. Desktop search is integrated into the file chooser dialog. For laptops, power management has been improved along with battery monitoring. For developers, there is a new version of the GTK+ toolkit, better documentation, and improved development tools. With GNOME 2.22, the GVFS (GNOME Virtual File System) provides direct file manager support for virtual file systems, letting you access Samba shares and FTP sites directly.

Some of GNOME features added since version 2.0 are described in the following sections.

GNOME Desktop Features

➢ File Roller can now work on archives on networked systems. You can also copy and paste or drag and drop files between archives.

➢ For right-to-left languages, window, menu, and workspace components are now mirrored, also positioned right-to-left.

➢ GNOME documentation site is **http://library.gnome.org**, which organizes documentation into Users, Administrators, and Developers sections.

➢ An easy-to-use file permissions dialog allows changing permissions for all files in a folder.

➢ Basic window compositing is provided using drop shadows, live previews, and transparency effects. Support is included for 3-D effects for windows in Appearance Visual Effects panel (wobble, shrink, and explode).

➢ Home directories now have data specific folders set up including Pictures, Documents, Videos, and Music. Gnome applications may use these as defaults.

➢ GNOME automatically mounts removable devices at the **/media** directory.

GNOME Applications

➢ The Cheese application manages Web cam photos. For image collections, there is enhanced browsing.

> ➢ The GNOME video player, Totem, supports Web access, DVB, and DVD. It also provides YouTube and MythTV support.

> ➢ Tomboy note taker can now synchronize your notes from different computers. Connecting to a central server, all your notes from different systems can be integrated and synchronized, providing just one set of notes for all your systems.

> ➢ The International Clock Applet is now used for the time applet on the top GNOME panel. It lets you see the time at any location on the planet, as well as the weather.

> ➢ GNOME sound and video applications can now prompt the user to search for any needed codecs. The mechanism for finding and installing the codec is handled separately by the codec wizard.

> ➢ The Disk Usage Analyzer (Accessories | Disk Usage Analyzer) details disk and partition usage, as well as usage by directory, with totals for your entire file systems with space availability.

> ➢ GEdit has been reworked to adhere to the Multiple Documentation Interface specs. It now has a new syntax highlighting system for script languages like PHP, Ruby, and HTML.

> ➢ The Vinagre remote desktop viewer lets access desktops remotely

GNOME Administration Features

> ➢ Appearance administrative preferences integrates Theme, Background, Fonts, Interface, and Visual Effects into five panels in the Appearance Preferences window.

> ➢ Seahorse integrates GPG encryption, decryption, and signing of files and text (Applications | Accessories | Passwords and Encryption Keys. For Seahorse configuration you use System | Preferences | Keyrings and Encryption).

> ➢ Integration of PolicyKit controls for GNOME administration tools.

> ➢ User Profile Editor (Sabayon) allows administrators to create and mange user profiles, either on the current system or on remote ones. Profiles can contain personal information as well as application preferences, including OpenOffice.

> ➢ Integrated power management is controlled with Power Management Preferences.

> ➢ Preferred applications control panel now has an Accessibility panel with visual and mobility options.

> ➢ The GNOME Control Center (**gnome-control-center**) is integrated into Fedora as menu items in the System | Preferences menu. You can use System | Preferences | Look and Feel | Main Menu to add a Control Center entry to the System | Preferences menu

> ➢ Mouse accessibility options supporting different kinds of clicks is now integrated with the Mouse Preferences tool.

> ➢ The menu editor, Alacarte, lets you customize your menus easily. The disk usage analyzer, Baobab, lets you quickly see how much disk space is used.

> ➢ For developers, the Anjuta IDE provides integrated access to debuggers, Glade UI editor, and Valgrind analysis.

GNOME File Manager Features

Nautilus is the official file manager for the GNOME desktop. You can find out more about Nautilus from the Nautilus user's manual that is part of the GNOME User's Guide at **www.gnome.org**. The Nautilus file manager, as part of GNOME, also has several new features added.

➢ Nautilus File manger now includes disk usage chart when displaying properties for file systems. Images are displayed with their appropriate orientation using EXIF camera information.

➢ Nautilus is now more integrated into other applications such as File Roller for archives, the image viewer for pictures, and the GNOME media player for audio and video. You can now preview sound and video files within a Nautilus window.

➢ Nautilus uses GVFS (GNOME Virtual File System) for remote file systems, which replaces GnomeVFS. GVFS uses the GO object-based abstraction layer for I/0, GIO. With GVFS nautilus can support FUSE user based file system access. Applications no longer have to be written for GNOME virtual file system access. Any application can access a GVFS mounted file system.

➢ With GVFS, Nautilus now manages automounts for remote file systems. Access is stateful, requiring a user password only once, before granting continual access.

➢ Nautilus can burn files and ISO images to DVD/CD writers.

➢ Context-sensitive menus let you perform appropriate actions, such as extracting archive files. An Open With option lets you choose from a selection of appropriate applications. Multiple applications can now be registered for use with a file.

➢ The file manager can display network shares on local networks, using DNS-based service discovery. The file manager also supports access to password-protected FTP sites.

➢ The file manager can display audio tracks on music CDs with the **cdda://** protocol, and access connected digital cameras with the **gphoto2://** protocol.

GTK+

GTK+ is the widget set used for GNOME applications. Its look and feel was originally derived from Motif. The widget set is designed from the ground up for power and flexibility. For example, buttons can have labels, images, or any combination thereof. Objects can be dynamically queried and modified at runtime. It also includes a theme engine that enables users to change the look and feel of applications using these widgets. At the same time, the GTK+ widget set remains small and efficient.

The GTK+ widget set is entirely free under the Lesser General Public License (LGPL). The LGPL enables developers to use the widget set with proprietary software, as well as free software (the GPL would restrict it to just free software). The widget set also features an extensive set of programming language bindings, including C++, Perl, Python, Pascal, Objective C, Guile, and Ada. Internalization is fully supported, permitting GTK+-based applications to be used with other character sets, such as those in Asian languages. The drag-and-drop functionality supports drag-and-drop operations with other widget sets that support these protocols, such as Qt.

The GNOME Interface

The GNOME interface consists of the panel and a desktop, as shown in Figure 9-1. The panel appears as a long bar across the bottom of the screen. It holds menus, programs, and applets. (An *applet* is a small program designed to be run within the panel.) On the top panel is a menu labeled Applications. The menu operates like the Start menu lists entries for applications you can run on your desktop. You can display panels horizontally or vertically, and have them automatically hide to show you a full screen. The Applications menu is reserved for applications. Other tasks like opening a home directory window or logging out are located in the Places menu. The System menu holds the Preferences menu for configuring your GNOME interface, as well as the Administration menu for accessing the Fedora administrative tools.

Figure 9-1: GNOME with Preferences menu

Note: The current Fedora GNOME interface uses two panels, one on top for menus and notification tasks like your clock, and one on the bottom for interactive features for workspaces and docking applications. Three main menus are now used instead of one: an Applications menu, a Places menu, and the System. The System menu is used to log out of your session.

The remainder of the screen is the desktop. Here, you can place directories, files, or programs. You can create them on the desktop directly or drag them from a file manager window.

A click-and-drag operation will move a file from one window to another or to the desktop. A click and drag with the CTRL key held down will copy a file. A click-and-drag operation with the middle mouse button (two buttons at once on a two-button mouse) enables you to create links on the desktop to installed programs. Initially, the desktop holds only an icon for your home directory. Clicking it opens a file manager window to that directory. A right-click anywhere on the desktop displays a desktop menu with which you can open new windows and create new folders.

Tip: You can display your GNOME desktop using different themes that change the appearance of desktop objects such as windows, buttons, and scroll bars. GNOME functionality is not affected in any way. You can choose from a variety of themes. Many are posted on the Internet at **art.gnome.org**. Technically referred to as *GTK themes,* these allow the GTK widget set to change its look and feel. To select a theme, select Theme panel in the Appearance tool in the System | Preferences | Look And Feel menu. The default GNOME theme is Nadoka

GNOME Components

From a user's point of view, you can think of the GNOME interface as having four components: the desktop, the panel, the main menus, and the file manager.

In its standard default configuration, the GNOME desktop displays a Folder icon for your home directory in the upper-left corner, along with a trash can to delete items. In addition, the desktop also displays a Computer window for accessing the entire file system, CD/DVD drives, and network shares. Double-clicking the home directory icon will open the file manager, displaying files in your home directory. On Fedora Linux, you have two panels displayed, one used for menus, application icons, and running applets at the top of the screen, and one at the bottom of the screen used primarily for managing your windows and desktop spaces.

The top bar has several menus and application icons: the Applications menu, the Places menu, the System menu, the Mozilla Firefox Web browser (globe with fox), and the Evolution mail tool (envelope). To the right are the time and date icons. An update button will appear if updates are available. You can use the update icon to automatically update your system. The bottom bar holds icons for minimized windows as well as running applets. These include a Workspace Switcher (squares) placed to the right. An icon to the left lets you minimize all your open windows. When you open a window, a corresponding button for it will be displayed in the lower panel, which you can use to minimize and restore the window.

To start a program, you can select its entry in the Applications menu. You can also click its application icon in the panel (if there is one) or drag a data file to its icon. To add an icon for an application to the desktop, right-click on it entry in the Applications menu and select "Add this launcher to the desktop."

Quitting GNOME

To quit GNOME, you select the Logout or Shutdown entries in the System menu. The Logout entry quits GNOME, returning you to the login window (or command line shell, still logged in to your Linux account, if you started GNOME with **startx**). The Shut Down entry displays a dialog which allows you to hibernate, shutdown, cancel, or restart your system. A Restart entry shuts down and reboots your system. You must separately quit a window manager that is not GNOME-compliant after logging out of GNOME.

GNOME Help

The GNOME Help browser (Yelp) provides a browser-like interface for displaying the GNOME user's manual, Man pages, and info documents. You can select it from the System menu. It features a toolbar that enables you to move through the list of previously viewed documents. You can even bookmark specific items. A browser interface enables you to use links to connect to different documents. On the main page, expandable links for several Gnome desktop topics are displayed on left side, with entries for the Gnome User Manual, Administration Guide, and Fedora release notes on the right side. At the bottom of the left side listing are links for the Man and Info pages. You can use these links to display Man and Info pages easily. Use the Search box to quickly locate help documents. Special URL-like protocols are supported for the different types of documents: **ghelp**, for GNOME help; **man**, for man pages; and **info**, for the info documents, like **man:fstab** to display the Man page for the **fstab** file.

The GNOME Help Browser provides a detailed manual on every aspect of your GNOME interface. The left hand links display GNOME categories for different application categories like, like the System tools, Gnome Applets. The Gnome Applets entry will provide detailed descriptions of all available GNOME applets. Applications categories like Internet, Programming, System Tools, and Sound and Video will provide help documents for applications developed as part of the GNOME project, like the Evolution mail client, the Totem movie player, the Disk Usage Analyzer, and the GNOME System Monitor. Click on the Desktop entry at the top of the left hand list, to display links for Gnome User and Administration manuals

The GNOME Desktop

The GNOME desktop provides you with all the capabilities of GUI-based operating systems (see Figure 9-1). You can drag files, applications, and directories to the desktop, and then back to GNOME-compliant applications. If the desktop stops functioning, you can restart it by starting the GNOME file manager (Nautilus). The desktop is actually a back-end process in the GNOME file manager. But you needn't have the file manager open to use the desktop.

Note: As an alternative to using the desktop, you can drag any program, file, or directory to the panel and use the panel instead.

Drag and Drop Files to the Desktop

Any icon for an item that you drag from a file manager window to the desktop also appears on the desktop. However, the default drag-and-drop operation is a move operation. If you select a file in your file manager window and drag it to the desktop, you are actually moving the file from its current directory to the GNOME desktop directory, which is located in your home directory and holds all items on the desktop. For GNOME, the desktop directory is **DESKTOP**. In the case of dragging directory folders to the desktop, the entire directory and its subdirectories will be moved to the GNOME desktop directory. To remove an icon from the desktop, you move it to the trash.

You can also copy a file to your desktop by pressing the CTRL key and then clicking and dragging it from a file manager window to your desktop. You will see the small arrow in the upper-right corner of the copied icon change to a + symbol, indicating that you are creating a copy, instead of moving the original.

You can also create a link on the desktop to any file. This is useful if you want to keep a single version in a specified directory and just be able to access it from the desktop. You could also use links for customized programs that you may not want on the menu or panel. There are two ways to create a link. While hold down the CTRL AND SHIFT KEYS, CTRL-SHIFT, drag the file to where you want the like created. A copy of the icon then appears with a small arrow in the right corner indicating it is a link. You can click this link to start the program, open the file, or open the directory, depending on what kind of file you linked to. Alternatively, first click and drag the file out of the window, and after moving the file but before lifting up the mouse button, press the ALT key. This will display a pop-up menu with selections for Cut, Copy, and Link. Select the Link option to create a link.

GNOME's drag-and-drop file operation works on virtual desktops provided by the GNOME Workspace Switcher. The GNOME Workspace Switcher on the bottom panel creates icons for each virtual desktop in the panel, along with task buttons for any applications open on them.

Note: Although the GNOME desktop supports drag-and-drop operations, these normally work only for applications that are GNOME-compliant. You can drag any items from a GNOME-compliant application to your desktop, and vice versa.

Applications on the Desktop

In most cases, you only want to create on the desktop another way to access a file without moving it from its original directory. You can do this either by using a GNOME application launcher button or by creating a link to the original program. Application launcher buttons are the GNOME components used in menus and panels to display and access applications. The Open Office buttons on the top panel are application launcher buttons. To place an icon for the application on your desktop, you can simply drag the application button from the panel or from a menu. For example, to place an icon for the Firefox Web browser on your desktop, just drag the Web browser icon on the top panel to anywhere on your desktop space.

For applications that are not on the panel or in the menu, you can either create an application launcher button for it or create a direct link, as described in the preceding section. To create an application launcher, first right-click the desktop background to display the desktop menu. Then select the Create Launcher entry.

GNOME Desktop Menu

You can also right-click anywhere on the empty desktop to display the GNOME desktop menu. This will list entries for common tasks, such as creating an application launcher, creating a new folder, or organizing the icon display. Keep in mind that the New Folder entry creates a new directory on your desktop, specifically in your GNOME desktop directory (**DESKTOP**), not your home directory. The entries for this menu are listed in Table 9-2.

Window Manager

GNOME works with any window manager. However, desktop functionality, such as drag-and-drop capabilities and the GNOME workspace switcher (discussed later), works only with window managers that are GNOME-compliant. The current release of GNOME uses the Metacity window manager. It is completely GNOME-compliant and is designed to integrate with the

GNOME desktop without any duplication of functionality. Other window managers such as Enlightenment, IceWM, and Window Maker can also be used. Check a window manager's documentation to see if it is GNOME-compliant.

Menu Item	Description
Create Folder	Creates a new directory on your desktop, in your DESKTOP directory.
Create Launcher	Creates a new desktop icon for an application.
Create Document	Creates files using installed templates
Clean Up by Name	Arranges your desktop icons.
Keep Aligned	Aligns your desktop icons.
Cut, Copy, Paste	Cuts, copies, or pastes files, letting you move or copy files between folders.
Change Desktop Background	Opens a Background Preferences dialog to let you select a new background for your desktop.

Table 9-2: The GNOME Desktop Menu

For 3D support you can use compositing window managers like Compiz or Beryl. Windows are displayed using window decorators, allowing windows to wobble, bend, and move in unusual ways. They employ features similar to current Mac and Vista desktops. A compositing window manager relies on a graphics card OpenGL 3D acceleration support. Be sure your graphics card is supported. C Compiz is installed as the default 3D support, and can be activated by enabling desktop effects (System | Preferences | Look and Feel | Desktop Effects). See www.compiz-**fusion.org** for more information. Beryl was developed from Compiz and features its own window decorators. It is also available on the Fedora repository. You can find more about Beryl at **www.beryl-project.org**. Both projects plan to merge providing a single compositing window manager for Linux.

Metacity employs much the same window operations as used on other window managers. You can resize a window by clicking any of its sides or corners and dragging. You can move the window with a click-and-drag operation on its title bar. You can also right-click and drag any border to move the window, as well as ALT-click anywhere on the window. The upper-right corner shows the Maximize, Minimize, and Close buttons. Minimize creates a button for the window in the panel that you can click to restore it. You can right-click the title bar of a window to display a window menu with entries for window operations. These include workspace entries to move the window to another workspace (virtual desktop) or to all workspaces, which displays the window no matter to what workspace you move.

GNOME Volume Management

Managing DVD/CD-ROMs, card readers, floppy disks, digital cameras, and other removable media is now handled directly by GNOME. You not only can access removable media, but access all your mounted file systems, remote and local, including any Windows shared directories accessible from Samba. You can browse all your file systems directly from GNOME, which implements this capability with the gnome virtual file system (gnome-vfs) mapping to your drives, storage devices, and removable media. The GNOME uses HAL and udev to access removable media directly, and Samba to provide Windows networking support. Media are mounted by **gnome-mount**, a wrapper for accessing Hal and udev, which perform the mount (/etc/fstab is no longer used).

Figure 9-2: GNOME Computer window

You can access your file systems and removable media using the Computer icon on the desktop. This opens a top-level window showing icons for all removable media (mounted CD-ROMs, floppies, etc.), your local file system, and your network shared resources (see Figure 9-2). Double-click any icon to open a file manager window displaying its contents. The file system icon will open a window showing the root-level directory, the top directory for your file system. Access will be restricted for system directories, unless you log in as the root user.

Figure 9-3: GNOME Network window

To access your network resources on remote Windows or Linux systems, you click select the Network entry on the Places menu. This opens a Network window showing icons for all your connected network resources such as hosts, printers, and folders (see Figure 9-3). To add the Network icon to the desktop, click and drag its entry in the Places menu to the Desktop. Drag-and-drop operations are supported for all shared directories, letting you copy files and folders between a shared directory on another host with a directory on your system. To browse Windows systems on GNOME using Samba, you first have to configure your firewall to accept Samba connections. Using system-config-firewall (Firewall on the System | Administration menu) check the Samba entry, if you have not already done so. You also should set access through SELinux, On the SELinux panel, open Modify SELinux Policy, expand the Samba entry and click the two Allow entries.

Removable media will also appear automatically as icons directly on your desktop. A DVD/CD-ROM is automatically mounted when you insert it into your DVD/CD-ROM drive, displaying an icon for it with its label. The same kind of access is also provided for card readers, digital cameras, and USB drives. Be sure to unmount the USB drives before removing them so that data will be written.

You can then access the disk in the DVD/CD-ROM drive either by double-clicking it or by right-clicking and selecting the Open entry. A file manager window opens to display the contents of the CD-ROM disc. To eject a CD-ROM, you can right-click its icon and select Eject from the pop-up menu. The same procedure works for floppy disks, using the Floppy Disk icon. Be sure you don't remove a mounted floppy disk until you have first unmounted it, selecting the Eject entry in the pop-up menu.

Burning a data DVD/CD is a simple matter of placing a blank DVD in your drive. Nautilus automatically recognizes it as a blank disk and allows you to write to it. All Read/Write disks, even if they are not blank, are also recognized as writable disks and opened up in a DVD/CD writer window. To burn a disk, just drag the files you want to copy to the blank disk window and then click Write To Disk. A dialog will open up with buttons to set options like the write speed and disk label. After writing, a dialog then list buttons to eject, burn again, or close. Keep in mind that the newly written disk is not mounted. You can eject it at any time.

Nautilus can also burn ISO DVD and CD images. Just insert a blank DVD or CD disk and then drag to ISO disk image file to a blank CD/DVD icon on your desktop. A dialog will open up asking you if you want to burn the DVD/CD image. Nautilus works with ISO images, files ending with an **.iso** suffix. For other image files like **.img** you can just change the suffix to **.iso** and Nautilus will recognize and burn the image file normally.

GNOME will display icons for any removable media and perform certain default actions on them. For example, Audio CDs will be automatically played in the CD player. DVD movies can be started up in a DVD player. To set the preferences for how removable media are treated, you use the File Management tool, accessible from System | Preferences | Personal | File Management. Certain settings are already set.

Desktop Effects - Compiz-Fusion

For 3D desktop effects support you can use compositing window manager support provided by Compiz-fusion. Windows are displayed using window decorators, allowing windows to wobble, bend, and move in unusual ways. Desktops can also be accessed using 3D tools like the Desktop Wall or the Desktop Cube. They employ features similar to current Mac and Vista desktops. A compositing window manager support relies on a graphics card OpenGL 3D acceleration support. Be sure your graphics card is supported. Compiz-fusion is a merger of Compiz and Beryl compositing window managers. See **http://wiki.compiz-fusion.org** for more information. Several keyboard shortcuts are supported for popular effects (see Table 9-3).

Keys	Description
ALT-TAB	Switchers: Application, Shift, and Ring
CTRL-TAB-ARROW (LEFT, RIGHT, UP, DOWN)	Viewport switcher, moving to different workspaces
MOUSE SCROLL BUTTON, UP OR DOWN	Viewport switcher, moving to different workspaces
CTRL-ALT-(LEFT-MOUSE-CLICK AND DRAG)	Desktop Wall or Desktop Cube

Table 9-3: Compiz-Fusion Keyboard Shortcuts

Compiz-fusion is now integrated into your Fedora GNOME desktop. To enable Compiz-fusion effect, you use the Desktop Effects tool, System | Preferences | Look and Feel | Desktop Effects. On this dialog you click the Enable Effects button. Two options are listed, Wobble windows and Cube. These enable two basic effects, wobbling windows when you move windows, and the Cube desktop switcher, showing desktops on a Cube that you can rotate to choose a desktop. The Desktop Effects window is shown here.

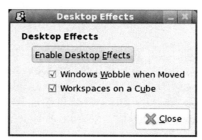

Figure 9-4: CompizConfig Settings Manager

Not all Compiz-Fusion features are enabled. Some will conflict, requiring other to be turned off. To enable specific Compiz-fusion effects, you should first install a Compiz configuration manager, the CompizConfig Settings Manager (**ccsm**). Install with PackageKit. Then access them from the System | Preferences | Look and Feel menu as CompizConfig Settings

Manager. The CompizConfig Settings Manager (CCSM) provides a detailed interface with all effects directly selectable with a separate configuration pane for each effect (see Figure 9-4). Select the effect you want. Conflicting features will be turned off automatically. Double click an effect entry to open a configuration pane with options for configuring the effect. The CCSM will use the original default keys for certain effects. For the Switchers, the CCSM will use the super-Tab keys for the Shift and Ring switchers. The super key is the Windows Start key or MAC options key found on most keyboards.

When configuring using CCSM, your changes are not immediately made. You have to restart CompizFusion using the Desktop Effects window. After making your changes on CCSM, the open the Desktop Effects window and click the Enable Desktop Effects button. Your CompizFusion window manager will be disabled and you will return to using Metacity. Then click the Enable Desktop Effects button again. CompizFusion will restart with the new settings. You will be prompted to use Previous Settings or your Current Settings. Click Current settings (Previous is the default). Your new configuration is now in effect.

Figure 9-5: CompizConfig Settings Manager Window operations

Enabling desktop effects will change window managers, from Metacity (GNOME default) to Compiz-fusion. Disabling the desktop effects returns to Metacity. Disable desktop effects if the Compiz-fusion window manager becomes unstable.

Keep in mind that CompizFusion runs its own window manager. To move, resize, minimize, or even display window components like title bars, these features have to be enabled by CompizFusion. In the Windows section of the CompizFusion Configuration Manager, you will find entries for these basic operations. Figure 9-5 shows settings for Move Window, Resize Window, and Shelf (minimize). In the Desktop section (see Figure 9-4) the Expo option enables access to virtual desktops.

Switchers

Compiz provides several switchers for browsing quickly through open windows, selecting the one you want. Alt-Tab views open windows in current workspace. To list windows in all your workspaces, press Ctrl-Alt-Tab. Should you have numerous windows open across several workspaces, this becomes a way to quickly browse through them, stopping at and selecting the one you want. On the CompizConfig Settings Manager you can choose the switcher you want from the Windows Management section (see Figure 9-5). The options are: Application Switcher, Static Application Switcher, Shift Switcher, and Ring Switcher

Application switcher will display a central dialog showing images of your open windows. If you have many windows open, the Application Switcher is a very fast way to locate and select a window. Press the Alt-Tab key to display the Application Switcher. Your current active window will be centrally displayed and highlighted. Continually pressing Alt-Tab will move you through the sequence of window images, making the next window the central and thereby selected one. The Shift-Alt-Tab keys will move you backward to the previous window.

A variation on the Application switcher, the Static Application Switcher, displays all windows side by side, but moves the highlighted selection across them, instead of moving the window images (see Figure 9-6)..

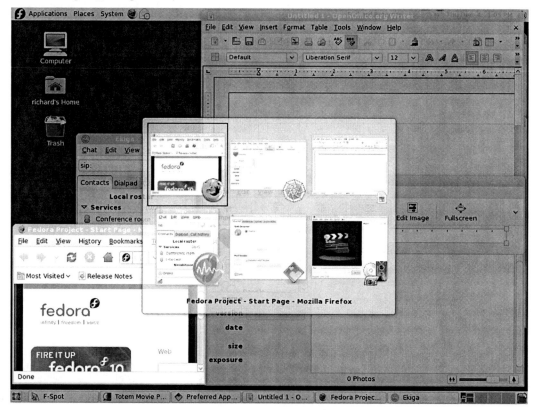

Figure 9-6: Static Applications switcher (Alt-Tab)

The Shift Switcher performs the same task as the Application Switcher, but will display the non-central windows stacked to the sides (see Figure 9-7). You use the super key with the Tab key. The super key is the Windows start key on Windows keyboards. The shift switcher displays non-selected windows on either side, whereas the Ring Switcher displays the windows in a ring, moving the ring of windows around to a central selected position.

Figure 9-7: Shift Switcher (Alt-Tab or Super-Tab, Super is Windows Start key)

Window previews

The Window Previews feature displays thumbnails of open windows as you pass the mouse over their taskbar labels on the panel (see Figure 9-8). It is turned off by default.

Figure 9-8: Windows previews, thumbnails of open windows as mouse passes over on lower panel

Viewport Switcher

The Viewport switcher lets you use the mouse scroll button or the Ctrl-Alt-Arrow keys to switch quickly between workspaces. Click on the desktop, deselecting any active windows, and then use the scroll button to move directly between workspaces. Scrolling up moves to the right, and scrolling down moves to the left. You can also use Ctrl-alt-arrow, right left up or down to move between workspaces. The Viewport switcher is designed to work with either the Desktop Wall or the Desktop Cube.

Desktop Wall

By default, compiz-fusion will enable the Desktop Wall for easy switching between workspaces. You can use Ctrl-Alt-arrow, right or left to quickly move from one workspace to another. Desktop Wall is incompatible with the Desktop Cube. Should you choose to use the Desktop Cube instead, then the Desktop Wall will be disabled. Desktop Wall is the more stable of the two, requiring only normal graphics card support.

As you move from one workspace to another, the Desktop Wall will display a small dialog containing boxes with simple arrow images for each desktop (see Figure 9-9). This is the Show Viewport Switcher Preview option which is enabled by default. You can configure the Desktop Wall using the CompizConfig Settings Manager to display an image of the desktop instead of just the arrow image. Enable the Show Live Viewport Previews option. For no desktop wall dialog deselect both. Desktop Wall will then just change desktops directly, without displaying a dialog,

Figure 9-9: Desktop Wall (Ctrl-Alt-arrow, arrow can be left, right, up, or down)

Desktop Cube with 3D and Deformation

The Desktop Cube displays your desktop workspaces on a cube. When in use, the cube is displayed on the entire screen, replacing your desktop display. The Desktop Cube is not active by default. It conflicts with Desktop Wall. You will have to use a configuration tool to turn it on, turning off Desktop Wall at the same time. To display the Desktop Cube be sure to also select the Rotate Cube option. Then you can display the Cube by pressing Ctrl-Alt with a mouse left-click and drag. As long as you hold the mouse button down, the cube is displayed. Move the mouse to move around the cube to different workspaces (see Figure 9-10).

You need to have more than two workspaces set up to see the cube (right-click on workspace switcher applet on bottom right panel and then add desktop columns).

The Viewport Switcher will work with Desktop Cube, letting you use the scroll button as well as Ctrl-Alt-arrow keys to move quickly between workspaces.

If you have 3d windows also selected (Effects section), then the open windows will be displayed above their respective workspaces (see Figure 9-10).

With the Cube Reflection and Deformation feature the cube is displayed as a circular sphere or cylinder. You can even set the top and bottom images or colors (see Figure 9-11).

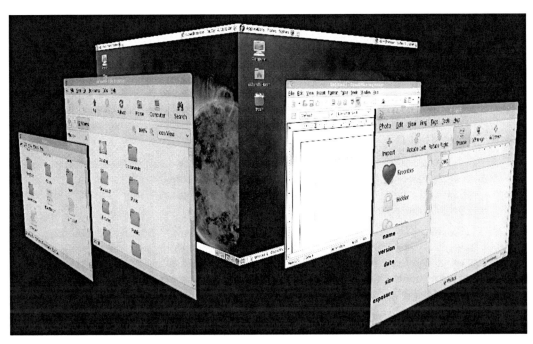

Figure 9-10: Cube with 3D Windows (Ctrl-Alt with mouse left-click and drag)

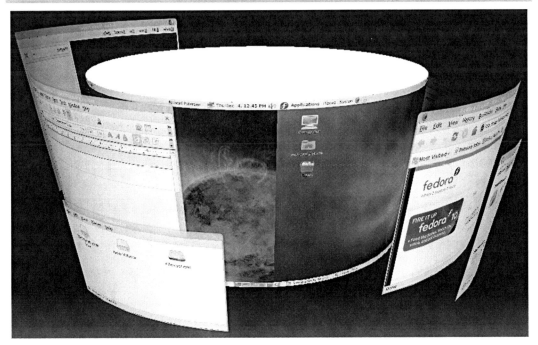

Figure 9-11: Cube with Deformation and 3D (Ctrl-Alt with mouse left-click and drag)

GNOME Preferences

Fedora provides several tools for configuring your GNOME desktop. These are listed in the System | Preferences menu. Configuration preference tools are organized into several submenus: Personal, Look and Feel, Internet and Network, Hardware, and System. Those that do not fall into any category are listed directly. The GNOME preferences are listed in Table 9-4. Several are discussed in different sections in this and other chapters. The Help button on each preference window will display detailed descriptions and examples. Some of the more important tools are discussed here.

Several appearances related configuration tasks have been combined into the Appearance tool. These include Themes, Background, Fonts, and menu and toolbar preferences. To change your theme or background image, or configure your fonts, use the Appearance tool (System | Preferences | Look and Feel | Appearance).

The keyboard shortcuts configuration (Personal | Keyboard Shortcuts) lets you map keys to certain tasks, like mapping multimedia keys on a keyboard to media tasks like play and pause. Just select the task and then press the key. There are tasks for the desktop, multimedia, and window management. With window management you can also map keys to perform workspace switching. Keys that are already assigned will be shown.

The File Management configuration (Personal | File Management) lets you determine the way files and directories are displayed along with added information to show in icon captions or list views. You can also specify double click behavior and files that can be previewed.

The Windows configuration (Look and Feel | Windows) is where you can enable features like window roll up, window movement key, and mouse window selection.

The Mouse and Keyboard preferences are the primary tools for configuring your mouse and keyboard (Hardware | Mouse). The Mouse preferences let you choose a mouse image, configure its motion, and hand orientation. The Keyboard preferences window shows several panels for selecting your keyboard model (layout), configuring keys (Layout Options), repeat delay (Keyboard), and even enforcing breaks from power typing as a health precaution.

To set the actual volume control and mixing for different sound sources like CD, speakers, microphone, and video, you use the GNOME Volume Control tool (Hardware | Volume Control). You can also invoke it with the Volume Control applet on your panel.

Personal

About Me	Personal information like image, addresses, and password (see About Me later in this chapter).
Assistive Technology Preferences	Enables features like screen reader, keyboard display, and magnifier
File Management	Default methods for file and director displays
Keyboard Accessibility	Set features like repeating, slow, and sticking, and mouse keys
Keyboard Shortcuts	Configure keys for special tasks, like multimedia operations.
Preferred Applications	Set default Web browser, Mail application, and Terminal window.
Sessions	Manage your session with start up programs and save options (see

Sessions later in this chapter).

Look and Feel

Appearance	Provides theme, background, font, and interface configuration panels. Choose a desktop background or theme. Change fonts and font sizes for different components on your desktop (see Desktop Font Sizes later in this chapter). Change simple menu and toolbar preferences.
Desktop Effects	Choose to use a 3d window manager like
Main Menu	Add or remove categories and menu items for the Applications and System menus.
Screensaver	Select and manage your screen saver
Windows	Enable certain window capabilities like roll up on title bar, movement key, window selection.

Internet and Network

Bluetooth Preferences	Bluetooth notification icon display options
Internet Proxy	Specify proxy configuration if needed: manual or automatic
Personal File Sharing	Permit sharing public files on network, can require password.
Remote Desktop	Allow remote users to view or control your desktop. Can control access with password.

Hardware

Default Printer	Choose a default printer if more than one.
Keyboard	Configure your keyboard: selecting options, models, and typing breaks.
Mouse	Mouse configuration: select hand orientation, mouse image, and motion.
Removable Drives and Media	Set removable drives and media preferences (see Using Removable Devices and Media later in this chapter).
Screen Resolution	Change your screen resolution, refresh rate, and screen orientation.
Sound	Select the sound driver for events, video and music, and conferencing. Also select sounds to use for desktop events.
Volume Control	Sound Mixer for setting volume control.

System

Power Management	Power management options for battery use and sleep options.
Search and Indexing	Set search and indexing preferences for Desktop searches.

Table 9-4: GNOME Desktop Preferences

To select a sound driver to use for different tasks, as well ad specify the sounds to use for desktop events, you use the Hardware Sound configuration tool (Hardware | Sound). On the

Devices panel you can select the sound driver to use, if more than one, for the Sound Events, Music and Videos, and conferencing. Defaults will already be chosen. On the Sounds tab you can enable alerts and sound effects. GNOME now uses sound themes to specify an entire set of sounds for different effects and alerts. You can turn effects and alerts on or off. The effects and alerts are listed in the Alerts and Sound Effects section. Each sound will have a default entry which you can click to open a pop-up menu with entries for default, disable, and custom. Selecting custom will open a window where you can select a sound file to use instead of the default.

Desktop Themes

You use the Themes panel on the Appearance Preferences tool to select or customize a theme. Themes control your desktop appearance. The Themes panel will list icons for currently installed themes (see Figure 9-12). The icons will show key aspects or each theme like window, folder, and button images, in effect previewing the theme for you. The Fedora theme is initially selected. You can move through the icons to select a different theme if you wish. If you have downloaded additional themes from sites like **http://art.gnome.org**, you can click the install button to locate and install them. Once installed, the additional themes will also be displayed in the Theme panel. If you download and install a theme or icon set from the Fedora repository, it will be automatically installed for you.

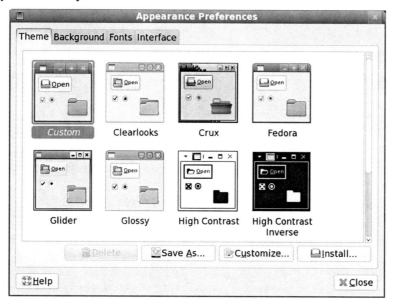

Figure 9-12: Theme selection on Appearance Preferences tool

The true power of Themes is shown in the ability it let users customize any given theme. Themes are organized into three components: controls, window border, and icons. Controls covers the appearance of window and dialog controls like buttons and slider bars. Window border specifies how title bars, borders, window buttons are displayed. Icons specify how all icons used on the desktop are displayed, whether on the file manager, desktop, or the panel. You can actually mix and match components from any installed theme to make your own theme. You can even download and install separate components like specific icon sets, which you can then use in a customized theme.

Clicking the customize button will open a Themes Details window with panels the different theme components. The ones used for the current theme will be already selected. The controls panel will list. An additional color panel lets you set the background and text colors for windows, input boxes, and selected items. In the control, window border, and icon panels you will see listings of the different themes. You can then mix and match different components from those themes, creating your own customized theme. Upon selecting a component, you desktop will automatically change showing you how it looks. If you have added a component, like a new icon set, it will also be listed.

One you have created a new customized theme, a Custom Theme entry will appear in the theme list. To save the customized theme, click the Save Theme button. This opens a dialog where you can enter a theme name, any notes, and specify whether you want to also keep the theme background. The saved theme then appears in the theme listing.

Themes and icons installed directly by a user are placed in the **.themes** and **.icons** directories in the user's home directory. Should you want these themes made available for all users, you can move them from the .themes and .icons directories to the **/usr/share/icons** and **/usr/share/themes** directories. Be sure to login as the root user. You then need to change ownership of the moved themes and icons to the root user.

```
chown  -R root:root   /usr/share/themes/newtheme
```

Fonts

Like most Linux distributions, Fedora uses the fontconfig method for managing fonts (**fontconfig.org**). You can easily change font sizes, add new fonts, and configure features like anti-aliasing. Both Gnome and KDE provide tools for selecting, resizing, and adding fonts.

Resizing Desktop Fonts

With very large monitors and their high resolutions becoming more common, one feature users find helpful is the ability to increase the desktop font sizes. On a large widescreen monitor, resolutions less than the native one tend not to scale well. A monitor always looks best in its native resolution. However, with a large native resolution like 1900 × 1200, text sizes become so small they are hard to read. You can overcome this issue by increasing the font size. The default size is 10; increasing it to 12 makes text in all desktop features like windows and menus much more readable.

Tip: You can use the Specimen Font Viewer to display your installed fonts, seeing what they look like (Applications | Graphics | Specimen Font Viewer).

To increase the font size, open the Font Preferences dialog by selecting the Fonts panel on the Appearance tool, System | Preferences | Look And Feel | Appearance. The Font panel is shown in Figure 9-13. You can even change the font itself as well as choose bold or italic. You can further refine your fonts display by clicking the Details button to open a window where you can set features like the dots-per-inch, hinting, and smoothing. To examine a font in more detail, click the Go To Fonts Folder button and click the font.

Adding Fonts

To add fonts you open the font viewer. You can do this directly by entering the **fonts:/** URL in any file manager window. Select Open Location from the File menu to open the URL box. Once the font viewer is open, you can add a font by simply dragging it to the font viewer window. When you restart, your font will be available for use on your desktop. KDE will have Personal and System folders for fonts, initially showing icons for each. For user fonts, open the Personal fonts window. Fonts that are Zip archived, should first be opened with the Archive manager and the can be dragged from the archive manager to the font viewer. To remove a font, right-click it in the font viewer select Move to Trash or Delete.

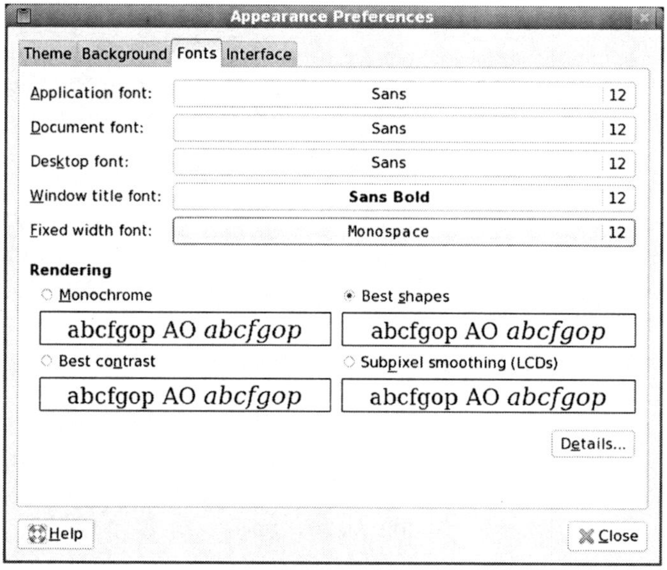

Figure 9-13: Setting Font Sizes on Appearance Preferences

User fonts will be installed to a user's **.fonts** directory. For fonts to be available to all users, they have to be installed in the **/usr/share/fonts** directory, making them system fonts. On KDE, you do this by opening the System folder, instead of the Personal folder when you start up the fonts viewer. You can do this from any user login. Then drag any fonts packages to this **fonts:/System** window. On Gnome, you have to login as the root user and manually copy fonts to the **/user/share/fonts** directory. If your system has installed both Gnome and KDE, you can install system fonts using KDE (Konqueror file manager) and they will be available on Gnome.

To provide speedy access to system fonts, you should create font information cache files for the **/usr/share/fonts** directory. To do this run **fc-cache** command as the root user.

Microsoft common Web fonts are freely available from **www.fontconfig.org**. These fonts are archived in Microsoft's cab format. You will need to download and install the **cabextract** tool (available from the Fedora repository) to extract the fonts. Once extracted, you can copy them to a folder in **/usr/share/fonts** directory to make them available to all users. If you have network access to a Windows system, can also directly copy fonts from the Windows fonts directory to your **/usr/share/fonts** directory.

Configuring Fonts

To better refine your font display, you can use the font rendering tool. Open the Font panel on the Appearance tool (System | Preferences | Look and Feel | Appearance). The Font Rendering section lists basic font rendering features like Monochrome, Best contrast, Best shapes, and Subpixel smoothing. Choose the one that works best. For LCDS choose subpixel smoothing. For detailed configuration, click on the Details button. Here you can set smoothing, hinting (anti-aliasing), and subpixel color order features. The sub-pixel color order is hardware dependent.

On KDE, in the KDE control center, select the Fonts entry under Appearance and Themes. Click on the "Use anti-aliasing for fonts" check box, and then click on the Configure button to open a window to let you select hinting and subpixel options.

On Gnome, clicking on a font entry in the Fonts panel will open a Pick a font dialog that will list all available fonts. On KDE, clicking any of the Choose buttons on the Control Center's Fonts panel will also open a window listing all available fonts. You can also generate a listing with the **fc-list** command. The list will be unsorted, so you should pipe it first to the sort command. You can use **fc-list** with any font name or name pattern to search for fonts, with options to search by language, family, or styles. See the **/etc/share/fontconfig** documentation for more details.

```
fc-list | sort
```

Sessions

You can configure your desktop to restore your previously opened windows and applications, as well as specify startup programs. When you log out, you may want the windows you have open and the applications you have running to be automatically started when you log back in. In effect, you are saving you current session, and having it restored it when you log back in. For example, if you are in the middle of working on a spread sheet, you can save your work, but not close the file. Then logout. When you log back in, your spreadsheet will be opened automatically to where you left off.

Saving sessions is not turned on by default. You use the Sessions preferences dialog's Session Options panel (System | Preferences | Personal | Sessions) to save sessions. You can save your current session manually, or opt to have all your sessions saved automatically when you logout, restoring them whenever you login.

You can also use the Sessions preferences dialog to select programs that you may want started up automatically. Some are already selected like the Packagekit Update applet and the SELinux troubleshooter. On the Startup Programs panel you can select programs you want started, as well as un-select the ones you don't want. Click the Add button to add a program to the list. You will be able to search for the application you want or enter it directly.

The GNOME Panel

The *panel* is the main component of the GNOME interface (see Figures 9-14 and 9-16). Through it you can start your applications, run applets, and access desktop areas. You can think of the GNOME panel as a type of tool you can use on your desktop. You can have several GNOME panels displayed on your desktop, each with applets and menus you have placed in them. In this respect, GNOME is flexible, enabling you to configure your panels any way you want. In fact, the default GNOME desktop that Fedora uses features two panels, a menu panel at the top for your applications and actions, and a panel at the bottom used for minimized windows and the workspace switcher. You can customize a panel to fit your own needs, holding applets and menus of your own selection. You may add new panels, add applications to the panel, and add various applets.

Panel configuration tasks such as adding applications, selecting applets, setting up menus, and creating new panels are handled from the Panel pop-up menu. Just right-click anywhere on your panel to display a menu with entries for Properties, New Panel, Add To Panel, and Delete This Panel, along with Help and About entries. New Panel lets you create other panels; Add To Panel lets you add items to the panel such as application launchers, applets for simple tasks like the Workspace Switcher, and menus like the main applications menu. The Properties entry will display a dialog for configuring the features for that panel, like the position of the panel and its hiding capabilities.

Figure 9-14: The GNOME panel, at the top of Fedora desktop

To add a new panel, select the New Panel entry in the Panel pop-up menu. A new expanded panel is automatically created and displayed on the side of your screen. You can then use the panel's properties box to set different display and background features, as described in the following sections.

Panel Properties

To configure individual panels, you use the Panel Properties dialog box. To display this dialog box, you right-click the particular panel and select the Properties entry in the pop-up menu. For individual panels, you can set general configuration features and the background. The Panel Properties dialog box includes a tabbed pane, General and Background. With version 2.4, GNOME abandoned the different panel types in favor of just one kind of panel with different possible features that give it the same capabilities as the old panel types.

Displaying Panels

On the General pane of a panel's properties box, you determine how you want the panel displayed. Here you have options for orientation, size, and whether to expand, auto-hide, or display hide buttons. The Orientation entry lets you select which side of screen you want the panel placed on. You can then choose whether you want a panel expanded or not. An expanded panel will fill the edges of the screen, whereas a non-expanded panel is sized to the number of items in the panel and shows handles at each end. Expanded panels will remain fixed to the edge of screen, whereas unexpanded panels can be moved, provided the Show Hide Buttons feature is not selected.

Moving and Hiding Expanded Panels

Expanded panels can be positioned at any edge of your screen. You can move expanded panels from one edge of a screen to another by simply dragging the panel to another edge. If a panel is already there, the new one will stack on top of the current one. You cannot move unexpanded panels in this way. Bear in mind that if you place an expanded panel on the side edge, any menus will be displayed across at the top corner to allow proper pop-up display. The panel on the side edge will expand in size to accommodate its menus. If you have several menus or a menu with a lengthy name, you could end up with a very large panel.

You can hide expanded panels either automatically or manually. These are features specified in the panel properties General box as Auto Hide and Show Hide Buttons. To automatically hide panels, select the Auto Hide feature. To redisplay the panel, move your mouse to the edge where the panel is located. You can enable or disable the Hide buttons in the panel's properties window.

If you want to be able to hide a panel manually, select the Show Hide Buttons. Two handles will be displayed at either end of the panel. You can further choose whether to have these handles display arrows or not. You can then hide the panel at any time by clicking either of the Hide buttons located on each end of the panel. The Hide buttons are thin buttons showing a small arrow. This is the direction in which the panel will hide.

Unexpanded Panels: Movable and Fixed

Whereas an expanded panel is always located at the edge of the screen, an unexpanded panel is movable. It can be located at the edge of a screen, working like a shrunken version of an Expanded panel, or you can move it to any place on your desktop, just as you would an icon.

An unexpanded panel will shrink to the number of its components, showing handles at either end. You can then move the panel by dragging its handles. To access the panel menu with its properties entry, right-click either of its handles.

To fix an unexpanded panel at its current position, select the Show Hide Buttons feature on its properties box. This will replace the handles with Hide buttons and make the panel fixed. Clicking a Hide button will hide the panel to the edge of the screen, just as with Expanded panels. If an expanded panel is already located on that edge, the button for a hidden unexpanded panel will be on top of it, just as with a hidden expanded panel. The Auto Hide feature will work for unexpanded panels placed at the edge of a screen.

If you want to fix an unexpanded panel to the edge of a screen, make sure it is placed at the edge you want, and then set its Show Hide Buttons feature.

Panel Background

With a panel's Background pane on its properties box, you can change the panel's background color or image. For a color background you click a color button to display a color selection window where you can choose a color from a color wheel or a list of color boxes, or else you can enter its number. Once your color is selected, you can use the Style slide bar to make it more transparent or opaque. To use an image instead of a color, select the image entry and use the Browse button to locate the image file you want. For an image, you can also drag and drop an image file from the file manager to the panel; that image then becomes the background image for the panel.

Panel Objects

A panel can contain several different types of objects. These include menus, launchers, applets, drawers, and special objects.

Menus   The Applications menu is an example of a panel menu. Launchers are buttons used to start an application or execute a command.

Launchers   The Web browser icon is an example of a launcher button. You can select any application entry in the Applications menu and create a launcher for it on the panel.

Applets   An applet is a small application designed to run within the panel. The Workspace Switcher showing the different desktops is an example of a GNOME applet.

Drawers   A drawer is an extension of the panel that can be open or closed. You can think of a drawer as a shrinkable part of the panel. You can add anything to it that you can to a regular panel, including applets, menus, and even other drawers.

Special objects   These are used for special tasks not supported by other panel objects. For example, the Logout and Lock buttons are special objects.

Moving, Removing, and Locking Objects

To move any object within the panel, right-click it and choose Move Entry. You can move it either to a different place on the same panel or to a different panel. For launchers, you can just drag the object directly where you want it to be. To remove an object from the panel, right-click it to display a pop-up menu for it, and then choose the Remove From Panel entry. To prevent an object from being moved or removed, you set its lock feature (right-click the object and select the Lock entry). To later allow it to be moved, you first have to unlock the object (right-click it and select Unlock).

Figure 9-15: Panel Add To Box listing panel objects

Tip: On the panel Add To list, common objects like the clock and the CD player are intermixed with object types like menus and applications. When adding a kind of object, like an application, you will have to search through the list to find the entry for that type; in the case of applications, it is the application launcher entry.

Adding Objects

To add an object to a panel, select the object from the panel's Add To box (see Figure 9-15). To display the Add To box, right-click on the panel and select the Add To Panel entry. This Add To box displays a lengthy list of common objects as well as object types. For example, it will display the Main menu as well as an entry for creating custom menus. You can choose to add an application that is already in the GNOME Application menu or to create an application launcher for one that is not. Launchers can be added to a panel by just dragging them directly. Launchers include applications, windows, and files.

Application Launchers

To Add an application that already has an application launcher to a panel is easy. You just have to drag the application launcher to the panel. This will automatically create a copy of the launcher for use on that panel. Launchers can be menu items or desktop icons. All the entries in your Application menu are application launchers. To add an application from the menu, just select it and drag it to the panel. You can also drag any desktop application icon to a panel to add a copy of it to that panel.

For any menu item, you can also go to its entry and right-click it. Then select the Add This Launcher To Panel entry. An application launcher for that application is then automatically added to the panel. Suppose you use Gedit frequently and want to add its icon to the panel, instead of having to go through the Application menu all the time. Right-click the Text Editor menu entry in the Accessories menu, and select the Add This Launcher To Panel option. The Gedit icon now appears in your panel.

You can also select the Add To Panel entry from the panel menu and then choose the Application Launcher entry. This will display a box with a listing of all the Application menu entries along with Preferences and Administration menus, expandable to their items. Just find the application you want added and select it. This may be an easier approach if you are working with many different panels.

Keep in mind that for any launcher that you previously created on the desktop, you can just drag it to the panel, to have copy of the launcher placed on the panel.

Folder and File Launchers

To add a folder to a panel, just drag it directly from the file manager window or from the desktop. To add a file, also drag it directly to the panel, but you will then have to create a launcher for it. The Create Launcher window will be displayed, and you can give the file launcher a name and select an icon for it.

Adding Drawers

You can also group applications under a Drawer icon. Clicking the Drawer icon displays a list of the different application icons you can then select. To add a drawer to your panel, right-click the panel and select the Add To Panel entry to display the Add To list. From that list select the Drawer entry. This will create a drawer on your panel. You can then drag any items from desktop, menus, or windows to the drawer icon on the panel to have them listed in the drawer.

If you want to add, as a drawer, a whole menu of applications on the main menu to your panel, right-click any item in that menu, and then select Entire Menu from the pop-up menu, and then select the Add This As Drawer To Panel entry. The entire menu appears as a drawer on your panel, holding icons instead of menu entries. For example, suppose you want to place the Internet Applications menu on your panel. Right-click any entry item, selecting Entire Menu, and select Add This As Drawer To Panel. A drawer appears on your panel labeled Internet, and clicking it displays a pop-up list of icons for all the Internet applications.

Adding Menus

A menu differs from a drawer in that a *drawer* holds application icons instead of menu entries. You can add menus to your panel, much as you add drawers. To add a submenu from the Applications menu to your panel, right-click any item and select Entire Menu, and then select the Add This As Menu To Panel entry. The menu title appears in the panel; you can click it to display the menu entries. You can also add a menu from the panel's Add To list, by selecting Custom menu.

Adding Folders

You can also add directory folders to a panel. Click and drag the Folder icon from the file manager window to your panel. Whenever you click this Folder button, a file manager window opens, displaying that directory. You already have a Folder button for your home directory. You can add directory folders to any drawer on your panel.

GNOME Applets

Applets are small programs that perform tasks within the panel. To add an applet, right-click the panel and select Add To Panel from the pop-up menu. This displays the Add To box listing common applets along with other types of objects, such as launchers. Select the one you want. For example, to add the clock to your panel, select Clock from the panel's Add To box. Once added, the applet will show up in the panel. If you want to remove an applet, right-click it and select the Remove From Panel entry.

GNOME features a number of helpful applets. Some applets monitor your system, such as the Battery Charge Monitor, which checks the battery in laptops, and System Monitor, which shows a graph indicating your current CPU and memory use. The Volume Control applet displays a small scroll bar for adjusting sound levels. The new Deskbar searches for files on your desktop.

Several helpful utility applets provide added functionality to your desktop. The Clock applet can display time in a 12- or 24-hour format. Right-click the Clock applet and select the Preferences entry to change its setup. The CPU Frequency Scaling Monitor displays CPU usage for CPUs like AMD and the new Intel processors that run at lower speeds when idle.

Workspace Switcher

The Workspace Switcher appears in the panel and shows a view of your virtual desktops (see Figure 9-16). Virtual desktops are defined in the window manager. On the current Fedora configuration, the Workspace Switcher is located on the right side of the lower panel. The Workspace Switcher lets you easily move from one desktop to another with the click of a mouse. It is a panel applet that works only in the panel. You can add the Workspace Switcher to any panel by selecting it from that panel's Add To box. If Compiz-fusion is enabled you can also use the scroll button on your mouse, or the Ctrl-Alt-arrow keys to move from one workspace to another.

The Workspace Switcher shows your entire virtual desktop as separate rectangles listed next to each other. Open windows show up as small colored rectangles in these squares. You can move any window from one virtual desktop to another by clicking and dragging its image in the Workspace Switcher. To configure the Workspace Switcher, right-click it and select Preferences to display the Preferences dialog box. Here, you can select the number of workspaces and name them. The default is two. If Compiz-Fusion is enables, then the Workspace Switcher Preferences shows a simple dialog with entries for column and rows number which can change to add workspaces.

Figure 9-16: Panel with workspace switcher and window list, at the bottom of the Fedora desktop

GNOME Window List

The Window List shows currently opened windows. The Window List arranges opened windows in a series of buttons, one for each window. A window can include applications such as a Web browser or a file manager window displaying a directory. You can move from one window to another by clicking its button. When you minimize a window, you can later restore it by clicking its entry in the Window List.

Right-clicking a window's Window List button opens a menu that lets you Minimize or Unminimize, Roll Up, Move, Resize, Maximize, or Close the window. The Minimize operation will reduce the window to its Window List entry. Right-clicking the entry will display the menu with an Unminimize option instead of a Minimize one, which you can then use to redisplay the window. The Roll Up entry will reduce the window to its title bar. The Close entry will close the window, ending its application.

If there is not enough space on the Window List applet to display a separate button for each window, then common windows will be grouped under a button that will expand like a menu, listing each window in that group. For example, all open terminal windows would be grouped under a single button, which when clicked would pop up a list of their buttons.

The Window List applet is represented by a small serrated bar at the beginning of the window button list. To configure the Window List, right-click on this bar and select the Properties entry. Here, you can set features such as the size in pixels, whether to group windows, whether to show all open windows or those from just the current workspace, or which workspace to restore windows to.

The GNOME File Manager

Nautilus is the GNOME file manager, supporting the standard features for copying, removing, and deleting items as well as setting permissions and displaying items. It also provides enhancements such as zooming capabilities, user levels, and theme support. You can enlarge or reduce the size of your file icons, select from novice, intermediate, or expert levels of use, and customize the look and feel of Nautilus with different themes. Nautilus also lets you set up customized views of file listings, enabling you to display images for directory icons and run component applications within the file manager window. Nautilus implements a spatial approach to file browsing. A new window is opened for each new folder. Nautilus is based on the GVFS (GNOME Virtual File System) which allows any application to access a virtually mounted file system. File system mounted with FUSE, the user base file systems access, will be displayed and accessed by Nautilus.

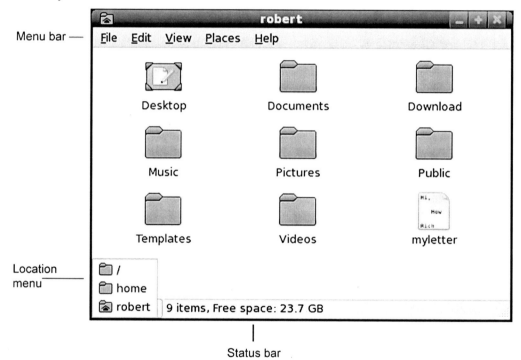

Figure 9-17: Default Nautilus window (spatial view)

Home Folder Subdirectories

Fedora uses the Common User Directory Structure (xdg-user-dirs at **www.freedesktop.org**) to set up subdirectories such as **Music** and **Video** in the user home directory. Folders will include Documents, Music, Pictures, and Videos. These localized user directories are used as defaults by many desktop applications. Users can change their directory names or place them within each other using the GNOME file browser. For example, Music can be moved into **Documents**, **Documents/Music**. Local configuration is held in the **.config/user-dirs.dirs** file. System-wide defaults are set up in the **/etc/xdg/user-dirs.defaults** file.

Nautilus Windows

Nautilus was designed as a desktop shell in which different components can be employed to add functionality. An image viewer can display images. The GNOME media player can run sound and video files. Archives can also be managed directly by the Nautilus file manager. With the implementation of GStreamer, multimedia tools such as the GNOME audio recorder are now more easily integrated into Nautilus.

By default, the Nautilus windows are displayed with the spatial view. This provides a streamlined display with no toolbars or sidebar (see Figure 9-17). Much of its functionality has been moved to menus and pop-up windows, leaving more space to display files and folders. You can, however, open a Nautilus window in the browser view, which will display the traditional menu bar and location toolbars. You can open a window in the browser view by right-clicking the folder icon and selecting Browse Folder from the pop-up menu.

The Spatial view of a Nautilus window displays a menu bar at the top with menus for managing your files. An information bar at the bottom displays information about the directory or selected files. To the lower left is a pop-up window displaying the parent directories for your current working directory. You can select any entry to open a window for that directory.

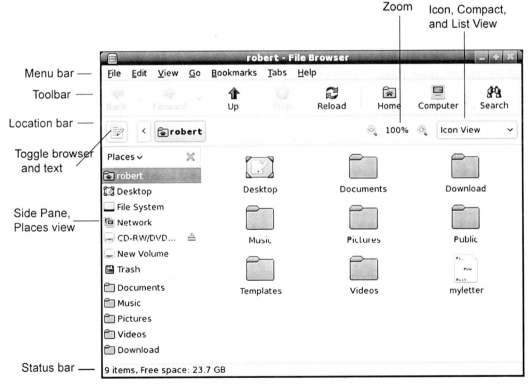

Figure 9-18: Nautilus file manager window with toolbars and sidebar (browser view)

With the Browser view, a Nautilus window displays toolbars, including a menu bar of file manager commands and a Location toolbar at the top which can toggle between a location box or button views (see Figure 9-18), along with a sidebar for file and directory information. The rest of the window is divided into two panes. The left pane is a side pane used to display information about the current working directory. The right pane is the main panel that displays the list of files and subdirectories in the current working directory. A status bar at the bottom of the window displays information about a selected file or directory. You can turn any of these elements on or off by selecting their entries in the View menu.

Next to the Location bar (box or button) is an element for zooming in and out of the view of the files. Click the + button to zoom in and the – button to zoom out. Next to the zoom element is a drop-down menu for selecting the different views for your files, such as icons, small icons, or details.

Nautilus Side Pane: Tree, History, and Notes

The side pane has several different views, selectable from a pop-up menu, for displaying additional information about files and directories: Places, Information, Tree, History, and Notes. Places show your file system locations that you would normally access, starting with your home directory. File System places you at top of the file system, letting you move to any accessible part of it. Information displays detailed information about the current directory or selected file. For example, if you double-click an image file, the Information pane will display detailed data on the image, while the window pane displays the full image. The Tree view will display a tree-based hierarchical view of the directories and files on your system, highlighting the one you have currently selected. You can use this tree to move to other directories and files. The tree maps all the directories on your system, starting from the root directory. You can expand or shrink any directory by clicking the + or – symbol before its name. Select a directory by clicking the directory name. The contents of that directory are then displayed in the main panel. The History view shows previous files or directories you have accessed, handy for moving back and forth between directories or files.

The Notes view will display notes you have entered about an item or directory. The Notes view opens an editable text window within the side pane. Just select the Notes view and type in your notes. To add a note for a particular item, such as an image or sound file, just double-click the item to display or run it, and then select the Note view to type in your note. You can also right-click the item, to display the item's pop-up menu and select preferences, from which you can click a Notes panel. After you have added a note, you will see a note image added to the item's icon in the Nautilus window.

Tabs

The GNOME file manager now supports tabs. You can open up several folders in the same file manager window. To open a tabbed pane, select New Tab from the File menu or press **Ctrl-t**. You can then use the entries in the Tabs menu to move from one tab to another, or to rearrange tabs. You can also use the Ctrl-PageUp and Ctrl-PageDown keys to move from one tab to another. Use the Shift-Ctrl-PageUp and Shift-Ctrl-PageDown keys to rearrange the tabs.

Displaying Files and Folders

You can view a directory's contents as icons, a compact list, or as a detailed list. In the spatial view, you select the different options from the View menu. In the Browser view, you use the pop-up menu located on the right side of the Location bar. The List view provides the name, permissions, size, date, owner, and group. In the "View as List" view, buttons are displayed for each field across the top of the main panel. You can use these buttons to sort the lists according to that field. For example, to sort the files by date, click the Date button; to sort by size, click Size.

In the Icon view, you can sort icons and preview their contents without opening them. To sort items in the Icon view, select the Arrange Items entry in the View menu (spatial or browser views) and then select a layout option. Certain types of file icons will display previews of their contents—for example, the icons for image files will display a small version of the image. A text file will display in its icon the first few words of its text. The Zoom In entry enlarges your view of the window, making icons bigger, and Zoom Out reduces your view, making them smaller. Normal Size restores them to the standard size. You can also use the + and – buttons on the Location bar to change sizes.

In both the spatial and browser views, you can also change the size of individual icons. Select the icon and then choose the Stretch entry from the Edit menu. Handles will appear on the icon image. Click and drag the handles to change its size. To restore the icon, select Restore Icon's Original Size in the Edit menu.

Menu Item	Description
Create Folder	Creates a new subdirectory in the directory.
Create Document	Creates a new document using installed templates.
Arrange Items	Displays a submenu to arrange files by name, size, type, date, or emblem.
Cut, Copy, Paste	Cuts, copies, or pastes files, letting you move or copy files between folders.
Zoom In	Provides a close-up view of icons, making them appear larger.
Zoom Out	Provides a distant view of icons, making them appear smaller.
Normal Size	Restores view of icons to standard size.
Properties	Opens the Properties panels for the directory opened in the window.
Clean Up by Name	Arranges icons by name.

Table 9-5: Nautilus File Manager Menu

To add an emblem to any file or directory icon, just select the Background & Emblems entry from the Edit menu to open the Background And Emblems window. Here you will see three icons to display panels for color and pattern backgrounds, as well as file and directory emblems. Click emblems to display the selection of emblems. To add an emblem to a file or directory icon, click and drag the emblem from the Emblem panel to the file or directory icon. The emblem will appear on that icon. If you want to add your own emblem, click the Add Emblem button to can search for an emblem image file by name, or browse your file system for the image you want to use (click the image icon).

Nautilus Menu

You can click anywhere on the main panel to display a pop-up menu with entries for managing and arranging your file manager icons (see Table 9-5). The menu is the same for both spatial and browser views. To create a new folder, select Create Folder. The Arrange Items entry displays a submenu with entries for sorting your icons by name, size, type, date, or even emblem.

The Manually entry lets you move icons wherever you want on the main panel. You can also cut, copy, and paste files to more easily move or copy them between folders.

Tip: To change the background used on the File Manager window, you now select "Background and Emblems" from the Edit menu, dragging the background you want to the file manager window. Choose from either colors or patterns.

Navigating Directories

The spatial and browser views use different tools for navigating directories. The spatial view relies more on direct window operations, whereas the browse view works more like a browser. Recall that to open a directory with the browser view, you need to right-click the directory icon and select Browse Folder.

Navigating in the Spatial View

In the spatial view, Nautilus will open a new window for each directory selected. To open a directory, either double-click it or right-click and select the Open entry. The parent directory pop-up menu at the bottom left lets you open a window for any parent directories, in effect, moving to a previous directory. To jump to a specific directory, select the Open Location entry from the File menu. This will, of course, open a new window for that directory. The Open Parent entry on the File menu lets you quickly open a new window for your parent. You will quickly find that moving to different directories entails opening many new windows.

Navigating in the Browser View

The browser view of the Nautilus file manager operates similarly to a Web browser, using the same window to display opened directories. It maintains a list of previously viewed directories, and you can move back and forth through that list using the toolbar buttons. The left arrow button moves you to the previously displayed directory, and the right arrow button moves you to the next displayed directory. The up arrow button moves you to the parent directory, and the Home button moves you to your home directory. To use a pathname to go directly to a given directory, you can type the pathname in the Location box and press ENTER. Use the toggle icon at the left of the location bar to toggle between box and button location views.

To open a subdirectory, you can double-click its icon or single-click the icon and select Open from the File menu. If you want to open a separate Nautilus browser view window for that directory, right-click the directory's icon and select Open In A New Window.

Managing Files

As a GNOME-compliant file manager, Nautilus supports GUI drag-and-drop operations for copying and moving files. To move a file or directory, click and drag from one directory to another as you would on Windows or Mac interfaces. The move operation is the default drag-and-drop operation in GNOME. To copy a file, click and drag normally while pressing the CTRL key.

Note: If you move a file to a directory on another partition (File System in Computer window), it will be copied instead of moved.

The File Manager pop-up Menu for files and directories

You can also perform remove, rename, and link creation operations on a file by right-clicking its icon and selecting the action you want from the pop-up menu that appears (see Table 9-6). For example, to remove an item, right-click it and select the Move To Trash entry from the pop-up menu. This places it in the Trash directory, where you can later delete it by selecting Empty Trash from the Nautilus File menu. To create a link, right-click the file and select Make Link from the pop-up menu. This creates a new link file that begins with the term "link."

Menu Item	Description
Open	Opens the file with its associated application. Directories are opened in the file manager. Associated applications will be listed.
Open In A New Window	Opens a file or directory in a separate window. Alternate view only.
Open With Other Application	Selects an application with which to open this file. A submenu of possible applications is displayed.
Cut, Copy, Paste files	Entries to cut, copy, paste files.
Make Link	Creates a link to that file in the same directory.
Rename	Renames the file.
Move To Trash	Moves a file to the Trash directory, where you can later delete it.
Create Archive	Archives file using File Roller.
Send To	Email the file
Properties	Displays the Properties dialog box for this file. There are three panels: Statistics, Options, and Permissions.

Table 9-6: The Nautilus File and Directory Pop-Up Menu

Renaming Files

To rename a file, you can either right-click the file's icon and select the Rename entry from the pop-up menu or click the name of the file shown below its icon. The name of the icon will be highlighted in a black background, encased in a small text box. You can then click the name and delete the old name, typing a new one. You can also rename a file by entering a new name in its Properties dialog box. Use a right-click and select Properties from the pop-up menu to display the Properties dialog box. On the Basic tab, you can change the name of the file.

File Grouping

File operations can be performed on a selected group of files and directories. You can select a group of items in several ways. You can click the first item and then hold down the SHIFT key while clicking the last item. You can also click and drag the mouse across items you want to select. To select separated items, hold the CTRL key down as you click the individual icons. If you want to select all the items in the directory, choose the Select All entry in the Edit menu. You can then click and drag a set of items at once. This enables you to copy, move, or even delete several files at once.

Applications and Files: MIME Types

You can start any application in the file manager by double-clicking either the application itself or a data file used for that application. If you want to open the file with a specific application, you can right-click the file and select the Open With entry. A submenu displays a list of possible applications. If your application is not listed, you can select Other Application to open a Select An Application dialog box where you can choose the application with which you want to open this file. You can also use a text viewer to display the bare contents of a file within the file manager window. Drag-and-drop operations are also supported for applications. You can drag a data file to its associated application icon (say, one on the desktop); the application then starts up using that data file.

To change or set the default application to use for a certain type of file, you open a file's Properties and select the Open With tab. Here you can choose the default application to use for that kind of file. Once you select your application, it will appear in the Open With list for this file. For example changing the default for an image file from Image Viewer to GwenView will make GwenView the default viewer for all image files. If there is an application you do not want listed in the Open With options, select it and click the Remove button.

If the application you want is not listed, click the Add button in the Open With panel to display a listing of applications. Choose the one you want. This displays an Add Application box and a Browse button. Commonly used applications are already listed. If you already know the full pathname of the application, you can enter it directly. If the application is not listed, you can click Browse to display a Select An Application box that will list applications you can choose. Initially, applications in the **/usr/bin** directory are listed, though you can browse to other directories. Once you select your application, it will appear in the Open With list for this file.

For example, to associate BitTorrent files, with the original BitTorrent application, you would right-click any BitTorrent file (one with a **.torrent** extension), select the Properties entry, and then select the Open With panel. A list of installed applications will be displayed, such as Ktorrent, Azureus, and BitTorrent. Click BitTorrent to use the original BitTorrent application, then close. BitTorrent is now the default for **.torrent** files.

Hint: The Preferred Applications tool will let you set default applications for Internet and System applications, namely the Web browser, mail client, and terminal window console. Available applications are listed in pop-up menus. You can even select from a list of installed applications for select a custom program. You access the Preferred Applications tool from the Personal submenu located in the System | Preferences menu.

Application Launcher

Certain files, such as shell scripts, are meant to be executed as applications. To run the file using an icon as you would other installed applications, you can create an application launcher for it. You can create application launchers using the Create Launcher tool. This tool is accessible either from the desktop menu as the Create Launcher entry or from the panel menu's Add To box as the Custom Application Launcher entry. When accessed from the desktop, the new launcher is placed on the desktop, and from the panel, it will be placed directly on the panel.

The Create Launcher tool will prompt you for the application name, the command that invokes it, and its type. For the type you have the choice for application, file, or file within a terminal. For shell scripts, you would use an Application In Terminal option, running the script within a shell.

Use the file type for a data file for which an associated application will be automatically started, opening the file, for example, a Web page, which will then start a Web browser. Instead of a command, you will be prompted to enter the location of the file.

For Applications and Applications In Terminal, you will be prompted to select the command to use. To select the command to use (the actual application or script file), you can either enter its pathname, if you know it, or use the Browse button to open a file browser window to select it.

To select an icon for your launcher, click the Icon button, initially labeled No Icon. This opens the Icon Browser window, listing icons from which you can choose.

Preferred Applications for Web, Mail, Accessibility, and terminal windows

Certain types of files will have default applications already associated with them. For example, double-clicking a Web page file will open the file in the Firefox Web browser. If you prefer to set a different default application, you can use the Preferred Applications tool (see Figure 9-19). This tool will let you set default applications for Web pages, Mail readers, and Terminal window. Available applications are listed in popup menus. In Figure 9-19 the default mail reader has been reset from Evolution to Thunderbird. You can even select from a list of installed applications for select a custom program. You access the Preferred Applications tool from the Personal submenu located in the Preferences menu (System | Preferences | Personal | Preferred Applications). The Preferred applications tool has panels for Internet, Multimedia, System, and Accessibility. On the Multimedia panel you can select default multimedia applications to run. The Accessibility panel has options for selecting a magnifier.

Figure 9-19: Preferred Applications tool

Default Applications for Media

Nautilus directly handles preferences for media operations. The Media panel of the File Management Preferences window (Edit | Preferences) lists entries for Cd Audio, DVD Video, Music Player, Photos, and Software (see Figure 9-20). Pop-up menus let you select the application to use for the different media (see Figure 9-21). You also have options for Ask what to do, Do Nothing, and Open folder. The Open Folder options will just open a window displaying the files on the disk. Audio CDs and video CDs will be played by the Totem player. There is currently no default for music players. Digital cameras will use gThumb or Fspot to import photos. You can change any of the default applications used for these actions, as well as turn off default operations, such as automatically mounting or playing Audio CDs. Keep in mind that Totem will not play commercial DVD Videos. You would have to install a DVD Video-enabled player for commercial discs or the MPlayer, Xine, or Totem-zine players.

Figure 9-20: File Management Preferences, Media

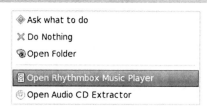

Figure 9-21: Multimedia media preferences

A segment labeled "Other media", lets you set up an association for less used media like Blu-Ray discs. Defaults are already setup for GNOME applications, like Rhythmbox Music Player for Cd Audio discs and Movie Player (Totem) for DVD Video. Photos are opened with the F-Spot Photo-manager. Software discs will run the autorun prompt.

When you insert removable media, like a CD Audio discs, its associated application is automatically started.

If you just want to turn off the startup for a particular kind of media, you can select the Do Nothing entry from its application pop-up menu. If you want to be prompted for options, then set the "Ask what to do" entry in the Media panel pop-up menu. When you insert a disc, a dialog with a pop-up menu for possible actions is displayed. The default application is already selected. You can select another application or select the Do Nothing or Open Folder options.

You can turn the automatic start up off for all media by checking the box for "Never prompt or start programs on media insertion" at the bottom of the Media panel. You can also enable the option "browse media when inserted" to just open a folder showing its files.

For certain devices like Digital Video devices, you can use the Removable Drives and Media Preferences tool, accessible with the Removable Drives And Media entry in the System | Preferences | Hardware menu (first install . This displays the Removable Drives And Media Preferences window with six panels: for storage devices, multimedia devices, cameras, PDAs, Printers and Scanners, and Input devices (see Figure 3-18). Certain settings are already set. Removable and hot plugged media will be automatically mounted. This includes floppy disks and data CD/DVDs. Blank CDs can be configured to be opened for burning by Nautilus.

File and Directory Properties

With the Properties dialog box, you can view detailed information on a file and set options and permissions (see Figure 9-22). A Properties box has five panels: Basic, Emblems, Permissions, Open With, and Notes. The *Basic* panel shows detailed information such as type, size, location, and date modified. The type is a MIME type, indicating the type of application associated with it. The file's icon is displayed at the top with a text box showing the file's name. You can edit the filename in this text box, changing that name. If you want to change the icon image used for the file or folder, just click the icon image on the Basic panel (next to the name). A Select Custom Icon dialog will open showing available icons you can use. You can select the one you want from that window. The **pixmaps** directory holds the set of current default images, though you can select your own images also. Click the image entry to see its icon displayed in the right panel. Double-clicking effects the icon image change.

The *Emblems* panel enables you to set the emblem you want displayed for this file, displaying all the emblems available. An emblem will appear in the upper-right corner of the icon, giving an indication of the file's contents or importance.

The *Permissions* panel for files shows the read, write, and execute permissions for owner, group, and other, as set for this file. You can change any of the permissions here, provided the file belongs to you. You configure access for owner, group, and others, using pop-up menus. You can set owner permissions as Read Only or Read And Write. For group and others, you can also set the None option, denying access. The group name expands to a pop-up menu listing different groups, allowing you to select one to change the file's group. If you want to execute this as an application (say a shell script) you check the Allow Executing File As Program entry. This has the effect of setting the execute permission.

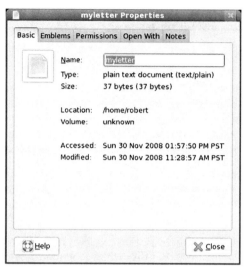

Figure 9-22: File properties on Nautilus

The *Permissions* panel for directories operates much the same way, but it includes two access entries, Folder Access and File Access. The Folder Access entry controls access to the folder with options for List Files Only, Access Files, and Create And Delete Files. These correspond to read, read and execute, and read/write/execute permissions given to directories. The File Access entry lets you set permissions for all those files in the directory. They are the same as for files: for the owner, Read or Read and Write; for the group and others, the entry adds a None option to deny access. To set the permissions for all the files in the directory accordingly (not just the folder), you click the Apply Permissions To Enclosed Files button.

The Open With panel lists all the applications associated with this kind of file. You can select which one you want as the default. This can be particularly useful for media files, where you may prefer a specific player for a certain file, or a particular image viewer for pictures. The *Notes* panel will list any notes you want to make for the file or directory. It is an editable text window, so you can change or add to your notes, directly.

Certain kind of files will have added panels, providing information about the item. For example, an audio file will have an *Audio* panel listing the type of audio file and any other information like the song title or compressions method used. An image file will have an *Image* panel listing the resolution and type of image. A video file will contain a *Video* panel showing the type of video file along with compression and resolution information.

Nautilus Preferences

You can set preferences for your Nautilus file manager in the Preferences dialog box. Access this dialog box by selecting the Preferences item in the Edit menu or select System | Preferences | Personal | File Management. The Preferences dialog box shows a main panel with a sidebar with several configuration entries, including Views, Behavior, Display, List Columns, and

Preview. You use these dialog boxes to set the default display properties for your Nautilus file manager.

> The Views panel allows you to select how files are displayed by default, such as the list or icon view.

> Behavior lets you choose how to select files, manage the trash, and handle scripts, as well as whether to use the Browse File alternate view as the default.

> Display lets you choose what added information you want displayed in an icon caption, like the size or date.

> List view lets you choose both the features to display in the detailed list and the order to display them in. In addition to the already-selected Name, Size, Date, and Type, you can add permissions, group, MIME type, and owner.

> The Preview panel lets you choose whether you want small preview content displayed in the icons, like beginning text for text files.

Tip: To display a Delete option on the file menus, on the Behavior panel of the File Management Preferences click the "Include a Delete Command that bypasses Trash" entry in the Trash section.

Nautilus as a FTP Browser

Nautilus works as an operational FTP browser. You can use the Location box (toggle to box view) or the Open Location entry on the File menu to access any FTP site. Just enter the URL for the FTP site in the Location box and press ENTER (you do not need to specify **ftp://**). Folders on the FTP site will be displayed, and you can drag files to a local directory to download them. The first time you connect to a site, an Authentication dialog will open letting you select either Anonymous access or access as a User. If you select User, you can then enter your username and password for that site. You can then choose to remember the password for just this session or permanently by storing it in a keyring.

Once you have accessed the site, you can navigate through the folders as you would with any Nautilus folder, opening directories or returning to parent directories. To download a file, just drag it from the ftp window to a local directory window. A small dialog will appear showing download progress. To upload a file, just drag it from your local folder to the window for the open ftp directory. Your file will be uploaded to that ftp site (should you have permission to do so). You can also delete files on the site's directories.

Note: Nautilus is not a functional Web browser. It is preferable that you use the Web browsers for access the Web.

GNOME Configuration

You can configure GNOME easily using the Preferences tools as described in this chapter. The GNOME Control Center also provides easy access to these tools. GNOME configuration is placed in both user and system directories. Many you can edit to tweak your interface, but it is not advisable. Also, for more lower level configuration, you can also use the GCONF configuration editor. Features for both application interfaces and the GNOME desktop can be easily managed.

GNOME Control Center

Both Preference and Administration tools can be accessed either from the System menu or from the GNOME Control Center (see Figure 9-23). The GNOME Control Center is not displayed by default. You can use the Main Menu tool to add it (System | Preferences | Look and Feel | Main Menu). You will find it in System | Preferences. Once displayed you can access the GNOME Control Center from the System | Preferences window. The GNOME Control Center opens a window with a sidebar for the Preferences and Administration (System) tools, and a pane listing the different tools by section. Click on an entry to open it. The GNOME Control Center also has a search capability for quickly locating a tool.

Figure 9-23: GNOME Control Center

GNOME Directories and Files

Fedora installs GNOME binaries in the **/usr/bin** directory on your system. GNOME libraries are located in the **/usr/lib** directory. GNOME also has its own **include** directories with header files for use in compiling and developing GNOME applications, **/usr/include/libgnome-2.0/libgnome** and **/usr/include/libgnomeui** (see Table 9-7). The directories located in **/usr/share/gnome** contain files used to configure your GNOME environment.

GNOME sets up several configuration files and directories in your home directory. The **.gnome2** and **.gconf** directories hold configuration files for different desktop components, such as **nautilus** for the file manager and **panel** for the panels. The **DESKTOP** directory holds all the items you placed on your desktop.

System GNOME Directories	Contents
`/usr/bin`	GNOME programs
`/usr/lib`	GNOME libraries
`/usr/include/libgnome-2.0/libgnome`	Header files for use in compiling and developing GNOME applications
`/usr/include/libgnomeui`	Header files for use in compiling and developing GNOME user interface components
`/usr/share/gnome`	Files used by GNOME applications
`/usr/share/doc/gnome*`	Documentation for various GNOME packages, including libraries
`/etc/gconf`	GConf configuration files
User GNOME Directories	**Contents**
`.gnome, .gnome2`	Holds configuration files for the user's GNOME desktop and GNOME applications.
`DESKTOP`	Directory where files, directories, and links you place on the desktop will reside
`.gnome2_private`	The user's private GNOME directory
`.gtkrc`	GTK+ configuration file
`.gconf`	GConf configuration database
`.gconfd`	GConf **gconfd** daemon management files
`.gstreamer`	GNOME GStreamer multimedia configuration files
`.nautilus`	Configuration files for the Nautilus file manager

Table 9-7: GNOME Configuration Directories

The GConf

GConf Configuration Editor provides underlying configuration support (not installed by default). GConf corresponds to the Registry used on Windows system. It consists of a series of libraries used to implement a configuration database for a GNOME desktop. This standardized configuration database allows for consistent interactions between GNOME applications. GNOME applications that are built from a variety of other programs, as Nautilus is, can use GConf to configure all those programs according to a single standard, maintaining configurations in a single database. Currently the GConf database is implemented as XML files in the user's **.gconf** directory. Database interaction and access is carried out by the GConf daemon, **gconfd**.

You can use the GConf editor to configure different GNOME applications and desktop functions. To start the GConf editor, enter `gconf-editor` in a terminal window, or select Configuration Editor from the Applications | System Tools menu (Applications menu). Be sure to install the gconf-editor package first (you can use PackageKit - Add/Remove Software).

Configuration elements are specified keys that are organized by application and program. You can edit the keys, changing their values. Figure 9-24 shows the GConf editor settings for the dialog display features used for the Epiphany Web browser.

The GConf editor has three panes (see Figure 9-24):

Tree A tree pane for navigating keys, with expandable trees for each application, is located on the left. Application entries expand to subentries, grouping keys into different parts or functions for the application. For example, the Epiphany entry expands to dialog, general, Web, and directories entries.

Modification A modification pane to the top right will display the keys for a selected entry. The name field will include an icon indicating its type, and the Value field is an editable field showing the current value. You can directly change this value.

Documentation The documentation field at the bottom right displays information about the selected key, showing the key name, the application that owns it, and a short and detailed description.

Results The results pane, displayed at the bottom, only appears when you do a search for a key.

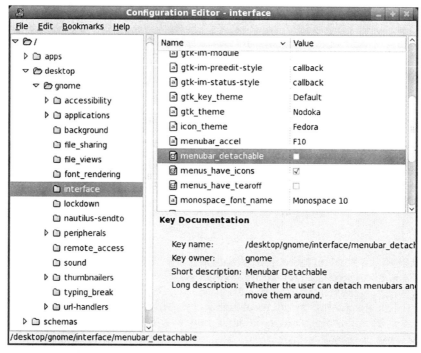

Figure 9-24: GConf editor

A key has a specific type such as numeric or string, and you will only be able to make changes using the appropriate type. Each key entry has an icon specifying its type, such as a check mark for the Boolean values, a number *1* for numeric values, and a letter a for string values. Some keys have pop-up menus with limited selections to choose from, represented by an icon with a row of lines. To change the value of a key, click its value field. You can then edit the value. For pop-up menus, you right-click the value field to display the menu.

There are many keys distributed over several applications and groups. To locate one, you can use the search function. Select Find from the Edit menu and enter a pattern. The results are displayed in a Results pane, which you can use to scroll through matching keys, selecting the one you want.

Changes can be made either by users or by administrators. Administrators can set default or mandatory values for keys. Mandatory values will prevent users from making changes. For user changes, you can open a Settings window by selecting Settings from the File menu. This opens an identical GConf Editor window. For administrative changes, you first log in as the root user. For default changes, you select the Default entry from the File menu, and for mandatory changes, select the Mandatory entry.

10. The K Desktop Environment: KDE 4

The *K Desktop Environment (KDE)* is a network-transparent desktop that includes the standard desktop features, such as a window manager and a file manager, as well as an extensive set of applications that cover most Linux tasks. KDE is an Internet-aware system that includes a full set of integrated network/Internet applications, including a mailer, a newsreader, and a Web browser. Fedora 10 uses the KDE 4 version of the K Desktop Environment. KDE 4 brings major changes, including a new file manager, window manager, and panel.

The KDE desktop is developed and distributed by the KDE Project, which is a large open group of hundreds of programmers around the world. KDE is entirely free and open software provided under a GNU Public License and is available free of charge along with its source code. KDE development is managed by a core group: the KDE Core Team. Anyone can apply, though membership is based on merit.

Numerous applications written specifically for KDE are easily accessible from the desktop. These include editors, photo and paint image applications, spreadsheets, and office applications. Such applications usually have the letter *K* as part of their name—for example, KWord or KMail. A variety of tools are provided with the KDE desktop. These include calculators, console windows, notepads, and even software package managers. On a system administration level, KDE provides several tools for configuring your system. With KUser, you can manage user accounts, adding new ones or removing old ones. Practically all your Linux tasks can be performed from the KDE desktop. KDE applications also feature a built-in Help application. Choosing the Contents entry in the Help menu starts the KDE Help viewer, which provides a Web page–like interface with links for navigating through the Help documents. KDE includes support for the office application suite KOffice, based on KDE's KParts technology. KOffice includes a presentation application, a spreadsheet, an illustrator, and a word processor, among other components. In addition, an integrated development environment (IDE), called KDevelop, is available to help programmers create KDE-based software.

Web Site	Description
`www.kde.org`	KDE Web site
`ftp.kde.org`	KDE FTP site
`www.kde-apps.org`	KDE software repository
`http://developer.kde.org`	KDE developer site
`www.trolltech.com`	Site for Qt libraries
`www.koffice.org`	KOffice office suite
`www.kde-look.org`	KDE desktop themes, select KDE entry
`http://lists.kde.org`	KDE mailing lists

Table 10-1: KDE Web Sites

KDE, initiated by Matthias Ettrich in October 1996, has an extensive list of sponsors, including SUSE, Red Hat, Fedora, Mandrake, O'Reilly, and others. KDE is designed to run on any UNIX implementation, including Linux, Solaris, HP-UX, and FreeBSD. The official KDE Web site is **www.kde.org**, which provides news updates, download links, and documentation. KDE software packages can be downloaded from the KDE FTP site at **ftp.kde.org** and its mirror sites. Several KDE mailing lists are available for users and developers, including announcements, administration, and other topics (see the KDE Web site to subscribe). A great many software applications are currently available for KDE at **www.kde-apps.org**. Development support and documentation can be obtained at **http://developer.kde.org**. Various KDE Web sites are listed in Table 10-1.

Currently, new versions of KDE are being released frequently, sometimes every few months. KDE releases are designed to enable users to upgrade their older versions easily. Your Fedora software updater will automatically update KDE from distribution repositories, as updates become available. Alternatively, you can download new KDE packages from your distribution's FTP site and install them manually.

Note: KDE uses as its library of GUI tools the Qt library, developed and supported by Trolltech (**www.trolltech.com**). Qt is considered one of the best GUI libraries available for Unix/Linux systems. Using Qt has the advantage of relying on a commercially developed and supported GUI library. Trolltech provides the Qt libraries as Open Source software that is freely distributable.

KDE 4

The KDE 4 release is a major reworking of the KDE desktop. IT is included with the Fedora 10 release. Check the KDE site for detailed information on KDE 4, including the visual guide.

```
www.kde.org/announcements/4.0/
```

For features added with KDE 4.1 (current Fedora edition), check:

```
www.kde.org/announcements/4.1/
```

Every aspect of KDE has been reworked with KDE4. There is a new files manager, desktop, theme, panel, and configuration interface. KDE Window manager supports advanced compositing effects. Oxygen artwork for user interface theme, icons, and windows.

Device interfaces are managed by Phonon for multimedia devices, and Solid for power, network, and bluetooth devices. Phonon multimedia framework provides can support different backends for media playback. Currently it uses the Xine backend. With Phonon you can direct media files to specific devices. Solid hardware integration framework integrates fixed and removable devices, as well as network and bluetooth connections. Solid also connects to your hardware's power management features. Threadweaver makes efficient use of multi-core processors.

New applications include the Okular document viewer for numerous document formats with various display features like zoom, page thumbnails, search, and bookmarks. It allows you to add notes to documents. Gwenview is the KDE image viewer with browsing, display, and slideshow features for your images. Terminal window supports tabbed panels, split views for large output, background transparency, and search dialog for commands. Large output can be scrolled.

Configuration and Administration Access with KDE

KDE uses a different set of menus and access points than GNOME for accessing system administration tools. There are also different ways to access KDE configuration tasks, as well as KDE system administration tools not available through GNOME.

Access Fedora system administration tools from the Applications | Administration entry. Here you will find system-config Fedora administration tools like Users and Groups, Printing, Display, and Network.

 ➤ **System Settings**   Accessible from Kickoff at Applications | Settings | System Settings, this is the comprehensive KDE configuration tool, which lists all the KDE configuration tools for your managing your desktop, file manager, and system, as well as KDE's own administration tools that could be used instead of the Fedora ones.

 ➤ **Administration**   Accessible from Applications | Administration, this is a collection of system tools corresponding to those found in your GNOME System Tools menu, with the addition of certain other Fedora administration tools, like Add/Remove Software and the Update System (PackageKit). Many Fedora tools, including Display, Samba, and Services, are repeated here.

 ➤ **Settings**   Accessible from Applications | Settings, this is a smaller collection of desktop configuration features for tasks such as setting the default printer or PDA devices. Also in this menu is the System Settings menu that lists all KDE configuration tools.

 ➤ **System**. Accessible from Applications | System, this is where you will find tools like the Disk Usage Analyzer and Terminal.

Keys	Description
ALT-F1	Kickoff menu
ALT-F2	Krunner, command execution, entry can be any search string for a relevant operation, including bookmarks and contacts, not just applications.
UP/DOWN ARROWS	Move among entries in menus, including Kickoff and menus
LEFT/RIGHT ARROWS	Move to submenus menus, including Kickoff and Quick Access submenus menus
ENTER	Select a menu entry, including a Kickoff or QuickAccess
PAGE UP, PAGE DOWN	Scroll up fast
ALT-F4	Close current window
ALT-F3	Window menu for current window
CTRL-ALT-F6	Command Line Interface
CTRL-ALT-F8	Return to desktop from command line interface
ALT-TAB	Cover Switch or Box Switch for open windows
CTRL-F8	Desktop Grid
CTRL-F9	Present Windows Current Desktop
CTRL-F10	Present Windows All Desktops

Table 10-2: Desktop and KWin Keyboard Shortcuts

Plasma: desktop, panel, and plasmoids (applets)

Plasma has containments and applets. Applets are referred to as plasmoids. These plasmoids are applets that operate within containments. On KDE4 there are two types of Plasma containments, the panel and the desktop. The desktop and the panel are now features of an underlying Plasma operation. They are not separate programs. Both can have plasmoids (applets). For each type you can several instances. You can have many different desktop containments, each with its own set of plasmoids installed. You could also have several panels on yoru desktop, using different collections of plasmoids.

Each containment will have its own toolbox for configuration. The desktop has a toolbox at the top right corner, and panels will have toolbox on the right side. The panel toolbox features configuration tools for sizing and positioning the panel. See Table 10-2 for keyboard shortcuts.

Fedora KDE4 also supports the Zoom User Interface (ZUI) with its support for multiple plasma desktop containments (Activities). The Toolbox icon shows only Add widgets, Zoom Out, and lock widgets entries. Use the Zoom In entry to access the ZUI interface: adding, removing, and selecting desktop containments.

The KDE Help Center

The KDE Help Center provides a browser-like interface for accessing and displaying both KDE Help files and Linux Man and info files (see Figure 10-1). You can start the Help Center by selecting its entry in Kickoff Applications menu. The Help window displays a sidebar that holds three tabbed panels, one listing contents, one providing a glossary, and the third for search options (boolean operators, scope, and number of results). The main pane displays currently selected documents. A help tree on the contents tab in the sidebar lets you choose the kind of Help documents you want to access. Here you can choose KDE manuals, Man pages, or info documents, even application manuals. The Help Center includes a detailed user manual, a FAQ, and KDE Web site access.

A navigation toolbar enables you to move through previously viewed documents. KDE Help documents use an HTML format with links you can click to access other documents. The Back and Forward commands move you through the list of previously viewed documents. The KDE Help system provides an effective search tool for searching for patterns in Help documents, including Man and info pages. Enter the search pattern in the Search box above the sidebar, or select the Find entry from the Edit menu or toolbar to display a page where you can enter a more detailed query.

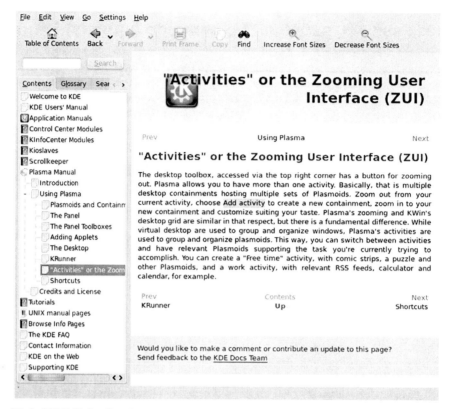

Figure 10-1: KDE Help Center

The KDE 4 Desktop

One of KDE's aims is to provide users with a consistent integrated desktop, where all applications use GUI interfaces (see Figure 10-2). To this end, KDE provides its own window manager (KWM), file manager (Dolphin), program manager, and desktop and panel (Plasma). You can run any other X Window System–compliant application, such as Firefox, in KDE, as well as any GNOME application. In turn, you can also run any KDE application, including the Dolphin file manager in GNOME. The KDE 4 desktop features the Plasma desktop shell with new panel, menu, and widgets, and adds a dashboard and zoom function. Plasma replaces desktop and Kicker panel, managing both the desktop and panel.

The desktop supports drag-and-drop operations. For example, to print a document, drag it to the Printer icon. You can place any directories on the desktop by simply dragging them from a file manager window to the desktop. A small menu will appear with options to copy or link the folder. To just create an icon on the desktop for the same folder, select the link entry.

The desktop also supports copy-and-paste operations, holding text you copied from one application in a desktop clipboard that you can then use to paste to another application. You can even copy and paste from a Konsole window.

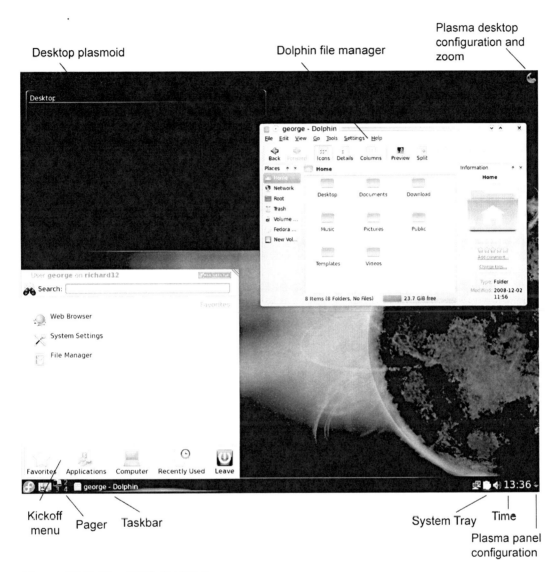

Desktop plasmoid

Dolphin file manager

Plasma desktop configuration and zoom

Kickoff menu

Pager

Taskbar

System Tray

Time

Plasma panel configuration

Figure 10-2: The KDE desktop

To configure your desktop, you use the Look & Feel tool in the System Settings window (Applications | Settings | System Settings). These include Appearance, Desktop, Notifications, and Window Behavior. Appearance holds the most configuration tasks, including Theme selection, Fonts, Styles, and Icons. Desktop is where you control Desktop Effects and the Screensaver. Windows Behavior controls window display features like shortcut keys, titlebar shading, and window movement. One key exception is the background. This is set by right-clicking on the desktop background to display the desktop menu and then selecting Configure Desktop. This entry only configures the background, called wallpaper in KDE. You can select other wallpaper from a drop-down menu, select your own image, and even download directly from **www.kde-look.org**, by clicking the New Wallpaper button.

For your desktop, you can also select a variety of different themes. A *theme* changes the look and feel of your desktop, affecting the appearance of GUI elements, such as scroll bars, buttons, and icons. For example, you use the Plastik theme to make your K Desktop look like a KDE 3.5 desktop. You can use the Theme Manager in the System Settings Appearance tool (System Settings | Look and Feel | Appearance | Themes) to select a theme and install new ones. Several will be installed for you. You can click the Get New Themes link to open the theme Web page at the **www.kde-look.org**. You can then download a new theme, and then click the Install New Theme button to locate the theme and install it.

Quitting KDE

To quit KDE, you first click the Leave button on the KDE Kickoff menu (see Figure 10-3). Here you will find options to logout, lock, switch user, quit and restart. You can also right-click anywhere on the desktop and select the Logout entry from the pop-up menu. If you leave any KDE applications or windows open when you quit, they are automatically restored when you start up again. If you just want to lock your desktop, you can select the Lock entry on the Kickoff Leave menu, and your screen saver will appear. To access a locked desktop, click on the screen and a box appears prompting you for your login password. When you enter the password, your desktop reappears.

Figure 10-3: The Kickoff menu Leave

KDE Kickoff menus

KickOff application launcher replaces the KDE main menu (see Figure 10-4). It organizes menu entries tabbed panels accessed by icons at the bottom of the menu window. There are panels for Favorites, Applications, Computer, Recently Used, and Leave. You can add and remove applications to the Favorites panel by right-clicking and selecting add or remove to favorites. The Applications panel shows application categories. The Computer button will open a window with all your fixed and removable storage. The Recently Used panel shows both documents and applications. KickOff also provides a Search box where you can search for a particular application, instead of working through menus.

Figure 10-4: The Kickoff menu Favorites

Figure 10-5: The Kickoff menu Computer

To configure KDE, you use the KDE System Settings referenced by the System Settings item in the Favorites, Computer, or Applications tab.

Use the Leave panel to logout or shut down (see Figure 10-3). There Session and System sections. The Session section has entries for Logout, Lock, and Switch User. The System section features system-wide operations, including Shutdown, Restart, and Suspend (either to RAM or Disk).

The Computer menu has Applications and Places sections (see Figure 10-5). The Applications section has entries for System Settings. The Places section is similar to the Places menu in GNOME, with entries for your home folder, network folder, root folder and the trash.

The Applications menu has most of the same entries as those found on GNOME. The entries have been standardized for both interfaces (see Figure 10-6). You can find entries for categories such as Internet, Graphics, and Office. These menus list both GNOME and KDE applications you can use. However, some of the KDE menus contain entries for a few more alternate KDE applications, like KMail on the Internet menu. Some entries will invoke the KDE version of a tool, like the Terminal entry in the System Tools menu, which will invoke the KDE terminal window, KConsole. There is no Preferences menu.

Figure 10-6: The Kickoff menu Applications

The Kickoff menu can be added to any panel or desktop by opening the Add Widgets dialog for that desktop or panel and selecting Applications Launcher. On the desktop, the Application Launcher appears as simple icon that when clicked opens a Kickoff menu as a dialog window. On Fedora, the Application Launcher icon is the Fedora logo. The Application Launcher Menu installs a traditional menu for applications, instead of Kickoff.

Krunner

For fast access to applications, bookmarks, contacts, and other desktop items, you can use Krunner. The Krunner plasmoid operates as a search tool for applications and other items. To find an application, enter a search pattern and an icon for the application is displayed. Click on the icon to start the application. For applications where you know the name, part of the name, or just its basic topic, Krunner is a very fast way to access the applications. To start Krunner, press Alt-F2, right-click on the desktop to display the desktop menu and select Run command. Enter the pattern for the application you want to search for and press enter. The pattern "software" or "package" would both display the Adept package manager icon. Entering the pattern "office" displays icons for all the OpenOffice.org applications (see Figure 10-7).

Figure 10-7: Krunner application search

Removable Devices: New Device Notifier

Installed on the panel to the left, next to the Fedora icon for the Kickoff menu, is the New Device Notifier plasmoid. When you insert a removable device like a CD/DVD-ROM disc or a USB drive, the New Device Notifier briefly displays a window showing all your removable devices, including the new one. You can click on the New Device Notifier any time to display this window. Figure 10-8 shows the New Device Notifier displayed on the panel and its applet icon.

Removable devices are not displayed as icons on your desktop. Instead, to open the devices, you use the New Device Notifier. Click on the New Device Notifier icon in the panel to open its dialog. Then click on the device you want to open, like your DVD/CD disc or yoru USB drive. A file manager window will open showing your device contents. A USB drive will be automatically mounted when you click on its New Device Notifier entry to open up a file manager window for it.

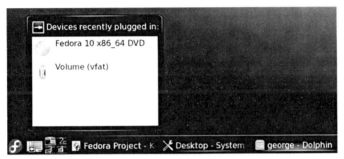

Figure 10-8: New Device Notifier on panel with applet

Figure 10-9: New Device Notifier dialog

You can use the New Device Notifier to eject a removable device. When you select the device entry, an eject button will appear. Clicking on an entry for a DVD/CD-ROM disc will physically eject it, whereas for a USB drive, the drive will be unmounted and prepared for removal.

You can then safely remove the USB drive. Figure 10-9 shows the window as it appears on the panel, the icon used for the New Device Notifier on the panel, a close up of the window with a USB drives selected with its eject button displayed.

Desktop Plasmoids (applets)

The KDE 4 desktop features the Plasma desktop that treats applets differently. Plasma designates its applets as plasmoids. It is designed to deal with plasmoids on the same level as windows and icons. Just as a desktop can display windows, it can also display plasmoids. Plasmoids, or applets, are taking on more responsibility in desktop operations, running essential operations, every replacing to a limited extent the need for file manager windows. To this end, the dashboard tool can hide all other desktop items, showing just the plasmoids. When you first login, your desktop will show one plasmoid, the Desktop folder view.

Managing desktop plasmoids

To add a widget (plasmoid) to the desktop, right-click anywhere on the desktop and select Add Widgets from the pop-up menu, or move your mouse to the desktop toolbox icon in the top right corner and select Add widgets from the displayed menu. This opens the Add Widgets window that lists widgets you can add (see Figure 10-10). A drop-down menu at the top of the window lets you see different widget categories like Date & Time, Online Services, and Graphics. You can also see recently used widgets as well as set up favorite widgets.

Figure 10-10: Adding a plasmoid: Add Widgets

Figure 10-11 shows Desktop, digital clock, calculator, and folder view plasmoids. The Desktop plasmoid is just a folder view plasmoid set to the Desktop folder. When you add a Folder View plasmoid, it will default to your home directory.

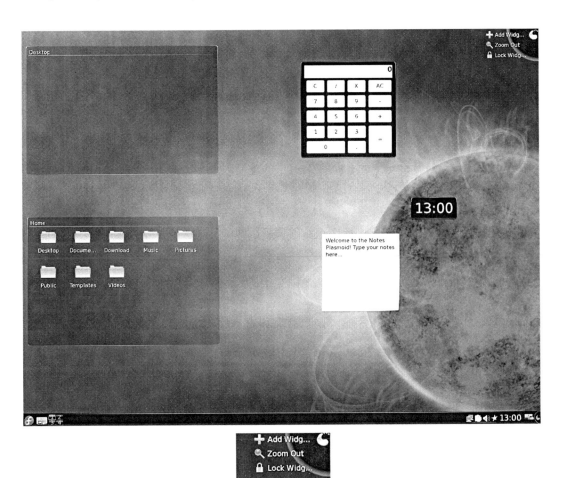

Figure 10-11: Desktop window, Folder window, Calculator, Digital clock, and Notetaker plasmoids. Also desktop toolbox entries to Add Widgets and Zoom Out.

When you pass your mouse over a plasmoid, its sidebar is displayed with button for resizing, refreshing, settings, and closing the plasmoid (see Figure 10-12). Click and drag the resize button to change the plasmoid size. Clicking the settings button (wrench icon) opens that plasmoid's settings dialog (see Figure 10-13). You can also use Plasma shortcut keys (see Table 10-3).

Figure 10-12: Analog Clock Plasmoid with task sidebar

Figure 10-13: Analog Clock Plasmoid Configuration

Keys	Description
CTRL- A	Open the Add Widgets window to add a plasmoid to the desktop
CTRL- L	Lock your widgets to prevent removal, adding new ones, or changing settings
CTRL--	Zoom out
CTRL-=	Zoom in
CTRL-N	Next Applet
CTRL-P	Previous applet
CTRL-]	Next Containment (activity)
CTRL-[	Previous Containment (activity)
CTRL-S	Open a selected plasmoid configuration settings
CTRL-R	Remove a selected plasmoid

Table 10-3: KDE Plasma Keyboard Shortcuts

Dashboard

The dashboard is designed to display plasmoids (applets) only. It hides all windows and icons, showing all your desktop plasmids. To start the dashboard, click the dashboard applet in the panel. On Fedora you will have to first install the dashboard plasmoid on the panel or desktop. On the Add Widgets window, select the Show Dashboard entry and click Add Widget. The Show Dashboard icon is shown in Figure 10-14.

When the dashboard is in use, the screen will display the Plasma Dashboard label at the top (see Figure 10-14). To return to the desktop, select Hide Dashboard from the top-right corner menu (Plasma desktop toolbox).

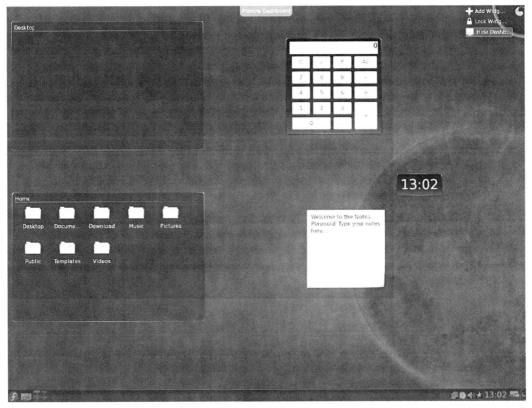

Figure 10-14: The Dashboard and Dashboard applet

Activities and ZUI (zoom)

Fedora KDE also supports multiple activities. Activities are different plasma desktop containments, each with it own set of plasmoids. An activity is not the same as virtual desktop. Virtual desktops affect windows, displaying a different set of windows on each desktop. An activity uses the current virtual desktop, but has its own set of plasmoids that are also displayed. You can use different activities, with different plasmoids on the same virtual desktop. Technically, each activity is a Plasma desktop containment that has its own collection of plasmoids. You can switch to a different activity (desktop containment) and display a different collection of plasmoids on your desktop.

An activity is a way to set up as set of plasmoids for a certain task. You could have one activity for office work, another for news, and yet another for media. Each activity could have its own set of appropriate plasmoids, like clock, calculator, dictionary, and document folder for an office activity. A media activity might have a now playing plasmoid for audio, picture frame for photos, news ticker for latest news. You could have an activity for home, one for office, one for work, or one for entertainment, each with its own set of plasmoids.

Multiple activities are managed using the Zooming User Interface (ZUI). This interface is accessed through the Zoom entries on the desktop toolbox menu. You zoom out to display your different activities, and zoom in to select an activity or move to a lower zoom level. There are two zoom out levels, the first showing a few activities (see Figure 10-15), and the second showing all of them. On the first level your mouse becomes a hand that can move to different activities (your screen shows only a few at a time). You can zoom out fully to display all your activities on a single screen (see Figure 10-16). Click on any activity toolbox (upper right corner of an activity), and then click on Zoom Out again.

Tip: The Zoomed display will still show any open windows on your original desktop using the entire screen as if it where one desktop. To fully see your zoomed activities (not having them blocked by open windows), you should close or minimize your windows before zooming.

Each activity will have its own toolbox in the upper right of its display. These toolboxes are all active. When you move your mouse to one, its menu is displayed. The menu will show added entries for zooming and to add an activity. The lower level zoom mode will have both Zoom Out and Zoom In entries, whereas the full zoom will have only a Zoom In mode. Your desktop will have only a Zoom Out entry.

```
Zoom In
Zoom Out
Add Activity
```

To add a new activity, move the mouse to any dashboard toolbox (initially you will have only one), and then select the Add Activity entry. This creates a new activity, which will be displayed as a desktop.

To use an activity, click on its toolbox and then select Zoom In from the toolbox menu. Your desktop will be restored to its original display, but now showing the desktop plasmoids for that activity.

To change from one activity to another, first select Zoom Out on the desktop toolbox to enter the Zoom Out mode. Find the activity you want (displayed as desktops with their different plasmoids). Then click on the activity's toolbox and select Zoom In. The new activity with its own set of plasmoids is then displayed on your desktop.

While in the Zoom Out mode, showing your multiple activities, you can manage plasmoids on any of the activities. You can move plasmoids to different positions within an activity, remove a plasmoid, or even configure it. As you pass your mouse over a plasmoid, its sidebar will be displayed with items for moving, resizing, removing, and configuring the plasmoid. To move a plasmoid, click and drag anywhere on its sidebar, except on the sidebar items.

Though you can manage plasmoids on any activity displayed on the Zoom out mode, you can only add plasmoids to the currently selected activity. To select an activity, you Zoom In on it. You can zoom in either from the top level Zoom out mode to the lower level Zoom out mode, or you can Zoom In from the lower level directly to your desktop. Either way, once selected, you can add plasmoids to that selected activity. Use the Add Widgets from the toolbox menu to add widgets as you normally would.

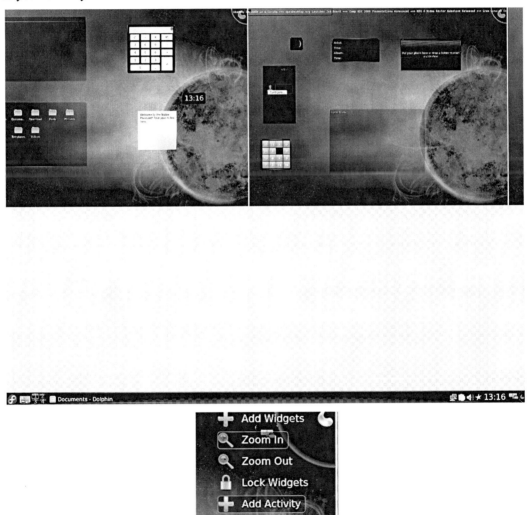

Figure 10-15: Zoom with added activities and toolbox Zoom entries

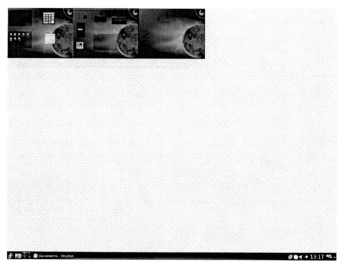

Figure 10-16: Full Zoom with multiple actions

KDE Windows

A KDE window has the same functionality you find in other window managers and desktops. You can resize the window by clicking and dragging any of its corners or sides. A click-and-drag operation on a side extends the window in that dimension, whereas a corner extends both height and width at the same time. The top of the window has a title bar showing the name of the window, the program name in the case of applications, and the current directory name for the file manager windows. The active window has the title bar highlighted. To move the window, click this title bar and drag it where you want. Right-clicking the window title bar displays a pop-up menu with entries for window operations, such as closing or resizing the window. Within the window, menus, icons, and toolbars for the particular application are displayed.

You can configure the appearance and operation of a window by selecting the Configure Window Behavior entry from the Window menu (right-click the title bar). Here you can set appearance (Window Decorations), button and key operations (Actions), the focus policy such as a mouse click on the window or just passing the mouse over it (Focus), how the window is displayed when moving it (Moving), and advanced features like moving a window directly to another virtual desktop, Active Desktop Borders. All these features can be configured also using the System Setting Look & Feel tools.

Opened windows are also shown as buttons on the KDE taskbar located on the panel. The taskbar shows the different programs you are running or windows you have open. This is essentially a docking mechanism that lets you change to a window or application just by clicking its button. When you minimize (iconify) a window, it is reduced to its taskbar button. You can then restore the window by clicking its taskbar button.

To the right of the title bar are three small buttons for minimizing, maximizing, or closing the window (down, up, and x symbols). You can switch to a window at any time by clicking its taskbar button. From the keyboard, you can use the ALT-TAB key combination to display a list of current open windows. Holding down the ALT key and sequentially pressing TAB moves you through the list.

Application and configuration windows may display a Help Notes button, shown next to the iconify button and displaying a question mark. Clicking this button changes your cursor to a question mark. You can then move the cursor to an item such as an icon on a toolbar, and then click it to display a small help note explaining what the item does. For example, moving the mouse to the Forward button in the file manager taskbar will show a note explaining that this button performs a browser forward operation.

Applications

You can start an application in KDE in several ways. If an entry for it is in the Kickoff Applications menu, you can select that entry to start the application. You can right-click on any application entry in the Applications menu to display a pop-up menu with "Add to Panel" and "Add to Desktop" entries. Select either to add a shortcut icon for the application to the desktop or the panel. You can then start an application by single clicking its desktop or panel icon.

An application icon on the desktop is implemented as desktop plasmoid. Passing the mouse over the application icon on the desktop displays a sidebar with the wrench icon for the icon settings. This opens a Setting window with tabs for general, permissions, application, and preview. On the general tab you can select an icon image and set the displayed name. The application tab references the actual application program file with possible options. Permissions set standard access permissions by the owner, group, or others.

You can also run an application by right-clicking on the desktop and selecting select Run Command (or press ALT-F2) which will display the Krunner tool consisting of a box to enter a single command. Previous commands can be accessed from a pop-up menu. You need only enter a pattern to search for the application. Results will be displayed in the Krunner window. Choose the one you want. A Show Options button will list options for running the program.

Virtual Desktops: Desktop Pager

KDE, like most Linux window managers, supports virtual desktops. In effect, this extends the desktop area on which you can work. You could have Mozilla running on one desktop and be using a text editor in another. KDE can support up to 16 virtual desktops, though the default is 4. Your virtual desktops can be displayed and accessed using the KDE Desktop Pager located on the panel. The KDE Desktop Pager represents your virtual desktops as miniature screens showing small squares for each desktop. It is made to look similar to the GNOME Workspace Switcher. By default, there are 4 squares, numbered 1, 2, 3, and 4. You can have up to 16. To move from one desktop to another, click the square for the destination desktop. Clicking 3 displays the third desktop, and clicking 1 moves you back to the first desktop. If you want to move a window to a different desktop, first open the window's menu by right-clicking the window's title bar. Then select the To Desktop entry, which lists the available desktops. Choose the one you want.

You can also configure KDE so that if you move the mouse over the edge of a desktop screen, it automatically moves to the adjoining desktop. You need to imagine the desktops arranged in a four-square configuration, with two top desktops next to each other and two desktops below them. You enable this feature by enabling the Active Desktop Borders feature in the System Settings | Window Behavior | Window Behavior | Advanced pane

Figure 10-17: Virtual desktop configuration

To change the number of virtual desktops, you right-click on the Desktop Pager on the panel, and the select the Configure Desktop entry in the pop-up menu. This opens the Multiple Desktops window with 20 possible desktops and four active ones (see Figure 10-17). The text box labeled "Number of Desktops" controls the number of active desktops. Use the arrows or enter a number to change the number of active desktops. You can change any of the desktop names by clicking an active name and entering a new one.

KDE Panel

The KDE panel, located at the bottom of the screen, provides access to most KDE functions (see Figure 10-18). The panel is a specially configured Plasma containment, just as the desktop is a specially configured Plasma containment. The panel includes icons for menus, directory windows, specific programs, and virtual desktops. These are plasmoids that are configured for use on the panel with size restrictions so they will fit. At the left end of the panel is a button for the Kickoff menu, a KDE *K* icon.

To add an application to the panel, right-click on its entry in the Kickoff menu to open a pop-up menu and select Add to Panel.

To add a widget to the panel, right-click anywhere on the panel and select Add Widgets from the pop-up menu. This opens the Add Widgets window that lists widgets you can add (see Figure 10-19). A drop-down menu at the top of the window lets you see different widget categories like Date & Time, Online Services, and Graphics. You can also see recently used widgets as well as set up favorite widgets. This is the same Add Widgets used for the desktop.

Figure 10-18: KDE panel

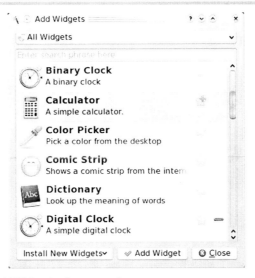

Figure 10-19: KDE Add Widgets for panel

The Plasma panel supports three kinds of Windows and Tasks widgets: taskbar, system tray, and pager. The system tray holds widgets for desktop operations like sound settings, date and time, network connections (NetworkManager), and clipboard, and trash (see Figure 10-20). You can also add application launcher like the Help button shown in Figure 10-20. This was added by locating its entry in the Kickoff menu (Applications tab) and right-clicking on it and choosing Add to panel. You can have more than one system tray on a panel. On the left side of the main panel, you also have a system tray with Application Launcher (Kickoff menu), desktop pager, and New Device Notifier.

Figure 10-20: KDE system tray

KDE Panel Configuration

To configure a panel, changing its position, size, and display features, you use the panel's toolbox. The panel toolbox is located at the right side of the panel. Click on it to open an additional panel configuration panel with buttons for adding widgets, moving the panel, changing its size and position, and with a More Settings menu for setting visibility and alignment features. Figure 10-21 shows the configuration panel as it will appear on your desktop. Figure 10-22 provides a more detailed description, including the More Settings menu entries.

Figure 10-21: KDE Panel Configuration

With the configuration panel activated, you can also move plasmoids around the panel. Clicking on a plasmoid will overlay a movement icon, letting you then move the plasmoid icon to a different location on the panel.

The lower part of the configuration panel is used for panel position settings. On the left side is a slider for positioning the panel on the edge of the screen. On the right side are two sliders for the minimum (bottom) and maximum (top) size of the panel.

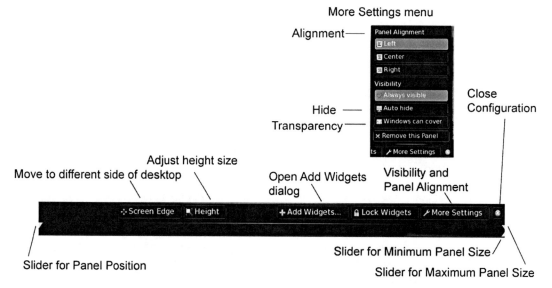

Figure 10-22: KDE Panel Configuration details and display features

The top part of the panel has button for changing the location and the size of the panel. The Screen Edge button lets you move the panel to another side of the screen (left, right, top, bottom). Just click and drag. The height button lets you change the panel size, larger or smaller.

The Add Widgets button will open the Add Widgets dialog letting you add new plasmoids to the panel.

The More Setting menu lets you set Visibility and Alignment features. You can choose and AutoHide setting that will hide the panel until you move the mouse to its location. The Windows can cover lets a window overlap the panel. For smaller panels, you can align to the right, left, or center of the screen edge.

The More Settings menu also has an entry to remove the panel. Use this entry to delete a panel you no longer want.

When you are finished with the configuration, click the red x icon the upper right side.

KDE Quick Access plasmoid

The QuickAcces menu is a plasmoid that will let you quickly access items like folder, files, bookmarks, or contacts. The Quick Access plasmoid is not installed by default. Install the **kde-plasma-quickaccess** package, and then you can choose Quick Access from the Add Widgets window. The QuickAccess plasmoid is set up for your home folder by default with a favorites icon. Clicking on it display a pop up dialog with entries for folders in your home folders as well as any files you may have there (see Figure 10-23). Click on a folder entry to open a file manger window on your desktop for that folder. For a file, its associated application will be opened with that file. Clicking on the upper right sort button lets you change the sort sequence of your items.

On the QuickAccess configuration dialog you can configure the folder to access (General tab), the icon to display (Appearance tab) and the display mode for the folder items (icon or list). The Preview tab enables previews of folders and files. On the Appearance tab, clicking on the Custom icon image opens an Icon source window where you can choose the icon you want to use.

Figure 10-23: The Quick Access applet customized with home folder image

KWin - Desktop Effects

KWin desktop effects can be enabled on the System Settings Desktop tool (System Settings | Desktop | Desktop Effects). The All Effects tab will list available effects (see Figure 10-24). The more dramatic effects are found in the Windows Management section.

Figure 10-24: Desktop Effect selection and configuration

Several Windows effects will be selected by default, depending on whether your graphics card can support them. A check mark is placed next to active effects. IF there is wrench icon in the effects entry, it means the effect can be configured. Click on the icon to open its configuration dialog. For several effects, you use certain keys to start them. The more commonly used effects are Cover Switch, Desktop Grid, and Present Windows. The keys for these effects are listed in Table 10-4.

KEY	Operation
ALT-TAB	Cover Switch or Box Switch for open windows
CTRL-F8	Desktop Grid
CTRL-F9	Present Windows Current Desktop
CTRL-F10	Present Windows All Desktops

Table 10-4: KWin desktop effects keyboard shortcuts

Most effects will occur automatically. The Taskbar Thumbnails effect will display a live thumbnail of window on the taskbar as your mouse passes over it, showing information on the widget in an expanded window (see Figure 10-25).

The Present Windows effect will display images of your open windows on your screen. The selected one will be highlighted (see Figure 10-26).

You can use your mouse to select another. This provides an easy way to browse your open windows. Use Ctrl-F9 to display windows just on your current desktop, and use Ctrl-F10 to display all your open windows across all your desktops.

Figure 10-25: Taskbar Thumbnails effect, showing thumbnails of minimized applications

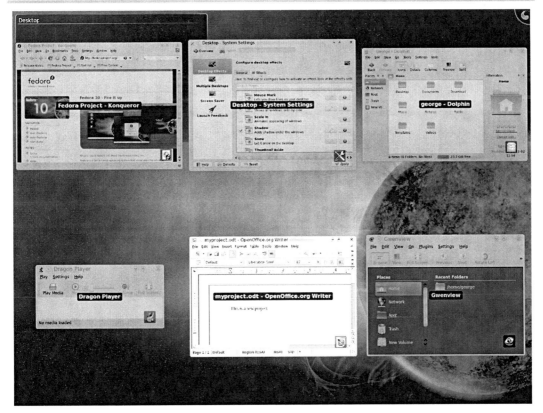

Figure 10-26: Present Windows (Windows effects), Ctrl-F9 for current desktop, Ctrl-f10 for all desktops

The Box Switch and Cover Switch effects let you quickly browse through and select an open window (Figures 10-27 and 10-28). Open windows are arranges in a sequence, with the selected one centered. Continuing to press Alt-Tab moves you through the sequence. Box Switch displays windows in a boxed dialog, whereas Cover switch arranges unselected windows stacked to the sides.

Figure 10-27: Box Switch - Alt-Tab

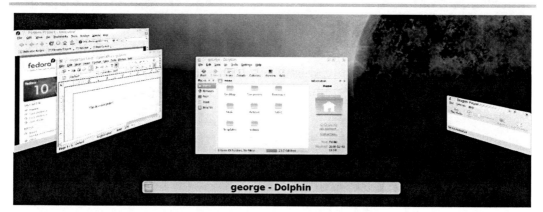

Figure 10-28: Cover Switch - Alt-Tab (Box Switch disabled)

Desktop Grid will show a grid of all your virtual desktops (Ctrl-F8), letting you see all your virtual desktops on the screen at once (see Figure 10-29). You can then move windows and open applications between desktops. Clicking on a desktop makes it the current one.

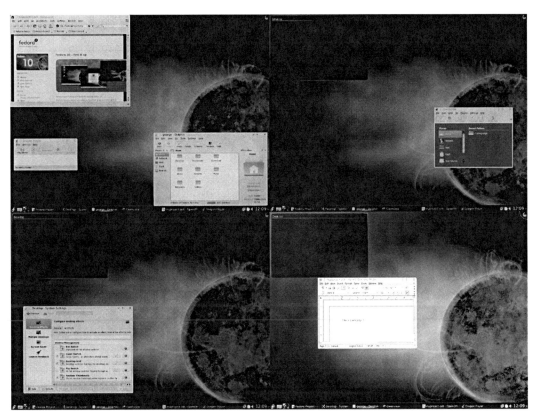

Figure 10-29: Desktop Grid - Ctrl-F8

KDE File Manager: Dolphin

Dolphin is KDE's dedicated file manager (Konqueror is used as a Web browser). A path for the current directory is displayed at the top of the file window and you can use it to move to different directories and their subdirectories (see Figure 10-30). With the split view you can open directories in the same window, letting you copy and move items between them. A side bar will display different panels. The Places panel will show icons for often used folders like Home, Network, and Trash, as well as removable devices. To add a folder to the Places panel, just drag it there. The files listed in a folder can be viewed in several different ways, such as icons, detailed listing, and columns (View | View Mode menu).

You can open a file either by clicking it or by selecting it and then choosing the Open entry in the File menu. If you want to select the file or directory, you need to hold down the CTRL key while you click it. A single-click opens the file. If the file is a program, that program starts up. If it is a data file, such as a text file, the associated application is run using that data file. For example, if you single-click a text file, the Kate application starts displaying that file. If Dolphin cannot determine the application to use, it opens a dialog box prompting you to enter the application name.

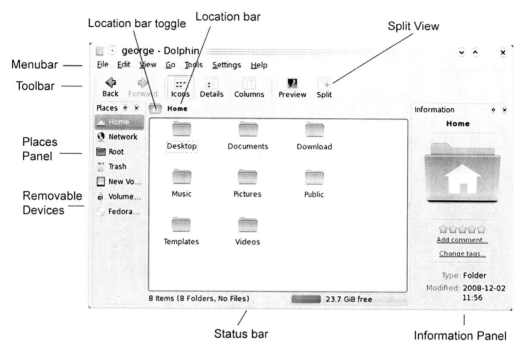

Figure 10-30: The KDE file manager (dolphin)

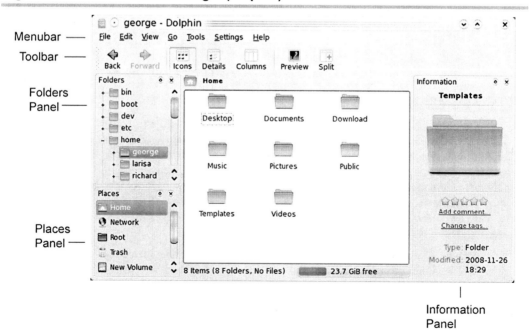

Figure 10-31: The KDE file manager panes

You can click the Browse button on this box to use a directory tree to locate the application program you want. To configure Dolphin, click Configure Dolphin from the Setting menu.

Tip: Configuration files, known as hidden files, are not usually displayed. To have the file manager display these files, select Show Hidden Files from the View menu (Ctrl-.). Dolphin also supports split views, letting you view different directories in the same window (Windows menu). You can split it vertically or horizontally.

You can display additional panels by selecting them from the View | Panels menu (see Figure 10-31). The Information panel will display detailed information about a selected file or folder, and the Folders panel will display a directory tree for the file system. The panels are detachable from the file manager window (see Figure 10-32). Dolphin file manager also features integrated desktop search and meta-data extraction.

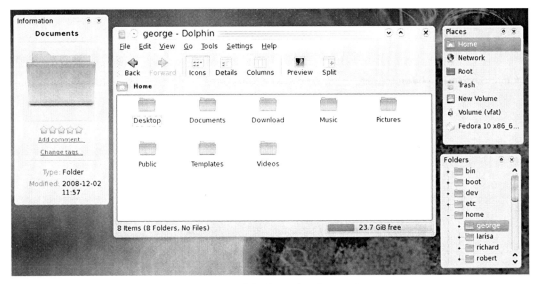

Figure 10-32: The KDE file manager with detached panels

Dolphin also supports split views, where you can open two different folders in the same window. Click the Split button in the toolbar. You can then drag folder and files from one folder to the other (see Figure 10-33).

The file manager can also extract tar archives and install RPM packages. An *archive* is a file ending in **.tar.gz**, **.tar**, or **.tgz**. Clicking the archive lists the files in it. You can extract a particular file simply by dragging it out of the window. Clicking a text file in the archive displays it with Kate, while clicking an image file displays it with GwenView. Selecting an RPM package opens it with the package-manager utility, which you can then use to install the package.

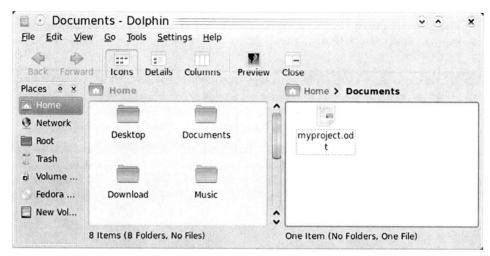

Figure 10-33: The KDE file manager with split views

Keys	Description
ALT-LEFT ARROW, ALT-RIGHT ARROW	Backward and Forward in History
ALT-UP ARROW	One directory up
ENTER	Open a file/directory
ESC	Open a pop-up menu for the current file
LEFT/RIGHT/UP/DOWN ARROWS	Move among the icons
SPACEBAR	Select/unselect file
PAGE UP, PAGE DOWN	Scroll up fast
CTRL-C	Copy selected file to clipboard
CTRL-V	Paste files from clipboard to current directory
CTRL-S	Select files by pattern
CTRL-L	Open new location
CTRL-F	Find files
CTRL-W	Close window

Table 10-5: KDE File Manager Keyboard Shortcuts

Search

To search for files, select the Find Files entry in the Tools menu. This opens the Kfind tool with several panes for searching files. There are three panes: Name/Location, Contents, and Properties. The Name/Location pane lets you perform a standard search on file and directory names. You can use wildcard matching symbols, such as *. The search results are displayed in a pane in the lower half of the Find window. You can click a file and have it open with its appropriate application. Text files are displayed by the Kate text editor. Images are displayed by

GwenView. Applications are run. The search program also enables you to save your search results for later reference.

On the Properties pane you can search by date, size, owner, or group, and on the Contents pane you can search files for phrases or words, even including their meta info.

Navigating Directories

Within a file manager window, a single-click on a directory icon moves to that directory and displays its file and subdirectory icons. To move back up to the parent directory, you click the up arrow button located on the left end of the navigation toolbar. A single-click on a directory icon moves you down the directory tree, one directory at a time. By clicking the up arrow button, you move up the tree. The Navigation bar can display either the directory path for the current folder or an editable location box where you can enter in a pathname. For the directory path, you can click on any displayed directory name to moving you quickly to an upper level folder. Initially only the directories in the path name are displayed. To use the location box, select Show Full Location in the View | Navigation Bar menu (or press Ctrl-L). The navigation bar changes to an editable text box where you can type a path name.

Like a Web browser, the file manager remembers the previous directories it has displayed. You can use the back and forward arrow buttons to move through this list of prior directories. You can also use several keyboard shortcuts to perform such operations, like Atl-uparrow to move up a directory, and the arrow keys to move to different icons.

Copy, Move, Delete, Rename, and Link Operations

To perform an operation on a file or directory, you first have to select it. To select a file or directory, you click the file's icon or listing. To select more than one file, continue to hold the CTRL key down while you click the files you want. You can also use the keyboard arrow keys to move from one file icon to another and then use the ENTER key to select the file you want.

To copy and move files, you can use the standard drag-and-drop method with your mouse. To copy a file, you locate it by using the file manager. Open another file manager window to the directory to which you want the file copied. Then click and drag the File icon to that window. A pop-up menu appears with selections for Move, Copy, or Link. Choose Copy. To move a file to another directory, follow the same procedure, but select Move from the pop-up menu. To copy or move a directory, use the same procedure as for files. All the directory's files and subdirectories are also copied or moved.

To rename a file, Ctrl-click its icon and press F2, or right-click the icon and select Rename from the pop-up menu. The name below the icon will become boxed, editable text that you can then change.

You delete a file either by selecting it and deleting it or placing it in the Trash folder to delete later. To delete a file, select it and then choose the Delete entry in the File menu (also SHIFT-DEL key). To place a file in the Trash folder, click and drag it to the Trash icon on your desktop or select Move To Trash from the Edit menu (DEL key). You can later open the Trash folder and delete the files. To delete all the files in the Trash folder, right-click the Trash icon in Dolphin file manager sidebar, and select Remove Trash from the pop-up menu. To restore any files in the Trash bin, open the Trash window and drag them out of the Trash folder.

Each file or directory has properties associated with it that include permissions, the filename, and its directory. To display the Properties window for a given file, right-click the file's icon and select the Properties entry. On the General panel, you see the name of the file displayed. To change the file's name, replace the name there with a new one. Permissions are set on the Permissions panel. Here, you can set read, write, and execute permissions for user, group, or other access to the file. The Group entry enables you to change the group for a file. The Meta Info panel lists information specific to that kind of file, for example, the number of lines and characters in a text file. An image file will list features like resolution, bit depth, and color.

Web and FTP Access: Konqueror

The KDE Konqueror is a full-featured Web browser and an FTP client. It includes a box for entering either a pathname for a local file or a URL for a Web page on the Internet or your intranet (see Figure 10-34). A navigation toolbar can be used to display previous Web pages. The Home button will always return you to your home page. When accessing a Web page, the page is displayed as on any Web browser. With the navigation toolbar, you can move back and forth through the list of previously displayed pages in that session.

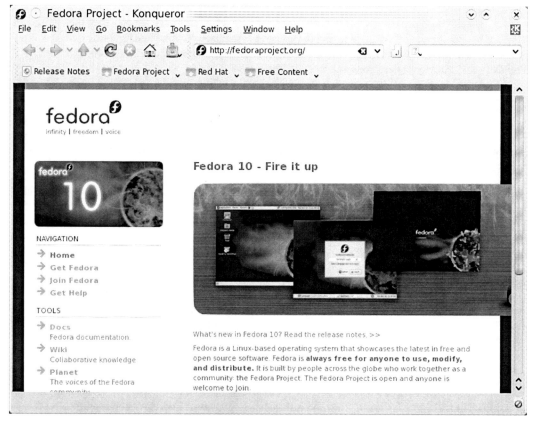

Figure 10-34: Konqueror

The Konqueror also operates as an FTP client. When you access an FTP site, you navigate the remote directories as you would your own. The operations to download a file are the same as copying a file on your local system. Just select the file's icon or entry in the file manager window and drag it to a window showing the local directory to which you want it downloaded. Then, select the Copy entry from the pop-up menu that appears.

Tip: KDE features the KGet tool for Konqueror, which manages FTP downloads, letting you select, queue, suspend, and schedule downloads, while displaying status information on current downloads.

To configure Konqueror, select Configure Konqueror from a Konqueror window Settings menu. You can perform configuration tasks like specifying proxies, and Web page displays, fonts to use, cookie management, and encryption methods. The History category lets you specify the number of history items and their expiration date. With the Plugins category you can see a listing of current browser plug-ins as well as scan for new ones.

Konqueror supports split views as well as a navigation sidebar. You can select vertical or horizontal split views from the Window menu. Also you can add split view icons to the toolbar by selecting Settings | Toolbar | Show Extra Toolbar (see Figure 10-35). With split views you can display two different Web sites at the same time in the same Konqueror window.

The Navigation sidebar can display bookmarks, folder links, and system tools. To show the Navigation sidebar, first display the Extra toolbar. Then click on Show Navigation bar. The navigation bar displays bookmarks, history, home folder, root folder, and network folder. In effect, Konqueror can be used as an alternative file manager to Dolphin.

Figure 10-35: Konqueror with split views and sidebar

Konqueror also supports tabbed displays. Instead of opening a folder or site in the same Konqueror window or a new one, you can open a new tab for it using the same Konqueror window. One tab can display the initial folder or site opened, and other tabs can be used for folders or sites opened later. You can then move from viewing one folder to another by simply clicking the latter folder's tab. This way you can view multiple folders or sites with just one Konqueror window. To open a folder as a tab, right-click its icon and select Open In New Tab. To later close the folder, right-click its tab label and select Close Tab. You can also detach a tab, opening it up in its own file manager window.

Konqueror can also operate as a file manger. To use Konqueror as a file manager, on the Konqeror window, choose Settings | Load View Profile | File Management. Konqueror will open to your home folder and the sidebar will list your file system directories (see Figure 10-36). You can also use split views on different folders, showing two or more open side by side. You can then move files directly between the displayed folders.

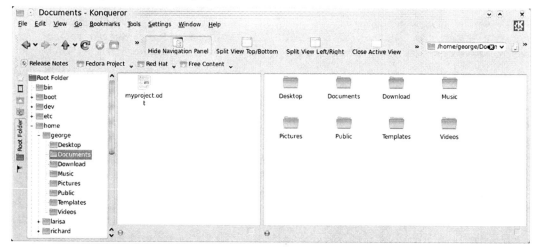

Figure 10-36: Konqueror as file manager profile with split views

KDE Configuration: KDE System Settings

With the KDE configuration panels, you can configure your desktop and system, changing the way it is displayed and the features it supports. The configurations are accessed on the System Settings window (See Figure 10-37). On the KDE desktop spin of Fedora, you can access this window from the System Settings entry in the Kickoff Favorites panel. From a standard Fedora 10 installation, where KDE is one of several available desktops, including GNOME, access to the System Settings window is more complicated.

From Applications, you would select Settings, and then from the Setting menu, you select System Settings. You should use the KDE System Settings tools to configure your KDE desktop. Keep in mind that most system configurations task are still performed by the GNOME-based Fedora administration tools. You can use the KDE versions if you wish.

The System Settings window shows two tabbed panels, one General and the other Advanced. The General panel is divided into icons for Personal, Look & Feel, Computer Administration, and Network & Connectivity. The Advanced panel has icons for System Administration and Advanced User Settings. Use the icons to display a window with sidebar icon list for configuration panels, with the panel selected shown on the right. The selected panel may have tabbed panels.

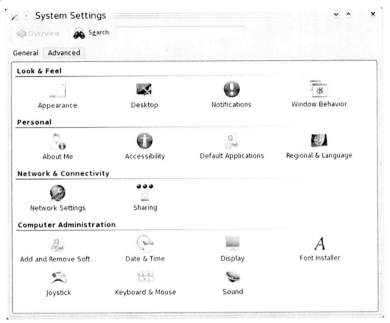

Figure 10-37: KDE System Settings

To change your theme, you would select the Appearance icon on the System Settings General panel located in the Look & Feel section. This opens an Appearances window with a sidebar listing icons for appearance features like fonts and styles (see Figure 10-38). To change the theme, select the Style icon. This displays the style pane on the right side of the window. There are three tabbed panels: Style, Effects, and Toolbar. On the Style panel you can select the widget style. For Icons you would use the Icon panel selected from the sidebar.

The Network and Connectivity segment holds icons for configuring the KDE file manager's network tools, including Web browser features as well as Samba (Windows) access and Wireless connectivity. Under Appearances & Themes, you can set different features for displaying and controlling your desktop. For example, the Background entry enables you to select a different background color or image for each one of your virtual desktops. Other icons enable you to configure components such as the screen saver, the language used, and the window style. The Peripheral segment holds entries that let you to configure your mouse, keyboard, and printer. The Sound and Multimedia segment contains icons for configuring sound components. From the System Settings, you can also access a set of specialized KDE system configuration tools. Currently these include a login manager and a font manager.

The Advanced panel tools for Advanced Users Settings like the Solid hardware interface for Bluetooth and HAL power management (see Figure 10-39). File Associations lets you associate file types with applications (MIME types). The Sessions manager allows you to configure sessions. The System segment has entries for Login manager and Samba. The login manager applies only to the KDE login manager (KDM), not GDM. You would have to first choose to use the KDM instead of GDM.

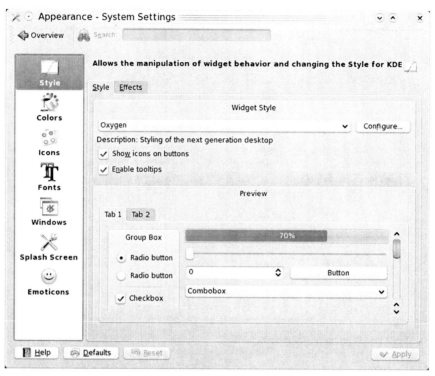

Figure 10-38: KDE Appearance Style panel

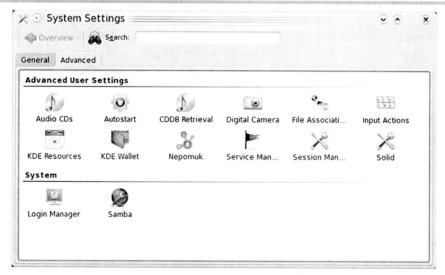

Figure 10-39: KDE System Settings Advanced Panel

KDE Directories and Files

When KDE is installed on your system, its system-wide application, configuration, and support files may be installed in the same system directories as other GUIs and user applications (see Table 10-6). On Fedora, KDE is installed in the standard system directories with some variations, such as **/usr/bin** for KDE program files, **/usr/lib/kde3**, which holds KDE libraries, and **/usr/include/kde**, which contains KDE header files used in application development.

System KDE Directories	Description
/usr/bin	KDE programs
/usr/lib/kde3	KDE libraries
/usr/include/kde	Header files for use in compiling and developing KDE applications
/usr/share/config	KDE desktop and application configuration files
/usr/share/mimelnk	Desktop files used to build the main menu
/usr/share/apps	Files used by KDE applications
/usr/share/icons	Icons used in KDE desktop and applications
/usr/share/doc	KDE Help system
User KDE Directories	**Description**
.kde/AutoStart	Applications automatically started up with KDE
.kde/share/config	User KDE desktop and application configuration files for user-specified features
.kde/share/mimelnk	Desktop files used to build the user's menu entries on the KDE main menu
.kde/share/apps	Directories and files used by KDE applications
Desktop	Desktop files for icons and folders displayed on the user's KDE desktop
Desktop/Trash	Trash folder for files marked for deletion

Table 10-6: KDE Installation Directories

Your **.kde** directory holds files and directories used to maintain your KDE desktop. As with GNOME, the **Desktop** directory holds KDE desktop files whose icons are displayed on the desktop. Configuration files are located in the **.kde/share/config** directory. Here you can find the general configuration files for different KDE components: **kwinrc** holds configuration commands for the window manager, **kmailrc** for mail, while **kdeglobals** holds keyboard shortcuts along with other global definitions. You can place configuration directives directly in any of these files; **.kde/share/mimelnk** holds the desktop files for the menu entries added by the user. The **.kde/share/apps** directory contains files and directories for configuring KDE applications, including **koffice**, **kmail**, and even **konqueror**.

The directories located in **share** directory contain files used to configure system defaults for your KDE environment (the system **share** directory is located at **/usr/share**). The **share/mimelnk** directory maps its files to KDE icons and specifies MIME type definitions. Their contents consist of desktop files having the extension **.desktop**, one for each menu entry. The **share/apps** directory contains files and directories set up by KDE applications; **share/config** contains the configuration files for particular KDE applications. These are the system-wide defaults that can be overridden by users' own configurations in their own **.kde/share/config** directories. The **share/icons** directory holds the default icons used on your KDE desktop and by KDE applications. As noted previously, in the user's home directory, the **.kde** directory holds a user's own KDE configuration for the desktop and its applications.

11. Shells

The Command Line

History

Filename Expansion: *, ?, [ ]

Standard Input/Output and Redirection

Linux Files

The File Structure

Listing, Displaying, and Printing Files

Managing Directories: mkdir, rmdir, ls, cd, pwd

File and Directory Operations: find, cp, mv, rm, ln

The *shell* is a command interpreter that provides a line-oriented interactive and non-interactive interface between the user and the operating system. You enter commands on a command line; they are interpreted by the shell and then sent as instructions to the operating system (the command line interface is accessible from Gnome and KDE through a Terminal windows – Applications/Accessories menu). You can also place commands in a script file to be consecutively executed much like a program. This interpretive capability of the shell provides for many sophisticated features. For example, the shell has a set of file expansion characters that can generate filenames. The shell can redirect input and output, as well as run operations in the background, freeing you to perform other tasks.

Shell	Web Site
`www.gnu.org/software/bash`	BASH Web site with online manual, FAQ, and current releases
`www.gnu.org/software/bash/manual/bash.html`	BASH online manual
`www.zsh.org`	Z shell Web site with referrals to FAQs and current downloads.
`www.tcsh.org`	TCSH Web site with detailed support including manual, tips, FAQ, and recent releases
`www.kornshell.com`	Korn shell site with manual, FAQ, and references

Table 11-1: Linux Shells

Several different types of shells have been developed for Linux: the Bourne Again shell (BASH), the Korn shell, the TCSH shell, and the Z shell. All shells are available for your use, although the BASH shell is the default. You only need one type of shell to do your work. Fedora Linux includes all the major shells, although it installs and uses the BASH shell as the default. If you use the command line shell, you will be using the BASH shell unless you specify another. This chapter discusses the BASH shell, which shares many of the same features as other shells.

You can find out more about shells at their respective Web sites as listed in Table 11-1. Also, a detailed online manual is available for each installed shell. Use the **man** command and the shell's keyword to access them, **bash** for the BASH shell, **ksh** for the Korn shell, **zsh** for the Z shell, and **tsch** for the TSCH shell. For example, the command **man bash** will access the BASH shell online manual.

Note: You can find out more about the BASH shell at **www.gnu.org/software/bash**. A detailed online manual is available on your Linux system using the **man** command with the **bash** keyword.

The Command Line

The Linux command line interface consists of a single line into which you enter commands with any of their options and arguments. From GNOME or KDE, you can access the command line interface by opening a terminal window. Should you start Linux with the command line interface, you will be presented with a BASH shell command line when you log in.

By default, the BASH shell has a dollar sign (**$**) prompt, but Linux has several other types of shells, each with its own prompt (like **%** for the C shell). The root user will have a different prompt, the #. A shell *prompt,* such as the one shown here, marks the beginning of the command line:

```
$
```

You can enter a command along with options and arguments at the prompt. For example, with an -1 option, the ls command will display a line of information about each file, listing such data as its size and the date and time it was last modified. In the next example, the user enters the ls command followed by a -1 option. The dash before the -1 option is required. Linux uses it to distinguish an option from an argument.

```
$ ls -l
```

If you wanted only the information displayed for a particular file, you could add that file's name as the argument, following the -1 option:

```
$ ls -l mydata
-rw-r--r-- 1 chris weather 207 Feb 20 11:55 mydata
```

Tip: Some commands can be complex and take some time to execute. When you mistakenly execute the wrong command, you can interrupt and stop such commands with the interrupt key—CTRL-C.

You can enter a command on several lines by typing a backslash just before you press ENTER. The backslash "escapes" the ENTER key, effectively continuing the same command line to the next line. In the next example, the cp command is entered on three lines. The first two lines end in a backslash, effectively making all three lines one command line.

```
$ cp -i \
mydata \
/home/george/myproject/newdata
```

You can also enter several commands on the same line by separating them with a semicolon (;). In effect the semicolon operates as an execute operation. Commands will be executed in the sequence they are entered. The following command executes an ls command followed by a date command.

```
$ ls ; date
```

You can also conditionally run several commands on the same line with the && operator. A command is executed only if the previous one is true. This feature is useful for running several dependent scripts on the same line. In the next example, the ls command is run only if the date command is successfully executed.

```
$ date && ls
```

TIP: Command can also be run as arguments on a command line, using their results for other commands. To run a command within a command line, you encase the command in back quotes, see Values from Linux Commands later in this chapter.

Command Line Editing

The BASH shell, which is your default shell, has special command line editing capabilities that you may find helpful as you learn Linux (see Table 11-2). You can easily modify commands you have entered before executing them, moving anywhere on the command line and inserting or deleting characters. This is particularly helpful for complex commands. You can use the CTRL-F or RIGHT ARROW key to move forward a character, or the CTRL-B or LEFT ARROW key to move back a character. CTRL-D or DEL deletes the character the cursor is on, and CTRL-H or BACKSPACE deletes the character before the cursor. To add text, you use the arrow keys to move the cursor to where you want to insert text and type the new characters.

Movement Commands	Operation
CTRL-F, RIGHT-ARROW	Move forward a character
CTRL-B, LEFT-ARROW	Move backward a character
CTRL-A or HOME	Move to beginning of line
CTRL-E or END	Move to end of line
ALT-F	Move forward a word
ALT-B	Move backward a word
CTRL-L	Clear screen and place line at top

Editing Commands	Operation
CTRL-D or DEL	Delete character cursor is on
CTRL-H or BACKSPACE	Delete character before the cursor
CTRL-K	Cut remainder of line from cursor position
CTRL-U	Cut from cursor position to beginning of line
CTRL-W	Cut previous word
CTRL-C	Cut entire line
ALT-D	Cut the remainder of a word
ALT-DEL	Cut from the cursor to the beginning of a word
CTRL-Y	Paste previous cut text
ALT-Y	Paste from set of previously cut text
CTRL-Y	Paste previous cut text
CTRL-V	Insert quoted text, used for inserting control or meta (Alt) keys as text, such as CTRL-B for backspace or CTRL-T for tabs
ALT-T	Transpose current and previous word
ALT-L	Lowercase current word
ALT-U	Uppercase current word
ALT-C	Capitalize current word
CTRL-SHIFT-_	Undo previous change

Table 11-2: Command Line Editing Operations

You can even cut words with the CTRL-W or ALT-D key and then use the CTRL-Y key to paste them back in at a different position, effectively moving the words. As a rule, the CTRL version of the command operates on characters, and the ALT version works on words, such as CTRL-T to transpose characters and ALT-T to transpose words. At any time, you can press ENTER to execute the command. For example, if you make a spelling mistake when entering a command, rather than reentering the entire command, you can use the editing operations to correct the mistake. The actual associations of keys and their tasks, along with global settings, are specified in the **/etc/inputrc** file.

The editing capabilities of the BASH shell command line are provided by Readline. Readline supports numerous editing operations. You can even bind a key to a selected editing operation. Readline uses the **/etc/inputrc** file to configure key bindings. This file is read automatically by your **/etc/profile** shell configuration file when you log in. Users can customize their editing commands by creating an **.inputrc** file in their home directory (this is a dot file). It may be best to first copy the **/etc/inputrc** file as your **.inputrc** file and then edit it. **/etc/profile** will first check for a local **.inputrc** file before accessing the **/etc/inputrc** file. You can find out more about Readline in the BASH shell reference manual at **www.gnu.org/manual/bash**.

Command and Filename Completion

The BASH command line has a built-in feature that performs command line and file name completion. Automatic completions can be effected using the TAB key. If you enter an incomplete pattern as a command or filename argument, you can then press the TAB key to activate the command and filename completion feature, which completes the pattern. Directories will have a / attached to their name. If more than one command or file has the same prefix, the shell simply beeps and waits for you to enter the TAB key again. It then displays a list of possible command completions and waits for you to add enough characters to select a unique command or filename. For situations where you know there are likely multiple possibilities, you can just press the ESC key instead of two TABs. In the next example, the user issues a `cat` command with an incomplete filename. When the user presses the TAB key, the system searches for a match and, when it finds one, fills in the filename. The user can then press ENTER to execute the command.

```
$ cat pre tab
$ cat preface
```

The automatic completions feature also works with the names of variables, users, and hosts. In this case, the partial text needs to be preceded by a special character, indicating the type of name. A listing of possible automatic completions follows:

> ➤ Filenames begin with any text or /.

> ➤ Shell variable text begins with a $ sign.

> ➤ User name text begins with a ~ sign.

> ➤ Host name text begins with a @.

> ➤ Commands, aliases, and text in files begin with normal text.

Variables begin with a **$** sign, so any text beginning with a dollar sign is treated as a variable to be completed. Variables are selected from previously defined variables, like system shell variables. User names begin with a tilde (~). Host names begin with a @ sign, with possible names taken from the **/etc/hosts** file. For example, to complete the variable HOME given just $HOM, simple enter a tab character.

```
$ echo $HOM <tab>
$ echo $HOME
```

If you entered just an H, then you could enter two tabs to see all possible variables beginning with H. The command line is redisplayed, letting you complete the name.

```
$ echo $H <tab> <tab>
$HISTCMD $HISTFILE $HOME $HOSTTYPE HISTFILE  $HISTSIZE $HISTNAME
$ echo $H
```

You can also specifically select the kind of text to complete, using corresponding command keys. In this case, it does not matter what kind of sign a name begins with.

Command (CTRL-R for listing possible completions)	Description
TAB	Automatic completion
TAB TAB or ESC	List possible completions
ALT-/, CTRL-R-/	Filename completion, normal text for automatic
ALT-$, CTRL-R-$	Shell variable completion, $ for automatic
ALT-~, CTRL-R-~	User name completion, ~ for automatic
ALT-@, CTRL-R-@	Host name completion, @ for automatic
ALT-!, CTRL-R-!	Command name completion, normal text for automatic

Table 11-3: Command Line Text Completion Commands

For example, the ALT-~ will treat the current text as a user name. ALT-@ will treat it as a host name, and ALT-$, as a variable. ALT-! will treat it as a command. To display a list of possible completions, use the CTRL-X key with the appropriate completion key, as in CTRL-X-$ to list possible variable completions. See Table 11-3 for a complete listing.

History

The BASH shell keeps a list, called a *history list,* of your previously entered commands. You can display each command, in turn, on your command line by pressing the UP ARROW key. The DOWN ARROW key moves you down the list. You can modify and execute any of these previous commands when you display them on your command line.

Tip: The capability to redisplay a previous command is helpful when you've already executed a command you had entered incorrectly. In this case, you would be presented with an error message and a new, empty command line. By pressing the UP ARROW key, you can redisplay your previous command, make corrections to it, and then execute it again. This way, you would not have to enter the whole command again.

History Events

In the BASH shell, the *history utility* keeps a record of the most recent commands you have executed. The commands are numbered starting at 1, and a limit exists to the number of commands remembered—the default is 500. The history utility is a kind of short-term memory, keeping track of the most recent commands you have executed. To see the set of your most recent commands, type `history` on the command line and press ENTER. A list of your most recent commands is then displayed, preceded by a number.

```
$ history
1 cp mydata today
2 vi mydata
3 mv mydata reports
4 cd reports
5 ls
```

History Commands	Description
CTRL-N or DOWN ARROW	Moves down to the next event in the history list
CTRL-P or UP ARROW	Moves up to the previous event in the history list
ALT-<	Moves to the beginning of the history event list
ALT->	Moves to the end of the history event list
ALT-N	Forward Search, next matching item
ALT-P	Backward Search, previous matching item
CTRL-S	Forward Search History, forward incremental search
CTRL-R	Reverse Search History, reverse incremental search
`fc` *event-reference*	Edits an event with the standard editor and then executes it **Options** -l List recent history events; same as **history** command -e *editor event-reference* Invokes a specified editor to edit a specific event
History Event References	
`!`*event num*	References an event with an event number
`!!`	References the previous command
`!`*characters*	References an event with beginning characters
`!?`*pattern*`?`	References an event with a pattern in the event
`!-`*event num*	References an event with an offset from the first event
`!`*num*`-`*num*	References a range of events

Table 11-4: History Commands and History Event References

Each of these commands is technically referred to as an event. An *event* describes an action that has been taken—a command that has been executed. The events are numbered according to their sequence of execution. The most recent event has the highest number. Each of these events can be identified by its number or beginning characters in the command.

The history utility enables you to reference a former event, placing it on your command line and enabling you to execute it. The easiest way to do this is to use the UP ARROW and DOWN ARROW keys to place history events on your command line, one at a time. You needn't display the list first with **history**. Pressing the UP ARROW key once places the last history event on your command line. Pressing it again places the next history event on your command. Pressing the DOWN ARROW key places the previous event on the command line.

You can use certain control and meta keys to perform other history operations like searching the history list. A meta key is the ALT key, and the ESC key on keyboards that have no ALT key. The ALT key is used here. ALT-< will move you to the beginning of the history list; ALT-N will search it. CTRL-S and CTRL-R will perform incremental searches, display matching commands as you type in a search string. Table 11-4 lists the different commands for referencing the history list.

Tip: If more than one history event matches what you have entered, you will hear a beep, and you can then enter more characters to help uniquely identify the event.

You can also reference and execute history events using the **!** history command. The **!** is followed by a reference that identifies the command. The reference can be either the number of the event or a beginning set of characters in the event. In the next example, the third command in the history list is referenced first by number and then by the beginning characters:

```
$ !3
mv mydata reports
$ !mv my
mv mydata reports
```

You can also reference an event using an offset from the end of the list. A negative number will offset from the end of the list to that event, thereby referencing it. In the next example, the fourth command, **cd mydata**, is referenced using a negative offset, and then executed. Remember that you are offsetting from the end of the list—in this case, event 5—up toward the beginning of the list, event 1. An offset of 4 beginning from event 5 places you at event 2.

```
$ !-4
vi mydata
```

To reference the last event, you use a following !, as in **!!**. In the next example, the command **!!** executes the last command the user executed—in this case, **ls**:

```
$ !!
ls
mydata today reports
```

Filename Expansion: *, ?, [ ]

Filenames are the most common arguments used in a command. Often you may know only part of the filename, or you may want to reference several filenames that have the same extension or begin with the same characters. The shell provides a set of special characters that search out, match, and generate a list of filenames. These are the asterisk, the question mark, and brackets (*, ?, []). Given a partial filename, the shell uses these matching operators to search for files and expand to a list of filenames found. The shell replaces the partial filename argument with the expanded list of matched filenames. This list of filenames can then become the arguments for commands such as `ls`, which can operate on many files. Table 11-5 lists the shell's file expansion characters.

Common Shell Symbols	Execution
ENTER	Execute a command line.
;	Separate commands on the same command line.
`` `command` ``	Execute a command.
$ (*command*)	Execute a command.
[ ]	Match on a class of possible characters in filenames.
\	Quote the following character. Used to quote special characters.
|	Pipe the standard output of one command as input for another command.
&	Execute a command in the background.
!	History command.

File Expansion Symbols	Execution
*	Match on any set of characters in filenames.
?	Match on any single character in filenames.
[ ]	Match on a class of characters in filenames.

Redirection Symbols	Execution
>	Redirect the standard output to a file or device, creating the file if it does not exist and overwriting the file if it does exist.
>!	The exclamation point forces the overwriting of a file if it already exists.
<	Redirect the standard input from a file or device to a program.
>>	Redirect the standard output to a file or device, appending the output to the end of the file.

Standard Error Redirection Symbols	Execution
2>	Redirect the standard error to a file or device.
2>>	Redirect and append the standard error to a file or device.
2>&1	Redirect the standard error to the standard output.

Table 11-5: Shell Symbols

Matching Multiple Characters

The asterisk (*) references files beginning or ending with a specific set of characters. You place the asterisk before or after a set of characters that form a pattern to be searched for in filenames.

If the asterisk is placed before the pattern, filenames that end in that pattern are searched for. If the asterisk is placed after the pattern, filenames that begin with that pattern are searched for. Any matching filename is copied into a list of filenames generated by this operation.

In the next example, all filenames beginning with the pattern "doc" are searched for and a list generated. Then all filenames ending with the pattern "day" are searched for and a list is generated. The last example shows how the * can be used in any combination of characters.

```
$ ls
doc1 doc2 document docs mydoc monday tuesday
$ ls doc*
doc1 doc2 document docs
$ ls *day
monday tuesday
$ ls m*d*
monday
$
```

Filenames often include an extension specified with a period and followed by a string denoting the file type, such as **.c** for C files, **.cpp** for C++ files, or even **.jpg** for JPEG image files. The extension has no special status and is only part of the characters making up the filename. Using the asterisk makes it easy to select files with a given extension. In the next example, the asterisk is used to list only those files with a **.c** extension. The asterisk placed before the **.c** constitutes the argument for **ls**.

```
$ ls *.c
calc.c main.c
```

You can use * with the **rm** command to erase several files at once. The asterisk first selects a list of files with a given extension, or beginning or ending with a given set of characters, and then it presents this list of files to the **rm** command to be erased. In the next example, the **rm** command erases all files beginning with the pattern "doc":

```
$ rm doc*
```

Tip: Use the * file expansion character carefully and sparingly with the **rm** command. The combination can be dangerous. A misplaced * in an **rm** command without the **-i** option could easily erase all the files in your current directory. The **-i** option will first prompt the user to confirm whether the file should be deleted.

Matching Single Characters

The question mark (?) matches only a single incomplete character in filenames. Suppose you want to match the files **doc1** and **docA**, but not the file **document**. Whereas the asterisk will match filenames of any length, the question mark limits the match to just one extra character. The next example matches files that begin with the word "doc" followed by a single differing letter:

```
$ ls
doc1 docA document
$ ls doc?
doc1 docA
```

Matching a Range of Characters

Whereas the * and ? file expansion characters specify incomplete portions of a filename, the brackets ([]) enable you to specify a set of valid characters to search for. Any character placed within the brackets will be matched in the filename. Suppose you want to list files beginning with "doc", but only ending in *1* or *A*. You are not interested in filenames ending in *2* or *B*, or any other character. Here is how it's done:

```
$ ls
doc1 doc2 doc3 docA docB docD document
$ ls doc[1A]
doc1 docA
```

You can also specify a set of characters as a range, rather than listing them one by one. A dash placed between the upper and lower bounds of a set of characters selects all characters within that range. The range is usually determined by the character set in use. In an ASCII character set, the range "a-g" will select all lowercase alphabetic characters from *a* through *g*, inclusive. In the next example, files beginning with the pattern "doc" and ending in characters *1* through *3* are selected. Then, those ending in characters *B* through *E* are matched.

```
$ ls doc[1-3]
doc1 doc2 doc3
$ ls doc[B-E]
docB docD
```

You can combine the brackets with other file expansion characters to form flexible matching operators. Suppose you want to list only filenames ending in either a **.c** or **.o** extension, but no other extension. You can use a combination of the asterisk and brackets: * [co]. The asterisk matches all filenames, and the brackets match only filenames with extension **.c** or **.o**.

```
$ ls *.[co]
main.c  main.o  calc.c
```

Matching Shell Symbols

At times, a file expansion character is actually part of a filename. In these cases, you need to quote the character by preceding it with a backslash to reference the file. In the next example, the user needs to reference a file that ends with the **?** character, **answers?**. The **?** is, however, a file expansion character and would match any filename beginning with "answers" that has one or more characters. In this case, the user quotes the **?** with a preceding backslash to reference the filename.

```
$ ls answers\?
answers?
```

Placing the filename in double quotes will also quote the character.

```
$ ls "answers?"
answers?
```

This is also true for filenames or directories that have white space characters like the space character. In this case you could either use the backslash to quote the space character in the file or directory name, or place the entire name in double quotes.

```
$ ls My\ Documents
My Documents
$ ls "My Documents"
My Documents
```

Generating Patterns

Though not a file expansion operation, {} is often useful for generating names that you can use to create or modify files and directories. The braces operation only generates a list of names. It does not match on existing filenames. Patterns are placed within the braces and separated with commas. Any pattern placed within the braces will be used to generate a version of the pattern, using either the preceding or following pattern, or both. Suppose you want to generate a list of names beginning with "doc", but only ending in the patterns "ument", "final", and "draft". Here is how it's done:

```
$ echo doc{ument,final,draft}
document docfinal docdraft
```

Since the names generated do not have to exist, you could use the {} operation in a command to create directories, as shown here:

```
$ mkdir {fall,winter,spring}report
$ ls
fallreport springreport winterreport
```

Standard Input/Output and Redirection

The data in input and output operations is organized like a file. Data input at the keyboard is placed in a data stream arranged as a continuous set of bytes. Data output from a command or program is also placed in a data stream and arranged as a continuous set of bytes. This input data stream is referred to in Linux as the *standard input,* while the output data stream is called the *standard output.* There is also a separate output data stream reserved solely for error messages, called the *standard error* (see the section "Redirecting and Piping the Standard Error: >&, 2>" later in this chapter).

Because the standard input and standard output have the same organization as that of a file, they can easily interact with files. Linux has a redirection capability that lets you easily move data in and out of files. You can redirect the standard output so that, instead of displaying the output on a screen, you can save it in a file. You can also redirect the standard input away from the keyboard to a file, so that input is read from a file instead of from your keyboard.

When a Linux command is executed that produces output, this output is placed in the standard output data stream. The default destination for the standard output data stream is a device—in this case, the screen. *Devices,* such as the keyboard and screen, are treated as files. They receive and send out streams of bytes with the same organization as that of a byte-stream file. The screen is a device that displays a continuous stream of bytes. By default, the standard output will send its data to the screen device, which will then display the data.

For example, the `ls` command generates a list of all filenames and outputs this list to the standard output. Next, this stream of bytes in the standard output is directed to the screen device. The list of filenames is then printed on the screen. The `cat` command also sends output to the standard output. The contents of a file are copied to the standard output, whose default destination is the screen. The contents of the file are then displayed on the screen.

Redirecting the Standard Output: > and >>

Suppose that instead of displaying a list of files on the screen, you would like to save this list in a file. In other words, you would like to direct the standard output to a file rather than the screen. To do this, you place the output redirection operator, the greater-than sign (>) , followed by the name of a file on the command line after the Linux command. Table 11-6 lists the different ways you can use the redirection operators. In the next example, the output of the `ls` command is redirected from the screen device to a file:

```
$ ls -l *.c > programlist
```

The redirection operation creates the new destination file. If the file already exists, it will be overwritten with the data in the standard output. You can set the `noclobber` feature to prevent overwriting an existing file with the redirection operation. In this case, the redirection operation on an existing file will fail. You can overcome the `noclobber` feature by placing an exclamation point after the redirection operator. You can place the `noclobber` command in a shell configuration file to make it an automatic default operation. The next example sets the `noclobber` feature for the BASH shell and then forces the overwriting of the **oldarticle** file if it already exists:

```
$ set -o noclobber
$ cat myarticle >! oldarticle
```

Although the redirection operator and the filename are placed after the command, the redirection operation is not executed after the command. In fact, it is executed before the command. The redirection operation creates the file and sets up the redirection before it receives any data from the standard output. If the file already exists, it will be destroyed and replaced by a file of the same name. In effect, the command generating the output is executed only after the redirected file has been created.

In the next example, the output of the `ls` command is redirected from the screen device to a file. First the `ls` command lists files, and in the next command, `ls` redirects its file list to the **listf** file. Then the `cat` command displays the list of files saved in **listf**. Notice the list of files in **listf** includes the **listf** filename. The list of filenames generated by the `ls` command includes the name of the file created by the redirection operation—in this case, **listf**. The **listf** file is first created by the redirection operation, and then the `ls` command lists it along with other files. This file list output by `ls` is then redirected to the **listf** file, instead of being printed on the screen.

```
$ ls
mydata intro preface
$ ls > listf
$ cat listf
mydata intro listf preface
```

You can also append the standard output to an existing file using the `>>` redirection operator. Instead of overwriting the file, the data in the standard output is added at the end of the file. In the next example, the **myarticle** and **oldarticle** files are appended to the **allarticles** file. The **allarticles** file will then contain the contents of both **myarticle** and **oldarticle**.

```
$ cat myarticle >> allarticles
$ cat oldarticle >> allarticles
```

Command	Execution
ENTER	Execute a command line.
;	Separate commands on the same command line.
command *opts args*	Enter backslash before carriage return to continue entering a command on the next line.
`` `command` ``	Execute a command.

Special Characters for Filename Expansion	Execution
*	Match on any set of characters.
?	Match on any single characters.
[]	Match on a class of possible characters.
\	Quote the following character. Used to quote special characters.

Redirection	Execution
command > filename	Redirect the standard output to a file or device, creating the file if it does not exist and overwriting the file if it does exist.
command < filename	Redirect the standard input from a file or device to a program.
command >> filename	Redirect the standard output to a file or device, appending the output to the end of the file.
command 2> filename	Redirect the standard error to a file or device
command 2>> filename	Redirect and append the standard error to a file or device
command 2>&1	Redirect the standard error to the standard output in the Bourne shell.
command >& filename	Redirect the standard error to a file or device in the C shell.

Pipes	Execution
*command	command*	Pipe the standard output of one command as input for another command.

Table 11-6: The Shell Operations

Tip: Errors occur when you try to use the same filename for both an input file for the command and the redirected destination file. In this case, because the redirection operation is executed first, the input file, because it exists, is destroyed and replaced by a file of the same name. When the command is executed, it finds an input file that is empty.

The Standard Input

Many Linux commands can receive data from the standard input. The standard input itself receives data from a device or a file. The default device for the standard input is the keyboard. Characters typed on the keyboard are placed in the standard input, which is then directed to the Linux command. Just as with the standard output, you can also redirect the standard input, receiving input from a file rather than the keyboard. The operator for redirecting the standard input is the less-than sign (<). In the next example, the standard input is redirected to receive input from the **myarticle** file, rather than the keyboard device (use CTRL-D to end the typed input). The contents of **myarticle** are read into the standard input by the redirection operation. Then the cat command reads the standard input and displays the contents of **myarticle**.

```
$ cat < myarticle
hello Christopher
How are you today
$
```

You can combine the redirection operations for both standard input and standard output. In the next example, the cat command has no filename arguments. Without filename arguments, the cat command receives input from the standard input and sends output to the standard output. However, the standard input has been redirected to receive its data from a file, while the standard output has been redirected to place its data in a file.

```
$ cat < myarticle > newarticle
```

Pipes: |

You may find yourself in situations in which you need to send data from one command to another. In other words, you may want to send the standard output of a command to another command, not to a destination file. Suppose you want to send a list of your filenames to the printer to be printed. You need two commands to do this: the ls command to generate a list of filenames and the lpr command to send the list to the printer. In effect, you need to take the output of the ls command and use it as input for the lpr command. You can think of the data as flowing from one command to another. To form such a connection in Linux, you use what is called a *pipe*. The *pipe operator* (|, the vertical bar character) placed between two commands forms a connection between them. The standard output of one command becomes the standard input for the other. The pipe operation receives output from the command placed before the pipe and sends this data as input to the command placed after the pipe. As shown in the next example, you can connect the ls command and the lpr command with a pipe. The list of filenames output by the ls command is piped into the lpr command.

```
$ ls | lpr
```

You can combine the **pipe** operation with other shell features, such as file expansion characters, to perform specialized operations. The next example prints only files with a **.c** extension. The ls command is used with the asterisk and ".c" to generate a list of filenames with the **.c** extension. Then this list is piped to the lpr command.

```
$ ls *.c | lpr
```

In the preceding example, a list of filenames was used as input, but what is important to note is that pipes operate on the standard output of a command, whatever that might be. The contents of whole files or even several files can be piped from one command to another. In the next example, the `cat` command reads and outputs the contents of the **mydata** file, which are then piped to the `lpr` command:

```
$ cat mydata | lpr
```

Linux has many commands that generate modified output. For example, the `sort` command takes the contents of a file and generates a version with each line sorted in alphabetic order. The `sort` command works best with files that are lists of items. Commands such as `sort` that output a modified version of its input are referred to as *filters*. Filters are often used with pipes. In the next example, a sorted version of **mylist** is generated and piped into the `more` command for display on the screen. Note that the original file, **mylist**, has not been changed and is not itself sorted. Only the output of `sort` in the standard output is sorted.

```
$ sort mylist | more
```

The standard input piped into a command can be more carefully controlled with the standard input argument (-). When you use the dash as an argument for a command, it represents the standard input.

List, Display, and Print Files: ls, cat, more, less, and lpr

One of the primary functions of an operating system is the management of files. You may need to perform certain basic output operations on your files, such as displaying them on your screen or printing them. The Linux system provides a set of commands that perform basic file-management operations, such as listing, displaying, and printing files, as well as copying, renaming, and erasing files. These commands are usually made up of abbreviated versions of words. For example, the `ls` command is a shortened form of "list" and lists the files in your directory. The `lpr` command is an abbreviated form of "line print" and will print a file.

Command or Option	Execution
`ls`	This command lists file and directory names.
`cat` *filenames*	This filter can be used to display a file. It can take filenames for its arguments. It outputs the contents of those files directly to the standard output, which, by default, is directed to the screen.
`more` *filenames*	This utility displays a file screen by screen. Press the SPACEBAR to continue to the next screen and **q** to quit.
`less` *filenames*	This utility also displays a file screen by screen. Press the SPACEBAR to continue to the next screen and **q** to quit.
`lpr` *filenames*	Sends a file to the line printer to be printed; a list of files may be used as arguments. Use the **-P** option to specify a printer.
`lpq`	Lists the print queue for printing jobs.
`lprm`	Removes a printing job from the print queue.

Table 11-7: Listing, Displaying, and Printing Files

The `cat`, `less`, and `more` commands display the contents of a file on the screen. Table 11-7 lists these commands with their different options. When you log in to your Linux system, you may want a list of the files in your home directory. The `ls` command, which outputs a list of your file and directory names, is useful for this. The `ls` command has many possible options for displaying filenames according to specific features.

Displaying Files: cat, less, and more

You may also need to look at the contents of a file. The `cat` and `more` commands display the contents of a file on the screen. The name `cat` stands for *concatenate.*

```
$ cat mydata
computers
```

The `cat` command outputs the entire text of a file to the screen at once. This presents a problem when the file is large because its text quickly speeds past on the screen. The `more` and `less` commands are designed to overcome this limitation by displaying one screen of text at a time. You can then move forward or backward in the text at your leisure. You invoke the `more` or `less` command by entering the command name followed by the name of the file you want to view (`less` is a more powerful and configurable display utility).

```
$ less mydata
```

When `more` or `less` invoke a file, the first screen of text is displayed. To continue to the next screen, you press the F key or the SPACEBAR. To move back in the text, you press the B key. You can quit at any time by pressing the Q key.

Printing Files: lpr, lpq, and lprm

With the printer commands such as `lpr` and `lprm`, you can perform printing operations such as printing files or canceling print jobs (see Table 11-7). When you need to print files, use the `lpr` command to send files to the printer connected to your system. In the next example, the user prints the **mydata** file:

```
$ lpr mydata
```

If you want to print several files at once, you can specify more than one file on the command line after the `lpr` command. In the next example, the user prints out both the **mydata** and **preface** files:

```
$ lpr mydata preface
```

Printing jobs are placed in a queue and printed one at a time in the background. You can continue with other work as your files print. You can see the position of a particular printing job at any given time with the `lpq` command, which gives the owner of the printing job (the login name of the user who sent the job), the print job ID, the size in bytes, and the temporary file in which it is currently held.

If you need to cancel an unwanted printing job, you can do so with the `lprm` command, which takes as its argument either the ID number of the printing job or the owner's name. It then removes the print job from the print queue. For this task, `lpq` is helpful, for it provides you with the ID number and owner of the printing job you need to use with `lprm`.

Managing Directories: mkdir, rmdir, ls, cd, pwd

You can create and remove your own directories, as well as change your working directory, with the `mkdir`, `rmdir`, and `cd` commands. Each of these commands can take as its argument the pathname for a directory. The `pwd` command displays the absolute pathname of your working directory. In addition to these commands, the special characters represented by a single dot, a double dot, and a tilde can be used to reference the working directory, the parent of the working directory, and the home directory, respectively. Taken together, these commands enable you to manage your directories. You can create nested directories, move from one directory to another, and use pathnames to reference any of your directories. Those commands commonly used to manage directories are listed in Table 11-8.

Command	Execution
`mkdir` *directory*	Creates a directory.
`rmdir` *directory*	Erases a directory.
`ls -F`	Lists directory name with a preceding slash.
`ls -R`	Lists working directory as well as all subdirectories.
`cd` *directory name*	Changes to the specified directory, making it the working directory. **cd** without a directory name changes back to the home directory: **$ cd reports**
`pwd`	Displays the pathname of the working directory.
directory name / filename	A slash is used in pathnames to separate each directory name. In the case of pathnames for files, a slash separates the preceding directory names from the filename.
`..`	References the parent directory. You can use it as an argument or as part of a pathname: **$ cd ..** **$ mv ../larisa oldarticles**
`.`	References the working directory. You can use it as an argument or as part of a pathname: **$ ls .**
~/pathname	The tilde is a special character that represents the pathname for the home directory. It is useful when you need to use an absolute pathname for a file or directory: **$ cp monday ~/today**

Table 11-8: Directory Commands

Creating and Deleting Directories

You create and remove directories with the `mkdir` and `rmdir` commands. In either case, you can also use pathnames for the directories. In the next example, the user creates the directory **reports**. Then the user creates the directory **articles** using a pathname:

```
$ mkdir reports
$ mkdir /home/chris/articles
```

You can remove a directory with the `rmdir` command followed by the directory name. In the next example, the user removes the directory **reports** with the `rmdir` command:

```
$ rmdir reports
```

To remove a directory and all its subdirectories, you use the `rm` command with the `-r` option. This is a very powerful command and could easily be used to erase all your files. You will be prompted for each file. To simply remove all files and subdirectories without prompts, add the `-f` option. The following example deletes the **reports** directory and all its subdirectories:

```
rm -rf reports
```

Displaying Directory Contents

You have seen how to use the `ls` command to list the files and directories within your working directory. To distinguish between file and directory names, however, you need to use the `ls` command with the `-F` option. A slash is then placed after each directory name in the list.

```
$ ls
weather reports articles
$ ls -F
weather reports/ articles/
```

The `ls` command also takes as an argument any directory name or directory pathname. This enables you to list the files in any directory without first having to change to that directory. In the next example, the `ls` command takes as its argument the name of a directory, **reports**. Then the `ls` command is executed again, only this time the absolute pathname of **reports** is used.

```
$ ls reports
monday tuesday
$ ls /home/chris/reports
monday tuesday
$
```

Moving Through Directories

The `cd` command takes as its argument the name of the directory to which you want to change. The name of the directory can be the name of a subdirectory in your working directory or the full pathname of any directory on the system. If you want to change back to your home directory, you only need to enter the `cd` command by itself, without a filename argument.

```
$ cd props
$ pwd
/home/dylan/props
```

Referencing the Parent Directory

A directory always has a parent (except, of course, for the root). For example, in the preceding listing, the parent for **travel** is the **articles** directory. When a directory is created, two entries are made: one represented with a dot (.), and the other with double dots (. .). The dot represents the pathnames of the directory, and the double dots represent the pathname of its parent directory. Double dots, used as an argument in a command, reference a parent directory. The single dot references the directory itself.

You can use the single dot to reference your working directory, instead of using its pathname. For example, to copy a file to the working directory retaining the same name, the dot can be used in place of the working directory's pathname. In this sense, the dot is another name for the working directory. In the next example, the user copies the **weather** file from the **chris** directory to the **reports** directory. The **reports** directory is the working directory and can be represented with the single dot.

```
$ cd reports
$ cp /home/chris/weather .
```

The .. symbol is often used to reference files in the parent directory. In the next example, the **cat** command displays the **weather** file in the parent directory. The pathname for the file is the .. symbol followed by a slash and the filename.

```
$ cat ../weather
raining and warm
```

Tip: You can use the **cd** command with the .. symbol to step back through successive parent directories of the directory tree from a lower directory.

File and Directory Operations: find, cp, mv, rm, ln

As you create more and more files, you may want to back them up, change their names, erase some of them, or even give them added names. Linux provides you with several file commands that enable you to search for files, copy files, rename files, or remove files (see Tables 11-5). If you have a large number of files, you can also search them to locate a specific one. The commands are shortened forms of full words, consisting of only two characters. The **cp** command stands for "copy" and copies a file, **mv** stands for "move" and renames or moves a file, **rm** stands for "remove" and erases a file, and **ln** stands for "link" and adds another name for a file, often used as a shortcut to the original. One exception to the two-character rule is the **find** command, which performs searches of your filenames to find a file. All these operations can be handled by the GUI desktops, like GNOME and KDE.

Searching Directories: find

Once you have a large number of files in many different directories, you may need to search them to locate a specific file, or files, of a certain type. The **find** command enables you to perform such a search from the command line. The **find** command takes as its arguments directory names followed by several possible options that specify the type of search and the criteria for the search; it then searches within the directories listed and their subdirectories for files that meet these criteria. The **find** command can search for a file by name, type, owner, and even the time of the last update.

```
$ find directory-list -option criteria
```

Tip: From the GNOME desktop you can use the "Search" tool in the Places menu to search for files. From the KDE Desktop you can use the find tool in the file manager. Select find from the file manager (Konqueror) tools menu.

The **-name** option has as its criteria a pattern and instructs **find** to search for the filename that matches that pattern. To search for a file by name, you use the **find** command with the directory name followed by the **-name** option and the name of the file.

```
$ find directory-list -name filename
```

The **find** command also has options that merely perform actions, such as outputting the results of a search. If you want **find** to display the filenames it has found, you simply include the **-print** option on the command line along with any other options. The **-print** option is an action that instructs **find** to write to the standard output the names of all the files it locates (you can also use the **-ls** option instead to list files in the long format). In the next example, the user searches for all the files in the **reports** directory with the name **monday**. Once located, the file, with its relative pathname, is printed.

```
$ find reports -name monday -print
reports/monday
```

The **find** command prints out the filenames using the directory name specified in the directory list. If you specify an absolute pathname, the absolute path of the found directories will be output. If you specify a relative pathname, only the relative pathname is output. In the preceding example, the user specified a relative pathname, **reports**, in the directory list. Located filenames were output beginning with this relative pathname. In the next example, the user specifies an absolute pathname in the directory list. Located filenames are then output using this absolute pathname.

```
$ find /home/chris -name monday -print
/home/chris/reports/monday
```

Tip: Should you need to find the location of a specific program or configuration file, you could use **find** to search for the file from the root directory. Log in as the root user and use **/** as the directory. This command searched for the location of the **more** command and files on the entire file system: **find / -name more -print**.

Searching the Working Directory

If you want to search your working directory, you can use the dot in the directory pathname to represent your working directory. The double dots would represent the parent directory. The next example searches all files and subdirectories in the working directory, using the dot to represent the working directory. If you are located in your home directory, this is a convenient way to search through all your own directories. Notice the located filenames are output beginning with a dot.

```
$ find . -name weather -print
./weather
```

You can use shell wildcard characters as part of the pattern criteria for searching files. The special character must be quoted, however, to avoid evaluation by the shell. In the next example, all files with the **.c** extension in the **programs** directory are searched for and then displayed in the long format using the **-ls** action:

```
$ find programs -name '*.c' -ls
```

Locating Directories

You can also use the **find** command to locate other directories. In Linux, a directory is officially classified as a special type of file. Although all files have a byte-stream format, some files, such as directories, are used in special ways. In this sense, a file can be said to have a file type. The **find** command has an option called **-type** that searches for a file of a given type. The **-type** option takes a one-character modifier that represents the file type. The modifier that represents a directory is a **d**. In the next example, both the directory name and the directory file type are used to search for the directory called **travel**:

```
$ find /home/chris -name travel -type d -print
/home/chris/articles/travel
$
```

Command or Option	Execution
find	Searches directories for files according to search criteria. This command has several options that specify the type of criteria and actions to be taken.
-name *pattern*	Searches for files with the *pattern* in the name.
-lname *pattern*	Searches for symbolic link files.
-group *name*	Searches for files belonging to the group *name*.
-gid *name*	Searches for files belonging to a group according to group ID.
-user *name*	Searches for files belonging to a user.
-uid *name*	Searches for files belonging to a user according to user ID.
-size *numc*	Searches for files with the size *num* in blocks. If **c** is added after *num*, the size in bytes (characters) is searched for.
-mtime *num*	Searches for files last modified *num* days ago.
-newer *pattern*	Searches for files modified after the one matched by *pattern*.
-context *scontext*	Searches for files according to security context (SE Linux).
-print	Outputs the result of the search to the standard output. The result is usually a list of filenames, including their full pathnames.
-type *filetype*	Searches for files with the specified file type. File type can be **b** for block device, **c** for character device, **d** for directory, **f** for file, or **l** for symbolic link.
-perm *permission*	Searches for files with certain permissions set. Use octal or symbolic format for permissions.
-ls	Provides a detailed listing of each file, with owner, permission, size, and date information.
-exec *command*	Executes command when files found.

Table 11-9: The find Command

File types are not so much different types of files as they are the file format applied to other components of the operating system, such as devices. In this sense, a device is treated as a type of file, and you can use `find` to search for devices and directories, as well as ordinary files. Table 11-9 lists the different types available for the `find` command's `-type` option.

You can also use the find operation to search for files by ownership or security criteria, like those belonging to a specific user or those with a certain security context. The user option lets to locate all files belonging to a certain user. The following example lists all files that the user **chris** has created or owns on the entire system. To list those just in the users' home directories, you would use **/home** for the starting search directory. This would find all those in a user's home directory as well as any owned by that user in other user directories.

```
$ find / -user chris -print
```

Copying Files

To make a copy of a file, you simply give `cp` two filenames as its arguments (see Table 11-10). The first filename is the name of the file to be copied—the one that already exists. This is often referred to as the *source file.* The second filename is the name you want for the copy. This will be a new file containing a copy of all the data in the source file. This second argument is often referred to as the *destination file.* The syntax for the `cp` command follows:

```
$ cp source-file destination-file
```

In the next example, the user copies a file called **proposal** to a new file called **oldprop**:

```
$ cp proposal oldprop
```

You could unintentionally destroy another file with the `cp` command. The `cp` command generates a copy by first creating a file and then copying data into it. If another file has the same name as the destination file, that file is destroyed and a new file with that name is created. By default Fedora configures your system to check for an existing copy by the same name (`cp` is aliased with the `-i` option). To copy a file from your working directory to another directory, you only need to use that directory name as the second argument in the `cp` command. In the next example, the **proposal** file is overwritten by the **newprop** file. The **proposal** file already exists.

```
$ cp newprop proposal
```

You can use any of the wildcard characters to generate a list of filenames to use with `cp` or `mv`. For example, suppose you need to copy all your C source code files to a given directory. Instead of listing each one individually on the command line, you could use an `*` character with the **.c** extension to match on and generate a list of C source code files (all files with a **.c** extension). In the next example, the user copies all source code files in the current directory to the **sourcebks** directory:

```
$ cp *.c sourcebks
```

If you want to copy all the files in a given directory to another directory, you could use `*` to match on and generate a list of all those files in a `cp` command. In the next example, the user copies all the files in the **props** directory to the **oldprop** directory. Notice the use of a **props** pathname preceding the `*` special characters. In this context, **props** is a pathname that will be appended before each file in the list that `*` generates.

```
$ cp props/* oldprop
```

You can, of course, use any of the other special characters, such as ., ?, or []. In the next example, the user copies both source code and object code files (.c and .o) to the **projbk** directory:

```
$ cp *.[oc] projbk
```

When you copy a file, you may want to give the copy a different name than the original. To do so, place the new filename after the directory name, separated by a slash.

```
$ cp filename directory-name/new-filename
```

Moving Files

You can use the **mv** command either to rename a file or to move a file from one directory to another. When using **mv** to rename a file, you simply use the new filename as the second argument. The first argument is the current name of the file you are renaming. If you want to rename a file when you move it, you can specify the new name of the file after the directory name. In the next example, the **proposal** file is renamed with the name **version1**:

```
$ mv proposal version1
```

As with **cp**, it is easy for **mv** to erase a file accidentally. When renaming a file, you might accidentally choose a filename already used by another file. In this case, that other file will be erased. The **mv** command also has an **-i** option that checks first to see if a file by that name already exists.

You can also use any of the special characters to generate a list of filenames to use with **mv**. In the next example, the user moves all source code files in the current directory to the **newproj** directory:

```
$ mv *.c newproj
```

If you want to move all the files in a given directory to another directory, you can use * to match on and generate a list of all those files. In the next example, the user moves all the files in the **reports** directory to the **repbks** directory:

```
$ mv reports/* repbks
```

Note: The easiest way to copy files to a CD-R/RW or DVD-R/RW disc is to use the built-in Nautilus burning capability. Just insert a blank disk, open it as a folder, and drag and drop files on to it. You will be prompted automatically to burn the files.

Copying and Moving Directories

You can also copy or move whole directories at once. Both **cp** and **mv** can take as their first argument a directory name, enabling you to copy or move subdirectories from one directory into another (see Table 11-10). The first argument is the name of the directory to be moved or copied, while the second argument is the name of the directory within which it is to be placed. The same pathname structure used for files applies to moving or copying directories.

You can just as easily copy subdirectories from one directory to another. To copy a directory, the **cp** command requires you to use the **-r** option. The **-r** option stands for "recursive." It directs the **cp** command to copy a directory, as well as any subdirectories it may contain. In other words, the entire directory subtree, from that directory on, will be copied. In the next example, the **travel** directory is copied to the **oldarticles** directory. Now two **travel** subdirectories exist, one in **articles** and one in **oldarticles**.

```
$ cp -r articles/travel oldarticles
$ ls -F articles
/travel
$ ls -F oldarticles
/travel
```

Command	Execution
cp *filename filename*	Copies a file. **cp** takes two arguments: the original file and the name of the new copy. You can use pathnames for the files to copy across directories:
cp -r *dirname dirname*	Copies a subdirectory from one directory to another. The copied directory includes all its own subdirectories:
mv *filename filename*	Moves (renames) a file. The **mv** command takes two arguments: the first is the file to be moved. The second argument can be the new filename or the pathname of a directory. If it is the name of a directory, then the file is literally moved to that directory, changing the file's pathname:
mv *dirname dirname*	Moves directories. In this case, the first and last arguments are directories:
ln *filename filename*	Creates added names for files referred to as links. A link can be created in one directory that references a file in another directory:
rm *filenames*	Removes (erases) a file. Can take any number of filenames as its arguments. Literally removes links to a file. If a file has more than one link, you need to remove all of them to erase a file:

Table 11-10: File Operations

Erasing Files and Directories: the rm Command

As you use Linux, you will find the number of files you use increases rapidly. Generating files in Linux is easy. Applications such as editors, and commands such as **cp**, easily create files. Eventually, many of these files may become outdated and useless. You can then remove them with the **rm** command. The **rm** command can take any number of arguments, enabling you to list several filenames and erase them all at the same time. In the next example, the user erases the file **oldprop**:

```
$ rm oldprop
```

Be careful when using the **rm** command, because it is irrevocable. Once a file is removed, it cannot be restored (there is no undo). With the **-i** option, you are prompted separately for each file and asked whether to remove it. If you enter **y**, the file will be removed. If you enter anything else, the file is not removed. In the next example, the **rm** command is instructed to erase the files **proposal** and **oldprop**. The **rm** command then asks for confirmation for each file. The user decides to remove **oldprop,** but not **proposal**.

```
$ rm -i proposal oldprop
Remove proposal? n
Remove oldprop? y
$
```

Links: the In Command

You can give a file more than one name using the `ln` command. You might want to reference a file using different filenames to access it from different directories. The added names are often referred to as *links*. Linux supports two different types of links, hard and symbolic. *Hard* links are literally another name for the same file, whereas *symbolic* links function like shortcuts referencing another file. Symbolic links are much more flexible and can work over many different file systems, whereas hard links are limited to your local file system. Furthermore, hard links introduce security concerns, as they allow direct access from a link that may have public access to an original file that you may want protected. Links are usually implemented as symbolic links.

Symbolic Links

To set up a symbolic link, you use the `ln` command with the `-s` option and two arguments: the name of the original file and the new, added filename. The `ls` operation lists both filenames, but only one physical file will exist.

```
$ ln -s original-file-name added-file-name
```

In the next example, the **today** file is given the additional name **weather**. It is just another name for the **today** file.

```
$ ls
today
$ ln -s today weather
$ ls
today weather
```

You can give the same file several names by using the `ln` command on the same file many times. In the next example, the file **today** is given both the names **weather** and **weekend**:

```
$ ln -s today weather
$ ln -s today weekend
$ ls
today weather weekend
```

If you list the full information about a symbolic link and its file, you will find the information displayed is different. In the next example, the user lists the full information for both **lunch** and **/home/george/veglist** using the `ls` command with the `-l` option. The first character in the line specifies the file type. Symbolic links have their own file type, represented by an l. The file type for **lunch** is l, indicating it is a symbolic link, not an ordinary file. The number after the term "group" is the size of the file. Notice the sizes differ. The size of the **lunch** file is only four bytes. This is because **lunch** is only a symbolic link—a file that holds the pathname of another file—and a pathname takes up only a few bytes. It is not a direct hard link to the **veglist** file.

```
$ ls -l lunch /home/george/veglist
lrw-rw-r-- 1 chris group 4 Feb 14 10:30 lunch
-rw-rw-r-- 1 george group 793 Feb 14 10:30 veglist
```

To erase a file, you need to remove only its original name (and any hard links to it). If any symbolic links are left over, they will be unable to access the file. In this case, a symbolic link would hold the pathname of a file that no longer exists.

Hard Links

You can give the same file several names by using the **ln** command on the same file many times. To set up a hard link, you use the **ln** command with no **-s** option and two arguments: the name of the original file and the new, added filename. The **ls** operation lists both filenames, but only one physical file will exist.

```
$ ln original-file-name added-file-name
```

In the next example, the **monday** file is given the additional name **storm**. It is just another name for the **monday** file.

```
$ ls
today
$ ln monday storm
$ ls
monday storm
```

To erase a file that has hard links, you need to remove all its hard links. The name of a file is actually considered a link to that file—hence the command **rm** that removes the link to the file. If you have several links to the file and remove only one of them, the others stay in place and you can reference the file through them. The same is true even if you remove the original link—the original name of the file. Any added links will work just as well. In the next example, the **today** file is removed with the **rm** command. However, a link to that same file exists, called **weather**. The file can then be referenced under the name **weather**.

```
$ ln today weather
$ rm today
$ cat weather
The storm broke today
and the sun came out.
$
```

Part 4: Administration

Fedora System Tools
System Administration
Network Configuration
Printing

12. Fedora System Tools

GNOME System Monitor

Managing Processes

Terminal Window

Scheduling Tasks

System Log

Disk Usage Analyzer

Virus Protection

Hardware Sensors

SELinux Configuration

SELinux Troubleshooting

Additional useful system tools as well as user specific configuration tools can be found in the Applications | System Tools menu and the System | Preferences menu (see Table 12-1).

Fedora System Tools	Applications	System Tools menu	Description
system-config-selinux	SELinux Management	Manages and configures SELinux policy
gpk-update	Update System	Package Updater (see Chapter 4)
gnome-system-monitor	System Monitor	GNOME System Monitor
gnome-system-log	System Log	GNOME system log viewer
gnome-terminal	Terminal	GNOME Terminal Window
baobab	Disk Usage Analyzer	Baobab disk usage analyzer
sealert	SELinux Trouble Shooter	setroubleshoot, SELinux alert browser.
gnome-power-statistics	Power Statistics	Power usage
Schedule	Scheduled Tasks	GNOME Cron schedule manager

Table 12-1: Fedora System Tools, Application | System Tools

The System Tools menu holds tools like the System Monitor for checking on resource usage by processes and storage devices, whereas the Preferences menu holds user specific tools for customizing your desktop and device usage (see Chapter 3). In particular, mouse and keyboard configurations are handled by GNOME or KDE directly (System | Preferences | Hardware). Software management is handled by the PackageKit software manager (System | Administration | Add/Remove Software System | Administration | Update System)

GNOME System Monitor

Fedora provides the GNOME System Monitor for displaying system information and monitoring system processes, accessible from Applications | System Tools | System Monitor. There are four panels, one for system information, one for processes, one for resources, and one for file systems (see Figure 12-1). The System panel shows the amount of memory, available disk space, and the type of CPU on your system.

The Resources panel displays graphs for CPU, Memory and Swap memory, and Network usage. Your File Systems panel lists your file systems, where they are mounted, and their type, as well as the amount of disk space used and how much is free. The Processes panel lists your processes, letting you sort or search for processes. You can use field buttons to sort by name, process ID, user, and memory. The View pop-up menu lets you select all processes, just your own, or active processes. You can easily stop any process by selecting it and then clicking the End Process button. Right-clicking an item displays actions you can take on the process such as stopping or hiding it. The Memory Maps display, selected from the View menu, shows information on virtual memory, inodes, and flags.

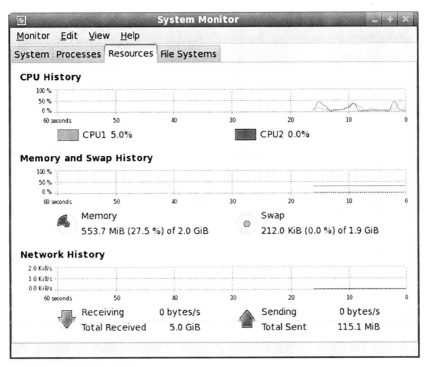

Figure 12-1: GNOME System Monitor

Managing Processes

Should you have to force a process or application to quit, you can use the Gnome System Monitor Processes tab to find, select, and stop the process. You should be sure of the process you want to stop. Ending a critical process could cripple your system. Application processes will bear the name of the application, and you can use those to force an application to quit. Ending processes manually is usually preformed for open ended operations that you are unable to stop normally. In Figure 12-2, the firefox application has been selected. Clicking the End Process button on the lower right will then force the Firefox Web browser to end.

You can also use the kill command in a terminal window to end a process. The **kill** command takes as its argument a process number. Be sure you obtain the correct one. Use the **ps** command to display a process id. Entering in the incorrect process number could also cripple your system. The **ps** command with the **-C** option searches for a particular application name. The **-o pid=** will display only the process id, instead of the process id, time, application name, and tty. Once you have the process id, you can use the kill command with the process id as its argument to end the process.

```
$ ps -C firefox -o pic=
5555
$ kill 5555
```

One way to insure the correct number is to use the **ps** command to return the process number directly as an argument to a **kill** command. In the following example, an open ended process was started to record a program from channel 12 from a digital video broadcast device, using the **getatsc** command.

```
getatsc -dvb 0 12 > my.ts
```

The process is then stopped by first executing the **ps** command to obtain the process id for the **getatsc** process (backquotes), and then using that process id in the **kill** command to end the process. The **-o pid=** option displays only the process id.

```
kill `ps -C getatsc -o pid=`
```

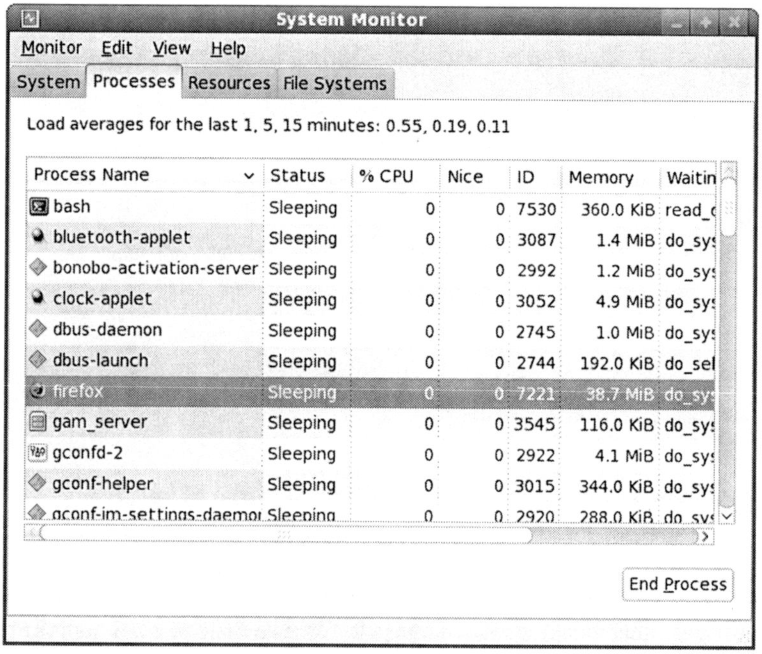

Figure 12-2: GNOME System Monitor, Processes tab

Terminal Window

The Terminal window allows you to enter Linux commands on a command line. It also provides you with a shell interface for using shell commands instead of your desktop (see Chapter 11). The command line is editable, allowing you to use the backspace key to erase characters on the line. Pressing any key will insert the key. You can use the left and right arrow keys to move anywhere on the line, and then press keys to insert characters, or use backspace to delete characters (see Figure 12-3).

The terminal window will remember the previous commands you entered. Use the up and down arrows to have those commands displayed in turn. Press the ENTER key to re-execute the currently displayed command. You can even edit a previous command before running it, allowing you to execute a modified version of a previous command.

The terminal window will display all your previous interactions and commands for that session. Use the scrollbar to see any previous commands you ran and their displayed results.

Figure 12-3: Terminal Window

You open as many terminal windows as you want, each working in its own shell. This way you run several command line operations at once, each in their own terminal window using their own shell. Instead of opening a separate window for each new shell you may want, you can open several shells in the same window, using tabbed panels. Select Open Tab from the File menu to open a new panel, (**Shift-Ctrl-t**). You can use the Tabs menu to move to different tabs, or just click on its panel to select it. Each panel runs a separate shell, letting you enter different commands in each (see Figure 12-4).

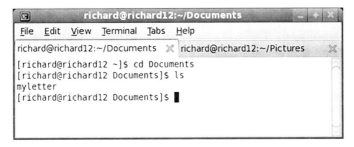

Figure 12-4: Terminal Window with Tabs

The terminal window is also supports GNOME desktop cut/copy and paste operations. You can copy a line from a Web page and then paste it to the terminal window (you may have to use the Copy entry on the Terminal window's Edit menu). The command will appear and then you can press ENTER to execute the command. This is useful for command line operations that may be displayed on an instructional Web page. Instead of typing in a complex command yourself, just copy from the Web page directly, and then paste to the Terminal window. Perform any edits if needed.

Schedule Tasks

Scheduling regular maintenance tasks, such as backups, is managed by the **cron** service on Linux, and implemented by a **cron** daemon. A daemon is a continually running server that constantly checks for certain actions to take. These tasks are listed in the **crontab** file. The **cron** daemon constantly checks the user's **crontab** file to see if it is time to take these actions. Any user can set up a **crontab** file of his or her own. The root user can set up a **crontab** file to take system administrative actions, such as backing up files at a certain time each week or month.

Creating cron entries can be a complicated task, using the crontab command to make changes to crontab files in the **/etc/crontab** directory. Instead you can use several GUI cron scheduler tools to easily set up cron actions. Two of the more useful tools are KCron and GNOME Schedule which create an easy to use interface for creating scheduled commands.

GNOME Schedule

GNOME Schedule is a more recent tool that also creates and easy to use interface for managing scheduled tasks (See Figure 12-5). Once installed you can access it from the Applications | System Tools menu as Scheduled Tasks.

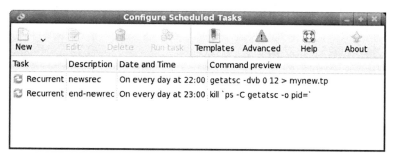

Figure 12-5: GNOME Schedule

Use the New button to schedule a task. You are first asked if you want to create the task as a recurrent item, one time task, or from a template. The Create a New Scheduled Task window then open where you can specify the time and date, and whether to repeat weekly or monthly (see Figure 12-6). You can use the Basic button to set defaults for Hourly, Daily, Weekly, or Monthly entries. Then click Advanced to specify a time.

The template feature lets you set up a new schedule with information for a previous one, using the same or similar commands but different time. Click the Template button to add a new template. This opens a window similar to the Create task window in Figure 12-6. Once you have created the template you can use it to create scheduled tasks. When creating a task, from the initial menu, choose "A task from a predefined template. This opens the Choose template window (see Figure 12-7). Clicking the Use template button opens the Create task window where you can modify your task.

To delete a task, just select the entry in the Scheduled Tasks window and click the Delete button. To run a task immediately, select and click the Run task button.

On the Scheduled Tasks window you can click the Advanced button to see the actual cron entries created by GNOME Schedule.

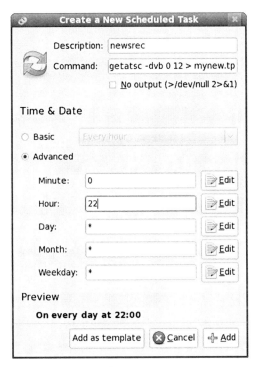

Figure 12-6: GNOME Schedule new task

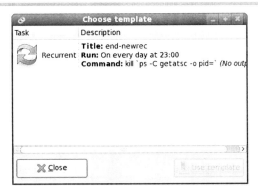

Figure 12-7: GNOME Schedule templates

KCron (KDE4)

KCron which creates and easy to use interface for creating scheduled commands. KCron is a KDE desktop tool and will require installation of supporting KDE libraries (selected automatically for you when you install KCron). To run KCron, login to the KDE desktop. Use the New entry in the Edit menu to schedule a command, specifying the time and date, and whether to repeat weekly or monthly.

System Log

Various system logs for tasks performed on your system are stored in the **/var/log** directory. Here you can find logs for mail, news, and all other system operations, such as Web server logs. The **/var/log/messages** file is a log of all system tasks not covered by other logs (see Figure 12-8). This usually includes startup tasks, such as loading drivers and mounting file systems.

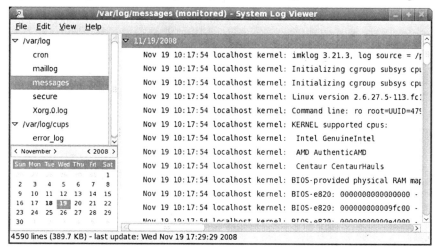

Figure 12-8: GNOME System Log Viewer

If a driver for a card failed to load at startup, you find an error message for it here. Logins are also recorded in this file, showing you who attempted to log in to what account. The **/var/log/maillog** file logs mail message transmissions and news transfers.

To view these logs you can use the GNOME Log Viewer, Applications | System Tools | System Logs. A side panel lists different logs. Selecting one will display the log on the panel to the right.

Disk Usage Analyzer

The disk usage analyzer lets you see how much disk space is used and available on all your mounted hard disk partitions (see Figure 12-9). It will also check all LVM and RAID arrays. Usage is shown in simple graph, letting you see how much overall space is available and where it is. When you san the file system (Scan Filesystem button in toolbar), disk usage for all your directories is analyzed and displayed in the left pane, and on a graph in the right pane. Passing your mouse over a section in the graph will display its directory name and disk usage. In the left hand listing, each files system is first shown with a graph for its usage, as well as its size and number of top-level directories and files. Then the directories are shown, along with their size and contents (files and directories).

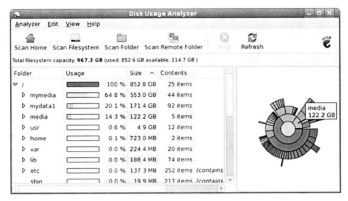

Figure 12-9: Disk Usage Analyzer, Applications | System Tools | Disk Usage Analyzer

Virus Protection

For virus protection you can use the Linux version of ClamAV, **www.clamav.org**. This Virus scanner is included on the Fedora main repository. You will have to download and install it using Synaptic. Choose the clamav, clamav-base, clamav-freshclam, and clamav-data. In addition you may want either ClamTK (clamtk package, GNOME) or Klamav (KDE) front ends. You can access ClamTK from the Applications | System Tools menu as Virus Scanner. With ClamTK, you can scan specific files and directories, as well as your home directory (see Figure 12-10). Searches can be recursive, including subdirectories. You have the option to also check dot configuration files. Infected files are quarantined.

Figure 12-10: The clamtk tool for ClamAV virus protection.

To update your virus definitions, you need to run **clamtk** with administrative access. Open a terminal window and enter the following. You will be prompted for your user password.

```
gksu clamtk
```

You can then go to the Help menu and select Update Signatures to update your definitions.

You can also install the clam-daemon which works with your email application to detect viruses.

Hardware Sensors

Another concern with many users is the temperatures and usage of computer components. The GNOME hardware monitor display detected temperatures for your CPU, system, hard drives, and, if available, for your graphics card, as well as any other sensors your computer may support, like fan speeds. You can also detect the extent your CPU is being used. You install different software packages to enable certain sensors (see Table 12-2).

Sensor application	Description
`lm-sensors`	Detects and accesses computer (motherboard) sensors like CPU and fan speed. Run **sensors-detect** once to configure.
`hddtemp`	Detects hard drive temperatures
`powernowd`	Detects CPU usage
`gnome-applet-sensors`	GNOME applet to display sensor information for all sensors, **gnome-applet-sensors**. Also called **Hardware Sensors Monitor**.
`ksenors`	KDE sensor applet

Table 12-2: Sensor packages and applications

For CPU, system, fan speeds, and any other motherboard supported sensors, you use the **lm-sensors** service. Download and install the **lm-sensors** package. First you have to configure your sensor detection. In a terminal window login as the root user (**su root**) and enter following and answer yes to the prompts:

```
sensors-detect
```

This service will detect hardware sensors on your computer. It will run as the Hardware Monitor service in System | Administration | Services.

For hard drive temperature detection you install **hddtemp**. During the installation, you will be prompted to configure the hddtemp service to start automatically. Upon installing the hddtemp package, you need to configure the **/etc/sysconfig/hddtemp** file to detect your hard drives. Add the device name of the drives, using **[abcd]** to match on the last letter, as in **/dev/sd[abcd]** for the sda, sdb, sdc, and sdd hard drives. In the following example, the device names, **/dev/sd[adcd]**, were inserted to the HDDTEMP_OPTIONS entry after **127.0.0.1**, the localhost IP address used to reference your system.

```
HDDTEMP_OPTIONS="-l 127.0.0.1 /dev/sd[abcd]"
```

You will also need to enable the **hddtemp** daemon using System | Administration | Services. Upon restart, your hard drive temperature sensor should be available in the GNOME sensors applet (Hardware Sensors Monitor) on its Preferences Sensors tab (see Figure 12-11).

You can then download and install the **sensors-applet** package, the GNOME applet for displaying sensor information (use KSensors for KDE desktop). Once the applet is installed, you can add it to the panel as the **Hardware Sensors Monitor**. You can right-click the applet icon and open its preferences window, where you can set the temperature scale and display information (see

Figure 12-12). You can then use the GNOME sensors applet to display any sensor information (Sensors tab). They will be group by the service providing the sensor access, usually lmsensors, hddtemp, and a graphics driver if supported, like Nvidia. In Figure 12-9, the CPU, System, CPU fan, graphics card, and two hard drives are selected for display.

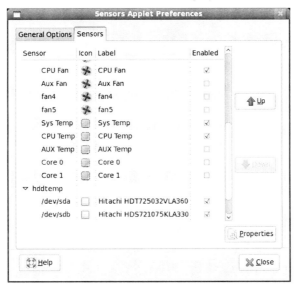

Figure 12-11: GNOME Sensor configuration

The hardware sensor information will then be displayed on the panel. You can configure the sensors applet to use either centigrade or Fahrenheit temperatures. Fan speeds can also be displayed, if your computer detects them. Figure 12-6 shows CPU fan speed, the System temperature, the CPU temperature, and two hard drive temperatures.

1520 RPM 39 °C 36 °C 34 °C 38 °C

Figure 12-12: Hardware sensor display on GNOME panel

Another useful applet is the CPU Frequency Scaling Monitor, which will display CPU usage (See Figure 12-13). This applet used the **powernowd** service to detect how much of the CPU is being used. Most current CPUs support frequency scaling, which will lower the CPU frequency when it has few tasks to perform. Intel CPUs will scale down to 60 percent and AMD by 50 percent.

60% 1.20 GHz

Figure 12-13: CPU Frequency Scaling Monitor

SELinux: Configuration with system-config-selinux

With system-config-selinux you can manage and configure your SELinux policies, though you cannot create new policies. You can access system-config-selinux from the System | Administration menu by selecting the SELinux Management entry. The system-config-selinux window will list several panes with a sidebar menu for Status, Boolean, File Labeling, User Mapping, SELinux User, Translation, Network Port, and Policy Module (see Figure 12-14). system-config-selinux will invoke the SELinux management tools like sestatus and semanage with appropriate options to make configuration changes.

User Mapping shows the mapping of user login names to SELinux users. Initially there will be two mappings: the root user and the default user.

The Boolean pane lists various options for targeted services like Web and FTP servers, NFS, and Samba. With these you can further modify how each service is controlled. There are expandable menus for different services like FTP, Apache Web server, and Samba. For example, the FTP entry lets you choose whether to allow access to home directories or to NFS transfers..

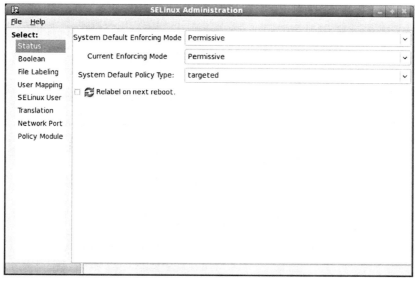

Figure 12-14: The system-config-selinux, Applications | System Tools | SELinux Management

The File Labeling pane will list your system directories and files, showing their security contexts and types. You can edit a file's properties by selecting the entry and then clicking Properties. This displays a dialog with the File Name, Type, SELinux Type, and MLS Level. You can change the SELinux type or the MLS level. For a permissive policy, the MLS level will be s0, allowing access to anyone. You can also add or delete entries.

The SELinux Users pane shows the different kinds of SELinux users. Initially there will be several user types including root, system_u, and user_u (see Figure 12-15). The root user is the root user, which has full and total administrative access to the entire system. The system_u user allows users to take on administrative access where needed. The user_u user is used for normal users. Each entry lists its SELinux User, SELinux prefix, MLS level, MLS range, and SELinux roles. MLS level is the access level (s0 on a permissive policy), and MLS range is the range of access from SystemLow to SystemHigh. A given user has certain roles available. The root user has the system_r, sysadm_r, and staff_r roles, allowing it system access, administration capability, and staff user access. The user_u users also have a system_r role, allowing the user to perform system administration if that user has the root user password.

Figure 12-15: system-config-selinux SELinux Boolean pane

The Translation pane lets you set MLS symbols. Initially you will have symbols for SystemHigh and the SystemLow–SystemHigh range. You change the MLS levels for a mapping, changing security level access across the system

The Network Port pane lists the network protocol, the SELinux type, and the MLS security level for ports on your system. Select an entry and click Properties to change the SELinux type or the MLS level for the port. The Group View button will display the SELinux type along with a list of the ports they apply to. This view does not display the MLS level, as these apply to ports individually.

The Policy modules pane lists the different SELinux policy modules. Here you will see modules for different applications like Thunderbird and Evolution, as well as device service like USB and HAL. Listed also are desktops like GNOME. The pane allows you to add or remove a module. You can also enable or additional audit rules for a module for logging.

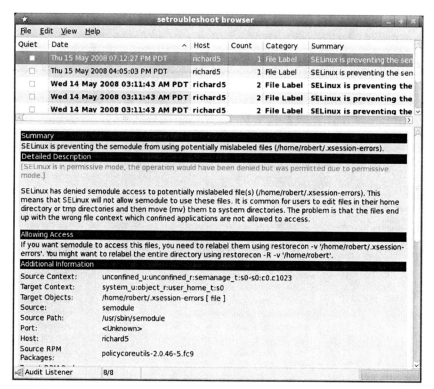

Figure 12-16: SELinux troubleshooter, Applications | System Tools | Trouble Shooter

SELinux Troubleshooting

Fedora includes the SELinux troubleshooter which notifies problems that SELinux detects. Whenever SELinux denies access to a file or application, the kernel issue an AVC notice. These are analyzed by SELinux troubleshooter to detect problems that users may have to deal with. When a problem is detected, the SELinux troubleshooter notification will be displayed in the desktop notification area along with the troubleshooter icon. Clicking on the icon or notice will open the SELinux troubleshooter window. You can also access it at any time from System | Administration | SELinux troubleshooter. You can find out more information about SELinux troubleshooter at **http://fedoraproject.org/wiki/SELinux/Troubleshooting**.

The SELinux troubleshooter window will display a list of notices, along with their date, the number of times it has occurred, its category, and brief explanation. The Filter entry lets you turn off future notification of this event. Selecting and entry will display detailed information about the notice in four sections: Summary, Detailed Description, Allowing Access, and Additional Information (see Figure 12-16)

In many cases the problem may be simple to fix, as shown in the Allowing Access section. Often, the security context of a file has to be renamed to allow access. You use the **chcon** command to change a file's security context. The SELinux troubleshooter will take no action of its own.

Instead it recommends possible actions. In this example, the user just issues the following **chcon** command.

```
chcon -R -t samba_share_t
```

fedora

13. System Administration

To make effective use of your Fedora Linux system, you will have to know how to configure certain features and services. Administrative operations such as adding users and installing software can now be performed with user-friendly system tools. This chapter discusses basic system administration operations that you need to get your system up and running, as well as to perform basic maintenance such as adding new users or setting up printers. You can make changes or additions easily using the administrative tools described in this chapter.

Fedora Administration Menus	Description
System | Administration	Fedora menu for accessing administrative tools
System | Preferences | Hardware	Fedora menu for desktop device configuration like mouse or screen resolution
Applications | System Tools	Fedora menu for accessing specialized administrative applications and configuration tools, see Chapter 12.

Fedora Administration Tools	System | Administration Menu	Description
`system-config-authentication`	Authentication	Sets authentication settings
`system-config-boot`	Bootloader	Sets operating system to boot default
`system-config-date`	Date & Time	Changes system time / date
`system-config-display`	Display	Manual Fedora display configuration tool (detection is normally automatic)
`system-config-firewall`	Firewall	Configures your network firewall
`system-config-keyboard`	Keyboard	Select basic the keyboard type
`system-config-language`	Languages	Selects a language to use
`system-config-lvm`	Logical Volume Management	Configures LVM file system volumes
`system-config-network`	Network	Configures your network interfaces
`system-config-printer`	Printing	Printer configuration tool
`system-config-rootpassword`	Root Password	Changes the root user password
`system-config-samba`	Samba	Configures Samba
`system-config-nfs`	Server Settings | nfs	Configures your network interfaces
`system-config-services`	Services	Manages services such as starting and stopping servers.
`system-config-users`	Users & Groups	User and Group configuration tool

Table 13-1: Administration Tools on System | Administration

Configuration operations can be performed from a GUI interface such as GNOME or KDE, or they can be performed using a simple shell command line at which you type configuration commands. You can also manually access system configuration files, editing them and making entries yourself. For example, some file system mount configuration entries are kept in the **/etc/fstab.conf** file. You can edit this file and type in the mount operations for file systems.

Most administration tools can be found in three menus on the Fedora desktop, as listed here. The primary administrative tools described in this chapter can be found in the System | Administration menu.

TIP: If you have difficulties with your system configuration, check the **www.fedorasolved.org** site for possible solutions. The site offers helpful solutions ranging from video and network problems to games, browsers, and multimedia solutions,

Note: Configuration tools are accessible only to the root user. Though these tools are accessible from any user account, you will be first prompted for the root user password before you can use them. Alternatively, you could just log in as the root user, using **root** as the username and providing the root password you specified during installation.

Fedora Administrative Tools

On Fedora, administration is handled by a set of separate specialized administrative tools developed and supported by Fedora, such as those for user management and printer configuration (see Table 13-1). The Fedora administration tools are accessible from the System | Administration menu. Here you will find tools to set the time and date, manage users, configure printers, and setup network connections. Users & Groups lets you create and modify users and groups. Printing lets you install and reconfigure printers. All tools provide very intuitive graphical user interfaces that are easy to use. In the Administration menu, tools are identified by simple descriptive terms, whereas their actual names normally begin with the term *system-config*. For example, the printer configuration tool is listed as **Printing**, but its actual name is **system-config-printer**. You can separately invoke any tool by entering its name in a terminal window.

Note: Many configuration tasks can also be handled on a command line, invoking programs directly. To use the command line, open a terminal window by selecting the Terminal entry in the Applications | System Tools menu. This opens a terminal window with a command line prompt. Commands like **rpm** and **yum** will require a terminal window.

Simple Administrative Tasks

Certain simple administrative tasks can be performed using some of the system-config tools. Most of these have obvious entries in the Administration menu. Others like Login Window use their own configuration tools.

system-config-rootpassword (Root Password)   Use this tool to change your root password, something you may want to do regularly.

system-config-date (Date & Time)   Use this to set the date and time, as well as select a time server for automatic time settings.

system-config-boot (Bootloader)   Use this tool if you have set up a dual-boot system, with several operating systems on the same hard disks. This will list your operating systems and let you choose the default. Useful for selecting either Window or Linux on the same computer, or, say, a stable or test kernel. If you install a new kernel, it will become the default. Use system-config-boot to set the default back to the one you want.

Mouse configuration and display of logs are now handled by desktop tools, on GNOME as System | Preferences | Hardware | Mouse. Check GNOME preferences for mouse configuration, and Applications | System Tools | System Log (**gnome-system-log**) to display logs.

Login window (GDM) configuration is not currently supported, but may be supported in later updates (possibly as **gdmsetup**).

Superuser Control: the Root User

To perform system administration operations, you will have to supply the root user password, making you the superuser. Because a superuser has the power to change almost anything on the system, such a password is usually a carefully guarded secret, changed very frequently, and given only to those whose job is to manage the system. With the correct password, you can log in to the system as a system administrator and configure the system in different ways. You can also access administrative tools for specific tasks from any account, temporarily giving you superuser access for just that administrative operation. As a superuser, you can perform tasks like starting up and shutting down the system, as well as changing to a different operating mode, such as a single-user mode. You can also add or remove users, add or remove whole file systems, back up and restore files, and even designate the system's name and address.

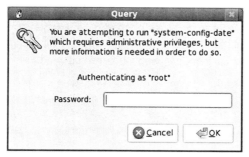

Figure 13-1: Administrative access

Administrative access from normal user accounts

Normally to access an administrative tool, you simply login to a normal account, and then choose the tool you want from the System | Administration menu. A dialog will then be displayed that will prompt you to enter the root user password. Once you do so, the administrative tool you choose will start up, allowing its functions to have full root user access. For example, to create a new user, you can login to any normal account, then choose Users & Groups from the System | Administration menu. A dialog window will appear prompting you to enter in the root user password (see Figure 31-1). Once you do, the Users & Groups tool starts up and you can create a new user on the system, as well as perform any other tasks supported by the Users & Groups tool.

The same kind of permission is required for updates. Logged into any normal account, you will be notified of any new updates. When you try the Update System, you will be first prompted by the same dialog for a root user password. For each different administrative tool you start up, you will have to separately enter the root user password.

Logging into the root user account directly: su

There are situations where you may want to login directly to the root user account. This provides total control over the system and is considered to be risky. But if you are performing several administrative tasks at once or if you need to modify configuration files directly, root user account access may work best. The root user is a special account reserved for system management operations with unrestricted access to all components of your Linux operating system. You can log in as the root user from either from a terminal window or the command line login prompt. From the command line and su access, you will only be able to use command line command.

If you log in from the command line interface, you can run corresponding administrative commands like `rpm` to install packages or `useradd` to add a new user. From your GUI desktop, you can also run command line administrative tools using a terminal window. The command line interface for the root user uses a special prompt, the sharp sign, #. In the next example, the user logs in to the system as the root user and receives the # prompt.

```
login: root
password:
#
```

su

When logged in as a normal user, you can then log in as a **root** user using a terminal window and the **su** command. This is helpful if you just need to quickly run a command as a **root** user. You can use the **su** command with the root user name, or just the **su** command alone (the root user name will be assumed). You will be prompted to enter the **root** user password.

```
su root
password:
```

In the following example, the user logs in as the root user the runs the **/etc/init.d/nmb** script which requires root user access.

```
su
password:
/etc/init.d/nmb start
```

To exit from a **su** login operation, when you are finished on that account, just enter **exit**.

```
exit
```

Note: The **su** command can actually be used to login to any user, provided you have that user's password.

root password

Because a superuser has the power to change almost anything on the system, the **root** user password is usually a carefully guarded secret, changed very frequently, and given only to those whose job it is to manage the system. With the correct password, you can log in to the system as a system administrator and configure the system in different ways. You can also add or remove users, add or remove whole file systems, back up and restore files, and even designate the system's name and address.

To change the root user password, you can use the System | Administration | Root Password tool on the GNOME desktop. You can also use the **passwd** command in a Terminal window, once you have logged in as the **root** user. Both will check your password to see if you've selected one that can be easily cracked.

Controlled Administrative Access: sudo

With the sudo tool you can allow ordinary users to have limited root user–level administrative access for any specified task. This allows other users to perform specific superuser operations without having full root level control. You can find more about sudo at **www.sudo.ws**. Normal users are not configured for sudo access by default, though the root user, if specified, is. For normal user access, you will have to first specify that a user can have sudo access. This requires editing the **/etc/sudoers** file. Once you have sudo access, you can use GNOME tools as the root user, giving you direct root user access with GNOME capabilities for editing and fiel browsing.

sudo configuration

Access is controlled by the **/etc/sudoers** file. This file lists users and the commands they can run, along with the password for access. If the NOPASSWD option is set, then users will not need a password. ALL, depending on the context, can refer to all hosts on your network, all root-level commands, or all users. To make changes or add entries, you have to edit the file with the special sudo editing command **visudo**. This invokes the Vi editor to edit the **/etc/sudoers** file.Unlike a standard editor, **visudo** will lock the **/etc/sodoers** file and check the syntax of your entries. You are not allowed to save changes unless the syntax is correct. Use Vi editing commands to make changes (see Chapter 5). If you want to use a different editor, you can assign it to the EDITOR shell variable. Login first as the root user, using the **su** command, then enter **visudo**.

```
visudo
```

A **sudoers** entry has the following syntax. The host is a host on your network. You can specify all hosts with the ALL term. The command can be a list of commands, some or all qualified by options such as whether a password is required. To specify all commands, you can also use the ALL term.

```
user    host=command
```

The following gives the user **george** full root-level access to all commands on all hosts:

```
george  ALL = ALL
```

Use VI commands to edit the file.You can move to the root user entry, and then press the **o** command to open a new line. Type in the new user entry and then press the **ESC** key. Press **Shift-ZZ** when finished editting.

In addition, you can let a user run as another user on a given host. Such alternate users are placed within parentheses before the commands. For example, if you want to give **george** access to the **beach** host as the user **mydns**, you use the following:

```
george beach = (mydns) ALL
```

By default sudo will deny access to all users, including the root. For this reason, the default **/etc/sudoers** file sets full access for the root user to all commands. The ALL=(ALL) ALL entry allows access by the root to all hosts as all users to all commands.

```
root    ALL=(ALL)    ALL
```

To specify a group name, you prefix the group with a **%** sign, as in **%mygroup**. This way, you can give the same access to a group of users. The **/etc/sudoers** file contains samples for a **%wheel** group.

To give **robert** access on all hosts to the **date** command, you would use

```
robert ALL=/usr/bin/system-config-date
```

If a user wants to see what commands he or she can run, that user would use the **sudo** command with the **-l** option.

```
sudo -l
```

Using sudo and sudoedit

Once the user is configured, the user can use sudo to run an administrative command. The user precedes the command with the **sudo** command. The user is then issued a time-sensitive ticket to allow access.

```
sudo date
```

The **sudo** command becomes very useful when you need to perform an otherwise ordinary task with root user access. This allows you to avoid having to login as the root user, yet still have extensive root user access over the system. One very common use is to use the Gedit graphical text editor to edit system configuration files. There is no specific administrative tool to do this, so ordinarily would have to login as the root user to perform this task. With the **sudo** command, though, you can edit any system configuration file from a normal account. The following example would let you edit the **/etc/fstab** file, used for automatic file system mounting. Open a terminal window and enter the command. You will be prompted for the user password, and then Gedit will start up as a functional GUI editor.

```
sudo gedit /etc/fstab
```

You could even run the file manager as a sudo operation, allowing the file manager full administrative access from any normal account. The file manager will open up to the **root** user account.

```
sudo nautilus
```

If you are familiar with the Vi editor, you can use the **sudoedit** command to edit any text file.

```
sudoedit /etc/fstab
```

PolicyKit

PolicyKit will control access to certain applications and devices. There is no direct access to PolicyKit configuration. You have to open a terminal window and enter to **polkit-gnome-authorization** command (see Figure 13-2). This will display the PolicyKit window with entries for different components you can control. Whenever you try to change an authorization, you will be prompted to enter the root user password (access can be remembered). The left pane holds and expandable tree with currently supported authorizations. The right pane shows those authorizations and allows you to change them. You can either change Implicit Authorizations (click the Edit button), or grant access to particular users (the Grant button).

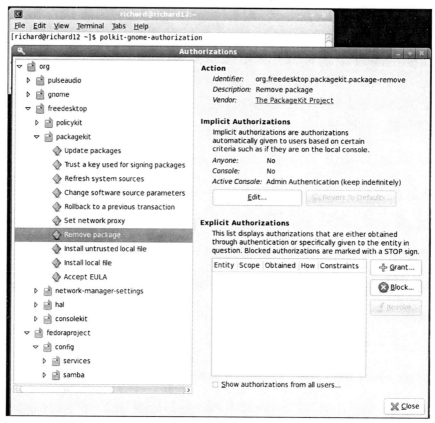

Figure 13-2: PolicyKit

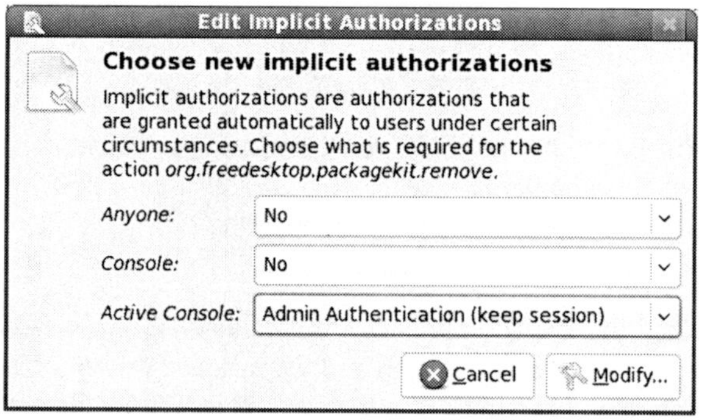

Figure 13-3: PolicyKit Implicit Authorizations

Before authorization changes can be made, you will be asked to enter the root password (see Figure 13-4).

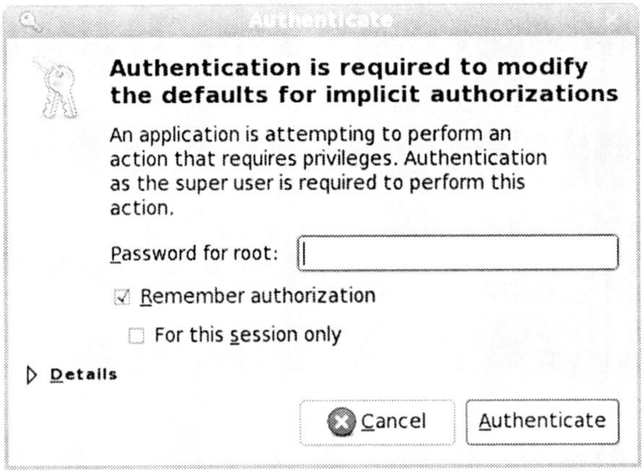

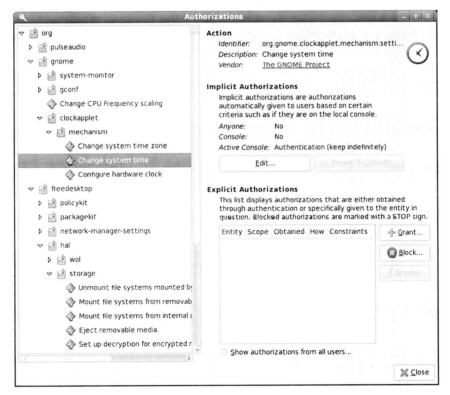

Figure 13-4: PolicyKit authentication for changes

Figure 13-5: PolicyKit supported components

The implicit authorization Edit button will open a window where you can set the implicit authorization level. For most components this is Admin Authentication (keep indefinitely). This only requires a root password authentication the first time a user tries to use the component. This is the case for the PackageKit Add/Remove software application. Another option, as shown in Figure 13-3 is to keep the authorization only for that user session. All the authorizations are listed in the pop-up menu on the Edit Implicit Authorizations window. You can also set authorization for any console for any user (whether at the active console of not). The Grant operation for Explicit Authorizations provides authorizations for particular users.

PolicyKit currently supports access to components maintained by PulseAudio, GNOME, Freedekstop.org, and the Fedora Project. GNOME provides support for the System Monitor, the Clock, and GNOME configuration (gconf). Freedesktop provides support for policykit, PackageKit, Network Manager, HAL (hardware storage, device access, and power management), and consolekit (system stop and restart). The Fedora Project provides PolicyKit support for access to service management (system-config-services) and Samba configuration. PulseAudio, PackageKit, HAL hardware storage and device access, power management, and the GNOME system monitor and clock applet (see Figure 13-5).

Date and Time

You can set the system time and date using the GNOME international date applet as discussed in Chapter 3, the shell `date` command, or the Fedora administrative tool system-config-date. You probably set the time and date when you first installed your system. You should not need to do so again. If you entered the time incorrectly or moved to a different time zone, though, you could use this utility to change your time.

Using the system-config-date Utility

The preferred way to set the system time and date is to use the Fedora Date and Time Properties utility (system-config-date). Select the System | Administration | Date & Time entry. There are three panels, one for the date and time, one for the Network Time Protocol, and one for the time zone (see Figure 13-6). Use the calendar to select the year, month, and date. Then use the Time box to set the hour, minute, and second. The Time Zone panel shows a map with locations. Select the one nearest you to set your time zone.

The Network Time Protocol (NTP) allows a remote server to set the date and time, instead of using local settings. NTP allows for the most accurate synchronization of your system's clock. It is often used to manage the time and date for networked systems, freeing the administrator from having to synchronize clocks manually. You can download current documentation and NTP software from the **www.ntp.org** site.

On the Network Time Protocol panel you can choose to enable NTP and select the server to use. NTP servers operate through pools that will randomly select an available server to increase efficiency. A set of pools designated for use by Fedora are already installed for you, beginning with **0.fedora.pool.ntp.org**. If access with one pool is slow, you change to another. The **http://pool.ntp.org** pool servers support worldwide access. Pools for specific geographical locations can be found at the NTP Public Services Project site (Time Servers link), **http://ntp.isc.org**. A closer server could be faster.

Using the date Command

You can also use the **date** command on your root user command line to set the date and time for the system. As an argument to **date**, you list (with no delimiters) the month, day, time, and year. In the next example, the date is set to 2:59 P.M., April 6, 2008 (04 for April, 06 for the day, 1459 for the time, and 08 for the year 2008):

```
# date 0406145908
Sun Mar 6 02:59:27 PST 2008
```

Figure 13-6: Date & Time: system-config-date

Users and Groups

Currently, the easiest and most effective way to add new users on Fedora is to use system-config-users, also known as the Fedora User Manager. You can access it from the GNOME Desktop menu, System | Administration menu | Users and Groups entry. The system-config-users window will display panels for listing both users and groups (see Figure 13-7). A button bar will list various tasks you can perform, including creating new users or groups, editing current ones (Edit), or deleting a selected user or group.

New Users

To create a new user, click Add User. This opens a window with entries for the username, password, and login shell; along with options to create a home directory and a new group for that user (see Figure 13-8).

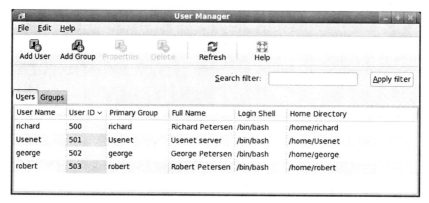

Figure 13-7: Users and Groups: system-config-users

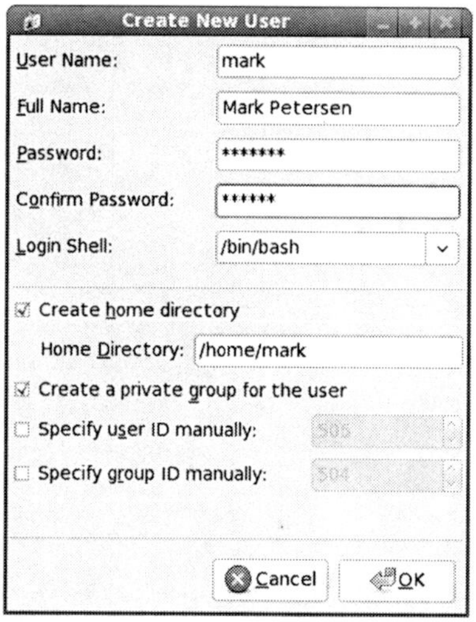

Figure 13-8: Users and Groups: Create New User

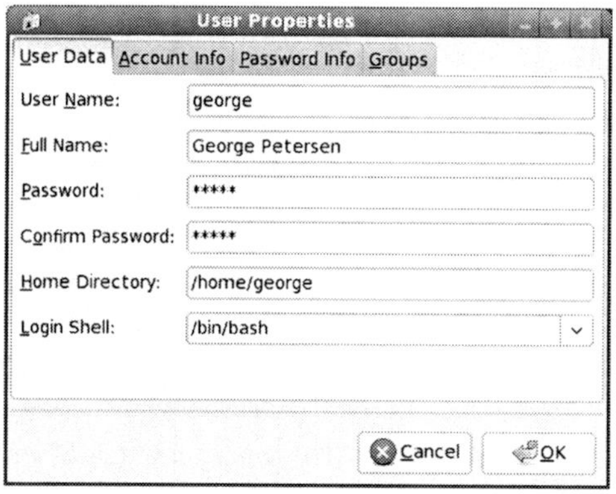

Figure 13-9: User Properties window: User Data

Once you have created a user, you can edit its properties to add or change features. Select the user's entry and click Properties. This displays a window with tabbed panels for User Data, Account Info, Password Info, and Groups (see Figure 13-9).

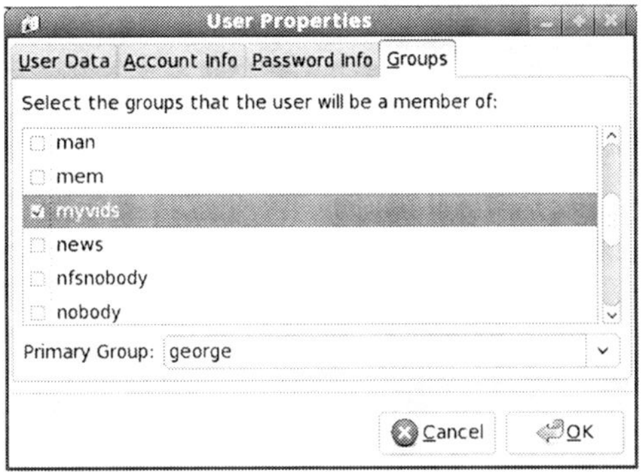

Figure 13-10: User Properties: Add groups to a user

On the Groups panel, you can select the groups that the user belongs to, adding or removing group memberships (see Figure 13-10). The Accounts Info panel lets you set an expiration date for the user, as well as lock the local password. Password Info can enable password expiration, forcing users to change their passwords at certain intervals.

Alternatively, you can use the `useradd` command in a terminal window or command line to add user accounts and the `userdel` command to remove them. The following example adds the user **dylan** to the system:

```
$ useradd dylan
```

Groups

To add a group, just click the Add Group button. This opens a small window where you can enter the group name. The new group will be listed in the Groups listing (see Figure 13-11).

Figure 13-11: Users and Groups: Groups panel

To add users as members of the group, select the group's entry and click the Properties button. This opens a window with tabbed panels for Group Data and Group Users. The Group Users panel lists all current users with check boxes (see Figure 13-12). Click the check boxes for the users you want to be members of this group.

If you want to remove a user as member, click the check box to remove its check. Click OK to effect your changes. If you want to remove a group, just select its entry in the Groups panel and then click the Delete button.

You can also add groups to a user by selecting the user in the Users panel, and opening their Properties window. Then select the Groups panel (see Figure 13-12). Select the groups you wan that user to belong to.

Figure 13-12: Group Properties: Group Users panel

Passwords

One common operation performed from the command line is to change a password. The easiest way to change your password on the GNOME desktop is to use the About Me utility (System | Preferences | Personal | About Me). Click on the Change Password button. A dialog opens up in which you enter your current password, and then the new password.

Alternatively you can use the `passwd` command. If you are using GNOME or KDE you first have to open a terminal window (Applications | System Tools | Terminal). Then, at the shell prompt, enter the `passwd` command. The command prompts you for your current password. After entering your current password and pressing ENTER, you are then prompted for your new password. After entering the new password, you are asked to reenter it. This is to make sure you actually entered the password you intended to enter.

```
$ passwd
Old password:
New password:
Retype new password:
$
```

Tip: You can use the system-config-rootpassword tool (Root Password on System | Administration) to change the password for the root user.

Display Configuration

The GUI interface for your desktop display is implemented by the X Window System. The version used on Fedora is X.org (**x.org**). X.org provides its own drivers for various graphics cards and monitors. You can find out more about X.org at **www.x.org**.

X.org will automatically detect most hardware. The **/etc/X11/Xorg**.conf file will usually hold only keyboard and graphics card information. All other information such as monitors will be automatically determined. Should you want to change the screen resolution, use the Screen Resolution tool accessible from System | Preferences | Hardware | Screen Resolution. You can configure your display settings using the system-config-display tool to change screen resolution settings, as well as select monitor or video card drivers.

Vendor drivers

As an alternative, you could download and install the drivers and video configuration tools supplied by graphics card vendors like ATI or Nvidia. These are provided by RPMFusion **nonfree** repository (**http://rpmfusion.org**). Due to licensing issues they are not part of the Fedora repository. Once installed you can use their own configurations tools to configure your display (Applications | System Tools menu). The vendor drivers often provide many more options such as 3d acceleration, than the X.org drivers, though the X.org drivers tend to be more stable.

Because the vendor drivers are designed to work across all distributions, they may conflict with the Fedora X Window System configuration. It is recommended you use the RPM Fusion packages for the ATI (AMD) or Nvidia drivers. These are the same vendor drivers, but with slight configuration modification to ensure Fedora compatibility.

RPM Fusion also provides the Livna Display Configuration tool for enabling AIGLX and XGL. AIGLX is Accelerated indirect GLX which is required for the compiz and beryl OpenGL window managers. Unlike XGL, AIGLX is fully open source and integrated into the X.org drivers.

xorg.conf

All configuration tools will generate an X Window System configuration file called **/etc/X11/xorg.conf**. This is the file the X Window System uses to start up. Fedora uses the X.org drivers for the X Window System. You can find out more about X.org at **www.x.org**. Whenever you change your settings, your current configuration is saved to **/etc/X11/xorg.backup.conf**. Should need to restore your old settings manually, you can just replace your current **xorg.conf** with the backup file.

You can also manually backup your **xorg.conf** file. In a terminal window you could enter something like the following. Backups have to be made as the root user.

```
cp /etc/X11/xorg.conf  /etc/X11/xorg.mybackup
```

This way, should the new configuration fail, you can restore the original by copying over the current **xorg.conf** file with the saved version.

```
cp /etc/X11/xorg.mybackup  /etc/X11/xorg.conf
```

If your X Windows system fails to start at all, you can login to the command line interface version (runlevel) by editing your boot loader and placing a **3** at the end of the kernel line. Use **e** key to edit a line, and **b** to boot when finished.

system-config-display: manual X configuration

If you want to manually change your display settings for the Xorg drivers, or if you are having trouble with your X Window System configuration, you can use the older system-config-display to change your configuration.

Before using system-config-display, be sure to backup your original **xorg.conf** file first. The system-config-display tool will overwrite your current **xorf.conf** file. In a terminal window you could enter something like the following. Backups have to be made as the root user.

You can run system-config-display by selecting Display on the System | Administration menu. The system-config-display tool opens a Display Settings window with three panels: Settings, Hardware, and Dual Head. The Settings panel shows pop-up menus for selecting your resolution and color depth. Your current resolution and color depth will already be selected.

Figure 13-13: Manual Display Settings

To change your monitor or video card settings, click the Hardware tab (see Figure 13-13). This displays a panel with entries for Monitor and Video Card. Each will have a Configure button. Clicking the Video Card Configure button displays a list of supported video cards. Initially only Generic CRT and LCD entries will show. Click the Show All Available Monitors check box to display a complete listing with expandable vendor entries (see Figure 13-14). A Reset default button will return to your default entries. The Video card configuration should not normally be used, though it can be useful for switching between different drivers for the same card, for instance, the X.org nv NVIDIA driver and the NVIDIA-supplied nvidia driver.

For video cards that support dual-head connections, you can use the Dual Head panel to configure your second monitor. First you enable dual head, and then you can configure the monitor connected to the second connection. For the Desktop Layout, you can have individual desktops or a spanning desktop over both monitors.

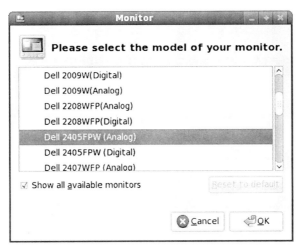

Figure 13-14: Screen Resolution

Bluetooth

Fedora Linux now provides Bluetooth support for both serial connections and BlueZ protocol–supported devices. Bluetooth is a wireless connection method for locally connected devices such as keyboards, mice, printers, and even PDAs and Bluetooth-capable cell phones. You can think of it as a small local network dedicated to your peripheral devices, eliminating the needs for wires. Bluetooth devices can be directly connected through your serial ports or through specialized Bluetooth cards connected to USB ports or inserted in a PCI slot. BlueZ is the official Linux Bluetooth protocol and is integrated into the Linux kernel. The BlueZ protocol was developed originally by Qualcomm and is now an open source project, located at **bluez.sourceforge.net**. It is included with Fedora in the bluez-utils and bluez-libs packages, among others. Check the BlueZ site for a complete list of supported hardware, including adapters, PCMCIA cards, and serial connectors.

Both GNOME and KDE provide Bluetooth configuration and management tools. GNOME provides the GNOME Bluetooth subsystem, which features a device manager, a plug-in for Nautilus to let the GNOME file browser access Bluetooth devices, and a file server. GNOME Bluetooth subsystem provides a GNOME interface for administering your Bluetooth devices, available at System | Preferences | Hardware | Bluetooth. For detected Bluetooth adapters the Adapter tab will list Visibility settings, a friendly name, and a list of Known devices for this adapter. Click on Setup new deivce to start the Blutetooth Device Wizerd to configure a new device. There are also buttons to Disconnect and Trust devices.

You can enable Bluetooth file sharing on the Personal File Sharing preferences (System | Preferences | Internet and Network | File Sharing Preferences). GVFS now supports Bluetooth devices. This means that Fedora can view files and folders on a Bluetooth device using the Nautilus file manager. To browse Bluetooth devices, right-click on the Bluetooth icon on the desktop panel.

For KDE, the KDE Bluetooth Utilities provides similar tools for accessing Bluetooth devices. To connect mobile phones to a system using Bluetooth, you can use the GNOME Phone Manager or KDE's K68 tool.

Managing Services

You can select certain services to run and the runlevel at which to run them. Most services are servers like a Web server or proxy server. Other services provide security, such as SSH or Kerberos. You can decide which services to use with the **chkconfig**, **service**, or system-config-services tools.

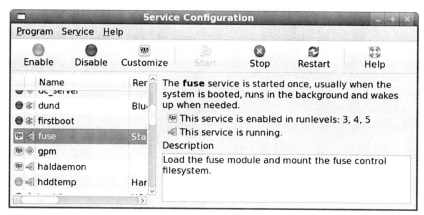

Figure 13-15: Services: system-config-services

system-config-services

The system-config-services tool provides an interface displaying a simple list of services from which you can select the ones you want to start up (System | Administration | Services) and have started automatically. On the system-config-services tool, the side pane displays a listing of installed daemons and servers (see Figure 13-15). A status ions indicate whether a service is enabled or not (green or red), and if they it is running. The right pane will display the current status of a selected service and its description.

Several services are already selected by default, like **network** which runs your network connections and **haldaemon** which detects your hardware. Others like Wine which runs the Windows emulator, and **smb** which runs Samba Windows network support, are optional. You can use system-config-services to run them.

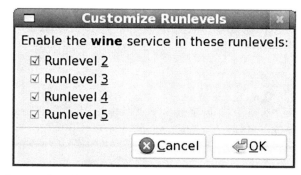

Figure 13-16: Service runlevel customization

Before a service can be run, it must be enabled. If disabled, a service's status icon will be red. To enable a service, select its entry and click the Enable button on the Toolbar. You will see the status icon turn green. You can then click the Start button to start the service manually.

To have a service start automatically, it has to be configured to run at standard runlevels, at least runlevel 5 and 3. Most services are configured to run at runlevels 2, 3, 4, and 5, when you enable them. Some are not. You can customize service to run at different runlevels. Select the service's entry and then click the Customize button. This opens a window listing all the runlevels with check boxes for each (see Figure 13-16). Click the runlevels you want the service to start at.

chkconfig

To configure a service to start up automatically, you can also use the `chkconfig` tool, which is run on a command line. The `chkconfig` command uses the `on` and `off` options to select and deselect services for startup.

```
chkconfig httpd on
```

Manual service control

To start and stop services manually, you can use either system-config-services or the service's script in the **/etc/init.d** directory with the **service** command. Use the service's script with the `stop` argument to stop it, the `start` argument to start it, and the `restart` argument to restart it. The scripts are run from a Terminal window. You will have to first login as the **root** user, using the **su** command. You can use the **service** command with the service script name and the argument. The following will restart the nmb Samba service.

```
service nmb start
```

Instead of the **service** command, you can reference the service script in the **/etc/init.d** directory directly.

```
/etc/init.d/nmb start
```

If, for some reason, system-config-services is not able to manually start or restart a service, you may have to use this method.

File System Access

Various file systems can be accessed on Fedora easily. Any additional internal hard drive partitions on your system, both Linux and Windows NTFS, will be automatically detected and can be automatically mounted, providing immediate and direct access from your desktop. In addition you can access remote Windows shared folders and make your own shared folders accessible.

Access Linux File Systems on Internal Drives

Other Linux file systems on internal hard drives will be detect by Fedora automatically. Icons for them will be displayed on Computer window. Initially they will not be mounted. You will have to first validate your authorization to mount a disk. To mount a file system for the first time, double click on its icon. A Policykit authorization window will appear similar to that in Figure 13-1. You then enter your user password. The option to Remember authorization is checked, keeping the authorization indefinitely. Whenever you start up your system again, the file system will be mounted for you automatically.

Your file system is then mounted, displaying its icon both in the Computer window and the desktop. The file system will be mounted under the **/media** directory and given folder with the name of the file system label, or, if unlabeled, with the device name like **sda3** for the third partition on the first SATA drive.

Once granted, authentication access will remain in place for a limited time, allowing you to mount other file systems without having to enter your password. These file systems will then be automatically be mounted also, provided you had left the Remember Authorization checked in the Authenticate window.

Any user with administrative access on the primary console is authorized to mount file systems. You can use PolicyKit agent to expand or restrict this level of authorization, as well as enabling access for specific users.

In addition, your partitions will automatically be displayed on the desktop and in the computer window as disks. Select Computer from the Places menu.

Access to Local Windows NTFS File Systems

If you have installed Fedora on a dual-boot system with Windows XP, NT, or 2000, or otherwise need access to NTFS partitions, Linux NTFS file system support is installed automatically. Your NTFS partitions are mounted using FUSE, file system in user space. The same authentication control used for Linux file systems applies to NTFS file systems. Icons for the NTFS partitions will be displayed in the Computer window (Computer in Places menu). The first time you access the file system, you may be asked to provide authorization, as in Figure 13-1. Your NTFS file system is then mounted with icons displayed in the Computer widow and on the desktop. Whenever you start up your system, they will be automatically mounted for you. The partitions will be mounted under the **/media** directory with their labels used as folder names. If they have no labels, then they are given the name **disk**, and then numbered as **disk0**, **disk1**, and so on for additional partitions (unlabeled removable devices may also share these names). The NTFS partitions are mounted using **ntfs-3g** drivers.

Access to Local Network Windows NTFS File Systems

Shared Windows folders and printers on any of the computers connected to your local network are automatically accessible from your Fedora desktop. The DNS discovery service (Ahavi) automatically detects hosts on your home or local network and will let you access directly any of their shared folders.

To access the shared folders, select Network from the Places menu to open the Network Places window (see Figure 13-17 want to access, just click on its icon, otherwise, click on the Windows network icon to see just the Windows machines (see Figure 13-18).

However, local systems cannot access your shared folders until you install a sharing server, Samba for Windows systems and NFS for Linux/Unix systems. Should you attempt to share a directory, an error notice will be displayed asking you to install Samba or NFS. Once selected, the shared folders will be shown.

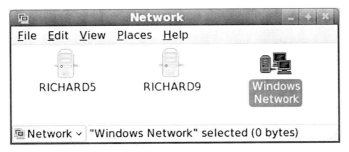

Figure 13-17: Network Places

Figure 13-18: Remote shares

Permissions on GNOME

On GNOME, you can set a directory or file permission using the Permissions panel in its Properties window (see Figure 13-19).

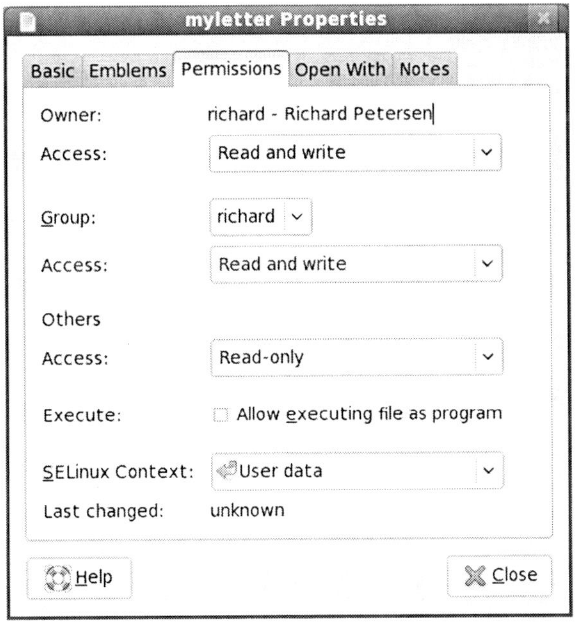

Figure 13-19: File Permissions

For files, right-click the file icon or entry in the file manager window and select Properties. Then select the Permissions panel. Here you will find pop-up menus for read and write permissions, along with rows for Owner, Group, and Other. You can set owner permissions as Read Only or Read And Write. For the group and others, you can also set the None option, denying access. The group name expands to a pop-up menu listing different groups; select one to change the file's group. If you want to execute this as an application (say, a shell script) check the Allow Executing File As Program entry. This has the effect of setting the execute permission

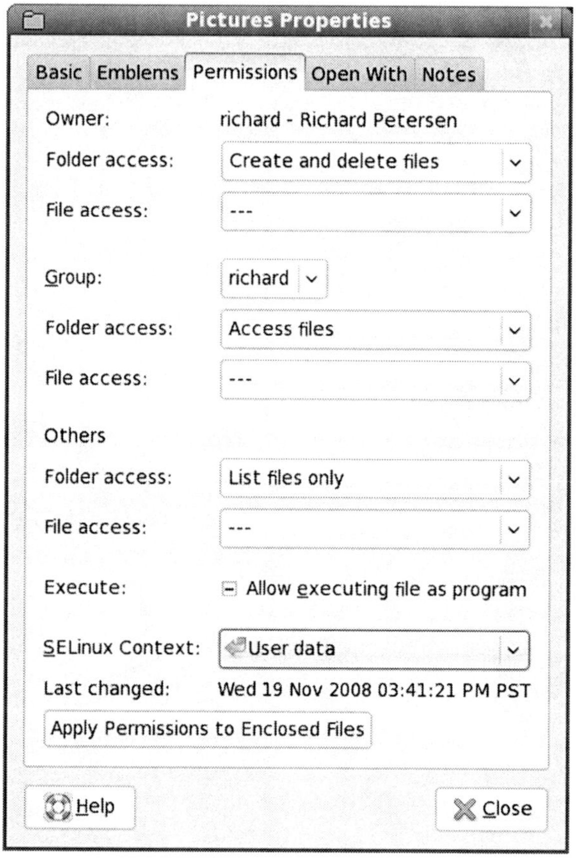

Figure 13-20: Folder Permissions

The Permissions panel for directories operates much the same way, but it includes two access entries, Folder Access and File Access (see Figure 13-20). The Folder Access entry controls access to the folder with options for List Files Only, Access Files, and Create And Delete Files. These correspond to the read, read and execute, and read/write/execute permissions given to directories. The File Access entry lets you set permissions for all those files in the directory. They are the same as for files: for the owner, Read or Read and Write; for the group and others, the entry adds a None option to deny access. To set the permissions for all the files in the directory accordingly (not just the folder), click the Apply Permissions To Enclosed Files button.

Automatic file system mounts with /etc/fstab

Though most file systems are automatically mounted for you, there may be instances where you need to have a file system mounted manually. Using the mount command you can do this directly, or you can specify the mount operation in the **/etc/fstab** file to have it mounted automatically. Make sure your file system is labeled. Fedora now uses labels to identify file systems, not device names. If you need to find out the device name of an unlabeled disk, you can use the fdisk command, the GParted or QTparted tools to list all your hard disks, their partitions, and their current device names. You can then use the **ext2label** command to label a file system. GParted and QTParted are not installed by default, but are available on the Fedora Software repository (use Add/Remove Software to install them).

All file systems are uniquely identified with their UUID (Universally Unique IDentifier). These are listed in the **/dev/disk/by-id** directory (or with the **sudo blkid** command). Fedora will use the UUID to identify any unlabeled file system. In the **/etc/fstab** file, the file system partition devices are listed as a comment, and then followed by the actual file system mount operation using the UUID. The following example mounts the boot file system on partition identified as 81acc8a8-128a-4860-bae3-999bfee5e0f5 to the **/boot** directory as an **ext3** file system with default options (**defaults**).

```
UUID=81acc8a8-128a-4860-bae3-999bfee5e0f5 /boot ext3 defaults 1
```

Keep in mind that any LVM file systems are already labeled. If you installed Fedora 10 as fresh install (not an upgrade), you may have to use a mount operation to mount any LVM file systems you already have. In this case, you would place an entry for the mount operation in the /etc/fstab file. The LVM device name is in the **/etc/fstab** file.

In the following example, the Linux file system labeled **mydata1** is mounted to the **/mydata1** directory as an ext3 file system type. In addition, an LVM file system, **mymedia**, is mounted to the **/mymedia** directory. LVM file system device names are located in the **/dev** directory with a directory for the volume group and device names within that directory for each logical volume in that group. So the logical volume **mymedia** is part of the logical group, **mymedia**, which is a directory it the **/dev** directory, **/dev/mymedia/myvideo**.

/etc/fstab

```
dev/VolGroup00/LogVol01      /           ext3      defaults      1 1
UUID=81acc8a8-128a-4860-bae3-999bfee5e0f5 /boot ext3 defaults   1 2
tmpfs                        /dev/shm    tmpfs     defaults      0 0
devpts                       /dev/pts    devpts    gid=5,mode=620 0 0
sysfs                        /sys        sysfs     defaults      0 0
proc                         /proc       proc      defaults      0 0
/dev/VolGroup00/LogVol00     swap        swap      defaults      0 0
/dev/mymedia/myvideo         /mymedia    ext3      defaults      1 1
LABEL=mydata1                /mydata1    ext3      defaults      1 1
```

To mount manually, use the **mount** command and specify the type with the **-t ext3** option. Use the **-L** option to mount by label. List the file system first and then the directory name to which it will be mounted. For a NTFS partition you would use the type **ntfs**. The mount option has the format:

```
mount -t type  file-system  directory
```

The following example mounts the **mydata1** file system to the **/mydata1** directory

```
mount -t ext3  -L mydata1  /mydata1
```

Editing Configuration Files Directly

Though the administrative tools will handle all configuration settings for you, there may be times when you will need to make changes by directly editing configuration files. These are usually text files in the **/etc** directory or dot files in a user home directory, like **.bash_profile**. System configuration files are normally located in the /etc, /usr/share, and /boot/grub directories. To change system configuration files you will need administrative access, requiring you to first log in as the **root** user. User configuration files are located in dot files in the user's home directory, and not require any administrative access. They can be accessed directly by the user.

To edit any of the system wide configuration files, like those in the **/etc** directory, you will first need root user access. You can login as the root user from a terminal window using the **su** command (alternatively you can use the **sudo** command once sudo is configured).

```
su
```

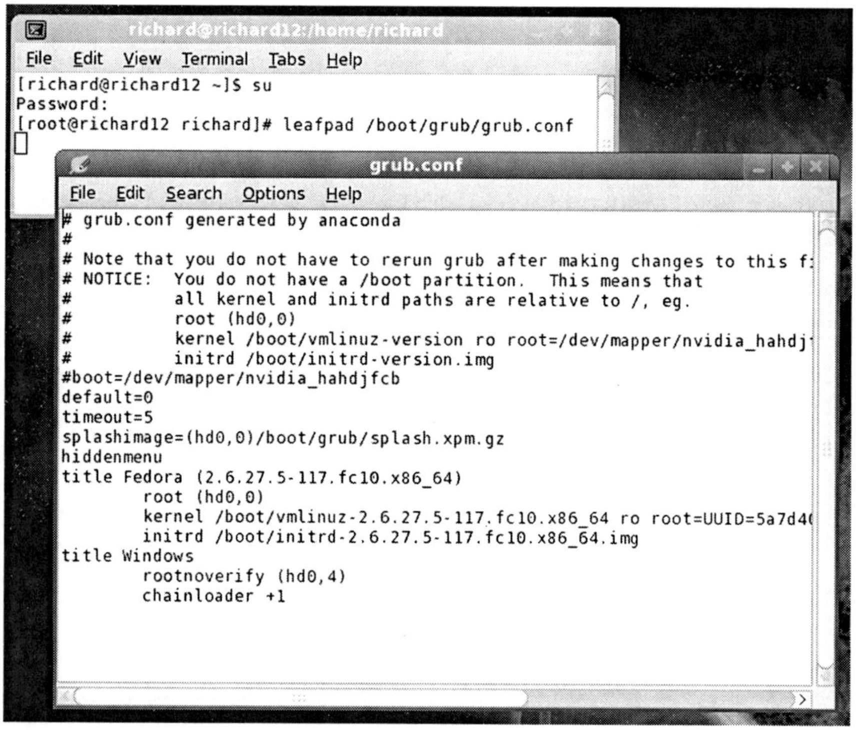

Figure 13-21: Leafpad editor and system configuration files

To edit system files, you can use a standard editor such as Vi or Emacs, though one of the easiest ways to edit them is to use the Leafpad editor from a terminal window on the GNOME desktop. Leafpad provides basic mouse support, letting you edit a file easily. Enter the command leafpad in a terminal window with the name of the file you want to edit. Be sure to login as the root user first using the **su** command. The following command would edit the **grub.conf** file (see Figure 13-21). If you use the **sudo** command (with sudo configured), you can use **gedit** instead.

```
su
leafpad /boot/grub/grub.conf
```

You can no longer use the Gedit text editor to edit system configuration files. Nor can you login as the root user with the GNOME or KDE desktops.

Select Text Editor from the Accessories menu. This opens a Gedit window. Click Open to open a file browser where you can move through the file system to locate the file you want to edit.

User configuration files, dot files, can be changed by individual users directly. To edit user configuration files, you can use a standard editor such as Vi or Emacs, though one of the easiest ways to edit them is to use the Gedit editor on the GNOME desktop. For Gedit, user configuration files do not show up automatically. Dot files like **.bash_profile** have to be chosen from the file manager window, not from the Gedit open operation. First configure the file manager to display dot files. Open any file manager window, and, from the View menu, choose Show Hidden Files. All your user configuration files will be displayed.

Caution: Be careful when editing your configuration files. Editing mistakes can corrupt your configurations. It is advisable to make a backup of any configuration files you are working on first, before making major changes to the original.

Gedit will let you edit several files at once, opening a tabbed pane for each. You can use Gedit to edit any text file, including ones you create yourself. In Figure 13-22 three configuration files are opened: **.bash_profile**, **.bashrc**, and **.bash_logout**.

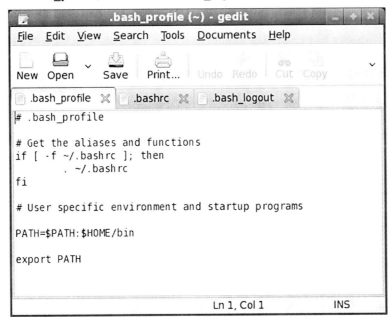

Figure 13-22: Gedit text editor and configuration files

Backup Management: rsync, Amanda, and dump/restore

Backup operations have become an important part of administrative duties. Several backup tools are provided on Linux systems, including Anaconda and the traditional dump/restore tools, as well as the **rsync** command for making individual copies. Anaconda provides server-based backups, letting different systems on a network back up to a central server. BackupPC provides network and local backup using configured rsync and tar tools. The dump tools let you refine your backup process, detecting data changed since the last backup. Table 13-2 lists websites for Linux backup tools.

Website	Tools
`rsync.samba.org`	rsync remote copy backup
`amanda.org`	Amanda network backup
`dump.sourceforge.net`	dump and restore tools
`backuppc.sourceforge.net`	BackupPC network or local backup using configured rsync and tar tools.

Table 13-2: Backup Resources

Individual Backups: archive and rsync

You can back up and restore particular files and directories with archive tools like **tar**, restoring the archives later. For backups, **tar** is usually used with a tape device. To automatically schedule backups, you can schedule appropriate **tar** commands with the **cron** utility. The archives can be also compressed for storage savings. You can then copy the compressed archives to any medium, such as a DVD disc, a floppy, or tape. On GNOME you can use File Roller to create archives easily (Archive Manager under System Tools). The Kdat tool on KDE will back up to tapes, a front end to **tar**. See Chapter 10 for a discussion of compressed archives.

If you want to remote-copy a directory or files from one host to another, making a particular backup, you can use **rsync**, which is designed for network backups of particular directories or files, intelligently copying only those files that have been changed, rather than the contents of an entire directory. In archive mode, it can preserve the original ownership and permissions, providing corresponding users exist on the host system. The following example copies the **/home/george/myproject** directory to the **/backup** directory on the host **rabbit**, creating a corresponding **myproject** subdirectory. The -**t** specifies that this is a transfer. The remote host is referenced with an attached colon, **rabbit:**.

```
rsync -t /home/george/myproject   rabbit:/backup
```

If, instead, you wanted to preserve the ownership and permissions of the files, you would use the -**a** (archive) option. Adding a -**z** option will compress the file. The -**v** option provides a verbose mode.

```
rsync -avz  /home/george/myproject   rabbit:/backup
```

A trailing slash on the source will copy the contents of the directory, rather than generating a subdirectory of that name. Here the contents of the **myproject** directory are copied to the **george-project** directory.

```
rsync -avz  /home/george/myproject/   rabbit:/backup/george-project
```

The `rsync` command is configured to use SSH remote shell by default. You can specify it or an alternate remote shell to use with the `-e` option. For secure transmission you can encrypt the copy operation with ssh. Either use the `-e ssh` option or set the `RSYNC_RSH` variable to ssh.

```
rsync -avz -e ssh  /home/george/myproject   rabbit:/backup/myproject
```

As when using `rcp`, you can copy from a remote host to the one you are on.

```
rsync -avz  lizard:/home/mark/mypics/  /pic-archice/markpics
```

You can also run rsync as a server daemon. This will allow remote users to sync copies of files on your system with versions on their own, transferring only changed files rather than entire directories. Many mirror and software FTP sites operate as rsync servers, letting you update files without have to download the full versions again. Configuration information for rsync as a server is kept in the **/etc/rsyncd.conf** file. On Fedora, rsync as a server is managed through **xinetd**, using the **/etc/xinetd.d/rsync** file, which starts **rsync** with the `--daemon` option. In the **/etc/services** file, it is listed to run on port 873. It is off by default, but you can enable it with system-config-services On Demand Services panel or `chkconfig`.

```
chkconfig rsync on
```

Tip: Though it is designed for copying between hosts, you can also use **rsync** to make copies within your own system, usually to a directory in another partition or hard drive. In fact there are eight different ways of using **rsync**. Check the **rsync** Man page for detailed descriptions of each.

BackupPC

BackupPC provides an easily managed local or network backup of your system or hosts on a system using configured rsync or tar tools. There is no client application to install, just configuration files. BackupPC can back up hosts on a network, including servers, or just a single system. Data can be backed up to local hard disks or to network storage such as shared partitions or storage servers. You can configure BackupPC using your Web page configuration interface. This is the host name of your computer with the /backuppc name attached, like **http://rabbit.turtle.com/backuppc**. Detailed documentation is installed at **/usr/share/doc/BackupPC**. You can find out more about BackupPC at **backuppc.sourceforge.net**.

BackupPC uses both compression and detection of identical files to significantly reduce the size of the backup, allowing several hosts to be backed up in limited space. Once an initial backup is performed, BackupPC will only back up changed files, reducing the time of the backup significantly.

BackupPC has its own service script with which you start the BackupPC service, **/etc/init.d/backuppc**. Configuration files are located at **/etc/BackupPC**. The **config.pl** file holds BackupPC configuration options and the hosts file lists hosts to be backed up.

Amanda

To back up hosts connected to a network, you can use the Advanced Maryland Automatic Network Disk Archiver (Amanda) to archive hosts. Amanda uses tar tools to back up all hosts to a single host operating as a backup server. Backup data is sent by each host to the host operating as the Amanda server, where they are written out to a backup medium such as tape. With an Amanda server, the backup operations for all hosts become centralized in one server, instead of each host having to perform its own backup. Any host that needs to restore data simply requests it from the Amanda server, specifying the file system, date, and filenames. Backup data is copied to the server's holding disk and from there to tapes. Detailed documentation and updates are provided at **amanda.org**. For the server, be sure to install the Amanda-server package, and for clients you use the amanda-clients package.

Amanda is designed for automatic backups of hosts that may have very different configurations, as well as operating systems. You can back up any host that supports GNU tools, including Mac OS X and Windows systems connected through Samba.

14. Network Configuration

With Fedora 10, network configuration is now managed primarily by the Network Manager, though the standard tools from previous releases are still used. Network configuration differs depending on whether you are connected to a local area network (LAN) with an Ethernet card or are using a DSL or ISDN modem, a wireless connection, or a dial-up modem connection. You had the opportunity to enter your LAN network settings during the installation process. For modifying your LAN settings and for configuring other kinds of interfaces such as DSL, wireless, or ISDN connections, you can configure your network connection using system-config-network, as well as add a new connection. Table 14-1 lists several different network configuration tools.

Network Information: Dynamic and Static

If you are on a network, you may need to obtain certain information to configure your interface. Most networks now support dynamic configuration using either the older Dynamic Host Configuration Protocol (DHCP) or the new IPv6 Protocol and its automatic address configuration. In this case, you need only check the DHCP entry in most network configuration tools. For IPv6, you would check the Enable IPv6 configuration entry in the system-config-network device configuration window (see Figure 14-3 later in this chapter).

Network Configuration Tool	Description
Network Manager	Automates wireless and standard network connection selection and notification.
system-config-network	Fedora network configuration tool for all types of connections.
KNetworkManager	KDE version of Network Manager, automates wireless and standard network connection selection and notification.
system-control-network	Fedora network device control tool for turning network connections on an off.
system-config-services	Starts and stops servers, including network servers (smb for Samba, httpd for Web, bind for DNS, and nfs for NFS).
system-config-firewall	Sets up a network firewall.
system-config-bind	Configures a domain name server.
system-config-samba	Configures Samba shares.
system-config-nfs	Configures NFS shares.
system-config-httpd	Configures an Apache Web server.
system-config-netboot	Configures diskless workstations and network installation.
wvdial	PPP modem connection, enter on a command line.

Table 14-1: Fedora Network Configuration Tools

If your network does not support DHCP or IPv6 automatic addressing, you will have to provide detailed information about your connection. Such connections are known as static connections, whereas DCHP and IPv6 connections are dynamic. In a static connection, you need to manually enter your connection information such as your IP address and DNS servers, whereas in a dynamic connection this information is automatically provided to your system by a DHCP server or generated by IPv6 when you connect to the network. For DHCP, a DHCP client on each host will obtain the information from a DHCP server serving that network. IPv6 generates its addresses directly from the device and router information such as the device hardware MAC address.

In addition, if you are using a DSL dynamic, ISDN, or modem connection, you will also have to supply provider, login, and password information, whether your system is dynamic or static. You may also need to supply specialized information such as DSL or modem compression methods, dialup number, or wireless channels to select.

You can obtain most of your static network information from your network administrator or from your ISP (Internet service provider). You would need the following information:

The device name for your network interface   For LAN and wireless connections, this is usually an Ethernet card with the name **eth0** or **eth1**. For a modem, DSL, or ISDN connection, this is a PPP device named **ppp0** (**ippp0** for ISDN). Virtual private network (VPN) connections are also supported.

Hostname   Your computer will be identified by this name on the Internet. Do not use localhost; that name is reserved for special use by your system. The name of the host should be a simple word, which can include numbers, but not punctuation such as periods and backslashes. The hostname includes both the name of the host and its domain. For example, a hostname for a machine could be **turtle**, whose domain is **mytrek.com**, giving it a hostname of **turtle.mytrek.com**.

Domain name   This is the name of your network.

The Internet Protocol (IP) address assigned to your machine   This is needed only for static Internet connections. Dynamic connections use the DHCP protocol to automatically assign an IP address for you. Every host on the Internet is assigned an IP address. Traditionally, this address used an IPv4 format consisting of a set of four numbers, separated by periods, which uniquely identifies a single location on the Internet, allowing information from other locations to reach that computer. Networks are now converting to the new IP protocol version 6, IPv6, which uses a new format with a much more complex numbering sequence.

Your network IP address   Static connections only. This address is usually similar to the IP address, but with one or more zeros at the end.

The netmask   Static connections only. This is usually 255.255.255.0 for most networks. If, however, you are part of a large network, check with your network administrator or ISP.

The broadcast address for your network, if available (optional)   Static connections only. Usually, your broadcast address is the same as your IP address with the number 255 added at the end.

The IP address of your network's gateway computer   Static connections only. This is the computer that connects your local network to a larger one like the Internet.

Name servers   Static connections only. The IP address of the name servers your network uses. These enable the use of URLs.

NIS domain and IP address for an NIS server   Necessary if your network uses an NIS server (optional).

User login and password information   Needed for dynamic DSL, ISDN, and modem connections.

User network configuration: Network Manager, System | Preferences | Network Configuration

Network Manager will automatically detect your network connections, both wired and wireless. Network Manager makes use the automatic device detection capabilities of udev and HAL to configure your connections. Should you instead need to configure your network connections manually, you still use Network Manager, selecting the manual options and entering the required network connection information.

Network Manager is user specific. When a user logs in, it selects the network connection preferred by that user. The first time a user runs NetworkManager, the notification applet will display a list of current possible connections. The user can then choose one. For wired connections, a connection can be started automatically, when the system starts up. Initial settings will be supplied from system-wide configuration.

Fedora 10 uses an enhanced version of Network Manager which can also manually configure any network connection. To configure all your network connections. This includes wired, wireless, and all manual connections. The network-admin tool has been dropped. Network Interface Connection (NIC cards) hardware is detected using HAL. Information provided by Network Manager is made available to other applications over D-Bus.

Network Manager will display a Network applet icon to the right on the top panel. Left-click to see a list of all possible network connections; including all available wireless connections (see Figure 14-1). Password-protected access points will display a lock next to them. The VPN Connection entry submenu will list configured VPN connection for easy access. The Configure VPN eatery will open Network Manager to the VPN tab where you can then add, edit, or delete VPN connections. The Disconnect VPN entry will end the current active VPN connection.

Figure 14-1: NetworkManager network connections menu and applet icon

Right-click to have the option of editing your connection, shutting off your connection (enable networking), or to see information about the connection. Select Edit connections to use Network Manager's own manual network configuration capability, which includes both wired connections and wireless 3G configuration (see Figure 14-2).

Figure 14-2: NetworkManager GNOME options

Note: The KDE version of Network Manager, knetworkmanager, also detects network connections. In addition it allows you to configure PPP dial up connections as well as manage wireless connections. To start kdenetworkmanager, select its entry in Applications | Network Tools.

You can also select the System | Preferences | Network Configuration menu entry.

With multiple wireless access points for Internet connections, a system could have several different network connections to choose from, instead of a single-line connection like DSL or cable. This is particularly true for notebook computers that could access different wireless connections at different locations. Instead of manually configuring a new connection each time one is encountered, the Network Manager tool can automatically configure and select a connection to use.

By default, an Ethernet connection will be preferred if available. Direct lines that support Ethernet connections are normally considered faster than wireless ones. For wireless connections, you will need to choose the one you want.

Network Manager is designed to work in the background, providing status information for your connection and switching from one configured connection to another as needed. For initial configuration, it detects as much information as possible about the new connection. It operates as a GNOME Panel applet, monitoring your connection, and can work on any Linux distribution.

Network Manager operates as a daemon with the name NetworkManager. If no Ethernet connection is available, Network Manager will scan for wireless connections, checking for Extended Service Set Identifiers (ESSIDs). If an ESSID identifies a previously used connection, then it is automatically selected. If several are found, then the most recently used one is chosen. If only a new connection is available, then Network Manager waits for the user to choose one. A connection is selected only if the user is logged in. If an Ethernet connection is later made, then Network Manager will switch to it from wireless.

Network Manager operates as a daemon with the name NetworkManager. It is managed with the NetworkManager service script, which you can start and stop using the Services tool in System | Administration | Services, or by using the service command in a terminal window.

```
service NetworkManager start
```

To have it start up automatically, you can use the Services tool, System | Administration | Services, or use **chkconfig**.

```
chkconfig NetworkManager on
```

Network Interface Connection (NIC cards) hardware is detected using HAL. Information provided by Network Manager is made available to other applications over D-Bus. Features currently under development include VPN and application notification. Network Manager uses the DHCP6c client to gather network information. For user interaction and notification, it uses NetworkManagerInfo.

Note: The KDE version of Network Manager, knetworkmanager, also detects network connections. To start kdenetworkmanager, select its entry in Applications | Network Tools.

Network Manager manual configuration for all network connections

Should you need to edit any network connection, wired or wireless, you right-click on the Network Manager icon and select Edit Network Connections (see Figure 14-2). This opens Network Manager's Network Connections window as shown in Figure 14-3. Established connections will be listed, with Add, Edit, and Delete buttons for adding, editing, and removing network connections. Your current network connections should already be listed, having been automatically detected by udev and HAL. In the Figure 14-3 a wired Ethernet connection referred to as **eth0** is listed, the first Ethernet connection.

Tip: There is no longer a Networking entry in the System | Administration menu. To configure your network, access Network Manager by clicking its top panel applet, the black computer icon.

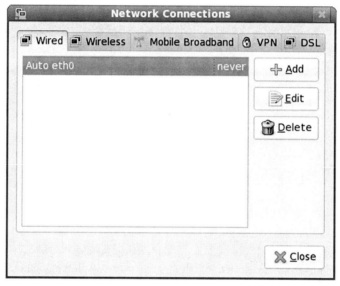

Figure 14-3: Network configuration

On the Network Connections window there are three tabs: Wired, Wireless, Mobile Broadband, VPN, and DSL.

➢ **Wired**: The wired connection is used for the standard IPv4 and IPv6 Ethernet connections, featuring support for DHCP and manual Ethernet settings.

➢ **Wireless**: The Wireless tab is where you enter in wireless configuration data like your ESSID, password, and encryption method.

➢ **Mobile Broadband**: The mobile broadband tab is the wireless 3G configuration, with selection for the service you are using.

➢ **VPN**: The VPN tab lets you specify a virtual private network

➢ **DSL**: The DSL tab lets you set up a direct DSL connection.

Each tab will list their configured network connections. Click on the ADD or EDIT buttons to configure a new network connection of that type, or edit an existing one.

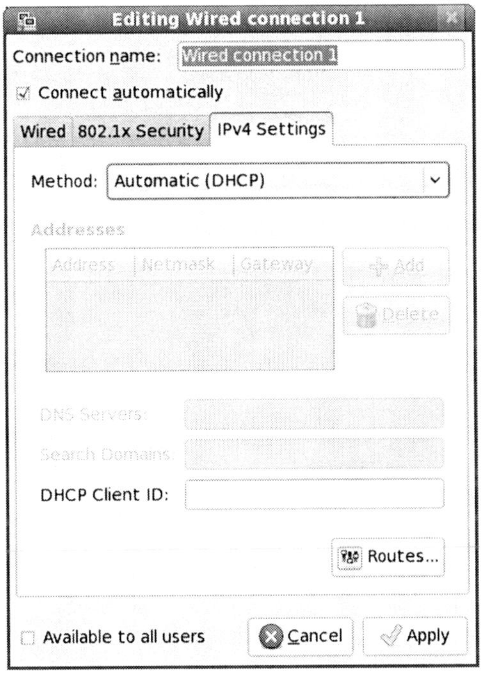

Figure 14-4: DHCP Wired Configuration

Wired Configuration

To edit a wired connection, select the connection and click the EDIT buttons on the Wired tab. This opens an Editing window as shown in Figure 14-4.

The ADD button is used to add a new connection and opens a similar window, with no settings. The Wired tab lists the MAC hardware address and the MTU. The MTU is usually set to automatic. Figure 14-4 shows the standard default configuration for a wired Ethernet connection using DHCP. Connect automatically will set up the connection when the system starts up.

There are three tabs, Wired, 8.02.1x Security, and IPv4 Settings.

The IPv4 Setting tab lets you select the kind of wired connection you have. The options are:

➢ **Automatic (DHCP)**: DHCP connection. Address information is blocked out.

➢ **Automatic (DHCP) addresses only**: DHCP that lets you specify your DNS server addresses.

➢ **Manual**: Enter your IP, network, and gateway addresses along with your DNS server addresses and your network domain name.

> ➤ **Link-local only**: IPv6 private local network (like IPv4 192.18.0 addresses). All address entries are blocked out.

> ➤ **Shared to other computers**: All address entries are blocked out.

Figure 14-5: Manual Wired Configuration

Figure 14-5 shows the manual configuration entries for a wired Ethernet connection. Click the Add button to enter the IP address, network mask, and gateway address. Then enter the address for the DNS servers and your network search domains.

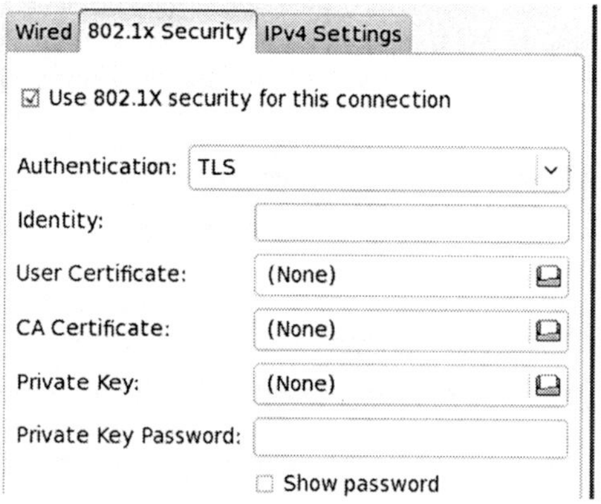

Figure 14-6: 802.1 Security Configuration

The Routes button will open a window where you can manually enter any network routes.

The 802.1 tab allows you to configure 802.1 security, if your network supports it (see Figure 14-6).

Wireless Configuration

For wireless connections, you click ADD or EDIT on the Network Connections window's Wireless tab. The Editing Wireless connection window opens with tabs for your wireless information, security, and IPv4 settings (See Figure 14-7). On the Wireless tab you specify your SSID, along with your Mode and MAC address.

Figure 14-7: Wireless configuration

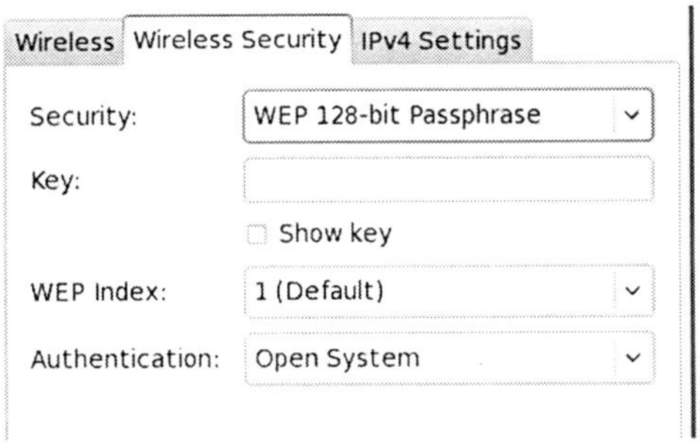

Figure 14-8: Wireless Security

On the Wireless Security tab you enter your wireless connection security method (see Figure 14-8). The commonly used method, WEP, is supported, along with WPA personal. The WPA personal method only requires a password. More secure connections like Dynamic WEP and Enterprise WPA are also supported. These will require much more configuration information like authentication methods, certificates, and keys.

On the IPv4 Settings tab you enter your wireless connection's network address settings. This tab is the same as the IPv4 Setting on the Wired connection (see Figures 14-5 and 14-6). You have the same options: DHCP, DHCP with DNS addresses, Manual, Link-local only, and Shared.

DSL Configuration

For a direct DSL connection, you click ADD or EDIT on the Network Connections window's DSL tab. The DSL connection window will open, showing tabs for both DSL and wired PPP connections. Here you enter your DSL user name, service provider, and password (see Figure 14-9).

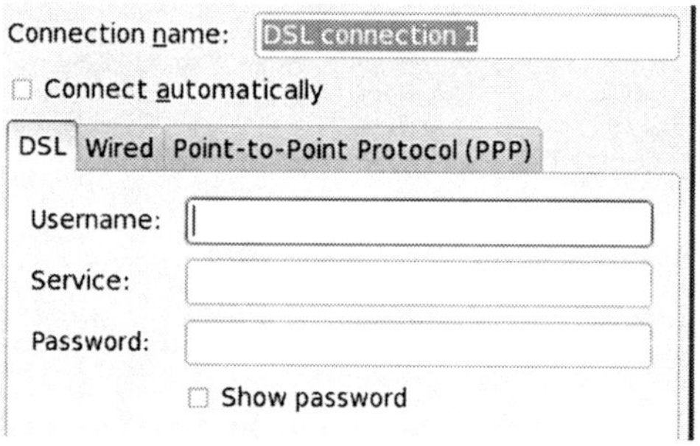

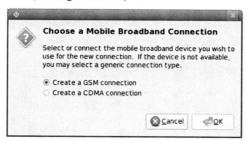

Figure 14-9: DSL manual configuration

Mobile Broadband: 3G Support

To set up a Mobile Broadband 3G connections, you select the Mobile Broadband tab in the Network Connections window, and click the ADD or EDIT button. You first choose either a CDMA or GSM 3G connection (see Figure 14-10).

Figure 14-10: Selecting 3G Support

The connection window for each will provide panels for both Mobile Broadband and PPP. On the Mobile Broadband panel you can enter your number, user name, and password.

The GSM connection window has advanced options including the APN, Network, PIN, and PUK (see Figure 14-11). The PPP tab lets you set up your connection configuration.

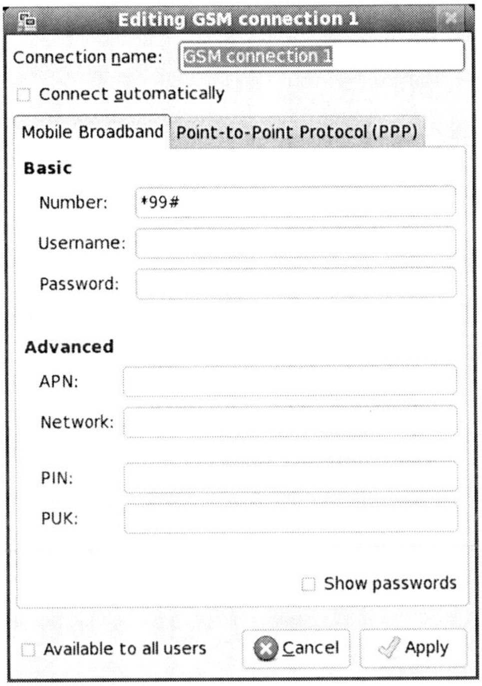

Figure 14-11: 3G GSM Support

For CDMA connections, the Mobile Broadband tab provides entries for just the number, username, and password (see Figure 14-12).

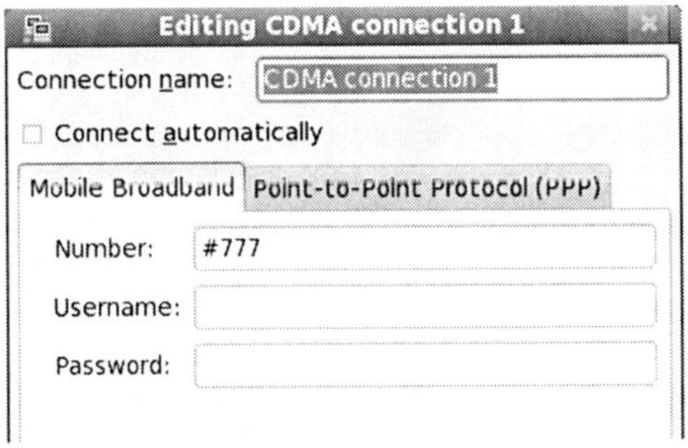

Figure 14-12: 3G CDMA Support

Once a service is selected, you can further edit the configuration by clicking its entry in the Mobile Broadband tab and clicking the EDIT button. The Editing window opens with tabs for Mobile Broadband and PPP. On the Mobile Broadband panel you can enter your number, user name, and password. Advance options including the APN, Network, type, PIN, and PUK. The APN should already be entered.

PPP Configuration

For either Wireless Broadband or DSL connections you can also specify PPP information. The PPP tab is the same for both (See Figure 14-13). There are sections Authentication, Compressions, and the Echo option. Check what features are supported by your particular PPP connection.

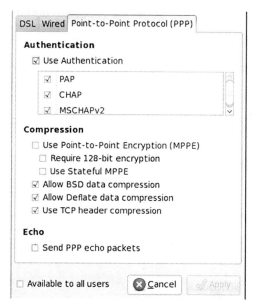

Figure 14-13: PPP Configuration

System wide network configuration: system-config-network, System | Administration | Network

Fedora 10 still provides the older system-config-network tools for easy system-wide configuration and activation of your network interfaces. You will be prompted for administrative access, and changes will be made system-wide. You can use this tool to configure and control any kind of network connection, including Ethernet cards, modems, DSL and ISDN modems, and wireless connections. All are supported with standard configuration tabs like those for IP address settings, along with specialized panels used only for a particular kind of connection, such as Compression for modem connections or Wireless Settings for a wireless card. New connections are initially configured using the Internet Configuration Wizard, which will detect and prompt for basic configuration information and then place you in the system-config-network tool to let you refine your configuration, making or changing entries as you require.

You can access the system-config-network tool directly from the System Administration menu (Network entry), System | Administration | Network. This tool opens a Network Configuration window that has five tabbed panels: Devices, Hardware, IPsec, Hosts, and DNS (see Figure 14-14). These panels are used for configuring the network settings for your entire system. The Devices panel lists all your network connections, and Hardware lists all the network components on your system, such as Ethernet cards and modems. The DNS panel is where you enter your own system's hostname and your network's name server addresses. The Hosts panel lists static host IP addresses and their domain names, including those for your own system. The IPsec panel is used to create virtual private networks (VPNs), creating secure connections between hosts and local networks across a larger network such as the Internet. It appears only if you have installed IPsec tools and support on your system.

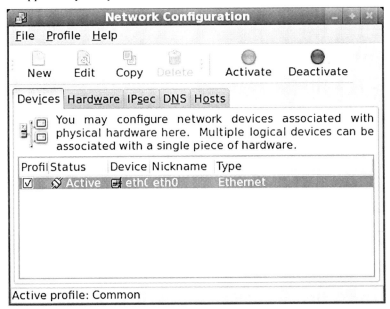

Figure 14-14: The system-config-network Network Configuration window showing Devices panel

DNS Settings

The DNS panel has a box at the top, labeled Hostname (see Figure 14-15). Here, you enter your system's fully qualified domain name. There are boxes for entering the IP addresses for your system's primary, secondary, and tertiary DNS servers, needed for static configurations. You can then list your search domain. Both the search domain and the name server addresses are saved in the **/etc/resolv.conf** file.

Hosts

You use the Hosts panel to associate static IP addresses with certain hosts. The panel has a single pane with New, Edit, Copy, and Delete buttons. This panel lists entries that associate hostnames with static IP addresses. You can also add aliases (nicknames). The Hosts panel actually displays the contents of the **/etc/hosts** file and saves any entries you make to that file. To add an entry, click New. A window opens with boxes for the hostname, IP address, and nicknames. When you finish, the entry is added to the Hosts list. To edit an entry, click Edit and a similar window opens, enabling you to change any of the fields. To delete an entry, select it and click Delete.

Note: If you are having trouble connecting with an Ethernet device using a static network connection, make sure that the Hosts panel lists your hostname and IP address, not just localhost. If your hostname is not there, add it.

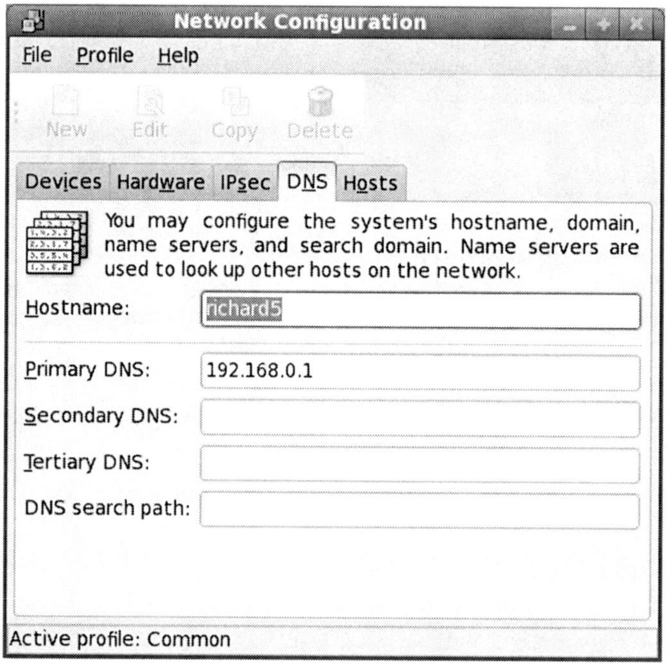

Figure 14-15: The system-config-network DNS panel

Device Configuration: Automatic or Static

The Devices panel will list the configured network devices on your system. An entry shows the device name and its type. Use the New, Edit, Copy, and Delete buttons to manage the device entries. To edit a device, you can just double-click its entry. For example, when you edit an Ethernet device, you open a tabbed panel for configuring it, enabling you to specify whether it is dynamic or static (see Figure 14-16). There is an entry for automatically activating it when the system starts. You can choose to use IPv6 for automatic addressing. For DHCP you can automatically obtain DNS information. For a static connection you will be able to enter an IP address, netmask, and gateway. A Hardware panel will let you choose the actual hardware device to use. The configuration panels will differ depending on the device you edit. For example, a modem device will add panels for provider, compression, and modem options, whereas a DSL connection will have panels for provider, route (gateway), and hardware device. An Ethernet connection will have only general, route, and hardware device panels. Making entries here performs the same function as `ifconfig`.

When you finish and are ready to save your configuration, select the Save entry from the File menu. If you want to abandon the changes you made, you can close without saving. You can run system-config-network at any time to make changes in your network configuration.

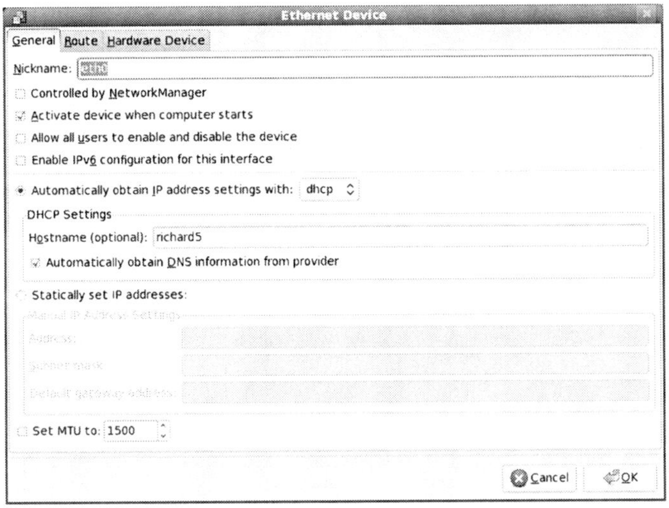

Figure 14-16: Device configuration in system-config-network

Profiles

The system-config-network tool also supports profiles. *Profiles* are commonly used for portable computers that may be moved from one environment to another. For example, at your office you could have an Office profile that uses an Ethernet card to connect to the office LAN. At home, you could use a Home profile that uses a modem to connect to the Internet. Profiles are integrated into the configuration process, with a Common profile functioning as the default configuration. The Common profile will be inherited by all other profiles, so make your basic configuration with that profile.

Profiles are accessed from the Profile menu. Select the profile you want, or select New to create a new profile. The name of the currently selected profile will be displayed at the bottom of the Network Configuration screen. The Delete entry in the Profile menu will delete the current profile. By default, the Common profile will be selected. To create a profile, click the New entry and enter the name of the profile. It will be added to the Profile menu. You can also remove or rename a profile. The new profile will inherit the setting of the common profile. Once you have selected a profile, you can then select devices or change DNS or host information. On the Devices panel of system-config-network, each device entry will have a check box. Selecting this check box selects the device for the current profiles. To select a device for a given profile, first be sure to select the profile you are configuring, and then click the device's check box. For other profiles, the device will be unchecked. Select the Save entry from the File menu when you are finished. The changes you make will be part of that profile, and not of any other.

Configuring Replaced or Unsupported Ethernet Cards

If you change your Ethernet card or if your card is not supported and you need to manually load a driver for it, you will have to manually configure the card. For supported cards, Kudzu will automatically detect the card when your system starts up and prompt you to configure it. For dynamic connections, simply select DHCP to automatically determine your network configuration. For static connections, enter the required network information, such as your IP address and DNS servers.

If the device is not supported or if you elected not to configure it with Kudzu, you can use system-config-network to manually create a new device for the card. For unsupported devices, make sure you have first obtained the required Linux kernel module for it and have installed as a kernel module (check the install instructions provided by the vendor, you may have to reboot). Then, start up system-config-network and click the New button in the Device panel. Select Ethernet as the type of device and then select the Ethernet card from the list provided. On the Configure Network Setting panel, click Automatically Obtain IP Address, and select the method from the drop-down menu, usually DHCP. Also click Automatically Obtain DNS Information. For static connections, enter the required information, such as your IP and DNS server addresses. Your new device will now appear in the Devices panel. To activate it, select it and then click Activate.

If your network hardware was not detected and did not show up in the Hardware panel after loading its module, you can try manually adding it, specifying its parameters and identification yourself. Click the Hardware panel and then click New. This opens a Choose Hardware Type dialog with a pop-up menu for different types of network cards. Choosing one opens a Network Adapter Configuration screen, where you select the kind of adapter, its device name, and resources used, such as IRQ.

Configuring New Network Devices Manually

If the device was detected but not configured, you will need to configure it manually. In this case the Hardware device will appear in the Hardware panel, but not in the Devices panel. To configure a new network connection manually, first open system-config-network to the Devices panel and click New. The Add New Device Type window opens and displays a list of all possible network connections (see Figure 14-17). When you select an entry, panels will prompt you to enter basic information about a connection; this will include phone number, username, and password for modem, DSL, and ISDN connections, whereas Ethernet connections will prompt only for IP addresses. The type of connections currently supported are Ethernet (**eth**), ISDN (**ippp**), Modem (**ppp**), xDSL (**ppp**), Token Ring (**tr**), and wireless connections (**eth**). After completing your entries, the wizard will configure your connection setting and the new connection will be ready for use.

Modem Configuration

You can also use a modem with telephone lines to connect to a network. For a modem connection, the Internet Configuration Wizard will probe and detect your modem. A window will then display entries for the serial device, baud rate, hardware control, and modem volume, which you can modify. You are then prompted to enter the phone number, provider, username, and password for your ISP account. The system-config-network tool is then started up, listing your modem device as a **ppp** connection (**ppp** stands for the *Point-to-Point Protocol [PPP]* protocol that transmits IP communications across telephone lines). You can then edit the **ppp** device to modify your settings and enter any other settings; for instance, you can enter IP addresses for static connections, specify compression methods, or list your DNS servers.

DSL and ISDN Configuration

To configure DSL, you will need to provide login and password information for DSL (Digital Subscriber Line) and ISDN. In other respects, DSL and ISDN connections operate much like a local area network (LAN), treating a host as an integrated part of a network. On Fedora, you can use the Internet Configuration Wizard to set up a DSL or ISDN connection. For DSL, the Internet Configuration Wizard will display a dialog box with entries for entering your login name, your password, and the Ethernet interface your DSL modem is attached to. You will also need to enter the IP addresses for the DNS servers provided by your ISP. You can elect to have the connection automatically made up when your system starts up (depending upon your selected network profile).

Figure 14-17: Add a new network device

Wireless Configuration

Wireless connections are now detected and configured by Network Manager, both automatically and manually. Should you need to, you can also configure a wireless connection manually for system wide settings with the Internet Wizard as shown here. A wireless connection operates much like a standard Ethernet connection, requiring only an IP address and DNS server information to connect to the Internet. In addition, you will have to specify wireless connection information such as the network name and channel used. To add a new wireless connection, you start the Internet Configuration Wizard (from the System Tools menu) and select the wireless connection. If system-config-network is open, you can click Add on the Devices panel to start the Internet Configuration Wizard. You are prompted to select your wireless card.

On the Configure Wireless Connection panel, you then configure your wireless connection, selecting the mode, network name, channel, transmit, and key information.

➢ **Mode**   Normally, you can leave this on Auto. For a simple network, one that does not require roaming, the mode is usually Ad Hoc. Managed networks allow roaming among different access points.

➢ **Network Name (SSID)**   Can be left on Auto for a simple network. The Network Name is used to identify a cell as part of a virtual network.

➢ **Channel**   Starting from 1, choose one with least interference.

➢ **Transmit Rate**   Usually set to Auto to adjust automatically to degraded transmissions. But you can set a specific rate such as 11M or 1M from the pop-up menu.

➢ **Key**   This is the encryption key for your wireless network. It must be the same for each cell on your network.

On the Configure Network Settings panel, you specify your IP address, whether it is obtained automatically with DHCP or one you enter yourself. For most company wireless networks, the IP address will be obtained automatically. Normally, the DNS servers are also provided. You can, if you wish, also specify a host name.

If you are setting up a local or home network, you will most likely use static IP addresses you select yourself from the private IP pool, beginning with 192.168, such as 192.168.0.1. The static subnet mask for a small local network is usually 255.255.255.0. The Gateway is the IP address for the computer on your network that connects to the Internet, or to a larger network.

You can later edit a wireless connection, making changes. Wireless configuration has the same General and Hardware Device panels as an Ethernet or DSL connection, but instead of a Route panel, it has a Wireless Settings panel, where you can set your mode and network name along with channel, transmit, and key information.

Your configuration setting will be saved in an Ethernet configuration file in the **/etc/sysconfig/network-scripts** directory. For example, if your wireless card is designated **eth1**, then its configuration information is saved in the **ifcfg-eth1** file. Here you will find the standard Ethernet connection parameters such as the IP address and gateway, as well as wireless parameters such as the channel used, the mode specified, and the encryption key. The standard setting can be modified using system-config-network on that device. You could also modify this file directly to enter additional parameters, like the frequency (FREQ) or sensitivity level (SENS). You can also specify any of the `iwconfig` parameters using the IWCONFIG option. Enter `IWCONFIG` followed by and assignment of an option with a value. For example, the following option sets the fragment threshold for packets:

```
IWCONFIG="frag 512"
```

Virtual Private Networks

A virtual private network lets you create your own private logical network on top of physical network connections, such as the Internet. Using encryption, your private network transmissions are kept secure from the physical network. Though a virtual private network (VPN) has no physical connections of its own and is not an actual network, the secure transmissions it sends have the effect of operating as if the network did exist as separate entity. VPNs make use of tunneling, in which secure transmissions are sent directly through interconnecting systems on a large network like the Internet without being intercepted or, at any point, translated. To implement a VPN, each node has to use the same encryption support software. On Fedora you can choose to use either the IPsec tools. To use IPsec to set up a VPN, you click the IPsec panel in system-config-network and create a new connection.

Interface Configuration Scripts: /etc/sysconfig/network-scripts

Network configuration implemented by the Internet Configuration Wizard and system-config-network are saved in interface configuration scripts located in the **/etc/sysconfig/network-scripts** directory. You can edit these scripts directly, changing specific parameters, as discussed previously for wireless connection. Interface configuration files bear the names of the network interfaces currently configured, such as **ifcfg-eth0** for the first Ethernet device, or **ifcfg-ppp0** for the first PPP modem device. These files define shell variables that hold information on the interface, such as whether to start them at boot time. For example, the **ifcfg-eth0** file holds definitions for NETWORK, BROADCAST, and IPADDR, which are assigned the network, broadcast, and IP addresses that the device uses. You can also manually edit these interface configuration files, making changes as noted previously for the wireless connection. A sample **ifcfg-eth0** file is shown here using a DHCP address.

/etc/sysconfig/network-scripts/ifcfg-eth0

```
DEVICE=eth0
BOOTPROTO=DHCP
HWDADDR=00:00:00:EF:AF:00
ONBOOT=yes
TYPE=Ethernet
```

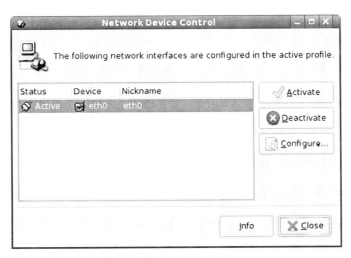

Figure 14-18: Network Device Control

system-control-network: System | Administration | Network Device Control

If you want to manually turn on or off your network connections, you use the Network Device Control tool (system-control-network), System | Administration | Network Device Control (see Figure 14-18). All your connections will be listed (many systems will have only one). You can click the Deactivate button to turn off a selected active connection, and the Activate button to turn it on. Clicking the Configure button will start up system-config-network allowing you to configure the selected device (see the following section).

Command Line PPP Access: wvdial

If, for some reason, you have been unable to set up a modem connection on your Desktop, you may have to set it up from the command line interface. For a dial-up PPP connection, you can use the wvdial dialer, which is an intelligent dialer that not only dials up an ISP service but also performs login operations, supplying your username and password.

Variable	Description
Inherits	Explicitly inherits from the specified section. By default, sections inherit from the [Dialer Defaults] section.
Modem	The device wvdial should use as your modem. The default is **/dev/modem**.
Baud	The speed at which wvdial communicates with your modem. The default is 57,600 baud.
Init1...Init9	Specifies the initialization strings to be used by your modem; wvdial can use up to 9. The default is "ATZ" for Init1.
Phone	The phone number you want wvdial to dial.
Area Code	Specifies the area code, if any.
Dial Prefix	Specifies any needed dialing prefix—for example, 70 to disable call waiting or 9 for an outside line.
Dial Command	Specifies the dial operation. The default is "ATDT".
Login	Specifies the username you use at your ISP.
Login Prompt	If your ISP has an unusual login prompt, you can specify it here.
Password	Specifies the password you use at your ISP.
Force Address	Specifies a static IP address to use (for ISPs that provide static IP addresses to users).
Auto Reconnect	If enabled, wvdial attempts to reestablish a connection automatically if you are randomly disconnected by the other side. This option is on by default.

Table 14-2: Variables for wvdial

The wvdial program first loads its configuration from the **/etc/wvdial.conf** file. In here, you can place modem and account information, including modem speed and serial device, as well as ISP phone number, username, and password. The **wvdial.conf** file is organized into sections, beginning with a section label enclosed in brackets. A section holds variables for different parameters that are assigned values, such as `username = chris`. The default section holds default values inherited by other sections, so you needn't repeat them. Table 14-2 lists the wvdial variables.

You can use the wvdialconf utility to create a default **wvdial.conf** file for you automatically; wvdialconf will detect your modem and set default values for basic features. You can then edit the **wvdial.conf** file and modify the Phone, Username, and Password entries with your ISP dial-up information. Remove the preceding semicolon (;) to unquote the entry. Any line beginning with a semicolon is ignored as a comment.

```
$ wvdialconf
```

You can also create a named dialer, such as *myisp* in the following example. This is helpful if you have different ISPs you log in to. The following example shows the **/etc/wvdial.conf** file:

To start wvdial, enter the command `wvdial`, which then reads the connection configuration information from the **/etc/wvdial.conf** file; wvdial dials the ISP and initiates the PPP connection, providing your username and password when requested.

```
$ wvdial
```

/etc/wvdial.conf

```
[Modem0]
Modem = /dev/ttyS0
Baud = 57600
Init1 = ATZ
SetVolume = 0
Dial Command = ATDT

[Dialer Defaults]
Modem = /dev/ttyS0
Baud = 57600
Init1 = ATZ
SetVolume = 0
Dial Command = ATDT

[Dialer myisp]
Username = chris
Password = mypassword
Modem = /dev/ttyS0
Phone = 555-5555
Area Code = 555
Baud = 57600
Stupid mode = 0
```

You can set up connection configurations for any number of connections in the **/etc/wvdial.conf** file. To select one, enter its label as an argument to the `wvdial` command, as shown here:

```
$ wvdial myisp
```

Manual Wireless Configuration with iwconfig

NetworkManager will automatically detect and configure your wireless connections for both GNOME and KDE desktops. You can manually configure your connections with wireless tools on Network Manager, as well as system-config-network (wireless properties) and ifwconfig. Wireless configuration using Network Manager and system-config-network was discussed in the previous sections.

Wireless configuration makes use of the same set of Wireless Extensions. The Wireless Tools package is a set of network configuration and reporting tools for wireless devices installed on a Linux system. They are currently supported and developed as part of the Linux Wireless Extension and Wireless Tools Project, an open source project maintained by Hewlett-Packard.

Wireless Tools

Wireless Tools consists of the configuration and report tools listed here:

Tool	Description
iwconfig	Sets the wireless configuration options basic to most wireless devices.
iwlist	Displays current status information of a device.
iwspy	Sets the list of IP addresses in a wireless network and checks the quality of their connections.
iwpriv	Accesses configuration options specific to a particular device.

The wireless LAN device will have an Ethernet name just like an Ethernet card. The appropriate modules will automatically be loaded, listing their aliases in the **/etc/modprobe.conf** file.

iwconfig

The **iwconfig** command works much like **ifconfig**, configuring a network connection. It is the tool used by the Internet Connection Wizard and by system-config-network to configure a wireless card. Alternatively, you can run **iwconfig** directly on a command line, specifying certain parameters. Added parameters let you set wireless-specific features such as the network name (nwid), the frequency or channel the card uses (freq or channel), and the bit rate for transmissions (rate). See the **iwconfig** Man page for a complete listing of accepted parameters. Some of the commonly used parameters are listed in Table 14-3.

For example, to set the channel used for the wireless device installed as the first Ethernet device, you would use the following, setting the channel to 2:

```
iwconfig eth0 channel 2
```

You can also use **iwconfig** to display statistics for your wireless devices, just as **ifconfig** does. Enter the **iwconfig** command with no arguments or with the name of the device. Information such as the name, frequency, sensitivity, and bit rate is listed. Check also **/proc/net/wireless** for statistics.

Instead of using **iwconfig** directly to set parameters, you can specify them in the wireless device's configuration file. The wireless device configuration file will be located in the **/etc/sysconfig/network-scripts** directory and given a name like **ifcfg-eth1**, depending on the name of the device. This file will already contain many `iwconfig` settings. Any further setting can be set by assigning `iwconfig` values to the IWCONFIG parameter as shown here.

```
IWCONFIG="rate 11M"
```

Parameter	Description
essid	A network name
freq	The frequency of the connection
channel	The channel used
nwid or domain	The network ID or domain
mode	The operating mode used for the device, such as Ad Hoc, Managed, or Auto. Ad Hoc = one cell with no access point, Managed = network with several access points and supports roaming, Master = the node is an access point, Repeater = node forwards packets to other nodes, Secondary = backup master or repeater, Monitor = only receives packets
sens	The sensitivity, the lowest signal level at which data can be received
key or enc	The encryption key used
frag	Cut packets into smaller fragments to increase better transmission
bit or rate	Speed at which bits are transmitted. The auto option automatically falls back to lower rates for noisy channels
ap	Specify a specific access point
power	Power management for wakeup and sleep operations

Table 14-3: Commonly Used Parameters

iwpriv

The `iwpriv` command works in conjunction with `iwconfig`, allowing you set options specific to a particular kind of wireless device. With `iwpriv`, you can also turn on roaming or select the port to use. You use the *private-command* parameter to enter the device-specific options. The following example sets roaming on:

```
iwpriv eth0 roam on
```

iwspy

Your wireless device can check its connection to another wireless device it is receiving data from, reporting the quality, signal strength, and noise level of the transmissions. Your device can maintain a list of addresses for different devices it may receive data from. You use the `iwspy` tool to set or add the addresses that you want checked. You can list either IP addresses or the hardware versions. A + sign will add the address, instead of replacing the entire list:

```
iwspy eth0 +192.168.2.5
```

To display the quality, signal, and noise levels for your connections, you use the `iwspy` command with just the device name:

```
iwspy eth0
```

iwlist

To obtain more detailed information about your wireless device, such as all the frequencies or channels available, you use the `iwlist` tool. Using the device name with a particular parameter, you can obtain specific information about a device, including the frequency, access points, rate, power features, retry limits, and encryption keys used. You can use iwlist to obtain information about faulty connections. The following example will list the frequencies used on the **eth0** wireless device.

```
iwlist eth0 freq
```

linux-wlan

The linux-wlan project (**www.linux-wlan.org**) has developed a separate set of wireless drivers designed for Prism-based wireless cards supporting the new 802.11 wireless standard. The linux-wlan drivers are not currently included with Fedora; you will have to download the drivers. The original source code package is available from the wlan-linux site at **www.linux-wlan.org**. The current package is linux-wlan-ng. You will have to unpack and compile the drivers.

The drivers will install WLAN devices, with device configurations placed in the **/etc/sysconfig/network-scripts** directory. For example, the configuration for the first WLAN device will be in the **ifcfg-wlan0** script. General wireless options are placed in the **/etc/wlan.conf** configuration file.

Setting Up Your Firewall: system-config-firewall

To set up your firewall, run system-config-firewall on your system (Firewall in the System Administration window and menu). Fedora 10 uses a new system configuration tool called system-config-firewall, to set up your firewall (see Figure 14-19). This replaces system-config-securitylevel which is no longer available (SELinux is configured with a separate tool called system-config-selinux).

You can run your firewall on a stand-alone system directly connected to the Internet, or on a gateway system that connects a local network to the Internet. Most networks now use dedicated routers for Internet access which have their own firewalls. If, instead, you decide to use a Linux system as a gateway, it will have at least two network connections, one for the local network and an Internet connection device for the Internet. Make sure that the firewall is applied to the Internet device, not to your local network.

The top button bar has buttons for a Firewall wizard, Apply button to effect any changes, Reload to restore your saved firewall, and Disable and Enable buttons. You can enable or disable your firewall with the Enable and Disable buttons (see Figure 14-19). If the Firewall is active, only the Disable button can be used, and visa versa.

A default configuration will already be in place. To create your own basic custom configuration just run the Wizard, by clicking the Wizard button.

You can also make changes directly to different firewall components. The Firewall Configuration window will show several panes, selected from entries on a sidebar. The panes are Trusted Services, Other Ports, Trusted Interfaces, Masquerading, and Custom Rules.

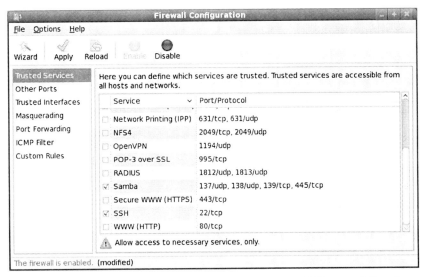

Figure 14-19: The system-config-firewall showing Firewall Trusted Services

The features many users may want to change are the Trusted services. A Linux system will often be used to run servers for a network. If you are creating a strong firewall but still want to run a service such as a Web server, allow users to perform FTP file transfers on the Internet, permit Samba desktop browsing, or allow remote encrypted connections such as SSH, you will have to specify them in the Trusted Services panel. Samba desktop browsing lets you access your Samba shares, like remote Windows file systems, from your GNOME or KDE desktops.

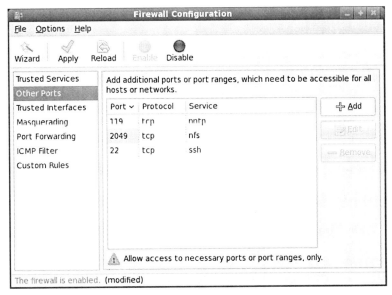

Figure 14-20: Firewall Other Ports configuration

The Other Ports section lets you specify ports that you may want opened for certain services, like BitTorrent (see Figure 14-20). Click the Add button to open a dialog where you can enter the port number along with the protocol to control (tcp or udp).

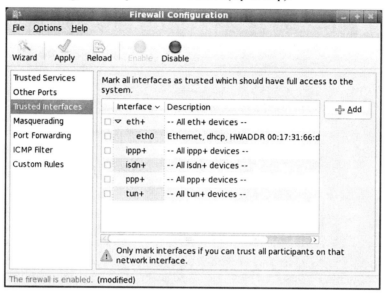

Figure 14-21: Firewall Trusted Interfaces

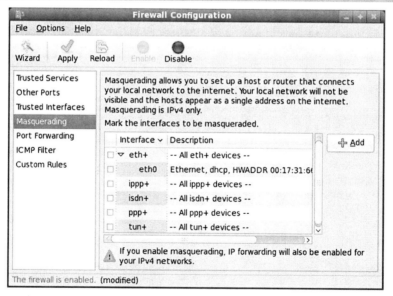

Figure 14-22: Firewall Masquerading

The Trusted interfaces panel lets you select those hardware network connections like NIC cards, modems, or wireless connections that can be trusted (see Figure 14-21). This is usually applied to interfaces connected to a local network or directly to a local router or server (like a print server). Interfaces connected to wider network like the Internet should not be trusted.

If your system is being used as gateway to the Internet for your local network, you can implement masquerading to hide your local hosts from outside access from the Internet (see Figure 14-22). This, though, also requires IP forwarding which is automatically enabled when you choose masquerading. Local hosts will still be able to access the Internet, but they will masquerade as your gateway system. You would select for masquerading the interface that is connected to the Internet. Masquerading is available only for IPv4 networks, not IPv6 networks.

The Custom Rules panel lets you load an IP-tables file that can hold customized firewall rules (see Figure 14-23). Instead of having to choose whether to use system-config-firewall or to create an entire set of rules in an IP-tables file, you can use system-config-firewall to automatically configure the standard firewall rules and then set up an IP-tables file that holds only customized rules for your system. These will be added to the standard set implemented by system-config-firewall. When you load the file you will also have to determine whether the IPtables fie holds IPv4 or IPv6 protocol rules (Address type). You will also have to select which table the firewall rules are meant for. There are three choices: filter (Netfilter rules), mangle (the mangle table used for rewriting addresses), and the nat table. Use the File entry to open a browser to locate the IPtables file you want to load.

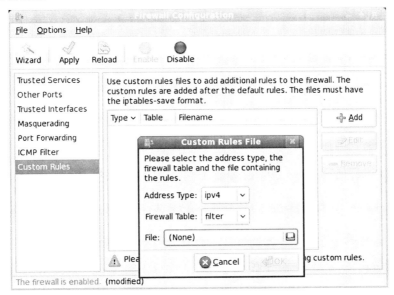

Figure 14-23: Firewall Custom Rules

Setting Up Windows Network Access: Samba

Most local and home networks may include some systems working on Microsoft Windows and others on Linux. You may need to let a Windows computer access a Linux system or vice versa. Windows, due to its massive market presence, tends to benefit from both drivers and applications support not found for Linux. Though there are equivalent applications on Linux, many of which are as good or better, some applications run best on Windows, if for no other reason than that the vendor only develops drivers for Windows.

One solution is to use the superior server and storage capabilities of Linux to manage and hold data, while using Windows systems with their unique applications and drivers to run applications. For example, you could use a Linux system to hold pictures and videos, while using Windows systems to show or run them. Video or pictures could be streamed through your router to the system that wants to run them. In fact many commercial DVR systems use a version of Linux to manage video recording and storage. Another use would be to enable Windows systems to use devices like printers that may be connected to a Linux system, or vice versa.

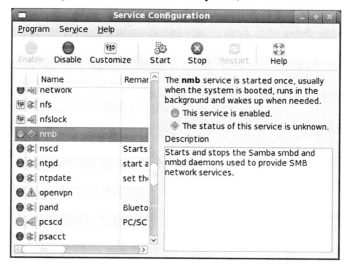

Figure 14-24: system-config-services for samba, System | Administration | Services

To allow Windows to access a Linux system, as well as Linux to access a Windows system, you use the Samba server. First be sure that Samba is installed along with the Services tool. Open the Add/Remove Software tool in the Administration menu (PackageKit). Click the Server entry or search for samba. On the left pane, and scroll down and locate the **Samba** and **system-config-samba** packages.

Be sure that the firewall on your Windows system is not blocking Samba. Run system-config-firewall (System | Administration | Firewall) and choose the Trusted services pane. Make sure that the Samba service and Samba client entries are checked, allowing Samba to operate on your system. To enable access immediately, restart your firewall. In the system-config-services window (System | Administration | Services), select IPtables and click Restart, then do the same for IPTables6. IPtables is the server name for your firewall. Also, make sure that Samba access is permitted by SELinux (system-config-selinux). Use the SELinux Management tool (System | Administration) and on the Boolean pane enable Samba access. Alternatively you could just disable SELinux by placing it in the Permissive mode (Status pane).

Samba has two methods of authentication, shares and users. User authentication requires that there be corresponding accounts in the Windows and Linux systems. They can have the same name, though a Windows user can be mapped to a Linux account. A share can be made open to any user and function as an extension of the user's storage space.

Use the system-config-services configuration (System | Administration | Services) to have Samba start up automatically (see Figure 14-24). Then on the Background Services panel click the check boxed for both the **smb** and **nmb** entries. Click Save to save the startup specification and click Restart to start the Samba server. Also, make sure firewall access

To set up simple file sharing on a Linux system, you first need to configure your Samba server. You can do this by directly editing the **/etc/samba/samba.conf** file or by using the **system-config-samba** configuration tool (System | Administration | Samba). If you just edit the **/etc/samba/samba.conf** file, you first need to specify the name of your Windows network.

system-config-samba

The system-config-samba tool provides a simple means to configure your Samba server, adding Samba users and specifying Samba shares. It will also automatically configure all the printers on your Linux system as Samba shared printers, allowing you to use them from any connected Windows system. You can start system-config-samba from the Samba entry in the System | Administration menu (see Figure 14-25). The system-config-samba tool will list all the shares for your server. You can use buttons at the top to manage your shares, adding new ones or deleting current ones. If you delete, the actual directories are not removed; they just lose their status as shared directories.

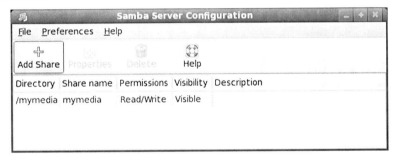

Figure 14-25: system-config-samba

Samba server configuration

To configure your Samba server, select Server Settings from the system-config-samba Preferences menu. This opens a window with two panels; Basic and Security (see Figure 14-26). On the Basic panel, you enter the Samba server workgroup name. This will be the same name used as the workgroup by all your Windows systems. The default names given by Windows are MSHOME or WORKGROUP. Use the name already given to your Windows network. For home networks, you can decide on your own. Just make sure all your computers use the same network name. Check your Windows Control Panel's System applet to make sure.

The description is the name you want displayed for your Samba server on your Windows systems. On the Security panel, you specify the authentication mode, the password encryption option, and the name of the guest account, along with the authentication server.

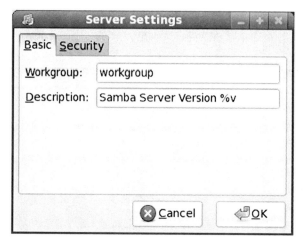

Figure 14-26: Samba Server Settings

By default User security is used. You could also use share or server security. These are more open, but both have been deprecated and may be dropped in later versions.

> The authentication mode specifies the access level, which can be user, share, server, ADS, or domain. User-level access restricts access by user password, whereas share access opens access to any guest.

> Normally, you would elect to encrypt passwords, rather than have them passed over your network in plain text.

> The Guest user is the name of the account used to allow access to shares or printers that you want open to any user, without having to provide a password. The pop-up menu will list all your current users, with "No Guest Account" as the selected default. Unless you want to provide access by everyone to a share, you would not have a Guest account.

Adding Samba Users

For user authentication you will have to associate a Windows user with a particular Samba user. Samba maintains its own password listing for users. To provide a user Samba access, you need to register the user as a Samba user. Select Samba Users from the Preferences menu to open the Samba Users window, clicking the Add User button. Here you enter the Unix Username, the Windows Username, and the Samba Password. There is an additional box for confirming the Samba password. The Unix Username is a pop-up window listing all the users on your Samba server.

Select Samba Users in the system-config-samba Preferences menu. This opens the Samba Users window listing all current Samba users. These correspond to user accounts already set up on your system. To add a Samba user, click the Add User button on the right. This opens a Create Samba User window with four entries (see Figure 14-27). Here you enter the Unix Username, the Windows Username, and the Samba Password. There is an additional box for confirming the Samba password. The Unix Username is a pop-up window listing all the users on the Linux system hosting your Samba server.

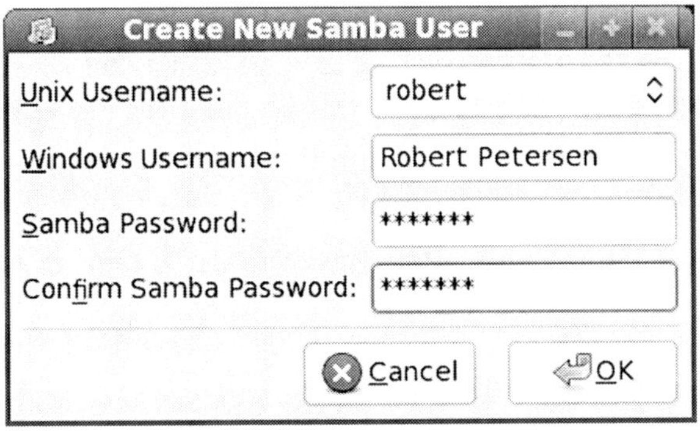

Figure 14-27: Adding Samba users

Select a Linux user to us from the Unix Username pop up menu, and then enter the corresponding Windows user. The Windows username can be different from the Linux account (Linux user name). You then a password that Windows user can use to access Linux. This is the Samba password for that user. Samba maintains its own set of passwords that users will need to access a Samba share. When a Windows user wants to access a Samba share, they will need their Samba password.

Once you create a Samba user, its name will appear in the list of Samba users on the Samba Users window. To later modify or delete a Samba user, Use the same Samba Users window, select the user from the list, and click the Edit User button to change entries like the password, or click the Delete User button to remove the Samba user.

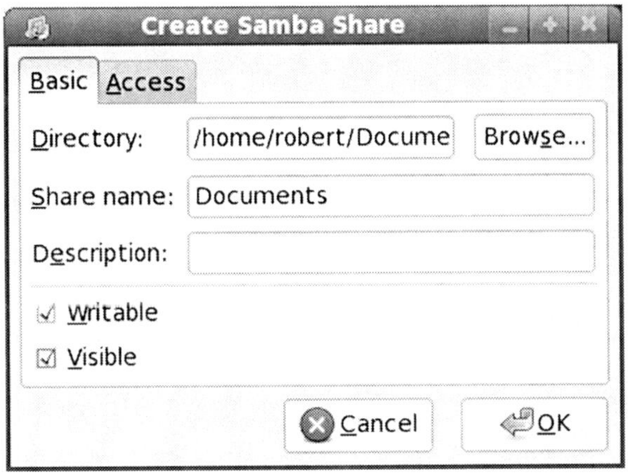

Figure 14-28: Create Samba Shares

Adding Samba shares on Linux systems

To set up a simple share, click Add Share, which opens a Create A Share window. On the Basic panel you select the Linux directory to share (click Browse to find it), and then specify whether it will be writable and visible. You also provide a name for the share, as well as any description you want (see Figure 14-28).

On the Access panel, you can restrict access to certain users or allow access to all users. All Samba users on your system will be listed with check boxes where you can select those you want to give access (see Figure 14-29).

Once created, the share will appear in the main system-config-samba window. The share's directory, share name, its visibility, read/write permissions, and description will be shown. To later modify a share, click on its entry and then click on the Properties menu. This opens an Edit samba share window with the same Basic and Access panels you used to create the share.

Accessing Samba shares

When a Windows user wants to access the share on the Linux system, they open their My Network Places and then "Add a network place" to add a network place entry for the share, or View workgroup computers to see computers on your Windows network. Selecting the Linux Samba server will display your Samba shares. To access the share, the user will be required to enter in the user Samba user name and the Samba password. You have the option of having the username and password remembered for automatic access.

Figure 14-29: Create Samba Shares: Access

On your Linux system, to restart Samba with your new configuration use the Services tool, restarting both **nmb** and **smb** (System | Administration | Services).

Note: As an alternative to system-config-samba, you can use SWAT, a Samba Web browser based tool that supports complex configurations. Install the swat package and the xinetd package. Be sure to also enable swat with the chkconfig tool. SWAT will be accessible at port 901 on the system hosting the samba server.

Network Analysis Tools

You can use a variety of network tools to perform tasks such as obtaining information about other systems on your network, accessing other systems, and communicating directly with other users. Network information can be obtained using utilities such as `ping`, `finger`, `traceroute`, and `host`. Talk and messenger clients like Ekiga for VoIP and CIQ enable you to communicate directly with other users on your network.

GNOME Network Tools: gnome-nettool

For the GNOME desktop, the **gnome-nettool** utility provides a GNOME interface for entering the `ping` and `traceroute` commands (see Figure 12-30), as well as Finger, Whois, and Lookup for querying users and hosts on the network (Applications | System Tools | Network Tools). Whois will provide domain name information about a particular domain, and Lookup will provide both domain name and IP addresses (see Figure 14-30). It also includes network status tools such as **netstat** and **portscan**. The first panel, Devices, describes your connected network devices, including configuration and transmission information about each device, such as the hardware address and bytes transmitted. Both IPv4 and IPv6 host IP addresses will be listed.

Network Information Tools	Description
`ping`	Detects whether a system is connected to the network.
`finger`	Obtains information about users on the network.
`who`	Checks what users are currently online.
`whois`	Obtains domain information.
`host`	Obtains network address information about a remote host.
`traceroute`	Tracks the sequence of computer networks and hosts your message passes through.
`ethereal`	Protocol analyzer to examine network traffic.
`gnome-nettool`	GNOME interface for various network tools including ping, finger, and traceroute.
`mtr` and `xmtr`	My traceroute combines both ping and traceroute operations (Traceroute on System Tools menu).

Table 14-4: Network Tools

Network Information: ping, finger, traceroute, and host

You can use the `ping`, `finger`, `traceroute`, and `host` commands to find out status information about systems and users on your network. The `ping` command is used to check if a remote system is up and running. You use `finger` to find out information about other users on your network, seeing if they are logged in or if they have received mail; `host` displays address information about a system on your network, giving you a system's IP and domain name addresses; and `traceroute` can be used to track the sequence of computer networks and systems your message passed through on its way to you. Table 14-4 lists various network information tools.

ping

The `ping` command detects whether a system is up and running. `ping` takes as its argument the name of the system you want to check. If the system you want to check is down, `ping` issues a timeout message indicating a connection could not be made. The next example checks to see if **www.redhat.com** is up and connected to the network:

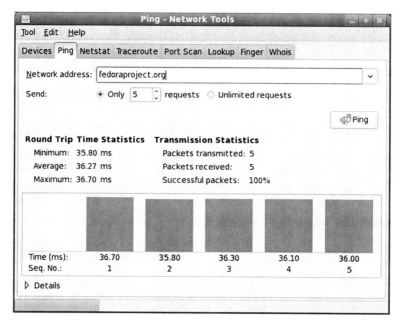

Figure 14-30: Gnome network tool

```
# ping www.redhat.com
PING www.redhat.com (209.132.177.50) 56(84) bytes of data.
64 bytes from www.redhat.com (209.132.177.50):icmp_seq=1 ttl=118 time=36.7ms
64 bytes from www.redhat.com (209.132.177.50):icmp_seq=2 ttl=118 time=36.9ms
--- www.redhat.com ping statistics ---
4 packets transmitted, 3 received, 25% packet loss, time 3000ms
rtt min/avg/max/mdev = 36.752/37.046/37.476/0.348 ms
```

You can also use `ping` with an IP address instead of a domain name. With an IP address, `ping` can try to detect the remote system directly without having to go through a domain name server to translate the domain name to an IP address. This can be helpful for situations where your network's domain name server may be temporarily down and you want to check if a particular remote host on your network is connected.

```
# ping 209.132.177.50
```

Note: A `ping` operation could also fail if `ping` access is denied by a network's firewall.

finger and who

You can use the `finger` command to obtain information about other users on your network and the `who` command to see what users are currently online on your system. The `who` and `w` commands lists all users currently connected, along with when, how long, and where they logged in. The `w` command provides more detailed information. It has several options for specifying the level of detail. The `who` command is meant to operate on a local system or network; `finger` can operate on large networks, including the Internet, though most systems block it for security reasons.

Note: Ethereal is a protocol analyzer that can capture network packets and display detailed information about them. You can detect what kind of information is being transmitted on your network as well as its source and destination. Ethereal is used primarily for network and server administration.

host

With the **host** command, you can find network address information about a remote system connected to your network. This information usually consists of a system's IP address, domain name address, domain name nicknames, and mail server. This information is obtained from your network's domain name server. For the Internet, this includes all systems you can connect to over the Internet.

The **host** command is an effective way to determine a remote site's IP address or URL. If you have only the IP address of a site, you can use **host** to find out its domain name. For network administration, an IP address can be helpful for making your own domain name entries in your **/etc/host** file. That way, you needn't rely on a remote domain name server (DNS) for locating a site.

```
# host gnomefiles.org
gnomefiles.org has address 67.18.254.188
gnomefiles.org mail is handled by 10 mx.zayda.net.
```

```
# host 67.18.254.188
188.254.18.67.in-addr.arpa domain name pointer gnomefiles.org.
```

traceroute

Internet connections are made through various routes, traveling through a series of interconnected gateway hosts. The path from one system to another could take different routes, some of which may be faster than others. For a slow connection, you can use **traceroute** to check the route through which you are connected to a host, monitoring the speed and the number of intervening gateway connections a route takes. The **traceroute** command takes as its argument the hostname or IP addresses for the system whose route you want to check. Options are available for specifying parameters like the type of service (**-t**) or the source host (**-s**). The **traceroute** command will return a list of hosts the route traverses, along with the times for three probes sent to each gateway. Times greater than five seconds are displayed with a asterisk, *.

```
traceroute rabbit.mytrek.com
```

You can also use the mtr or xmtr tools to perform both ping and traces (Traceroute on the System Tools menu).

15. Printing

Automatic Printer Detection

system-config-printer

Editing Printer Configuration

Printer Classes

Adding New Printers Manually

Published Printers

Remote Printers

Printers remotely accessed from Windows

This chapter covers the new version of the Printing configuration tool, system-config-printer, now used in Fedora 10. The configuration panes are similar to Fedora 9 with several important exceptions. When you select a printer driver, you can now choose to download it from the OpenPrinting repository. A separate dialog is now used to select both system-wide and personal default printers. In general, the configuration and management interface is organized into separate windows, instead of using a single window with selectable servers and printers.

Automatic printer detection

Whenever you first attach a local printer, like a USB printer, you will be asked to perform basic configuration such as confirming the make and model. Removable local printers are managed by udev and HAL, tools designed to automatically detect and configure removable devices. A message will appear like that shown in Figure 15-1, as soon as you connect your USB printer.

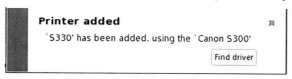

Printer added

`S330' has been added, using the `Canon S300'

Find driver

Figure 15-1: Printer detection notification

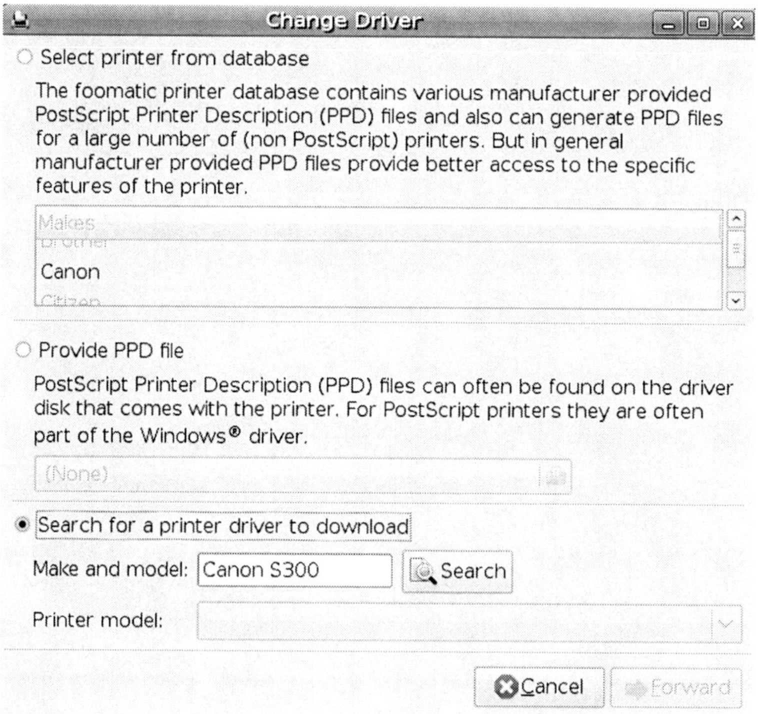

Change Driver

○ Select printer from database

The foomatic printer database contains various manufacturer provided PostScript Printer Description (PPD) files and also can generate PPD files for a large number of (non PostScript) printers. But in general manufacturer provided PPD files provide better access to the specific features of the printer.

> Makes
> brother
> Canon
> Citizen

○ Provide PPD file

PostScript Printer Description (PPD) files can often be found on the driver disk that comes with the printer. For PostScript printers they are often part of the Windows® driver.

(None)

● Search for a printer driver to download

Make and model: Canon S300   🔍 Search

Printer model:

❌Cancel   ➡ Forward

Figure 15-2: Change Printer driver

If a driver is available for your printer, it will be selected automatically for you. Should you want to use a different driver, or printer is being detected incorrectly, you can click on the Find diver button to select the driver. A Change Driver window opens up where you can enter in the printer configuration information (see Figure 15-2).

system-config-printer

To later change your configuration or to add a remote printer, you can use the printer configuration tool, system-config-printer. This utility enables you to select the appropriate driver for your printer, as well as set print options such as paper size and print resolutions. You can configure a printer connected directly to your local computer or a printer on a remote system on your network. You can start system-config-printer by selecting the Printing entry in the System | Administration menu.

Fedora 10 uses a more recent version of system-config-printer that has a slightly different interface. All the printer information and configuration formats are the same. You still have the same set of dialogs and panes for setting up a printer and displaying printer configuration. Instead of two panes you have a single window with icons for installed printers (see Figure 15-3).

Figure 15-3: system-config-printer tool

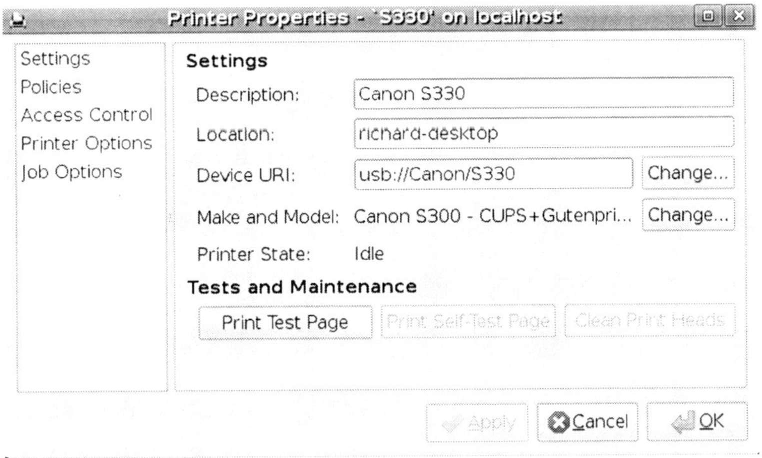

Figure 15-4: Printer properties window

To see the printer settings such as printer and job options, access controls, and policies, double-click on the printer icon or right-click and select Properties. The Printer Properties window opens up with five panes: Settings, Policies, Access Control, Printer Options, and Job Options (see Figure 15-4).

The Printer configuration window Printer menu lets you rename the printer, enable or disable it, and make it a shared printer. Select the printer icon and then click the Printer menu (see Figure 15-5). The Delete entry will remove a printer configuration. Use the Set As Default entry to make the printer a system-wide or personal default printer.

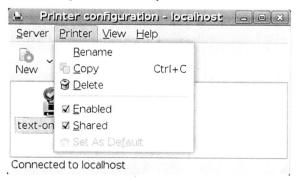

Figure 15-5: Printer configuration window Printer menu

The Printer icon menu is accesses by right-clicking on the printer icon (see Figure 15-6). It adds entries for accessing the printer properties and viewing the print queue. If the printer is already a default, there is no Set As Default entry. The properties entry opens the printer properties window for that printer.

Figure 15-6: Printer icon menu

The View Print Queue entry opens the Document print status window listing jobs for that printer. You can change the queue position as well as stop or delete jobs (see Figure 15-7). From the View menu you can choose to display printed jobs and the printer status. You will be notified if a job should fail. Click the Diagnose button to start the printing trouble- shooter to find the reason.

Figure 15-7: Printer queue

To check the server settings, select Settings from the Server menu. This opens a new window showing the CUPS printer server settings (see Figure 15-8).

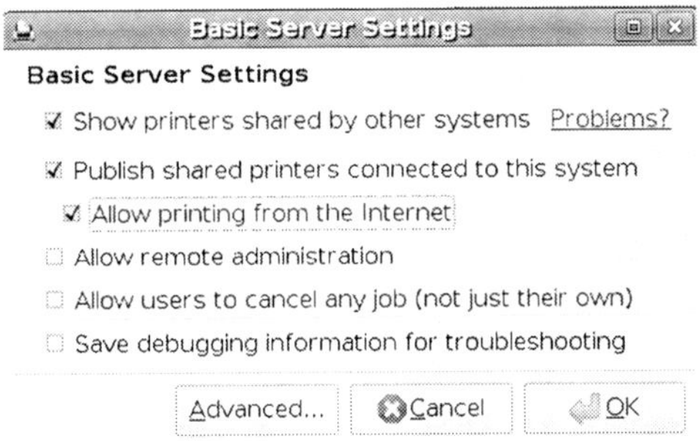

Basic Server Settings

Basic Server Settings

☑ Show printers shared by other systems Problems?

☑ Publish shared printers connected to this system

☑ Allow printing from the Internet

☐ Allow remote administration

☐ Allow users to cancel any job (not just their own)

☐ Save debugging information for troubleshooting

Advanced...   ✕ Cancel   ✓ OK

Figure 15-8: Server Settings

To select a particular CUPS server, select the Connect entry in the Server menu. This opens a "Connect to CUPS Server" window with a drop down menu listing all current CUPS servers from which to choose (see Figure 15-9).

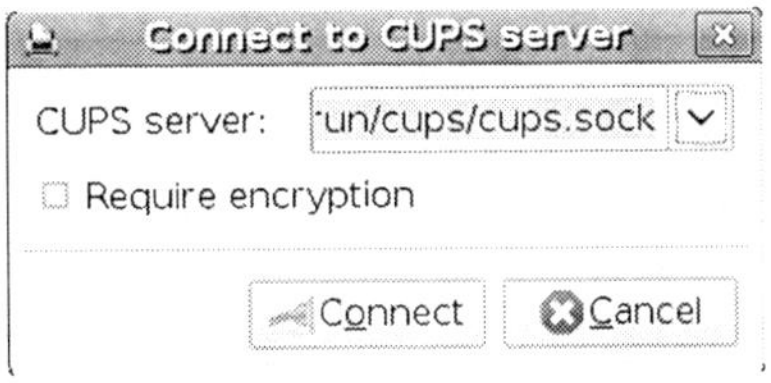

Connect to CUPS server

CUPS server: `un/cups/cups.sock` ⌄

☐ Require encryption

Connect   ✕ Cancel

Figure 15-9: Selecting a CUPS server

Editing Printer Configuration

To edit an installed printer, double click its icon in the Printer configuration window, or right-click and select the Properties entry. This opens a Printer Properties window for that printer. A sidebar lists configuration panes. Click on one to display that pane. There are configuration entries for Settings, Policies, Access Control, Printer Options, and Job Control (see Figure 15-10).

Once you have made your changes, you can click Apply to save your changes and restart the printer daemon. You can test your printer with a PostScript, A4, or ASCII test sheet selected from the Test menu.

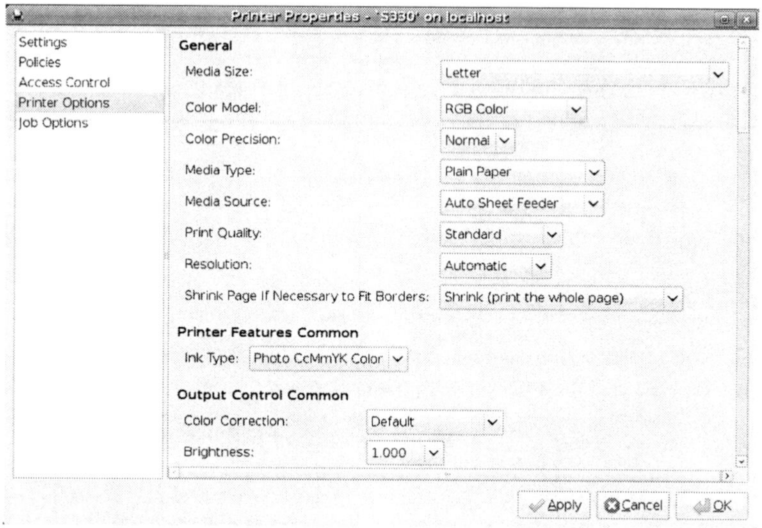

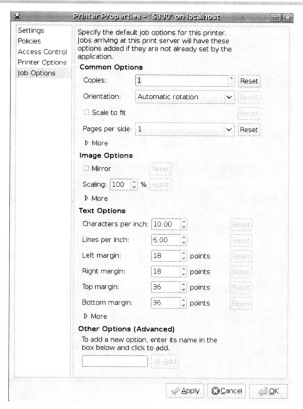

Figure 15-10: Printer Options pane

Figure 15-11: Jobs Options pane

On the Settings pane you can change configuration settings like the driver and the printer name, enable or disable the printer, or specify whether to share it or not (see Figure 15-4). Should you need to change the selected driver, click on the Change button next to the Make and Model entry. This will open printer model and driver windows like those described in the Add new printer manually section. There you can specify the model and driver you want to use, even loading your own driver.

The Policies pane lets you specify a start and end banner, as well as an error policy which specifies whether to retry or abort the print job, or stop the printer should an error occur. The Access Control pane allows you to deny access to certain users.

The Printer Options pane is where you set particular printing features like paper size and type, print quality, and the input tray to use (see Figure 15-11).

On the Job Options pane you can select default printing features (see Figure 15-8). A pop-up menu provides a list of printing feature categories to choose from. You then click the Add button to add the category, selecting a particular feature from a pop-up menu. You can set such features as the number of copies (copies); letter, glossy, or A4-sized paper (media); the kind of document, for instance, text, PDF, PostScript, or image (document format); and single- or double-sided printing (sides).

Default System-wide and Personal Printers

To make printer the default printer, either right-click on the printer icon and select "Set As Default", or single click on the printer icon and then from the Printer configuration window's Printer menu select the "Set As Default" entry (see Figure 15-5 and 15-6). A Set Default Printer dialog open with options for setting the system-wide default or setting the personal default (see Figure 15-12). The system-wide default printer is the default for your entire network served by your CUPS server, not just your local system.

Figure 15-12: Set Default Printer dialog

The system-wide default printer will have a green check mark emblem on its printer icon in the Printer configuration window.

Should you wish to use a different printer yourself as your default printer, you can designate it as your personal default. To make a printer your personal default, select the entry "Set as my personal default printer" in the Set Default Printer dialog. A personal emblem, a heart, will appear on the printer's icon in the Printer configuration window. In Figure 15-13, the S300-windows printer is the system-wide default, whereas the S330 printer is the personal default.

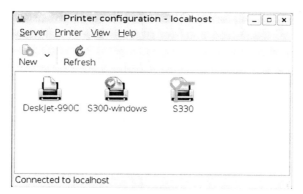

Figure 15-13: System-wide and personal default printers

If you have more than one printer on your system, you can make one the default by clicking Make Default Printer button in the printer's properties Settings pane.

Printer Classes

The Class entry in the New menu lets you create a printer class. You can access the New menu from the Server menu or from the New button. This feature lets you select a group of printers to print a job instead of selecting just one. That way, if one printer is busy or down, another printer can be automatically selected to perform the job. Installed printers can be assigned to different classes. When you click the Class entry in the New menu, a New Class window opens. Here you can enter the name for the class, any comments, and the location (your host name is entered by default). The next screen lists available printers on right side (Other printers) and the printers you assigned to the class on the left side (Printers in this class). Use the arrow button to add or remove printers to the class. Click Apply when finished. The class will appear under the Local Classes heading on the main system-config-printer window. Panes for a selected class are much the same as for a printer, with a members pane instead of a print control pane. In the Members pane you can change what printers belong to the class

Adding New Printers Manually

Printers are normally detected automatically, though in the case of older printers and network printers, you may need to add the printer manually. In this case click the New button and select Printer. A New Printer window opens up displaying series of dialog boxes where you select the connection, model, drivers, and printer name with location.

On the Select Connection screen, you select the appropriate printer connection information. Connected local printer brands will already be listed by name, such as Canon, whereas for remote printers you specify the type of network connection, like Windows printers via Samba for printers connected to a Windows system, AppSocket/HP Direct for HP printers connected directly to your network. The Internet Printing Protocol (ipp) for printers on Linux and Unix systems on your network.

For most connected printers, your connection is usually determined by the device hotplug services udev and HAL, which now manage all devices. Printers connected to your local system will be first entries on the list. A USB printer will simply be described as a USB printer, using the usb URI designation (see Figure 15-14 and 15-4).

Figure 15-14: Selecting a new printer connection

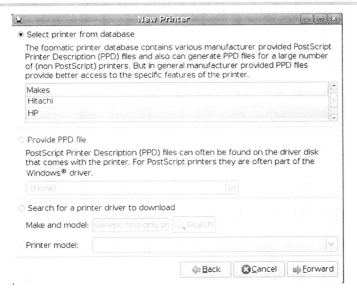

Figure 15-15: Printer manufacturer for new printers

For an older local printer, you will need to choose the port the printer is connected to, such as LPT1 for the first parallel port used for older parallel printers, or Serial Port #1 for a printer connected to the first serial port. For this example an older parallel printer will be set up, LPT #1.

On the next screen you select your printer manufacturer, choosing it from a printer database (See figure 3-15). You can also choose to load your own printer driver (PPD file).

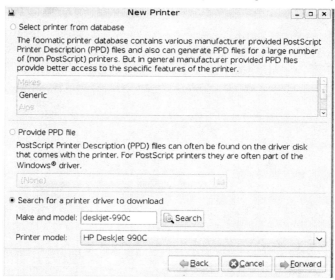

Figure 15-16: Searching for a printer driver from the OpenPrinting repository

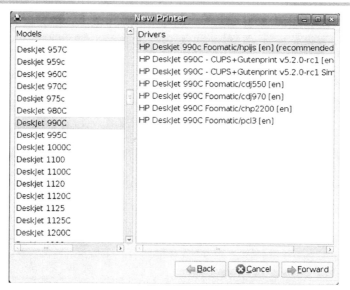

Figure 15-17: Printer Model and driver for new printers using local database

Instead of manually selecting the driver, you can try to search for it on OpenPrinting repository (see Figure 15-16). Click the Search for a printer driver to download entry. Enter the printer name and model and click the Search button. From the pop up menu labeled Printer model, select the driver for your printer. Then click Forward.

If you are selecting a printer from the database, then, on the next screen you select that manufacturer's model along with its driver (see Figure 15-17). For some older printer, though the driver can be located on the online repository, you will still choose it from the local database (the drivers are the same). The selected drivers for your printer will be listed. You can find out more about the printer and driver by clicking the Printer and Driver buttons at the bottom of the screen. Then click the Forward button.

You then enter in your printer name and location (see Figure 15-18). These will be entered for you using the printer model and your system's host name. You can change the printer name to anything you want. When ready, click Apply.

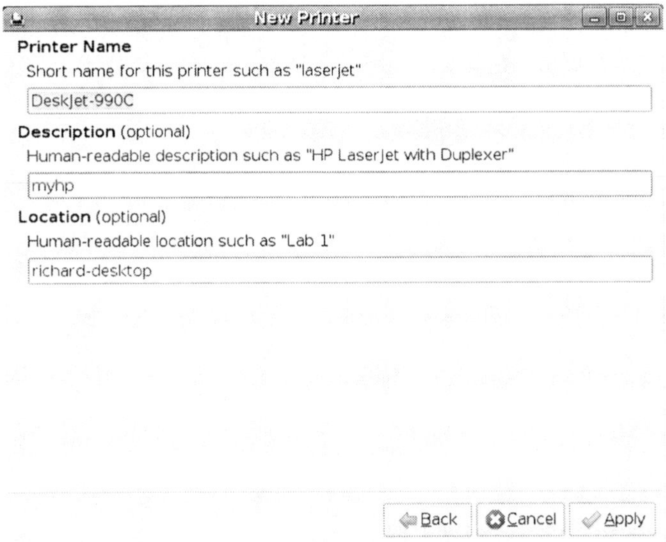

Figure 15-18: Printer Name and Location for new printers

You then see an icon for your printer displayed in the Printer configuration window. You are now ready to print.

Published Printers

If you choose to publish your local printers, then an added entry will appear for the printer in the Connections window (see Figure 15-19). The printer will be given an IPP protocol address by which it can be referenced by other hosts on your network. You can choose to publish printers by selecting the "Published shared printers connected to this system" entry in the Basic Server Settings dialog (see Figure 15-8). You can open the dialog by selecting Settings in the Printer configuration window Server menu.

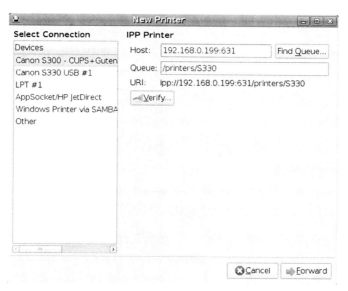

Figure 15-19: Printer Connection for new printers

Remote Printers

To install a remote printer that is attached to a Windows system or another Linux system running CUPS, you specify its location using special URI protocols. For a locally attached USB printer, the USB URI is uses, **usb**. For another CUPS printer on a remote host, the protocol used is **ipp**, for Internet Printing Protocol, whereas for a Windows printer, it would be **smb**. Older UNIX or Linux systems using LPRng would use the **lpd** protocol

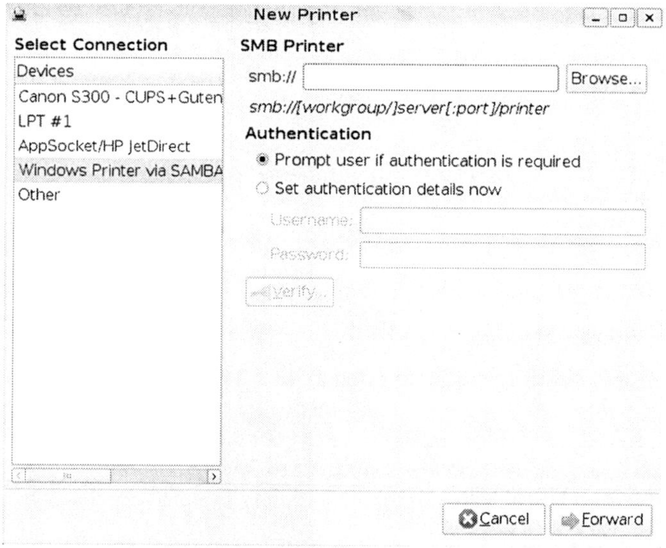

Figure 15-20: Selecting a Windows printer

You can also use system-config-printer to set up a remote printer on Linux, UNIX, or Windows networks. When you add a new printer or edit one, the New Printer/Select Connection dialog will list possible remote connection types. When you select a remote connection entry, a pane will be displayed where you can enter configuration information.

For a remote Linux or UNIX printer, select either Internet Printing Protocol (ipp), which is used for newer systems, or LPD/LPR Host or Printer, which is used for older systems. Both panes display entries for the Host name and the Printer name. For the Host name, enter the hostname for the system that controls the printer. For the Printer name, enter the device name on that host for the printer. The LPD/LPR dialog also has a probe button for detecting the printer.

For an Apple or HP jet direct printer on your network, select the AppSocket/HP jetDirect entry. You are prompted to enter the IP address and printer name.

A "Windows printer via Samba" is one located on a Windows network (see Figure 15-20). You need to specify the Windows server (host name or IP address), the name of the share, the name of the printer's workgroup, and the username and password. The format of the printer SMB URL is shown on the SMP Printer pane. The share is the hostname and printer name in the **smb** URI format *//workgroup/hostname/printername*. The workgroup is the windows network workgroup that the printer belongs to. On small networks there is usually only one. The hostname is the computer where the printer is located. The username and password can be for the printer resource itself, or for access by a particular user. The pane will display a box at the top where you can enter the share host and printer name as a **smb** URI.

You can click the Browse button to open a SMB Browser window, where you can select the printer from a listing of Windows hosts on your network (see Figure 15-21). For example, if your Windows network is WORKGROUP, then the entry WORKGROUP will be shown, which you can then expand to list all the Windows hosts on that network (if your network is MSHOME, then that is what will be listed).

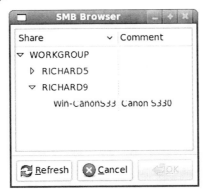

Figure 15-21: SMB Browser, selecting a remote windows printer

When you make your selection, the corresponding URL will show up in the **smb://** box (See Figure 15-22). If you are using the Firestarter firewall, be sure to turn it off before browsing a Windows workgroup for a printer, unless already configured to allow Samba access. Also on the pane, you can enter in any needed Samba authentication, if required, like user name or password. Check "Authentication required" to allow you to enter the Samba Username and Password.

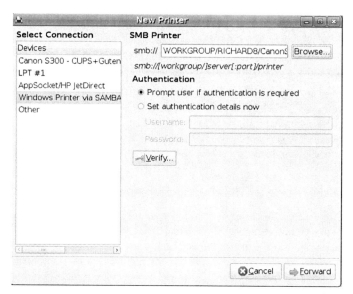

Figure 15-22: Remote windows printer connection configuration

You then continue with install screens for the printer model, driver, and name. Once installed, you can then access the printer properties just as you would any printer (see Figure 15-23).

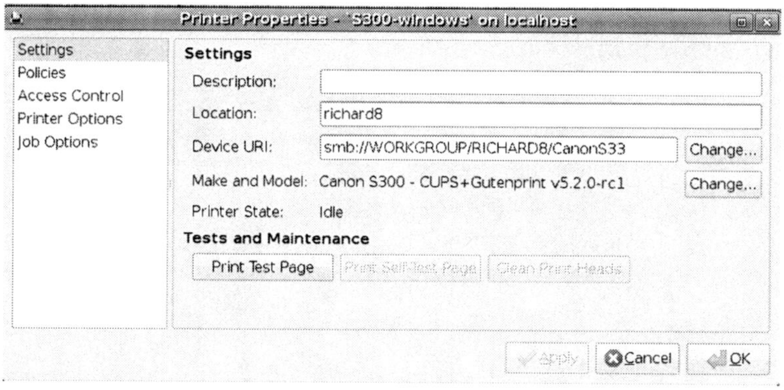

Figure 15-23: Remote Windows printer Settings

To access an SMB shared remote printer, you need to install Samba and have the Server Message Block services enabled using the smb and nmb daemons. The Samba service will be enabled by default. The service is enabled by checking the Windows Folders entry in the Gnome Services tool (System | Administration | Services). Printer sharing must, in turn, be enabled on the Windows network.

Linux Printers remotely accessed from Windows

On a Windows system, like WIndows XP, you can use the Add Printer Wizard to locate a shared printer on a Linux system (see Figure 15-24). Locate the Fedora system, click on it, and the shared printers on the Fedora system will be listed.

Tip: If the Windows driver for your printer on your Windows system should fail, you could just attach printer to a Linux system and use the Linux drivers, even remotely accessing the printer from your Windows system.

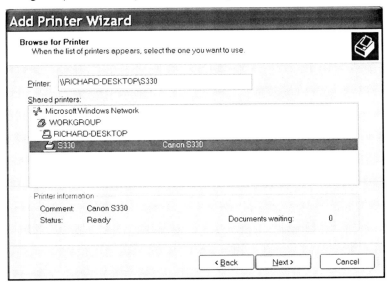

Figure 15-24: Remote Linux printer selection on Windows

Appendix A: Getting Fedora

The Fedora Linux distribution installs a professional-level and very stable Linux system along with the KDE and GNOME GUI interfaces, flexible and easy-to-use system configuration tools, an extensive set of Internet servers, a variety of different multimedia applications, and thousands of Linux applications of all kinds. You can find recent information about Red Hat Fedora Project at **http://fedoraproject.org**.

Most Fedora software is available for download from the Fedora repository. Install disks are available also, either as smaller desktop only installs, or larger server installs. You can every use the Live CD to install Fedora. Fedora distribution strategy relies on install disks with a selected collection of software, which can be later updated and enhanced from the very large collection of software on the Fedora repository. This means that the collection of software in an initial installation can be relatively small. Software on the Fedora repository is also continually updated, so any installation will likely have to undergo extensive updates from the repository.

Downloading Images

To obtain Fedora 10, just go to the Fedora Project Web site and click on the Get Fedora link. Here you will see links for both bittorrent or direct download for the different Fedora Install DVD and Fedora Live versions. The Direct downloads link to a currently available mirror site.

    http:// www.fedoraproject.org/get-fedora

You could also directly access a Fedora mirror site by entering the following URL. You would then need to navigate through the **releases** and **8** directories to find the Fedora and Live directories where the Fedora Install and Live iso images are kept.

    http://download.fedoraproject.org

You can also access a specific mirror at the following URL. Here will be listed the current Fedora mirror and their addresses.

    http://mirrors.fedoraproject.org

A detailed description for all the Fedora download options, including all the ISO discs you will need and links to mirror sites is available at the following URL. Check this site for the latest download procedures.

`http://www.fedoraproject.org/wiki/Distribution/Download`

Alternatively, you can also still download directly from the Fedora site using the following link at **http://download.fedora.redhat.com**. This site does not have the DVD, only the CDs and package files.

`http://download.fedora.redhat.com/pub/fedora/linux/releases/`

The direct downloads can be very fast with broadband DSL or cable, using an FTP client like **gFTP** (Applications | Internet menu). Web-client download with browsers like Firefox tend to be slower.

Install DVD and Live Images

To download Fedora 10 for installation from a DVD/CD-ROM drive, you download either the Fedora Install DVD image or a Fedora Live image. The Fedora Install and Live images are large files that have the extension .iso. The Fedora Install DVD resides within the Fedora subdirectory, under the respective version (i386, x86_64, or ppc), in an iso directory (Fedora/i386/iso). The Live images reside in the Live subdirectory, under the respective versions (i686, x86_64, and ppc). Once they are downloaded, you burn them to a disc using your CD or DVD writer and burner software, like the Nautilus file browser or K3b on Fedora.

There are ISO images for 64-bit system support and for the standard x86 (32-bit) support. Download the appropriate one. You cannot run a 64-bit version on an x86 (32-bit) system.

You do not have to download the images to a Linux system. You can just as easily download them on a Windows system and use Windows CD/DVD burner software to make the discs.

Using Jigdo

You can use any FTP or Web client, such as gFTP or Firefox, to download the CD image files. The DVD image, though, is a very large file that can take a long time to download, especially if the FTP site is very busy or if your have a slow Internet connection. An alternative for such very large files is to use BitTorrent. BitTorrent is a safe distributed download operation that is ideal for large files, letting many participants download and upload the same file, building a torrent that can run very fast for all participants. The Fedora 10 BitTorrent files are located both at **www.fedoraproject.org** and at

Using BitTorrent

You can use any FTP or Web client, such as gFTP or Firefox, to download the CD image files. The DVD image, though, is a very large file that can take a long time to download, especially if the FTP site is very busy or if your have a slow Internet connection. An alternative for such very large files is to use BitTorrent. BitTorrent is a safe distributed download operation that is ideal for large files, letting many participants download and upload the same file, building a torrent that can run very fast for all participants. The Fedora 10 BitTorrent files are located both at **http://fedoraproject.org** and at

```
http://torrent.fedoraproject.org/
```

You will first need to install the BitTorrent client. For Fedora, there are several BitTorrent clients available, including **transmission, azureus, rtorrent, ktorrent**, and the original **bittorrent**. A search on "bittorrent" in Add/Remove Software will display them (notice that bittorrent has two 't's and two 'r's in its spelling). Just install the ones you want.

Fedora Live Images

Fedora features a Live CDs with which you can run Fedora from a CD-ROM drive. Fedora provides both official and custom spins. The Live CD images are available from **www.fedoraproject.org/get-fedora** page, on the LiveCD segment. Fedora provides a GNOME and KDE desktop official Live CD spins.

Fedora Live: Available for i868, x86_64, and ppc. Includes Gnome desktop and productivity applications. 686 is a Live CD, x86_64 and ppc are DVDs.

Fedora KDE Live: Available for i686 and x86_64. Includes KDE desktop. 686 version is a CD, x86_64 is a DVD.

Fedora Custom Spins

Custom spins are also provided by supported special interest groups, see **http://fedoraproject.org/wiki/CustomSpins**. These can be downloaded from **http://spins.fedoraproject.org**, which lists torrent files on a Fedora Project Spins Tracker page. These include the following.

Fedora Developer Spin: i686 only. Includes GNOME desktop with development applications like Eclipse IDE, along with debugging and profiling tools, as well as documentation.

Fedora Electronic Lab (FEL): i686 only. CD. Designed for electronics engineers with tools for electronic component design and simulation.

Fedora Edu/Math Spin: Currently a Live DVD. Fedora configured for educational and math applications

XFCE Spin: Uses the Xfce desktop.

Once downloaded you can then burn the image to a DVD (CD for i686 version).

USB Live Disk

You can also install Fedora Live images to a USB disk. Your original data on the USB disk is preserved. To create a Live USB drive, you can either use the **liveusb-creator** application (**liveusb-creator** package), or the **livecd-iso-to-disk** command (**livecd-tools** package).

The liveusb-creator application is a GNOME application with an easy to use interface for creating a Live USB image from a Live CD iso image file. Once installed you can start liveusb-creator from Applications | System Tools | liveusb-creator. This opens the Fedora LiveUSB Creator window. Use the Browse button to locate the USB image or download one using the Download Fedora pop-up menu. The selected image will appear in the pane below. Use the Target Device pop-up menu to select the USB drive to use, if more than one. The Persistent Storage slider allows you to create an overlay memory segment on which changes and added data can be saved. When you are ready, just click the Create Live USB button on the bottom of the window.

To use the **livecd-iso-to-disk** command instead, first download **livecd-tools** package from the development repository, then use the **livecd-iso-to-disk** command to install the image. Use the Live image and the device name the USB disk as your arguments.

```
/usr/bin/livecd-iso-to-disk    F10-i686-Live.iso    /dev/sdb1
```

If you want to be able to save changes to the Fedora OS on the USB Live version, you set up overlay memory segment on the USB drive. To do this, use the **--overlay-size-mb** option with the size of the overlay in megabytes. Be sure your USB drive is large enough to accommodate both the overlay memory and the CD image. The following allows for 512 MB of persistent data.

```
livecd-iso-to-disk --overlay-size-mb 512  F10-i686-Live.iso  /dev/sbd1
```

Each Live CD also provides a **livecd-iso-to-disk** script in its LiveOS directory.

Appendix B: Additional Desktops

XFCE

LXDE

Sugar (OLPC)

Opendesktop

XFce4 Desktop

The XFce4 desktop is a lightweight desktop designed to run fast without the kind of overhead required for full featured desktops like KDE and GNOME. You can think of it as a window manager with desktop functionality. It includes its own file manger and panel, but the emphasis is on modularity and simplicity. Like GNOME, XFce4 is based on GTK+ GUI tools. The desktop consists of a collection of modules like the thunar file manager, xfce4-panel panel, and the xfwm4 window manager. Keeping with its focus on simplicity, XFce4 features only a few common applets on its panel. It small scale makes it appropriate for laptops or dedicated systems, that have no need for complex overhead found in other desktops.

The XFce4 desktop will display a top and bottom panel (see Figure B-1). The bottom panel has applets for launching applications, showing the time (clock), and logging out. The panel includes the applets: the Fedora application menu, terminal window, the text editor, file manager, Web browser, logout and shutdown, and the clock. The icon of the running person is the logout and shutdown button. The Fedora applications menu will let you choose an application to start.

The top panel holds the pager and the windows list. To the right are the applets for Network Manger, the sound, and trash. On the desktop will be icons for the trash, your home folder, and the file system folder.

Figure B-1: XFce desktop

Figure B-2: XFce Settings Manager

From the desktop pop-up menu or the Fedora applications menu, you can access all the installed applications on your system. A System submenu lets you access all the administrative tools. To quit or logout, right-click on the desktop background to display the desktop pop-up menu, and then select the Quit entry. You have the option to save your session.

Figure B-3: XFce Add Items to XFce Panel

You can configure your XFce4 desktop by right-clicking anywhere on the desktop background selecting Settings and then Settings Manager, or choosing Settings | Settings Manager from the Fedora applications menu. The Settings Manager window shows icons for your desktop, display, panel, user interface, among others (see Figure B-2). Use the user interface tool to resize fonts and select a theme. The Panel tool lets you add new panels and control features like fixed for freely movable and horizontally or vertically positioned.

XFce file manger it called Thunar. The file manager will open a side pane in the shortcuts view that lists entries for not just for the home directory, but also your file system, desktop, and trash contents. The File menu lets you perform file operations like renaming files or creating new directories. You can change the side pane view to a tree view of your file system by selecting from the menubar View | Side Pane | Tree, (Ctrl-t). The Shortcuts entry changes the view back (Ctrl-b).

You can add more items by right-clicking on the panel on any item and selecting Add new item from the popup menu. This opens a window with several applets like the clock and pager, as well as window list and icon box applets (see Figure B-3).

LXDE

The LXDE desktop provides another small desktop designed for use on minimal or low power systems like laptops, netbooks, or older computers. The desktop displays a single panel at the bottom with application applets to the right, followed by the windows taskbar, and system applets to the right (see Figure B-4). The desktop shows only the Documents folder for the user, not the home directory. Fro the Fedora applications menu you can access any applications.

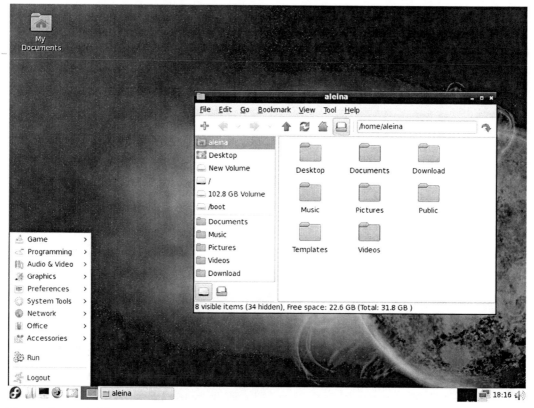

Figure B-4: LXDE desktop

The logout entry opens a dialog with buttons for logout, shutdown, suspend, hibernate, and restart.

The bottom panel shows applets for the Fedora applications menu, the PC-Man file manager, the terminal window, Web browser, minimize windows, desktop pager, window list. On the right side of the panel are the CPU monitor, the system tray with Network Manager, clock, and sound applets.

LXDE uses the PC-Man file manager as shown in Figure B-4. The button bar performs browser tasks like moving to backwards and forwards to previously viewed folders. The Home button moves you to your home folder. The plus button will open tabs, allowing you to open several folders in the same window. Next to the Home button, the Pane button opens and closes the side pane. The side pane has a location (Places) and directory tree view. You can switch between the two using the button at the bottom of the pane, the first being the directory tree and the second the locations view. You can also choose from the View | Side Pane menu.

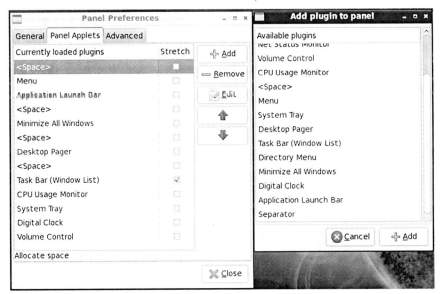

Figure B-5: LXDE Panel Preferences and Plugins

To configure your panel, right-click on the panel and select Panel Settings. This open the Panel Preferences window with tabs for General, Panel Applets, and Advanced (see Figure B-5). The General tab lets you set the position, background, font, and properties for the panel. The Applets tab is where you can add applets to the panel. The applets are referred to as plugins. Currently loaded applets are listed, along with format features like spaces. You have the option to stretch a particular applet to take up any available space on the panel. By default, only the Task Bar (Window List) is configured to do this. To remove an applet or feature, select it and click the Remove button. If an applet or feature can be configured, the Edit button will become active when you select the applet. You can then click the Edit button to open the applet's configuration dialog. This will vary among applets. To set the time display format, select the clock and click Edit to open the Digital Clock settings dialog. Applets settings can also be edited directly from the panel.

Right-click on the applet and choose the Settings entry, like "Digital Clock Settings" for the digital clock applet.

To add a new applet to the panel, click the Add button to open the "Add plugin to panel" window which with list all available applets and panel features like spaces and separators. Select the one you want and click the Add button (See Figure B-5).

To configure the desktop, right-click anywhere on the desktop and choose Desktop Settings from the pop-up menu. This opens the Preferences window with tabs fro General, Desktop, and Advanced (see Figure B-6). The Desktop tab lets you set the background. The General tab lets you set the icon size and file display.

Figure B-6: LXDE Desktop Preferences

Sugar

Though still under development, you can also run the Sugar desktop on Fedora. Sugar is designed for the OLPC (One Laptop Per Child) computers. The Sugar desktop initially displays a panel with a circular favorites menu (see Figure B-7). Each icon will start a simple applicaton, starting at the top with the calculator, text editor, chat, a moon description, terminal window, Web browser, and log. The top panel has button on the right for the circular favorites menu, or the list version. Fedora also provides a Fedora Sugar spin

For more detailed information on Sugar commands see the following link for Sugar instructions and information.

```
http://wiki.laptop.org/go/Sugar_Instructions
http://wiki.laptop.org/go/Getting_started
http://wiki.laptop.org/go/Activitie
```

To quit Sugar as run on Fedora 10, pass your mouse over your person image at the center of the main screen, and leave it there. A pop-up menu will appear with entries for logout, shutdown, restart, and also control panel.

Figure B-7: Sugar desktop: Favorites

You use the Frame to move around Sugar. The Frame works much like the Panel. It remains hidden until you choose to use it. Move the mouse to a corner or to the side, and the Frame will appear. In Figure B-7, the Frame is hidden. You can display the Frame from any activity. The top side of the Frame displays icons for accessing modes. The Home mode is your Home screen and uses the Circle around dot button. To the left are group and neighborhood mode buttons for displaying persons that many be accessible on your network. To the right are the activities button that displays all your current activities and the journal button. The top frame will also display buttons for all your currently running activities. You can use these buttons to quickly move between them (see Figure B-8).

The bottom side of the Frame shows device status. The left side is used as a clipboard. The right side shows any other accessible users in the neighborhood or group mode.

Below the person image is the journal icon. Use this as your file manager as well as bookmark and history capability. The Journal is a history of all activities performed on the laptop. All your previous activities are listed. You can change their names and select them for saving. Right-click on an activity to Resume, Copy, or Erase. Also, at the right side of an Activity entry is an arrow key that opens the activities properties. Here a panel at the top has buttons to Resume, Copy, or Erase. The screen has an image of the activity. There are also boxes labeled Description (for activity description), Tags (search terms), and Participants (shared projects).

To copy an activity, like a text file or image, to a USB drive, first insert the USB drive. A USB icon will appear on the lower left. Then just click and drag the activity to the USB icon.

Before removing the USB drive, place your mouse over it until a pop-up menu appears and select the Unmount entry. Select is, and the USB icon will disappear.

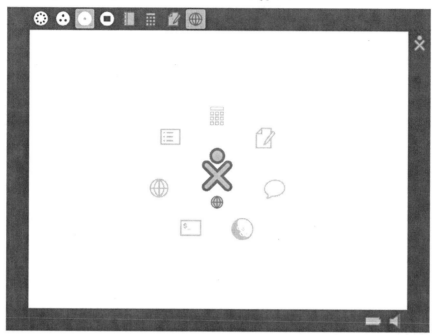

Figure B-8: Sugar desktop Frame

To return to the Home screen, move your mouse to a corner to display the Frame and then click the Home screen button (Circle around dot).

Figure B-9: Sugar text editor

When you run an activity, a button bar lets you choose different sets of actions, and those actions are displayed as button s, menus, or applets in a top panel. Activities are the equivalent of applications. The text editor will have buttons for Activity, Edit, Text, Image, Table, Format, and View (see Figure B-9). The panel on top will display different applets according to the button selected. The Text panel supports Undo and Redo, Cut and Paste, and Search operations; while the Fonts panel lets you set the font and size. Activities will have an Activity panel which you can use to save or quit. Click on the Journal icon to save your activity or press **Ctrl-s**. To quit, click on the octagonal shape on the right side of the panel, or press **Ctrl-q**.

To configure your desktop, first access the control panel. Place your mouse over your person image on the main screen and hold it there until the pop-up menu appears. Then select Control Panel. This opens a screen with icons for About Me, Network, Power, Date& Time, Language, Frame, and About my XO (see Figure B-10). The tasks are very simple. Date and Time sets the time zone. About Me lets you change your name and the color of your person icon. Network just lets you disable network connection to save power.

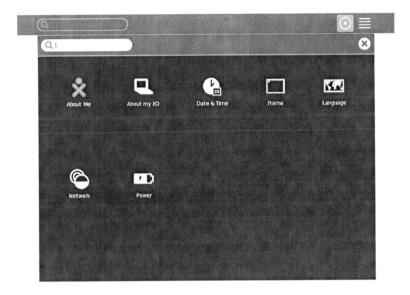

Figure B-10: Sugar Control Panel

Openbox

The Openbox desktop provides a very minimal interface. Openbox initially just displays the desktop background image. Access to all applications and system tools is obtained through the desktop menu. Right-click anywhere on the desktop to display the Openbox menu with entries for Applications, Preferences, Adminsitration, Terminal, exit and logout. Use Exit to return to the GDM login window. From the Applications menu you can start applications directly, like your Web browser. Also from the Applications | System Tools menu you can start desktop applications like the file manager (File Browser) or terminal window (see Figure B-11).

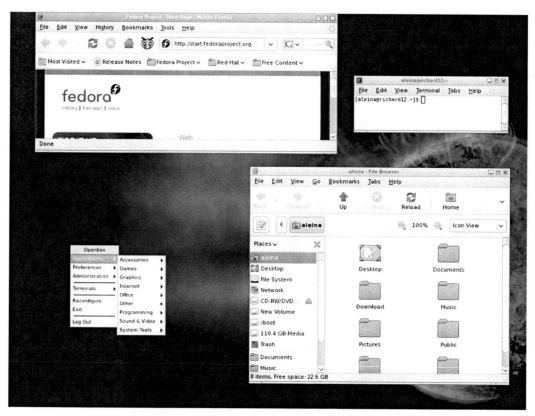

Figure B-11: Openbox desktop

Table Listing

Figure Listing

Index

Printed in the United States
139052LV00003B/65/P